CMake Cookbook

Building, testing, and packaging modular software
with modern CMake

Radovan Bast   **Roberto Di Remigio**

Pack<t>

BIRMINGHAM - MUMBAI

CMake Cookbook

Commissioning Editor: Smeet Thakkar
Acquisition Editor: Noyonika Das
Content Development Editor: Francis Carneiro
Technical Editor: Sachin Sunilkumar
Copy Editor: Safis Editing
Project Coordinator: Devanshi Doshi
Proofreader: Safis Editing
Indexer: Pratik Shirodkar
Graphics: Jason Monteiro
Production Coordinator: Aparna Bhagat

First published: September 2018

Production reference: 1240918

Published by Packt Publishing Ltd.
Livery Place
35 Livery Street
Birmingham
B3 2PB, UK.

ISBN 978-1-78847-071-1

www.packtpub.com

Mapt

Mapt is an online digital library that gives you full access to over 5,000 books and videos, as well as industry leading tools to help you plan your personal development and advance your career. For more information, please visit our website mapt.io.

Why subscribe?

- Spend less time learning and more time coding with practical eBooks and Videos from over 4,000 industry professionals

- Improve your learning with Skill Plans built especially for you

- Get a free eBook or video every month

- Mapt is fully searchable

- Copy and paste, print, and bookmark content

PacktPub.com

Did you know that Packt offers eBook versions of every book published, with PDF and ePub files available? You can upgrade to the eBook version at www.PacktPub.com and as a print book customer, you are entitled to a discount on the eBook copy. Get in touch with us at service@packtpub.com for more details.

At www.PacktPub.com, you can also read a collection of free technical articles, sign up for a range of free newsletters, and receive exclusive discounts and offers on Packt books and eBooks.

Contributors

About the authors

Radovan Bast works at the High Performance Computing Group at UiT - The Arctic University of Norway in Tromsø and leads the CodeRefinery project. He has a PhD in theoretical chemistry and contributes to a number of quantum chemistry programs as a code developer. He enjoys learning new programming languages and techniques, and teaching programming to students and researchers. He got in touch with CMake in 2008 and has ported a number of research codes and migrated a number of communities to CMake since then.

Roberto Di Remigio is a postdoctoral fellow in theoretical chemistry at UiT - The Arctic University of Norway in Tromsø, Norway and Virginia Tech, USA. He is currently working on stochastic methods and solvation models. He is a developer of the PCMSolver library and the Psi4 open source quantum chemistry program. He contributes or has contributed to the development of popular quantum chemistry codes and libraries: DIRAC, MRCPP, DALTON, LSDALTON, XCFun, and ReSpect. He usually programs in C++ and Fortran.

We would like to acknowledge the very valuable comments and suggestions from the reviewers, Eric Noulard and Shlomi Fish. In particular, Eric's feedback and input has improved the quality of the chapters significantly. We also thank Lori A. Burns for her comments and suggestions for chapters 8 through 11. Special thanks to the Tromsø Public Library for providing a wonderful space for writing and thinking. We are very grateful for the testing infrastructure and support provided by Travis CI, GmbH, Appveyor Systems Inc., and Circle Internet Services, Inc. – it is thanks to these infrastructure services that we can be confident that the examples work across the major operating systems.

About the reviewers

Holding an engineering degree from ENSEEIHT and a PhD in computer science from UVSQ in France, **Eric Noulard** has been writing and compiling source code in a variety of languages for 20 years. A user of CMake since 2006, he has also been an active contributor to the project for several years. During his career, Eric has worked for private companies and government agencies. He is now employed by Antidot, a software vendor developing and marketing high-end information retrieval technology and solutions.

Shlomi Fish is an Israeli software developer and writer. He has been contributing to various open source and open culture projects since at least 2000. Among other endeavors, he has initiated some solvers for games, which led to him maintaining the PySol FC suite of solitaire games, adopting fortune-mod, solving over 290 Project Euler problems, and writing several stories, essays, aphorisms, and other documents.

Packt is searching for authors like you

If you're interested in becoming an author for Packt, please visit `authors.packtpub.com` and apply today. We have worked with thousands of developers and tech professionals, just like you, to help them share their insight with the global tech community. You can make a general application, apply for a specific hot topic that we are recruiting an author for, or submit your own idea.

Table of Contents

Preface

Computer software is present in almost every aspect of our daily lives: it triggers our alarm clocks, fuels our communication, banking, weather forecasts, bus schedules, calendars, meetings, travel, photo albums, television, music streaming, social media, dinner and movie reservations, from dawn till dusk.

The software that surrounds us contains many layers: apps are built on top of frameworks, frameworks on top of libraries, libraries use smaller libraries and executables, all the way down to smaller and smaller software components. Libraries and executables in turn need to be built from source code. Often we only see the outermost layer, but all these layers need to be carefully organized and built. This book is about how to build libraries and executables from sources using CMake.

CMake and its siblings, CTest, CPack, and CDash, have emerged as the leading toolset for building software from sources, surpassing in usage and popularity many other similar tools, such as the venerated GNU Autotools and the more recent, Python-based, SCons build system.

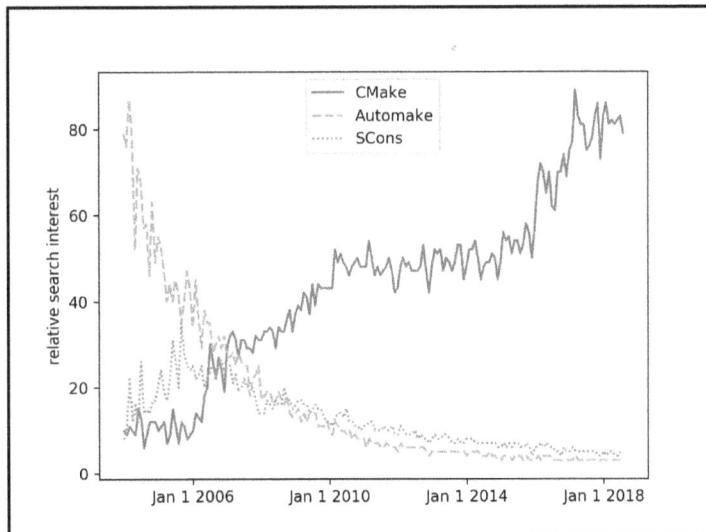

Search interest over time for three popular build systems: CMake, Automake, and SCons. The interest is measured using the number of searches for the relevant terms over time. The figure was obtained using data provided by Google Trends.

The history of the CMake project started in 1999, when Kitware, the company behind its development, was commissioned to design a new set of tools to simplify the day-to-day software work of researchers. The goal was clear: provide a set of tools that would make it easier to configure, build, test, and deploy the same project across different platforms. A fascinating account of the ensuing design choices in the CMake project can be found at `https://www.aosabook.org/en/cmake.html`.

CMake is a *build-system generator*, offering a powerful domain-specific language (DSL) to describe what the build system should achieve. In our opinion, this is one of the main strengths of CMake, because it allows the generation of *platform-native build systems* with the same set of CMake scripts. The CMake software toolset gives developers full control over the whole life cycle of a given project:

- **CMake** lets you describe how your project, whether building an executable, libraries, or both, has to be configured, built, and installed on all major hardware and operating systems.
- **CTest** allows you to define tests, test suites, and set how they should be executed.
- **CPack** offers a DSL for all your packaging needs, whether your project should be bundled and distributed in source code or platform-native binary form.
- **CDash** will be useful for reporting the results of tests for your project to an online dashboard.

An old adage goes that the deeper you dig, the more stones you will find. For the preparation of this book we have carefully been digging deeper through many software layers, with CMake being our quarry. The number of stones and artifacts that we have hit when building various software components and libraries on various platforms, each with their own quirks, has felt disheartening at times. But we believe we have cleared the ground of many stones and we are happy to share our findings and recipes with you, our readers. There will always be stones left but each stone will bring new insight and we encourage you to share this insight with the community.

Who this book is for

Writing software that can run natively, reliably, and efficiently on many different platforms is of paramount importance for all sectors of industry and society. Software build systems take center stage in this task. They are a crucial part in the management of the software development life cycle: from incubation and prototype development to testing and all the way till packaging, deployment, and distribution. CMake is designed to help you manage these operations: if you are a software developer who wishes to manage the build system using CMake or who would like to be able to understand and modify CMake code written by others, this book is for you.

What this book covers

We have written this book as a progressive sequence of tasks and recipes. At each point, we introduce enough information about CMake to show how to achieve our goals, without overwhelming you with details. By the end of the book, you will be able to tackle increasingly complex operations and leverage the contents of the recipes in your own real-world projects with confidence.

We will cover these topics:

- Configure, build, test, and install code projects using CMake
- Detect operating systems, processors, libraries, files, and programs for conditional compilation
- Increase the portability of your code
- Refactor a large code base into modules with the help of CMake
- Build multi-language projects
- Know where and how to tweak CMake configuration files written by somebody else
- Package projects for distribution
- Port projects to CMake

The workflow of a project managed by CMake happens in a number of stages, which we refer to as *times*. These can be summarized neatly in the following figure:

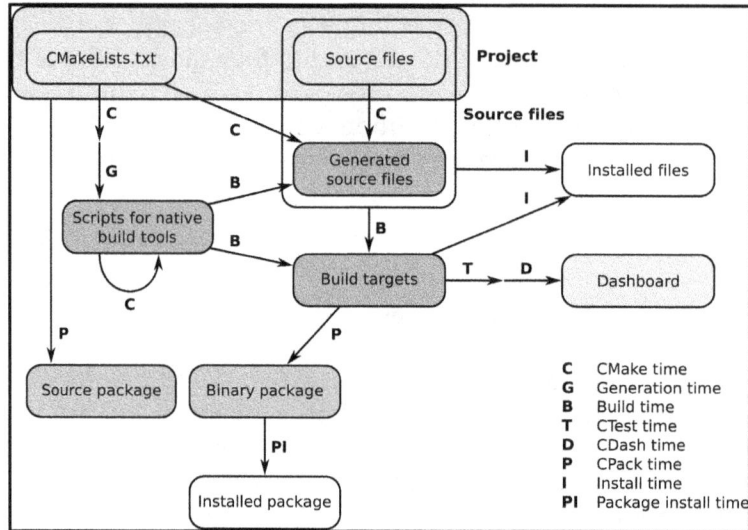

- **CMake time** or **configure time**. This is when CMake is running. In this phase CMake will process the CMakeLists.txt files in your project and configure it.
- **Generation time**. Upon successful configuration, CMake will generate the scripts needed by the native build tools to perform subsequent steps in the project.
- **Build time**. This is when the native build tools are invoked on the platform- and tool-native build scripts previously generated by CMake. At this point, the compiler will be invoked and the targets (executables and libraries) will be built in a specific build directory. Note the recursive CMake-time arrow: this can seem baffling, but it is a mechanism we will use many times throughout the book to achieve a truly platform-independent build.
- **CTest time** or **test time**. This is when we run the test suite of the project to check whether the targets perform as intended.
- **CDash time** or **report time**. This is when the results of testing the project are uploaded to a dashboard to be shared with other developers.
- **Install time**. This is when the project's targets, source files, executables, and libraries are installed from the build directory to an install location.
- **CPack time** or **packaging time**. This is when we package our project for distribution, either as source code or binary.
- **Package install time**. This is when the newly minted package is installed system-wide.

This book is organized as follows:

Chapter 1, From a Simple Executable to Libraries, shows how to get started configuring and building simple executables and libraries with CMake.

Chapter 2, Detecting the Environment, explains how to interact with the operating system and processor architecture using simple CMake commands.

Chapter 3, Detecting External Libraries and Programs, shows how CMake can simplify the detection of dependencies for your project.

Chapter 4, Creating and Running Tests, explains how to harness the power of CMake and CTest to define and run tests.

Chapter 5, Configure-time and Build-time Operations, shows how to perform custom operations at different stages of the build process with cross-platform CMake commands.

Chapter 6, Generating Source Code, discusses CMake commands to automatically generate source code.

Chapter 7, Structuring Projects, shows powerful CMake syntax for organizing your projects to make them more maintainable.

Chapter 8, The Superbuild Pattern, explains the powerful CMake superbuild pattern for managing critical project dependencies with control over side effects.

Chapter 9, Mixed-language Projects, shows how to build projects mixing different programming languages with the help of CMake.

Chapter 10, Writing an Installer, takes care of the installation of projects with the cross-platform power of CMake.

Chapter 11, Packaging Projects, shows how to use CPack to produce source and platform-native source archives and how to build Python and Conda packages for distribution.

Chapter 12, Building Documentation, shows how to use CMake to also build the documentation for your code.

Chapter 13, Alternative Generators and Cross-compilation, shows how to use CMake to cross-compile projects between platforms.

Chapter 14, Testing Dashboards, shows how to report the results of tests to an online dashboard.

Chapter 15, Porting a Project to CMake, shows best practices, tips, and tricks that will help you port a project to a CMake-based build system.

To get the most out of this book

This is a book written by programmers, for programmers. We have assumed basic knowledge and familiarity with the following:

- The command line for your favorite operating system
- Native tools for building software on your favorite operating system
- The compiled languages C++, C, or Fortran, and the corresponding compilers on your favorite operating system
- The Python programming language

Download the example code files

You can download the example code examples for this book from `https://github.com/dev-cafe/cmake-cookbook`. For more details please see the *Setting up Your System* section.

Download the color images

We also provide a PDF file that has color images of the screenshots/diagrams used in this book. You can download it here: `http://www.packtpub.com/sites/default/files/downloads/CMakeCookbook_ColorImages.pdf`.

Conventions used

There are a number of text conventions used throughout this book.

`CodeInText`: Indicates code commands in text, folder names, filenames, module names, and target names.

A block of code is set as follows:

```
cmake_minimum_required(VERSION 3.5 FATAL_ERROR)

project(recipe-01 LANGUAGES CXX)

add_executable(hello-world hello-world.cpp)
```

Any command-line input is written in bold and contains a **$** prompt in front of the command to type:

```
$ mkdir -p build
$ cd build
$ cmake ..
```

To distinguish command-line input and output, we keep output non-bold:

```
$ ./hello-world

Hello World!
```

Important notes appear like this.

Tips and tricks appear like this.

Additional reading resources

The documentation for CMake available online is comprehensive and we will refer to it throughout the book: https://cmake.org/documentation/

In preparing this book we have been inspired also by other resources:

- The presentation by Daniel Pfeifer, available on GitHub: https://github.com/boostcon/cppnow_presentations_2017/blob/master/05-19-2017_friday/effective_cmake__daniel_pfeifer__cppnow_05-19-2017.pdf
- The CMake tutorial by Eric Noulard, available on GitHub: https://github.com/TheErk/CMake-tutorial
- The CMake-related blog posts by Craig Scott: https://crascit.com/tag/cmake/

We can also recommend to browse the curated list of CMake resources, scripts, modules, and examples collected by Viktor Kirilov: `https://github.com/onqtam/awesome-cmake`.

It is also worth noting that our book is not the only one out there covering CMake:

- *Mastering CMake* by Ken Martin and Bill Hoffman, 2015, Kitware Inc.
- *Professional CMake* by Craig Scott: `https://crascit.com/professional-cmake/`

Get in touch

Feedback from our readers is always welcome.

Source code improvements and issues: Please direct pull requests towards `https://github.com/dev-cafe/cmake-cookbook` and report specific issues with recipes *via* `https://github.com/dev-cafe/cmake-cookbook/issues`.

General feedback: Email `feedback@packtpub.com` and mention the book title in the subject of your message. If you have questions about any aspect of this book, please email us at `questions@packtpub.com`.

Errata: Although we have taken every care to ensure the accuracy of our content, mistakes do happen. If you have found a mistake in this book, we would be grateful if you would report this to us. Please visit `www.packtpub.com/submit-errata`, selecting your book, clicking on the Errata Submission Form link, and entering the details.

Piracy: If you come across any illegal copies of our works in any form on the Internet, we would be grateful if you would provide us with the location address or website name. Please contact us at `copyright@packtpub.com` with a link to the material.

If you are interested in becoming an author: If there is a topic that you have expertise in and you are interested in either writing or contributing to a book, please visit `authors.packtpub.com`.

Reviews

Please leave a review. Once you have read and used this book, why not leave a review on the site that you purchased it from? Potential readers can then see and use your unbiased opinion to make purchase decisions, we at Packt can understand what you think about our products, and our authors can see your feedback on their book. Thank you!

For more information about Packt, please visit `packtpub.com`.

Setting up Your System

Before diving into CMake and the recipes in this book, you will need to set your system up to successfully run all of the examples. In this section, we will discuss the following topics:

1. How to obtain the code for the recipes
2. How to install all of the tools required to run the code samples on GNU/Linux, macOS, and Windows
3. How the automated testing for the repository works
4. How to report problems with the recipes and suggest improvements

We have strived to make our discussions of the topics in this book as accessible to novices as possible. However, this book does not start from absolute scratch. We assume that you have basic knowledge of the native tools for building software that are available on your platform of choice. It is also helpful (but not required) to have basic experience with version control using Git, to interact with the repository holding the recipe sources.

Obtaining the code

The source code for the recipes in this book is available on GitHub, at `https://github.com/dev-cafe/cmake-cookbook`. The code is licensed under the standard open source MIT license: this is a permissive software license, and you can reuse and remix the code in whatever way you see fit, as long as the original copyright and license notice are included in any copies of the software/source. The full text of the license is available at `https://opensource.org/licenses/MIT`.

In order to test the recipes by yourself, you will need a working installation of Git, obtained as follows:

- All major GNU/Linux distributions offer Git prepackaged, *via* their package managers. If that is not your case, a binary distribution can be downloaded from the Git project website at `https://git-scm.com`.
- On macOS, it is possible to use Homebrew or MacPorts to install Git.
- On Windows, you can download the Git executable from the Git project website at `https://git-scm.com`.

Alternatively, you can access the examples with the GitHub desktop client at `https://desktop.github.com`.

Yet another alternative is to download and extract the ZIP file from `https://github.com/dev-cafe/cmake-cookbook`.

Once you have Git installed, you can clone the repository to your local machine, as follows:

```
$ git clone https://github.com/dev-cafe/cmake-cookbook.git
```

This will create a folder named `cmake-cookbook`. The book and the repository are organized in chapters and recipes. The numbering of chapters and the order of recipes in the repository reflect the order in the text. Each recipe is further organized into example folders. Some of the recipes have more than one example, usually when similar CMake concepts are illustrated in different programming languages.

The recipes are tested on GNU/Linux, macOS, and Windows, using state-of-the-art continuous integration services. We will discuss the testing set up shortly.

We have tagged the precise versions that correspond to the examples printed in this book with the tag `v1.0`. For maximum overlap with the book text, you can fetch this particular version as follows:

```
$ git clone --single-branch -b v1.0
https://github.com/dev-cafe/cmake-cookbook.git
```

We expect to receive bug fixes and the GitHub repository to evolve. To get the latest updates, you may prefer to follow the `master` branch of the repository, instead.

Docker image

You will likely find that the easiest approach to testing the book's recipes in a software environment (which contains all of the dependencies preinstalled) is to use a Docker image that we have set up, based on Ubuntu 18.04. You can install Docker on your favorite operating system, following the official documentation at `https://docs.docker.com`.

Once Docker is installed, you can run our image and test the recipes with the full software environment in place, as follows:

```
$ docker run -it devcafe/cmake-cookbook_ubuntu-18.04
$ git clone https://github.com/dev-cafe/cmake-cookbook.git
$ cd cmake-cookbook
$ pipenv install --three
$ pipenv run python testing/collect_tests.py 'chapter-*/recipe-*'
```

Installing prerequisite software

An alternative to running the book recipes in a container is to install the dependencies directly on the host operating system. For this, we have assembled a minimal toolstack that can be used as a basic starting point for all of our recipes. You will have to install the following:

1. CMake
2. Language-specific tools, that is, the compilers
3. Build automation tools
4. Python

We will also detail how to install the additional dependencies required by some of the recipes.

Getting CMake

CMake 3.5 is the minimum required version of CMake for this book. Only a few, specific recipes and examples that demonstrate useful features that were introduced after version 3.5 will require a more recent version of CMake. The introduction to every recipe features an info box, pointing out where the code is available, which examples are given, and the minimum version of CMake required. The info boxes will look like the following box:

> The code for this recipe is available at `https://github.com/dev-cafe/cmake-cookbook/tree/v1.0/chapter-03/recipe-10`, and includes a C example. The recipe is valid with CMake version 3.5 (and higher) and has been tested on GNU/Linux, macOS, and Windows.

Some, if not most, of the recipes will still be valid with older versions of CMake. However, we have made no attempts to test this assumption, since we consider CMake 3.5 to be the default on most systems and distributions. We also consider upgrading to later versions of CMake to be a straightforward step.

CMake can be installed in a number of different ways. Downloading and extracting the binary distribution maintained by Kitware will work across all platforms. The download page is at `https://cmake.org/download/`.

Most GNU/Linux distributions have CMake available in their package managers. However, on some distributions, the packaged version can be rather old, so downloading the binary maintained by Kitware is still the preferred option. The following commands will download and install CMake 3.5.2 under $HOME/Deps/cmake (adjust this path to your preference), from the version packaged by CMake:

```
$ cmake_version="3.5.2"
$ target_path=$HOME/Deps/cmake/${cmake_version}
$
cmake_url="https://cmake.org/files/v${cmake_version%.*}/cmake-${cmake_version}-Linux-x86_64.tar.gz"
$ mkdir -p "${target_path}"
$ curl -Ls "${cmake_url}" | tar -xz -C "${target_path}" --strip-components=1
$ export PATH=$HOME/Deps/cmake/${cmake_version}/bin${PATH:+:$PATH}
$ cmake --version
```

Homebrew for macOS reliably ships the latest version of CMake:

```
$ brew upgrade cmake
```

On Windows, you can use Visual Studio 2017, which provides CMake support. The installation of Visual Studio 2017 is documented in *Chapter 13, Alternative Generators and Cross-compilation, Recipe 1, Building a CMake project using Visual Studio 2017*.

Alternatively, you can download the MSYS2 installer from https://www.msys2.org, follow the instructions given therein to update the list of packages, and then install CMake using the package manager, pacman. The following code assumes that we are building the 64-bit version:

```
$ pacman -S mingw64/mingw-w64-x86_64-cmake
```

For the 32-bit version, use the following (though we will only refer to 64-bit versions in future, for the sake of brevity):

```
$ pacman -S mingw64/mingw-w64-i686-cmake
```

Another nice feature of MSYS2 is that it provides a terminal on Windows that feels and behaves like a terminal on a Unix-like operating system, providing a useful development environment.

Compilers

We will need compilers for C++, C, and Fortran. These should be fairly recent, as we require support for recent language standards in most of the recipes. CMake offers very good support for many compilers, from both commercial and non-commercial vendors. To keep the recipes consistently cross-platform and as operating system independent as possible, we have worked with open source compilers:

- On GNU/Linux, the GNU Compiler Collection (GCC) is the obvious choice. It is free and available for all distributions. For example, on Ubuntu, you can install the compilers as follows:

  ```
  $ sudo apt-get install g++ gcc gfortran
  ```

- Clang, in the LLVM family, is also a good choice for C++ and C:

  ```
  $ sudo apt-get install clang clang++ gfortran
  ```

- On macOS, the LLVM compilers shipped with XCode will work for C++ and C. We have used the Fortran compiler from GCC in our macOS testing. This has to be installed separately, using the package manager. For example, the command for Homebrew is as follows:

  ```
  $ brew install gcc
  ```

- On Windows, you can use Visual Studio for the C++ and C recipes. Alternatively, you can use the MSYS2 installer and install the entire toolchain, including a C++, C, and Fortran compiler, with the following single command in an MSYS2 environment (for the 64-bit version):

  ```
  $ pacman -S mingw64/mingw-w64-x86_64-toolchain
  ```

Build-automation tools

These build-automation tools will provide the infrastructure for building and linking the projects presented in the recipes. What you will end up installing and using strongly depends on your operating system and your taste:

- On GNU/Linux, GNU Make will most likely be installed automatically, when installing the compilers.
- On macOS, XCode will provide GNU Make.

- On Windows, Visual Studio will provide you with the complete infrastructure. In the MSYS2 environment, GNU Make is installed as a part of the `mingw64/mingw-w64-x86_64-toolchain` package, which we installed previously.

For maximum portability, we have made the recipes as agnostic about these system-dependent details as possible. A clear advantage of this approach is that configuring, building, and linking are native to each platform and each set of compilers.

The Ninja program is a different build-automation tool that works on GNU/Linux, macOS, and Windows. Ninja is a new build tool, with a focus on speed, especially for incremental rebuilds. Prepackaged binaries for GNU/Linux, macOS, and Windows can be found on the project's GitHub repository at `https://github.com/ninja-build/ninja/releases`.

Using CMake and Ninja with Fortran projects requires some care. CMake 3.7.2 or later is required, along with the version of Ninja maintained by Kitware, available at `https://github.com/Kitware/ninja/releases`.

On GNU/Linux, you can install Ninja with the following series of commands:

```
$ mkdir -p ninja
$
ninja_url="https://github.com/Kitware/ninja/releases/download/v1.8.2.g3bbbe
.kitware.dyndep-1.jobserver-1/ninja-1.8.2.g3bbbe.kitware.dyndep-1.jobserver
-1_x86_64-linux-gnu.tar.gz"
$ curl -Ls ${ninja_url} | tar -xz -C ninja --strip-components=1
$ export PATH=$HOME/Deps/ninja${PATH:+:$PATH}
```

On Windows, using the MSYS2 environment (assuming the 64-bit version), executing the command:

```
$ pacman -S mingw64/mingw-w64-x86_64-ninja
```

We recommend reading the essay at `http://www.aosabook.org/en/posa/ninja.html` for an enlightening discussion of Ninja's history and design choices.

Python

This book is about CMake, but some of the recipes, along with the whole infrastructure powering testing, need Python. Thus, first and foremost, you will need a working installation of Python: the interpreter, header files, and libraries. The end of life for Python 2.7 was announced for 2020, and we will thus use Python 3.5.

On Ubuntu 14.04 LTS (this is the environment used by Travis CI which we will discuss later on), Python 3.5 can be installed as follows:

```
$ sudo apt-get install python3.5-dev
```

On Windows, using the MSYS2 environment, the Python environment can be installed as follows (assuming the 64-bit version):

```
$ pacman -S mingw64/mingw-w64-x86_64-python3
$ pacman -S mingw64/mingw-w64-x86_64-python3-pip
$ python3 -m pip install pipenv
```

Specific Python modules are also required, in order to run the testing machinery that we have put in place. These can be installed system-wide by using your favorite package manager, or in an isolated environment. The latter approach is highly recommended, as it offers the following advantages:

- You can install packages and clean up installations without affecting the system environment.
- Packages can be installed without administrator privileges.
- You lower the risk of version and dependency clashes.
- You gain much better control over package dependencies, for reproducibility.

We have prepared a `Pipfile` for this purpose. In combination with its `Pipfile.lock`, you can use Pipenv (`http://pipenv.readthedocs.io`) to generate an isolated environment, with all packages installed. To create this environment for the recipe example repository, run the following commands in the top-level directory of the repository:

```
$ pip install --user pip pipenv --upgrade
$ pipenv install --python python3.5
```

The `pipenv shell` command will drop you into a command-line environment with the specific version of Python and all of the packages available. Executing `exit` will bring you back to a clean environment. You can also use `pipenv run` to directly execute a command within the isolated environment.

Alternatively, the `requirements.txt` file in the repository can be used, in combination with Virtualenv (`http://docs.python-guide.org/en/latest/dev/virtualenvs/`) and `pip`, to achieve the same effect:

```
$ virtualenv --python=python3.5 venv
$ source venv/bin/activate
$ pip install -r requirements.txt
```

The virtual environment can be exited by using the `deactivate` command.

Yet another alternative is to use Conda environments. To do so, we suggest installing Miniconda. The following instructions will install the latest Miniconda to the directory $HOME/Deps/conda, for GNU/Linux (download from https://repo.continuum.io/miniconda/Miniconda3-latest-Linux-x86_64.sh) or macOS (download from https://repo.continuum.io/miniconda/Miniconda3-latest-MacOSX-x86_64.sh):

```
$ curl -Ls
https://repo.continuum.io/miniconda/Miniconda3-latest-Linux-x86_64.sh >
miniconda.sh
$ bash miniconda.sh -b -p "$HOME"/Deps/conda &> /dev/null
$ touch "$HOME"/Deps/conda/conda-meta/pinned
$ export PATH=$HOME/Deps/conda/bin${PATH:+:$PATH}
$ conda config --set show_channel_urls True
$ conda config --set changeps1 no
$ conda update --all
$ conda clean -tipy
```

On Windows, you can download the latest Miniconda from https://repo.continuum.io/miniconda/Miniconda3-latest-Windows-x86_64.exe. The package can be installed using PowerShell, as follows:

```
$basedir = $pwd.Path + "\"
$filepath = $basedir + "Miniconda3-latest-Windows-x86_64.exe"
$Anaconda_loc = "C:\Deps\conda"
$args = "/InstallationType=JustMe /AddToPath=0 /RegisterPython=0 /S
/D=$Anaconda_loc"
Start-Process -FilePath $filepath -ArgumentList $args -Wait -Passthru

$conda_path = $Anaconda_loc + "\Scripts\conda.exe"
$args = "config --set show_channel_urls True"
Start-Process -FilePath "$conda_path" -ArgumentList $args -Wait -Passthru
$args = "config --set changeps1 no"
Start-Process -FilePath "$conda_path" -ArgumentList $args -Wait -Passthru
$args = "update --all"
Start-Process -FilePath "$conda_path" -ArgumentList $args -Wait -Passthru
$args = "clean -tipy"
Start-Process -FilePath "$conda_path" -ArgumentList $args -Wait -Passthru
```

Once Conda is installed, the Python modules can be installed as follows:

```
$ conda create -n cmake-cookbook python=3.5
$ conda activate cmake-cookbook
$ conda install --file requirements.txt
```

Executing `conda deactivate` will drop you outside of the isolated environment.

Additional software

Some recipes will require additional software, which will be covered in the following sections.

BLAS and LAPACK

Most Linux distributions provide packages for BLAS and LAPACK. For example, on Ubuntu 14.04 LTS, you can run the following:

```
$ sudo apt-get install libatlas-dev liblapack-dev liblapacke-dev
```

On macOS, the Accelerate libraries, shipped with XCode, are enough for our purposes.

On Windows, using the MSYS2 environment, these libraries can be installed as follows (assuming the 64-bit version):

```
$ pacman -S mingw64/mingw-w64-x86_64-openblas
```

Alternatively, you can download the reference implementation of BLAS and LAPACK from GitHub (https://github.com/Reference-LAPACK/lapack) and compile the libraries from sources. Commercial vendors might offer packages for their own implementations of the BLAS and LAPACK APIs, available as installers for your platform.

Message passing interface (MPI)

There are many commercial and non-commercial implementations of MPI. For our introductory purposes, it is enough to install any of the freely available non-commercial implementations. On Ubuntu 14.04 LTS, we recommend OpenMPI. It can be installed with the following command:

```
$ sudo apt-get install openmpi-bin libopenmpi-dev
```

For macOS, Homebrew distributes MPICH:

```
$ brew install mpich
```

It is also possible to compile OpenMPI from the sources publicly available at https://www.open-mpi.org/software/.

For Windows, the Microsoft MPI implementation can be installed *via* https://msdn.microsoft.com/en-us/library/bb524831(v=vs.85).aspx.

The Eigen linear algebra template library

Some recipes will need the Eigen linear algebra template library, version 3.3 or later. If your package manager does not provide Eigen, you can install it from the online source archive (http://eigen.tuxfamily.org). For example, on GNU/Linux and macOS, you can install Eigen to the directory $HOME/Deps/eigen, as follows:

```
$ eigen_version="3.3.4"
$ mkdir -p eigen
$ curl -Ls http://bitbucket.org/eigen/eigen/get/${eigen_version}.tar.gz |
tar -xz -C eigen --strip-components=1
$ cd eigen
$ cmake -H. -Bbuild_eigen -DCMAKE_INSTALL_PREFIX="$HOME/Deps/eigen" &>
/dev/null
$ cmake --build build_eigen -- install &> /dev/null
```

The Boost libraries

Boost packages are available for every operating system; most Linux distributions have packages available through their package managers. On Ubuntu 14.04 LTS, for instance, the Boost Filesystem, Boost Python, and Boost Test libraries can be installed with the following command:

```
$ sudo apt-get install libboost-filesystem-dev libboost-python-dev
libboost-test-dev
```

For macOS, both MacPorts and Homebrew provide packages for recent versions of Boost. Our testing setup on macOS installs Boost as follows:

```
$ brew cask uninstall --force oclint
$ brew uninstall --force --ignore-dependencies boost
$ brew install boost
$ brew install boost-python3
```

Prebuilt binary distributions for Windows are also available for download from the Boost website at http://www.boost.org. Alternatively, you can download the sources from https://www.boost.org and compile the libraries yourself.

Cross-compilers

On Debian/Ubuntu-like systems, cross-compilers can be installed with the following command:

```
$ sudo apt-get install gcc-mingw-w64 g++-mingw-w64 gfortran-mingw-w64
```

On macOS, using Brew, the cross-compilers can be installed as follows:

```
$ brew install mingw-w64
```

Other package managers offer corresponding packages.

An alternative to using packaged cross-compilers is to build them from sources, using the M cross environment (https://mxe.cc).

ZeroMQ, pkg-config, UUID, and Doxygen

On Ubuntu 14.04 LTS, these packages can be installed as follows:

```
$ sudo apt-get install pkg-config libzmq3-dev doxygen graphviz-dev uuid-dev
```

On macOS, we recommend installing with Brew:

```
$ brew install ossp-uuid pkg-config zeromq doxygen
```

The pkg-config program and UUID library are only available on Unix-like systems.

On Windows, using the MSYS2 environment, these dependencies can be installed as follows (assuming the 64-bit version):

```
$ pacman -S mingw64/mingw-w64-x86_64-zeromq
$ pacman -S mingw64/mingw-w64-x86_64-pkg-config
$ pacman -S mingw64/mingw-w64-x86_64-doxygen
$ pacman -S mingw64/mingw-w64-x86_64-graphviz
```

Conda build and deployment tools

The recipes exploring packaging with Conda will need Miniconda and the Conda build and deployment tools installed on the system. The instructions for the installation of Miniconda were given previously. To install Conda build and deployment tools on GNU/Linux and macOS, run the following commands:

```
$ conda install --yes --quiet conda-build anaconda-client jinja2 setuptools
$ conda clean -tipsy
$ conda info -a
```

These tools can be installed on Windows as follows:

```
$conda_path = "C:\Deps\conda\Scripts\conda.exe"

$args = "install --yes --quiet conda-build anaconda-client jinja2
setuptools"
Start-Process -FilePath "$conda_path" -ArgumentList $args -Wait -Passthru

$args = "clean -tipsy"
Start-Process -FilePath "$conda_path" -ArgumentList $args -Wait -Passthru

$args = "info -a"
Start-Process -FilePath "$conda_path" -ArgumentList $args -Wait -Passthru
```

Testing the recipes

The recipes are tested on state-of-the-art continuous integration (CI) services: Travis (https://travis-ci.org) for GNU/Linux and macOS, Appveyor (https://www.appveyor.com) for Windows, and CircleCI (https://circleci.com) for additional GNU/Linux testing with commercial compilers. The configuration files for the CI services can be found in the repository (https://github.com/dev-cafe/cmake-cookbook/): .travis.yml for Travis, .appveyor.yml for Appveyor, and .circleci/config.yml for CircleCI. Additional installation scripts for Travis and Appveyor can be found in the folder testing/dependencies.

> We test the recipes with CMake 3.5.2 and CMake 3.12.1 on the Travis GNU/Linux infrastructure. CMake 3.12.1 is used on the Travis macOS infrastructure. On Appveyor, testing uses CMake 3.11.3. On Circle, CMake 3.12.1 is used.

The testing machinery is a set of Python scripts that are also contained in the testing folder. The script collect_tests.py will run tests and report their statuses. Recipes can be tested in isolation, or in batches; collect_tests.py accepts a regular expression as command-line input, for example:

```
$ pipenv run python testing/collect_tests.py
'chapter-0[1,7]/recipe-0[1,2,5]'
```

This command will run tests for Recipes 1, 2, and 5, in Chapters 1 and 7. A sample of the output looks as follows:

```
$ pipenv run python testing/collect_tests.py 'chapter-01/recipe-05'

recipe: Presenting options to the user

  /home/bast/tmp/cmake-cookbook/chapter-01/recipe-05/cxx-example
CMake Warning:
  Manually-specified variables were not used by the project:

    CMAKE_C_COMPILER
    CMAKE_Fortran_COMPILER


configuring ... OK
building configuration Debug ... OK
```

To get more verbose output, set VERBOSE_OUTPUT=ON:

```
$ env VERBOSE_OUTPUT=ON pipenv run python testing/collect_tests.py
'chapter-*/recipe-*'
```

Reporting problems and suggesting improvements

Please report issues at https://github.com/dev-cafe/cmake-cookbook/issues.

To contribute changes,we recommend forking the repository https://github.com/dev-cafe/cmake-cookbook and submitting changes using pull requests, following https://help.github.com/articles/creating-a-pull-request-from-a-fork/.

For non-trivial changes, we recommend to first describe and discuss the proposed change by opening an issue on https://github.com/dev-cafe/cmake-cookbook/issues before sending a pull request.

1

From a Simple Executable to Libraries

In this chapter, we will cover the following recipes:

- Compiling a single source file into an executable
- Switching generators
- Building and linking static and shared libraries
- Controlling compilation with conditionals
- Presenting options to the user
- Specifying the compiler
- Switching the build type
- Controlling compiler flags
- Setting the standard for the language
- Using control flow constructs

Introduction

The recipes in this chapter will walk you through fairly basic tasks needed to build your code: compiling an executable, compiling a library, performing build actions based on user input, and so forth. CMake is a *build system generator* particularly suited to being platform- and compiler-independent. We have striven to show this aspect in this chapter. Unless stated otherwise, all recipes are independent of the operating system; they can be run without modifications on GNU/Linux, macOS, and Windows.

The recipes in this book are mainly designed for C++ projects and demonstrated using C++ examples, but CMake can be used for projects in other languages, including C and Fortran. For any given recipe and whenever it makes sense, we have tried to include examples in C++, C, and Fortran. In this way, you will be able to choose the recipe in your favorite flavor. Some recipes are tailor-made to highlight challenges to overcome when a specific language is chosen.

Compiling a single source file into an executable

The code for this recipe is available at `https://github.com/dev-cafe/cmake-cookbook/tree/v1.0/chapter-01/recipe-01` and has C++, C, and Fortran examples. The recipe is valid with CMake version 3.5 (and higher) and has been tested on GNU/Linux, macOS, and Windows.

In this recipe, we will demonstrate how to run CMake to configure and build a simple project. The project consists of a single source file for a single executable. We will discuss the project in C++, but examples for C and Fortran are available in the GitHub repository.

Getting ready

We wish to compile the following source code into a single executable:

```
#include <cstdlib>
#include <iostream>
#include <string>

std::string say_hello() { return std::string("Hello, CMake world!"); }

int main() {
  std::cout << say_hello() << std::endl;
  return EXIT_SUCCESS;
}
```

How to do it

Alongside the source file, we need to provide CMake with a description of the operations to perform to configure the project for the build tools. The description is done in the CMake language, whose comprehensive documentation can be found online at `https://cmake.org/cmake/help/latest/`. We will place the CMake instructions into a file called `CMakeLists.txt`.

> The name of the file is *case sensitive*; it has to be called `CMakeLists.txt` for CMake to be able to parse it.

In detail, these are the steps to follow:

1. Open a text file with your favorite editor. The name of this file will be `CMakeLists.txt`.

2. The first line sets a minimum required version for CMake. A fatal error will be issued if a version of CMake lower than that is used:

   ```
   cmake_minimum_required(VERSION 3.5 FATAL_ERROR)
   ```

3. The second line declares the name of the project (recipe-01) and the supported language (CXX stands for C++):

   ```
   project(recipe-01 LANGUAGES CXX)
   ```

4. We instruct CMake to create a new *target*: the executable `hello-world`. This executable is generated by compiling and linking the source file `hello-world.cpp`. CMake will use default settings for the compiler and build automation tools selected:

   ```
   add_executable(hello-world hello-world.cpp)
   ```

5. Save the file in the same directory as the source file `hello-world.cpp`. Remember that it can only be named `CMakeLists.txt`.

6. We are now ready to configure the project by creating and stepping into a build directory:

   ```
   $ mkdir -p build
   $ cd build
   $ cmake ..

   -- The CXX compiler identification is GNU 8.1.0
   ```

```
-- Check for working CXX compiler: /usr/bin/c++
-- Check for working CXX compiler: /usr/bin/c++ -- works
-- Detecting CXX compiler ABI info
-- Detecting CXX compiler ABI info - done
-- Detecting CXX compile features
-- Detecting CXX compile features - done
-- Configuring done
-- Generating done
-- Build files have been written to: /home/user/cmake-
cookbook/chapter-01/recipe-01/cxx-example/build
```

7. If everything went well, the configuration for the project has been generated in the build directory. We can now compile the executable:

```
$ cmake --build .
```

```
Scanning dependencies of target hello-world
[ 50%] Building CXX object CMakeFiles/hello-world.dir/hello-
world.cpp.o
[100%] Linking CXX executable hello-world
[100%] Built target hello-world
```

How it works

In this recipe, we have used a simple CMakeLists.txt to build a "Hello world" executable:

```
cmake_minimum_required(VERSION 3.5 FATAL_ERROR)

project(recipe-01 LANGUAGES CXX)

add_executable(hello-world hello-world.cpp)
```

The CMake language is case *insensitive*, but the arguments are case *sensitive*.

In CMake, C++ is the default programming language. However, we suggest to always explicitly state the project's language in the project command using the LANGUAGES option.

To configure the project and generate its build system, we have to run CMake through its command-line interface (CLI). The CMake CLI offers a number of switches, cmake --help will output to screen the full help menu listing all of the available switches. We will learn more about them throughout the book. As you will notice from the output of cmake --help, most of them will let you access the CMake manual. The typical series of commands issued for generating the build system is the following:

```
$ mkdir -p build
$ cd build
$ cmake ..
```

Here, we created a directory, build, where the build system will be generated, we entered the build directory, and invoked CMake by pointing it to the location of CMakeLists.txt (in this case located in the parent directory). It is possible to use the following invocation to achieve the same effect:

```
$ cmake -H. -Bbuild
```

This invocation is cross-platform and introduces the -H and -B CLI switches. With -H. we are instructing CMake to search for the root CMakeLists.txt file in the current directory. -Bbuild tells CMake to generate all of its files in a directory called build.

> Note that the cmake -H. -Bbuild invocation of CMake is still undergoing standardization: https://cmake.org/pipermail/cmake-developers/2018-January/030520.html. This is the reason why we will instead use the traditional approach in this book (create a build directory, step into it, and configure the project by pointing CMake to the location of CMakeLists.txt).

Running the cmake command outputs a series of status messages to inform you of the configuration:

```
$ cmake ..

-- The CXX compiler identification is GNU 8.1.0
-- Check for working CXX compiler: /usr/bin/c++
-- Check for working CXX compiler: /usr/bin/c++ -- works
-- Detecting CXX compiler ABI info
-- Detecting CXX compiler ABI info - done
-- Detecting CXX compile features
-- Detecting CXX compile features - done
-- Configuring done
-- Generating done
-- Build files have been written to: /home/user/cmake-
cookbook/chapter-01/recipe-01/cxx-example/build
```

Running `cmake .` in the same directory as `CMakeLists.txt` would in principle be enough to configure a project. However, CMake would then write all generated files into the **root** of the project. This would be an *in-source build* and is generally undesirable, as it mixes the source and the build tree of the project. The *out-of-source* build we have demonstrated is the preferred practice.

CMake is a build system *generator*. You describe what type of operations the build system, such as Unix Makefiles, Ninja, Visual Studio, and so on, will have to run to get your code compiled. In turn, CMake *generates* the corresponding instructions for the chosen build system. By default, on GNU/Linux and macOS systems, CMake employs the Unix Makefiles generator. On Windows, Visual Studio is the default generator. We will take a closer look at generators in the next recipe and also revisit generators in *Chapter 13, Alternative Generators and Cross-compilation*.

On GNU/Linux, CMake will by default generate Unix Makefiles to build the project:

- `Makefile`: The set of instructions that `make` will run to build the project.
- `CMakeFiles`: Directory which contains temporary files, used by CMake for detecting the operating system, compiler, and so on. In addition, depending on the chosen *generator*, it also contains project-specific files.
- `cmake_install.cmake`: A CMake script handling install rules, which is used at install time.
- `CMakeCache.txt`: The CMake cache, as the filename suggests. This file is used by CMake when re-running the configuration.

To build the example project, we ran this command:

```
$ cmake --build .
```

This command is a generic, cross-platform wrapper to the native build command for the chosen *generator*, `make` in this case. We should not forget to test our example executable:

```
$ ./hello-world
```

```
Hello, CMake world!
```

Finally, we should point out that CMake does not enforce a specific name or a specific location for the build directory. We could have placed it completely outside the project path. This would have worked equally well:

```
$ mkdir -p /tmp/someplace
$ cd /tmp/someplace
$ cmake /path/to/source
$ cmake --build .
```

There is more

The official documentation at https://cmake.org/runningcmake/ gives a concise overview on running CMake. The build system generated by CMake, the Makefile in the example given above, will contain targets and rules to build object files, executables, and libraries for the given project. The hello-world executable was our only target in the current example, but running the command:

```
$ cmake --build . --target help

The following are some of the valid targets for this Makefile:
... all (the default if no target is provided)
... clean
... depend
... rebuild_cache
... hello-world
... edit_cache
... hello-world.o
... hello-world.i
... hello-world.s
```

reveals that CMake generates more targets than those strictly needed for building the executable itself. These targets can be chosen with the cmake --build . --target <target-name> syntax and achieve the following:

- all (or ALL_BUILD with the Visual Studio generator) is the default target and will build all other targets in the project.
- clean, is the target to choose if one wants to remove all generated files.
- depend, will invoke CMake to generate the dependecies, if any, for the source files.
- rebuild_cache, will once again invoke CMake to rebuild the CMakeCache.txt. This is needed in case new entries from the source need to be added.
- edit_cache, this target will let you edit cache entries directly.

For more complex projects, with a test stage and installation rules, CMake will generate additional convenience targets:

- test (or RUN_TESTS with the Visual Studio generator) will run the test suite with the help of CTest. We will discuss testing and CTest extensively in *Chapter 4, Creating and Running Tests*.
- install, will execute the installation rules for the project. We will discuss installation rules in *Chapter 10, Writing an Installer*.

- `package`, this target will invoke CPack to generate a redistributable package for the project. Packaging and CPack will be discussed in *Chapter 11, Packaging Projects*.

Switching generators

The code for this recipe is available at `https://github.com/dev-cafe/cmake-cookbook/tree/v1.0/chapter-01/recipe-02` and has a C++, C, and Fortran example. The recipe is valid with CMake version 3.5 (and higher) and has been tested on GNU/Linux, macOS, and Windows.

CMake is a build system generator and a single `CMakeLists.txt` can be used to configure projects for different toolstacks on different platforms. You describe in `CMakeLists.txt` the operations the build system will have to run to get your code configured and compiled. Based on these instructions, CMake will generate the corresponding instructions for the chosen build system (Unix Makefiles, Ninja, Visual Studio, and so on). We will revisit generators in *Chapter 13, Alternative Generators and Cross-compilation*.

Getting ready

CMake supports an extensive list of native build tools for different platforms. Both command-line tools, such as Unix Makefiles and Ninja, and integrated development environment (IDE) tools are supported. You can find an up-to-date list of the generators available on your platform and for your installed version of CMake by running the following:

```
$ cmake --help
```

The output of this command will list all options to the CMake command-line interface. At the bottom, you will find the list of available generators. For example, this is the output on a GNU/Linux machine with CMake 3.11.2 installed:

```
Generators

The following generators are available on this platform:
  Unix Makefiles               = Generates standard UNIX makefiles.
  Ninja                        = Generates build.ninja files.
  Watcom WMake                 = Generates Watcom WMake makefiles.
  CodeBlocks - Ninja           = Generates CodeBlocks project files.
```

```
CodeBlocks - Unix Makefiles = Generates CodeBlocks project files.
CodeLite - Ninja = Generates CodeLite project files.
CodeLite - Unix Makefiles = Generates CodeLite project files.
Sublime Text 2 - Ninja = Generates Sublime Text 2 project files.
Sublime Text 2 - Unix Makefiles = Generates Sublime Text 2 project files.
Kate - Ninja = Generates Kate project files.
Kate - Unix Makefiles = Generates Kate project files.
Eclipse CDT4 - Ninja = Generates Eclipse CDT 4.0 project files.
Eclipse CDT4 - Unix Makefiles= Generates Eclipse CDT 4.0 project files.
```

With this recipe, we will show how easy it is to switch generators for the same project.

How to do it

We will reuse `hello-world.cpp` and `CMakeLists.txt` from the previous recipe. The only difference is in the invocation of CMake, since we will now have to pass the generator explicitly with the -G CLI switch.

1. First, we configure the project using the following:

    ```
    $ mkdir -p build
    $ cd build
    $ cmake -G Ninja ..

    -- The CXX compiler identification is GNU 8.1.0
    -- Check for working CXX compiler: /usr/bin/c++
    -- Check for working CXX compiler: /usr/bin/c++ -- works
    -- Detecting CXX compiler ABI info
    -- Detecting CXX compiler ABI info - done
    -- Detecting CXX compile features
    -- Detecting CXX compile features - done
    -- Configuring done
    -- Generating done
    -- Build files have been written to: /home/user/cmake-
    cookbook/chapter-01/recipe-02/cxx-example/build
    ```

2. In the second step, we build the project:

    ```
    $ cmake --build .

    [2/2] Linking CXX executable hello-world
    ```

How it works

We have seen that the output of the configuration step was unchanged compared to the previous recipe. The output of the compilation step and the contents of the build directory will however be different, as every generator has its own specific set of files:

- `build.ninja` and `rules.ninja`: Contain all the build statements and build rules for Ninja.
- `CMakeCache.txt`: CMake always generates its own cache in this file, regardless of the chosen generator.
- `CMakeFiles`: Contains temporary files generated by CMake during configuration.
- `cmake_install.cmake`: CMake script handling install rules and which is used at install time.

Note how `cmake --build .` wrapped the `ninja` command in a unified, cross-platform interface.

See also

We will discuss alternative generators and cross-compilation in *Chapter 13, Alternative Generators and Cross-compilation*.

The CMake documentation is a good starting point to learn more about generators: `https://cmake.org/cmake/help/latest/manual/cmake-generators.7.html`.

Building and linking static and shared libraries

The code for this recipe is available at `https://github.com/dev-cafe/cmake-cookbook/tree/v1.0/chapter-01/recipe-03` and has a C++ and Fortran example. The recipe is valid with CMake version 3.5 (and higher) and has been tested on GNU/Linux, macOS, and Windows.

A project almost always consists of more than a single executable built from a single source file. Projects are split across multiple source files, often spread across different subdirectories in the source tree. This practice not only helps in keeping source code organized within a project, but greatly favors modularity, code reuse, and separation of concerns, since common tasks can be grouped into libraries. This separation also simplifies and speeds up recompilation of a project during development. In this recipe, we will show how to group sources into libraries and how to link targets against these libraries.

Getting ready

Let us go back to our very first example. However, instead of having one single source file for the executable, we will now introduce a class to wrap the message to be printed out to screen. This is our updated hello-world.cpp:

```
#include "Message.hpp"
#include <cstdlib>
#include <iostream>

int main() {
  Message say_hello("Hello, CMake World!");

  std::cout << say_hello << std::endl;

  Message say_goodbye("Goodbye, CMake World");

  std::cout << say_goodbye << std::endl;

  return EXIT_SUCCESS;
}
```

The Message class wraps a string, provides an overload for the << operator, and consists of two source files: the Message.hpp header file and the corresponding Message.cpp source file. The Message.hpp interface file contains the following:

```
#pragma once
#include <iosfwd>
#include <string>

class Message {
public:
  Message(const std::string &m) : message_(m) {}

  friend std::ostream &operator<<(std::ostream &os, Message &obj) {
    return obj.printObject(os);
  }
```

```
private:
  std::string message_;
  std::ostream &printObject(std::ostream &os);
};
```

The corresponding implementation is contained in `Message.cpp`:

```
#include "Message.hpp"
#include <iostream>
#include <string>

std::ostream &Message::printObject(std::ostream &os) {
  os << "This is my very nice message: " << std::endl;
  os << message_;

  return os;
}
```

How to do it

These two new files will also have to be compiled and we have to modify `CMakeLists.txt` accordingly. However, in this example we want to compile them first into a library, and not directly into the executable:

1. Create a new *target,* this time a static library. The name of the library will be the name of the target and the sources are listed as follows:

```
add_library(message
  STATIC
    Message.hpp
    Message.cpp
  )
```

2. The creation of the target for the `hello-world` executable is unmodified:

```
add_executable(hello-world hello-world.cpp)
```

3. Finally, tell CMake that the library target has to be linked into the executable target:

```
target_link_libraries(hello-world message)
```

4. We can configure and build with the same commands as before. This time a library will be compiled, alongside the `hello-world` executable:

```
$ mkdir -p build
$ cd build
$ cmake ..
$ cmake --build .

Scanning dependencies of target message
[ 25%] Building CXX object CMakeFiles/message.dir/Message.cpp.o
[ 50%] Linking CXX static library libmessage.a
[ 50%] Built target message
Scanning dependencies of target hello-world
[ 75%] Building CXX object CMakeFiles/hello-world.dir/hello-world.cpp.o
[100%] Linking CXX executable hello-world
[100%] Built target hello-world

$ ./hello-world

This is my very nice message:
Hello, CMake World!
This is my very nice message:
Goodbye, CMake World
```

How it works

The previous example introduced two new commands:

- `add_library(message STATIC Message.hpp Message.cpp)`: This will generate the necessary build tool instructions for compiling the specified sources into a library. The first argument to `add_library` is the name of the target. The same name can be used throughout `CMakeLists.txt` to refer to the library. The actual name of the generated library will be formed by CMake by adding the prefix `lib` in front and the appropriate extension as a suffix. The library extension is determined based on the second argument, `STATIC` or `SHARED`, and the operating system.

- `target_link_libraries(hello-world message)`: Links the library into the executable. This command will also guarantee that the `hello-world` executable properly depends on the message library. We thus ensure that the message library is always built before we attempt to link it to the `hello-world` executable.

After successful compilation, the build directory will contain the `libmessage.a` static library (on GNU/Linux) and the `hello-world` executable.

CMake accepts other values as valid for the second argument to `add_library` and we will encounter all of them in the rest of the book:

- `STATIC`, which we have already encountered, will be used to create static libraries, that is, archives of object files for use when linking other targets, such as executables.
- `SHARED` will be used to create shared libraries, that is, libraries that can be linked dynamically and loaded at runtime. Switching from a static library to a dynamic shared object (DSO) is as easy as using `add_library(message SHARED Message.hpp Message.cpp)` in `CMakeLists.txt`.
- `OBJECT` can be used to compile the sources in the list given to `add_library` to object files, but then neither archiving them into a static library nor linking them into a shared object. The use of object libraries is particularly useful if one needs to create both static and shared libraries in one go. We will demonstrate this in this recipe.
- `MODULE` libraries are once again DSOs. In contrast to `SHARED` libraries, they are not linked to any other target within the project, but may be loaded dynamically later on. This is the argument to use when building a runtime plugin.

CMake is also able to generate special types of libraries. These produce no output in the build system but are extremely helpful in organizing dependencies and build requirements between targets:

- `IMPORTED`, this type of library target represents a library located *outside* the project. The main use for this type of library is to model pre-existing dependencies of the project that are provided by upstream packages. As such `IMPORTED` libraries are to be treated as immutable. We will show examples of using `IMPORTED` libraries throughout the rest of the book. See also: `https://cmake.org/cmake/help/latest/manual/cmake-buildsystem.7.html#imported-targets`

- INTERFACE, this special type of CMake library is similar to an IMPORTED library, but is mutable and has no location. Its main use case is to model usage requirements for a target that is outside our project. We will show a use case for INTERFACE libraries in *Recipe 5, Distributing a project with dependencies as Conda package,* in *Chapter 11, Packaging Projects.* See also: https://cmake.org/cmake/help/latest/manual/cmake-buildsystem.7.html#interface-libraries
- ALIAS, as the name suggests, a library of this type defines an alias for a pre-existing library target within the project. It is thus not possible to choose an alias for an IMPORTED library. See also: https://cmake.org/cmake/help/latest/manual/cmake-buildsystem.7.html#alias-libraries

In this example, we have collected the sources directly using add_library. In later chapters, we demonstrate the use of the target_sources CMake command to collect sources, in particular in *Chapter 7, Structuring Projects.* See also this wonderful blog post by Craig Scott: https://crascit.com/2016/01/31/enhanced-source-file-handling-with-target_sources/ which further motivates the use of the target_sources command.

There is more

Let us now show the use of the object library functionality made available in CMake. We will use the same source files, but modify CMakeLists.txt:

```
cmake_minimum_required(VERSION 3.5 FATAL_ERROR)

project(recipe-03 LANGUAGES CXX)

add_library(message-objs
  OBJECT
    Message.hpp
    Message.cpp
  )

# this is only needed for older compilers
# but doesn't hurt either to have it
set_target_properties(message-objs
  PROPERTIES
    POSITION_INDEPENDENT_CODE 1
  )

add_library(message-shared
  SHARED
    $<TARGET_OBJECTS:message-objs>
  )
```

```
add_library(message-static
  STATIC
    $<TARGET_OBJECTS:message-objs>
  )

add_executable(hello-world hello-world.cpp)

target_link_libraries(hello-world message-static)
```

First, notice that the `add_library` command changed to `add_library(message-objs OBJECT Message.hpp Message.cpp)`. Additionally, we have to make sure that the compilation to object files generates position-independent code. This is done by setting the corresponding *property* of the `message-objs` target, with the `set_target_properties` command.

> The need to explicitly set the `POSITION_INDEPENDENT_CODE` property for the target might only arise on certain platforms and/or using older compilers.

This object library can now be used to obtain both the static library, called `message-static`, and the shared library, called `message-shared`. It is important to note the *generator expression syntax* used to refer to the object library: `$<TARGET_OBJECTS:message-objs>`. Generator expressions are constructs that CMake evaluates at generation time, right after configuration time, to produce configuration-specific build output. See also: `https://cmake.org/cmake/help/latest/manual/cmake-generator-expressions.7.html`. We will delve into generator expressions later in *Chapter 5, Configure-time and Build-time Operations*. Finally, the `hello-world` executable is linked with the static version of the `message` library.

Is it possible to have CMake generate the two libraries with the same name? In other words, can both of them be called `message` instead of `message-static` and `message-shared`? We will need to modify the properties of these two targets:

```
add_library(message-shared
  SHARED
    $<TARGET_OBJECTS:message-objs>
  )
set_target_properties(message-shared
  PROPERTIES
    OUTPUT_NAME "message"
  )

add_library(message-static
  STATIC
```

```
    $<TARGET_OBJECTS:message-objs>
  )
set_target_properties(message-static
  PROPERTIES
    OUTPUT_NAME "message"
  )
```

Can we link against the DSO? It depends on the operating system and compiler:

1. On GNU/Linux and macOS, it will work, regardless of the chosen compiler.
2. On Windows, it will not work with Visual Studio, but it will work with MinGW and MSYS2.

Why? Generating good DSOs requires the programmer to limit *symbol visibility*. This is achieved with the help of the compiler, but conventions are different on different operating systems and compilers. CMake has a powerful mechanism for taking care of this and we will explain how it works in *Chapter 10, Writing an Installer*.

Controlling compilation with conditionals

The code for this recipe is available at `https://github.com/dev-cafe/cmake-cookbook/tree/v1.0/chapter-01/recipe-04` and has a C++ example. The recipe is valid with CMake version 3.5 (and higher) and has been tested on GNU/Linux, macOS, and Windows.

So far, we have looked at fairly simple projects, where the execution flow for CMake was linear: from a set of source files to a single executable, possibly *via* static or shared libraries. To ensure complete control over the execution flow of all the steps involved in building a project, configuration, compilation, and linkage, CMake offers its own language. In this recipe, we will explore the use of the conditional construct `if-elseif-else-endif`.

The CMake language is fairly large and consists of basic control constructs, CMake-specific commands, and infrastructure for modularly extending the language with new functions. A complete overview can be found online here: `https://cmake.org/cmake/help/latest/manual/cmake-language.7.html`.

How to do it

Let us start with the same source code as for the previous recipe. We want to be able to toggle between two behaviors:

1. Build `Message.hpp` and `Message.cpp` into a library, static or shared, and then link the resulting library into the `hello-world` executable.
2. Build `Message.hpp`, `Message.cpp`, and `hello-world.cpp` into a single executable, without producing the library.

Let us construct `CMakeLists.txt` to achieve this:

1. We start out by defining the minimum CMake version, project name, and supported language:

   ```
   cmake_minimum_required(VERSION 3.5 FATAL_ERROR)

   project(recipe-04 LANGUAGES CXX)
   ```

2. We introduce a new variable, `USE_LIBRARY`. This is a logical variable and its value will be set to `OFF`. We also print its value for the user:

   ```
   set(USE_LIBRARY OFF)

   message(STATUS "Compile sources into a library? ${USE_LIBRARY}")
   ```

3. Set the `BUILD_SHARED_LIBS` global variable, defined in CMake, to `OFF`. Calling `add_library` and omitting the second argument will build a static library:

   ```
   set(BUILD_SHARED_LIBS OFF)
   ```

4. We then introduce a variable, `_sources`, listing `Message.hpp` and `Message.cpp`:

   ```
   list(APPEND _sources Message.hpp Message.cpp)
   ```

5. We then introduce an `if-else` statement based on the value of `USE_LIBRARY`. If the logical toggle is true, `Message.hpp` and `Message.cpp` will be packaged into a library:

   ```
   if(USE_LIBRARY)
     # add_library will create a static library
     # since BUILD_SHARED_LIBS is OFF
     add_library(message ${_sources})
   ```

```
    add_executable(hello-world hello-world.cpp)

    target_link_libraries(hello-world message)
else()
    add_executable(hello-world hello-world.cpp ${_sources})
endif()
```

6. We can again build with the same set of commands. Since USE_LIBRARY is set to OFF, the hello-world executable will be compiled from all sources. This can be verified by running the objdump -x command on GNU/Linux.

How it works

We have introduced two variables: USE_LIBRARY and BUILD_SHARED_LIBS. Both of them have been set to OFF. As detailed in the CMake language documentation, true or false values can be expressed in a number of ways:

- A logical variable is true if it is set to any of the following: 1, ON, YES, TRUE, Y, or a non-zero number.
- A logical variable is false if it is set to any of the following: 0, OFF, NO, FALSE, N, IGNORE, NOTFOUND, an empty string, or it ends in the suffix -NOTFOUND.

The USE_LIBRARY variable will toggle between the first and the second behavior. BUILD_SHARED_LIBS is a global flag offered by CMake. Remember that the add_library command can be invoked without passing the STATIC/SHARED/OBJECT argument. This is because, internally, the BUILD_SHARED_LIBS global variable is looked up; if false or undefined, a static library will be generated.

This example shows that it is possible to introduce conditionals to control the execution flow in CMake. However, the current setup does not allow the toggles to be set from outside, that is, without modifying CMakeLists.txt by hand. In principle, we want to be able to expose all toggles to the user, so that configuration can be tweaked without modifying the code for the build system. We will show how to do that in a moment.

> The () in else() and endif() may surprise you when starting to read and write CMake code. The historical reason for these is the ability to indicate the scope. For instance, it is possible instead to use if(USE_LIBRARY) ... else(USE_LIBRARY) ... endif(USE_LIBRARY) if this helps the reader. This is a matter of taste.

> When introducing the `_sources` variable, we have indicated to readers of this code that this is a local variable that should not be used outside the current scope by prefixing it with an underscore.

Presenting options to the user

> The code for this recipe is available at `https://github.com/dev-cafe/` `cmake-cookbook/tree/v1.0/chapter-01/recipe-05` and has a C++ example. The recipe is valid with CMake version 3.5 (and higher) and has been tested on GNU/Linux, macOS, and Windows.

In the previous recipe, we introduced conditionals in a rather rigid fashion: by introducing variables with a given truth value hardcoded. This can be useful sometimes, but it prevents users of your code from easily toggling these variables. Another disadvantage of the rigid approach is that the CMake code does not communicate to the reader that this is a value that is expected to be modified from outside. The recommended way to toggle behavior in the build system generation for your project is to present logical switches as options in your `CMakeLists.txt` using the `option()` command. This recipe will show you how to use this command.

How to do it

Let us have a look at our static/shared library example from the previous recipe. Instead of hardcoding `USE_LIBRARY` to `ON` or `OFF`, we will now prefer to expose it as an option with a default value that can be changed from the outside:

1. Replace the `set(USE_LIBRARY OFF)` command of the previous recipe with an option. The option will have the same name and its default value will be `OFF`:

   ```
   option(USE_LIBRARY "Compile sources into a library" OFF)
   ```

2. Now, we can switch the generation of the library by passing the information to CMake *via* its `-D` CLI option:

   ```
   $ mkdir -p build
   $ cd build
   $ cmake -D USE_LIBRARY=ON ..

   -- ...
   ```

```
-- Compile sources into a library? ON
-- ...

$ cmake --build .

Scanning dependencies of target message
[ 25%] Building CXX object CMakeFiles/message.dir/Message.cpp.o
[ 50%] Linking CXX static library libmessage.a
[ 50%] Built target message
Scanning dependencies of target hello-world
[ 75%] Building CXX object CMakeFiles/hello-world.dir/hello-
world.cpp.o
[100%] Linking CXX executable hello-world
[100%] Built target hello-world
```

The -D switch is used to set any type of variable for CMake: logicals, paths, and so forth.

How it works

The option command accepts three arguments:

```
option(<option_variable> "help string" [initial value])
```

- <option_variable> is the name of variable representing the option.
- "help string" is a string documenting the option. This documentation becomes visible in terminal-based or graphical user interfaces for CMake.
- [initial value] is the default value for the option, either ON or OFF.

There is more

Sometimes there is the need to introduce options that are dependent on the value of other options. In our example, we might wish to offer the option to either produce a static or a shared library. However, this option would have no meaning if the USE_LIBRARY logical was not set to ON. CMake offers the cmake_dependent_option() command to define options that depend on other options:

```
include(CMakeDependentOption)

# second option depends on the value of the first
cmake_dependent_option(
  MAKE_STATIC_LIBRARY "Compile sources into a static library" OFF
  "USE_LIBRARY" ON
  )
```

```
# third option depends on the value of the first
cmake_dependent_option(
  MAKE_SHARED_LIBRARY "Compile sources into a shared library" ON
  "USE_LIBRARY" ON
  )
```

If `USE_LIBRARY` is `ON`, `MAKE_STATIC_LIBRARY` defaults to `OFF`, while `MAKE_SHARED_LIBRARY` defaults to `ON`. So we can run this:

$ cmake -D USE_LIBRARY=OFF -D MAKE_SHARED_LIBRARY=ON ..

This will still not build a library, since `USE_LIBRARY` is still set to `OFF`.

As mentioned earlier, CMake has mechanisms in place to extend its syntax and capabilities through the inclusion of *modules*, either shipped with CMake itself or custom ones. In this case, we have included a module called `CMakeDependentOption`. Without the include statement, the `cmake_dependent_option()` command would not be available for use. See also `https://cmake.org/cmake/help/latest/module/CMakeDependentOption.html`.

> The manual page for any module can also be accessed from the command line using `cmake --help-module <name-of-module>`. For example, `cmake --help-option CMakeDependentOption` will print the manual page for the module just discussed.

Specifying the compiler

> The code for this recipe is available at `https://github.com/dev-cafe/cmake-cookbook/tree/v1.0/chapter-01/recipe-06` and has a C++/C example. The recipe is valid with CMake version 3.5 (and higher) and has been tested on GNU/Linux, macOS, and Windows.

One aspect that we have not given much thought to so far is the selection of compilers. CMake is sophisticated enough to select the most appropriate compiler given the platform and the generator. CMake is also able to set compiler flags to a sane set of defaults. However, often we wish to control the choice of the compiler, and in this recipe we will show how this can be done. In later recipes, we will also consider the choice of build type and show how to control compiler flags.

How to do it

How can we select a specific compiler? For example, what if we want to use the Intel or Portland Group compilers? CMake stores compilers for each language in the CMAKE_<LANG>_COMPILER variable, where <LANG> is any of the supported languages, for our purposes CXX, C, or Fortran. The user can set this variable in one of two ways:

1. By using the -D option in the CLI, for example:

   ```
   $ cmake -D CMAKE_CXX_COMPILER=clang++ ..
   ```

2. By exporting the environment variables CXX for the C++ compiler, CC for the C compiler, and FC for the Fortran compiler. For example, use this command to use clang++ as the C++ compiler:

   ```
   $ env CXX=clang++ cmake ..
   ```

Any of the recipes discussed so far can be configured for use with any other compiler by passing the appropriate option.

> CMake is aware of the environment and many options can either be set *via* the -D switch of its CLI or *via* an environment variable. The former mechanism overrides the latter, but we suggest to always set options explicitly with -D. **Explicit is better than implicit**, since environment variables might be set to values that are not suitable for the project at hand.

We have here assumed that the additional compilers are available in the standard paths where CMake does its lookups. If that is not the case, the user will need to pass the *full path* to the compiler executable or wrapper.

> We recommend to set the compilers using the -D CMAKE_<LANG>_COMPILER CLI options instead of exporting CXX, CC, and FC. This is the only way that is guaranteed to be cross-platform and compatible with non-POSIX shells. It also avoids polluting your environment with variables, which may affect the environment for external libraries built together with your project.

How it works

At configure time, CMake performs a series of platform tests to determine which compilers are available and if they are suitable for the project at hand. A suitable compiler is not only determined by the platform we are working on, but also by the generator we want to use. The first test CMake performs is based on the name of the compiler for the project language. For example, if cc is a working C compiler, then that is what will be used as the default compiler for a C project. On GNU/Linux, using Unix Makefiles or Ninja, the compilers in the GCC family will be most likely chosen by default for C++, C, and Fortran. On Microsoft Windows, the C++ and C compilers in Visual Studio will be selected, provided Visual Studio is the generator. MinGW compilers are the default if MinGW or MSYS Makefiles were chosen as generators.

There is more

Where can we find which default compilers and compiler flags will be picked up by CMake for our platform? CMake offers the --system-information flag, which will dump all information about your system to the screen or a file. To see this, try the following:

```
$ cmake --system-information information.txt
```

Searching through the file (in this case, information.txt), you will find the default values for the CMAKE_CXX_COMPILER, CMAKE_C_COMPILER, and CMAKE_Fortran_COMPILER options, together with their default flags. We will have a look at the flags in the next recipe.

CMake provides additional variables to interact with compilers:

- CMAKE_<LANG>_COMPILER_LOADED: This is set to TRUE if the language, <LANG>, was enabled for the project.
- CMAKE_<LANG>_COMPILER_ID: The compiler identification string, unique to the compiler vendor. This is, for example, GCC for the GNU Compiler Collection, AppleClang for Clang on macOS, and MSVC for Microsoft Visual Studio Compiler. Note, however, that this variable is not guaranteed to be defined for all compilers or languages.
- CMAKE_COMPILER_IS_GNU<LANG>: This logical variable is set to TRUE if the compiler for the language <LANG> is part of the GNU Compiler Collection. Notice that the <LANG> portion of the variable name follows the GNU convention: it will be CC for the C language, CXX for the C++ language, and G77 for the Fortran language.

- CMAKE_<LANG>_COMPILER_VERSION: This variable holds a string with the version of the compiler for the given language. The version information is given in the major[.minor[.patch[.tweak]]] format. However, as for CMAKE_<LANG>_COMPILER_ID, this variable is not guaranteed to be defined for all compilers or languages.

We can try to configure the following example CMakeLists.txt with different compilers. In this example, we will use CMake variables to probe what compiler we are using and what version:

```
cmake_minimum_required(VERSION 3.5 FATAL_ERROR)

project(recipe-06 LANGUAGES C CXX)

message(STATUS "Is the C++ compiler loaded? ${CMAKE_CXX_COMPILER_LOADED}")
if(CMAKE_CXX_COMPILER_LOADED)
  message(STATUS "The C++ compiler ID is: ${CMAKE_CXX_COMPILER_ID}")
  message(STATUS "Is the C++ from GNU? ${CMAKE_COMPILER_IS_GNUCXX}")
  message(STATUS "The C++ compiler version is:
${CMAKE_CXX_COMPILER_VERSION}")
endif()

message(STATUS "Is the C compiler loaded? ${CMAKE_C_COMPILER_LOADED}")
if(CMAKE_C_COMPILER_LOADED)
  message(STATUS "The C compiler ID is: ${CMAKE_C_COMPILER_ID}")
  message(STATUS "Is the C from GNU? ${CMAKE_COMPILER_IS_GNUCC}")
  message(STATUS "The C compiler version is: ${CMAKE_C_COMPILER_VERSION}")
endif()
```

Observe that this example does not contain any targets, so there is nothing to build and we will only focus on the configuration step:

```
$ mkdir -p build
$ cd build
$ cmake ..

...
-- Is the C++ compiler loaded? 1
-- The C++ compiler ID is: GNU
-- Is the C++ from GNU? 1
-- The C++ compiler version is: 8.1.0
-- Is the C compiler loaded? 1
-- The C compiler ID is: GNU
-- Is the C from GNU? 1
-- The C compiler version is: 8.1.0
...
```

The output will of course depend on the available and chosen compilers and compiler versions.

Switching the build type

The code for this recipe is available at `https://github.com/dev-cafe/` `cmake-cookbook/tree/v1.0/chapter-01/recipe-07` and has a C++/C example. The recipe is valid with CMake version 3.5 (and higher) and has been tested on GNU/Linux, macOS, and Windows.

CMake has the notion of build types or configurations, such as `Debug`, `Release`, and so forth. Within one configuration, one can collect related options or properties, such as compiler and linker flags, for a `Debug` or `Release` build. The variable governing the configuration to be used when generating the build system is `CMAKE_BUILD_TYPE`. This variable is empty by default, and the values recognized by CMake are:

1. `Debug` for building your library or executable without optimization and with debug symbols,
2. `Release` for building your library or executable with optimization and without debug symbols,
3. `RelWithDebInfo` for building your library or executable with less aggressive optimizations and with debug symbols,
4. `MinSizeRel` for building your library or executable with optimizations that do not increase object code size.

How to do it

In this recipe, we will show how the build type can be set for an example project:

1. We start out by defining the minimum CMake version, project name, and supported languages:

```
cmake_minimum_required(VERSION 3.5 FATAL_ERROR)

project(recipe-07 LANGUAGES C CXX)
```

2. Then, we set a default build type (in this case, `Release`) and print it in a message for the user. Note that the variable is set as a `CACHE` variable, so that it can be subsequently edited through the cache:

```
if(NOT CMAKE_BUILD_TYPE)
   set(CMAKE_BUILD_TYPE Release CACHE STRING "Build type" FORCE)
endif()

message(STATUS "Build type: ${CMAKE_BUILD_TYPE}")
```

3. Finally, we print corresponding compile flags set by CMake as a function of the build type:

```
message(STATUS "C flags, Debug configuration:
${CMAKE_C_FLAGS_DEBUG}")
message(STATUS "C flags, Release configuration:
${CMAKE_C_FLAGS_RELEASE}")
message(STATUS "C flags, Release configuration with Debug info:
${CMAKE_C_FLAGS_RELWITHDEBINFO}")
message(STATUS "C flags, minimal Release configuration:
${CMAKE_C_FLAGS_MINSIZEREL}")

message(STATUS "C++ flags, Debug configuration:
${CMAKE_CXX_FLAGS_DEBUG}")
message(STATUS "C++ flags, Release configuration:
${CMAKE_CXX_FLAGS_RELEASE}")
message(STATUS "C++ flags, Release configuration with Debug info:
${CMAKE_CXX_FLAGS_RELWITHDEBINFO}")
message(STATUS "C++ flags, minimal Release configuration:
${CMAKE_CXX_FLAGS_MINSIZEREL}")
```

4. Let us now verify the output of a default configuration:

```
$ mkdir -p build
$ cd build
$ cmake ..

...
-- Build type: Release
-- C flags, Debug configuration: -g
-- C flags, Release configuration: -O3 -DNDEBUG
-- C flags, Release configuration with Debug info: -O2 -g -DNDEBUG
-- C flags, minimal Release configuration: -Os -DNDEBUG
-- C++ flags, Debug configuration: -g
-- C++ flags, Release configuration: -O3 -DNDEBUG
-- C++ flags, Release configuration with Debug info: -O2 -g -
DNDEBUG
-- C++ flags, minimal Release configuration: -Os -DNDEBUG
```

5. And now, let us switch the build type:

```
$ cmake -D CMAKE_BUILD_TYPE=Debug ..

-- Build type: Debug
-- C flags, Debug configuration: -g
-- C flags, Release configuration: -O3 -DNDEBUG
-- C flags, Release configuration with Debug info: -O2 -g -DNDEBUG
-- C flags, minimal Release configuration: -Os -DNDEBUG
-- C++ flags, Debug configuration: -g
-- C++ flags, Release configuration: -O3 -DNDEBUG
-- C++ flags, Release configuration with Debug info: -O2 -g -
DNDEBUG
-- C++ flags, minimal Release configuration: -Os -DNDEBUG
```

How it works

We have demonstrated how to set a default build type and how to override it from the command line. With this, we can control whether a project is built with optimization flags or with all optimizations turned off, and instead debugging information on. We have also seen what kind of flags are used for the various available configurations, as this depends on the compiler of choice. Instead of printing the flags explicitly during a run of CMake, one can also peruse the output of running `cmake --system-information` to find out what the presets are for the current combination of platform, default compiler, and language. In the next recipe, we will discuss how to extend or adjust compiler flags for different compilers and different build types.

There is more

We have shown how the variable `CMAKE_BUILD_TYPE` (documented at this link: `https://cmake.org/cmake/help/v3.5/variable/CMAKE_BUILD_TYPE.html`) defines the configuration of the generated build system. It is often helpful to build a project both in `Release` *and* `Debug` configurations, for example when assessing the effect of compiler optimization levels. For *single-configuration* generators, such as Unix Makefiles, MSYS Makefiles or Ninja, this requires running CMake twice, that is a full reconfiguration of the project. CMake however also supports *multiple-configuration* generators. These are usually project files offered by integrated-development environments, most notably Visual Studio and Xcode which can handle more than one configuration simultaneously. The available configuration types for these generators can be tweaked with the `CMAKE_CONFIGURATION_TYPES` variable which will accept a list of values (documentation available at this link: `https://cmake.org/cmake/help/v3.5/variable/CMAKE_CONFIGURATION_TYPES.html`).

The following CMake invocation with the Visual Studio:

```
$ mkdir -p build
$ cd build
$ cmake .. -G"Visual Studio 12 2017 Win64" -D
CMAKE_CONFIGURATION_TYPES="Release;Debug"
```

will generate a build tree for both the `Release` and `Debug` configuration. You can then decide which of the two to build by using the `--config` flag:

```
$ cmake --build . --config Release
```

> **TIP**
>
> When developing code with single-configuration generators, create separate build directories for the `Release` and `Debug` build types, both configuring the same source. With this, you can switch between the two without triggering a full reconfiguration and recompilation.

Controlling compiler flags

> The code for this recipe is available at `https://github.com/dev-cafe/cmake-cookbook/tree/v1.0/chapter-01/recipe-08` and has a C++ example. The recipe is valid with CMake version 3.5 (and higher) and has been tested on GNU/Linux, macOS, and Windows.

The previous recipes showed how to probe CMake for information on the compilers and how to tune compiler optimizations for all targets in your project. The latter task is a subset of the general need to control which compiler flags are used in your project. CMake offers a lot of flexibility for adjusting or extending compiler flags and you can choose between two main approaches:

- CMake treats compile options as properties of targets. Thus, one can set compile options on a per target basis, without overriding CMake defaults.
- You can directly modify the `CMAKE_<LANG>_FLAGS_<CONFIG>` variables by using the `-D` CLI switch. These will affect all targets in the project and override or extend CMake defaults.

In this recipe, we will show both approaches.

Getting ready

We will compile an example program to calculate the area of different geometric shapes. The code has a `main` function in a file called `compute-areas.cpp`:

```cpp
#include "geometry_circle.hpp"
#include "geometry_polygon.hpp"
#include "geometry_rhombus.hpp"
#include "geometry_square.hpp"

#include <cstdlib>
#include <iostream>

int main() {
  using namespace geometry;

  double radius = 2.5293;
  double A_circle = area::circle(radius);
  std::cout << "A circle of radius " << radius << " has an area of " <<
A_circle
          << std::endl;

  int nSides = 19;
  double side = 1.29312;
  double A_polygon = area::polygon(nSides, side);
  std::cout << "A regular polygon of " << nSides << " sides of length " <<
side
          << " has an area of " << A_polygon << std::endl;

  double d1 = 5.0;
  double d2 = 7.8912;
  double A_rhombus = area::rhombus(d1, d2);
  std::cout << "A rhombus of major diagonal " << d1 << " and minor diagonal
" << d2
          << " has an area of " << A_rhombus << std::endl;

  double l = 10.0;
  double A_square = area::square(l);
  std::cout << "A square of side " << l << " has an area of " << A_square
          << std::endl;

  return EXIT_SUCCESS;
}
```

The implementations of the various functions are contained in other files: each geometric shape has a header file and a corresponding source file. In total, we have four header files and five source files to compile:

```
.
├───── CMakeLists.txt
├───── compute-areas.cpp
├───── geometry_circle.cpp
├───── geometry_circle.hpp
├───── geometry_polygon.cpp
├───── geometry_polygon.hpp
├───── geometry_rhombus.cpp
├───── geometry_rhombus.hpp
├───── geometry_square.cpp
└───── geometry_square.hpp
```

We will not provide listings for all these files but rather refer the reader to `https://github.com/dev-cafe/cmake-cookbook/tree/v1.0/chapter-01/recipe-08`.

How to do it

Now that we have the sources in place, our goal will be to configure the project and experiment with compiler flags:

1. We set the minimum required version of CMake:

   ```
   cmake_minimum_required(VERSION 3.5 FATAL_ERROR)
   ```

2. We declare the name of the project and the language:

   ```
   project(recipe-08 LANGUAGES CXX)
   ```

3. Then, we print the current set of compiler flags. CMake will use these for all C++ targets:

   ```
   message("C++ compiler flags: ${CMAKE_CXX_FLAGS}")
   ```

4. We prepare a list of flags for our targets. Some of these will not be available on Windows and we make sure to account for that case:

   ```
   list(APPEND flags "-fPIC" "-Wall")
   if(NOT WIN32)
     list(APPEND flags "-Wextra" "-Wpedantic")
   endif()
   ```

5. We add a new target, the `geometry` library and list its source dependencies:

```
add_library(geometry
  STATIC
    geometry_circle.cpp
    geometry_circle.hpp
    geometry_polygon.cpp
    geometry_polygon.hpp
    geometry_rhombus.cpp
    geometry_rhombus.hpp
    geometry_square.cpp
    geometry_square.hpp
  )
```

6. We set compile options for this library target:

```
target_compile_options(geometry
  PRIVATE
    ${flags}
  )
```

7. We then add a target for the `compute-areas` executable:

```
add_executable(compute-areas compute-areas.cpp)
```

8. We also set compile options for the executable target:

```
target_compile_options(compute-areas
  PRIVATE
    "-fPIC"
  )
```

9. Finally, we link the executable to the `geometry` library:

```
target_link_libraries(compute-areas geometry)
```

How it works

In this example, the warning flags `-Wall`, `-Wextra`, and `-Wpedantic` will be added to the compile options for the `geometry` target; both the `compute-areas` and `geometry` targets will use the `-fPIC` flag. Compile options can be added with three levels of visibility: `INTERFACE`, `PUBLIC`, and `PRIVATE`.

The visibility levels have the following meaning:

- With the PRIVATE attribute, compile options will only be applied to the given target and not to other targets consuming it. In our examples, compiler options set on the geometry target will not be inherited by the compute-areas, even though compute-areas will link against the geometry library.
- With the INTERFACE attribute, compile options on a given target will only be applied to targets consuming it.
- With the PUBLIC attribute, compile options will be applied to the given target and all other targets consuming it.

The visibility levels of target properties are at the core of a modern usage of CMake and we will revisit this topic often and extensively throughout the book. Adding compile options in this way does not pollute the CMAKE_<LANG>_FLAGS_<CONFIG> global CMake variables and gives you granular control over what options are used on which targets.

How can we verify whether the flags are correctly used as we intended to? Or in other words, how can you discover which compile flags are actually used by a CMake project? One approach is the following and it uses CMake to pass additional arguments, in this case the environment variable VERBOSE=1, to the native build tool:

```
$ mkdir -p build
$ cd build
$ cmake ..
$ cmake --build . -- VERBOSE=1

... lots of output ...

[ 14%] Building CXX object CMakeFiles/geometry.dir/geometry_circle.cpp.o
/usr/bin/c++ -fPIC -Wall -Wextra -Wpedantic -o
CMakeFiles/geometry.dir/geometry_circle.cpp.o -c /home/bast/tmp/cmake-
cookbook/chapter-01/recipe-08/cxx-example/geometry_circle.cpp
[ 28%] Building CXX object CMakeFiles/geometry.dir/geometry_polygon.cpp.o
/usr/bin/c++ -fPIC -Wall -Wextra -Wpedantic -o
CMakeFiles/geometry.dir/geometry_polygon.cpp.o -c /home/bast/tmp/cmake-
cookbook/chapter-01/recipe-08/cxx-example/geometry_polygon.cpp
[ 42%] Building CXX object CMakeFiles/geometry.dir/geometry_rhombus.cpp.o
/usr/bin/c++ -fPIC -Wall -Wextra -Wpedantic -o
CMakeFiles/geometry.dir/geometry_rhombus.cpp.o -c /home/bast/tmp/cmake-
cookbook/chapter-01/recipe-08/cxx-example/geometry_rhombus.cpp
[ 57%] Building CXX object CMakeFiles/geometry.dir/geometry_square.cpp.o
/usr/bin/c++ -fPIC -Wall -Wextra -Wpedantic -o
CMakeFiles/geometry.dir/geometry_square.cpp.o -c /home/bast/tmp/cmake-
cookbook/chapter-01/recipe-08/cxx-example/geometry_square.cpp
```

```
... more output ...

[ 85%] Building CXX object CMakeFiles/compute-areas.dir/compute-areas.cpp.o
/usr/bin/c++ -fPIC -o CMakeFiles/compute-areas.dir/compute-areas.cpp.o -c
/home/bast/tmp/cmake-cookbook/chapter-01/recipe-08/cxx-example/compute-
areas.cpp

... more output ...
```

The preceding output confirms that the compile flags were correctly set according to our instructions.

The second approach to controlling compiler flags involves no modifications to `CMakeLists.txt`. If one wants to modify compiler options for the `geometry` and `compute-areas` targets in this project, it is as easy as invoking CMake with an additional argument:

$ cmake -D CMAKE_CXX_FLAGS="-fno-exceptions -fno-rtti" ..

As you might have guessed, this command will compile the project, deactivating exceptions and runtime type identification (RTTI).

The two approaches can also be coupled. One can use a basic set of flags globally, while keeping control of what happens on a per target basis. We can use `CMakeLists.txt` and running this command:

$ cmake -D CMAKE_CXX_FLAGS="-fno-exceptions -fno-rtti" ..

This will configure the `geometry` target with `-fno-exceptions -fno-rtti -fPIC -Wall -Wextra -Wpedantic`, while configuring `compute-areas` with `-fno-exceptions -fno-rtti -fPIC`.

> In the rest of the book, we will generally set compiler flags on a per target basis and this is the practice that we recommend for your projects. Using `target_compile_options()` not only allows for a fine-grained control over compilation options, but it also integrates better with more advanced features of CMake.

There is more

Most of the time, flags are compiler-specific. Our current example will only work with GCC and Clang; compilers from other vendors will not understand many, if not all, of those flags. Clearly, if a project aims at being truly cross-platform, this problem has to be solved. There are three approaches to this.

The most typical approach will append a list of desired compiler flags to each configuration type CMake variable, that is, to CMAKE_<LANG>_FLAGS_<CONFIG>. These flags are set to what is known to work for the given compiler vendor, and will thus be enclosed in if-endif clauses that check the CMAKE_<LANG>_COMPILER_ID variable, for example:

```
if(CMAKE_CXX_COMPILER_ID MATCHES GNU)
   list(APPEND CMAKE_CXX_FLAGS "-fno-rtti" "-fno-exceptions")
   list(APPEND CMAKE_CXX_FLAGS_DEBUG "-Wsuggest-final-types" "-Wsuggest-
final-methods" "-Wsuggest-override")
   list(APPEND CMAKE_CXX_FLAGS_RELEASE "-O3" "-Wno-unused")
endif()

if(CMAKE_CXX_COMPILER_ID MATCHES Clang)
   list(APPEND CMAKE_CXX_FLAGS "-fno-rtti" "-fno-exceptions" "-Qunused-
arguments" "-fcolor-diagnostics")
   list(APPEND CMAKE_CXX_FLAGS_DEBUG "-Wdocumentation")
   list(APPEND CMAKE_CXX_FLAGS_RELEASE "-O3" "-Wno-unused")
endif()
```

A more refined approach does not tamper with the CMAKE_<LANG>_FLAGS_<CONFIG> variables at all and rather defines project-specific lists of flags:

```
set(COMPILER_FLAGS)
set(COMPILER_FLAGS_DEBUG)
set(COMPILER_FLAGS_RELEASE)

if(CMAKE_CXX_COMPILER_ID MATCHES GNU)
   list(APPEND CXX_FLAGS "-fno-rtti" "-fno-exceptions")
   list(APPEND CXX_FLAGS_DEBUG "-Wsuggest-final-types" "-Wsuggest-final-
methods" "-Wsuggest-override")
   list(APPEND CXX_FLAGS_RELEASE "-O3" "-Wno-unused")
endif()

if(CMAKE_CXX_COMPILER_ID MATCHES Clang)
   list(APPEND CXX_FLAGS "-fno-rtti" "-fno-exceptions" "-Qunused-arguments"
"-fcolor-diagnostics")
   list(APPEND CXX_FLAGS_DEBUG "-Wdocumentation")
   list(APPEND CXX_FLAGS_RELEASE "-O3" "-Wno-unused")
endif()
```

Later on, it uses generator expressions to set compiler flags on a per-configuration and per-target basis:

```
target_compile_option(compute-areas
  PRIVATE
    ${CXX_FLAGS}
    "$<$<CONFIG:Debug>:${CXX_FLAGS_DEBUG}>"
    "$<$<CONFIG:Release>:${CXX_FLAGS_RELEASE}>"
  )
```

We have shown both approaches in the current recipe and have clearly recommended the latter (project-specific variables and `target_compile_options`) over the former (CMake variables).

Both approaches work and are widely used in many projects. However, they have shortcomings. As we have already mentioned, `CMAKE_<LANG>_COMPILER_ID` is not guaranteed to be defined for all compiler vendors. In addition, some flags might become deprecated or might have been introduced in a later version of the compiler. Similarly to `CMAKE_<LANG>_COMPILER_ID`, the `CMAKE_<LANG>_COMPILER_VERSION` variable is not guaranteed to be defined for all languages and vendors. Although checking on these variables is quite popular, we think that a more robust alternative would be to check whether a desired set of flags works with the given compiler, so that only effectively working flags are actually used in the project. Combined with the use of project-specific variables, `target_compile_options`, and generator expressions, this approach is quite powerful. We will show how to use this check-and-set pattern in *Recipe 3, Writing a function to test and set compiler flags*, in *Chapter 7, Structuring Projects*.

Setting the standard for the language

The code for this recipe is available at `https://github.com/dev-cafe/cmake-cookbook/tree/v1.0/chapter-01/recipe-09` and has a C++ and Fortran example. The recipe is valid with CMake version 3.5 (and higher) and has been tested on GNU/Linux, macOS, and Windows.

Programming languages have different standards available, that is, different versions that offer new and improved language constructs. Enabling new standards is accomplished by setting the appropriate compiler flag. We have shown in the previous recipe how this can be done, either on a per-target basis or globally. With its 3.1 version, CMake introduced a platform- and compiler-independent mechanism for setting the language standard for C++ and C: setting the `<LANG>_STANDARD` property for targets.

Getting ready

For the following example, we will require a C++ compiler compliant with the C++14 standard or later. The code for this recipe defines a polymorphic hierarchy of animals. We use `std::unique_ptr` for the base class in the hierarchy:

```
std::unique_ptr<Animal> cat = Cat("Simon");
std::unique_ptr<Animal> dog = Dog("Marlowe);
```

Instead of explicitly using constructors for the various subtypes, we use an implementation of the factory method. The factory is implemented using C++11 *variadic templates*. It holds a map of creation functions for each object in the inheritance hierarchy:

```
typedef std::function<std::unique_ptr<Animal>(const std::string &)>
CreateAnimal;
```

It dispatches them based on a preassigned tag, so that creation of objects will look like the following:

```
std::unique_ptr<Animal> simon = farm.create("CAT", "Simon");
std::unique_ptr<Animal> marlowe = farm.create("DOG", "Marlowe");
```

The tags and creation functions are registered to the factory prior to its use:

```
Factory<CreateAnimal> farm;
farm.subscribe("CAT", [](const std::string & n) { return
std::make_unique<Cat>(n); });
farm.subscribe("DOG", [](const std::string & n) { return
std::make_unique<Dog>(n); });
```

We are defining the creation functions using C++11 *lambda* functions. Notice the use of `std::make_unique` to avoid introducing the naked `new` operator. This helper was introduced in C++14.

> This functionality of CMake was added in version 3.1 and is ever-evolving. Later versions of CMake have added better and better support for later versions of the C++ standard and different compilers. We recommend that you check whether your compiler of choice is supported on the documentation webpage: `https://cmake.org/cmake/help/latest/manual/cmake-compile-features.7.html#supported-compilers`.

How to do it

We will construct the `CMakeLists.txt` step by step and show how to require a certain standard (in this case C++14):

1. We state the minimum required CMake version, project name, and language:

```
cmake_minimum_required(VERSION 3.5 FATAL_ERROR)

project(recipe-09 LANGUAGES CXX)
```

2. We request all library symbols to be exported on Windows:

```
set(CMAKE_WINDOWS_EXPORT_ALL_SYMBOLS ON)
```

3. We need to add a target for the library. This will compile the sources into a shared library:

```
add_library(animals
  SHARED
    Animal.cpp
    Animal.hpp
    Cat.cpp
    Cat.hpp
    Dog.cpp
    Dog.hpp
    Factory.hpp
  )
```

4. We now set the `CXX_STANDARD`, `CXX_EXTENSIONS`, and `CXX_STANDARD_REQUIRED` properties for the target. We also set the `POSITION_INDEPENDENT_CODE` property, to avoid issues when building the DSO with some compilers:

```
set_target_properties(animals
  PROPERTIES
    CXX_STANDARD 14
    CXX_EXTENSIONS OFF
    CXX_STANDARD_REQUIRED ON
    POSITION_INDEPENDENT_CODE 1
  )
```

5. Then, we add a new target for the `animal-farm` executable and set its properties:

```
add_executable(animal-farm animal-farm.cpp)

set_target_properties(animal-farm
  PROPERTIES
    CXX_STANDARD 14
    CXX_EXTENSIONS OFF
    CXX_STANDARD_REQUIRED ON
  )
```

6. Finally, we link the executable to the library:

```
target_link_libraries(animal-farm animals)
```

7. Let us also check what our example cat and dog have to say:

```
$ mkdir -p build
$ cd build
$ cmake ..
$ cmake --build .
$ ./animal-farm

I'm Simon the cat!
I'm Marlowe the dog!
```

How it works

In steps 4 and 5, we set a number of properties for the `animals` and `animal-farm` targets:

- `CXX_STANDARD` mandates the standard that we would like to have.
- `CXX_EXTENSIONS` tells CMake to only use compiler flags that will enable the ISO C++ standard, without compiler-specific extensions.
- `CXX_STANDARD_REQUIRED` specifies that the version of the standard chosen is required. If this version is not available, CMake will stop configuration with an error. When this property is set to `OFF`, CMake will look for next latest version of the standard, until a proper flag has been set. This means to first look for C++14, then C++11, then C++98.

From a Simple Executable to Libraries

At the time of writing, there is no `Fortran_STANDARD` property available yet, but the standard can be set using `target_compile_options`; see `https://github.com/dev-cafe/cmake-cookbook/tree/v1.0/chapter-01/recipe-09`.

If the language standard is a global property shared by all targets, you can set the `CMAKE_<LANG>_STANDARD`, `CMAKE_<LANG>_EXTENSIONS`, and `CMAKE_<LANG>_STANDARD_REQUIRED` variables to their desired values. The corresponding properties on all targets will be set with these values.

There is more

CMake offers an even finer level of control over the language standard by introducing the concept of *compile features*. These are features introduced by the language standard, such as variadic templates and lambdas in C++11, and automatic return type deduction in C++14. You can ask for certain features to be available for specific targets with the `target_compile_features()` command and CMake will automatically set the correct compiler flag for the standard. It is also possible to have CMake generate compatibility headers for optional compiler features.

We recommend reading the online documentation for `cmake-compile-features` to get a complete overview of how CMake can handle compile features and language standards: `https://cmake.org/cmake/help/latest/manual/cmake-compile-features.7.html`.

Using control flow constructs

The code for this recipe is available at `https://github.com/dev-cafe/cmake-cookbook/tree/v1.0/chapter-01/recipe-10` and has a C++ example. The recipe is valid with CMake version 3.5 (and higher) and has been tested on GNU/Linux, macOS, and Windows.

We have used `if-elseif-endif` constructs in previous recipes of this chapter. CMake also offers language facilities for creating loops: `foreach-endforeach` and `while-endwhile`. Both can be combined with `break` for breaking from the enclosing loop early. This recipe will show you how to use `foreach` to loop over a list of source files. We will apply such a loop to lower the compiler optimization for a set of source files without introducing a new target.

[62]

Getting ready

We will reuse the geometry example introduced in *Recipe 8, Controlling compiler flags*. Our goal will be to fine-tune the compiler optimization for some of the sources by collecting them into a list.

How to do it

These are the detailed steps to follow in CMakeLists.txt:

1. As in *Recipe 8, Controlling compiler flags*, we specify the minimum required version of CMake, project name, and language, and declare the geometry library target:

```
cmake_minimum_required(VERSION 3.5 FATAL_ERROR)

project(recipe-10 LANGUAGES CXX)

add_library(geometry
  STATIC
    geometry_circle.cpp
    geometry_circle.hpp
    geometry_polygon.cpp
    geometry_polygon.hpp
    geometry_rhombus.cpp
    geometry_rhombus.hpp
    geometry_square.cpp
    geometry_square.hpp
  )
```

2. We decide to compile the library with the -O3 compiler optimization level. This is set as a PRIVATE compiler option on the target:

```
target_compile_options(geometry
  PRIVATE
    -O3
  )
```

3. Then, we generate a list of source files to be compiled with lower optimization:

```
list(
  APPEND sources_with_lower_optimization
    geometry_circle.cpp
    geometry_rhombus.cpp
  )
```

4. We loop over these source files to tune their optimization level down to -O2. This is done using their source file properties:

```
message(STATUS "Setting source properties using IN LISTS syntax:")
foreach(_source IN LISTS sources_with_lower_optimization)
  set_source_files_properties(${_source} PROPERTIES COMPILE_FLAGS -
O2)
  message(STATUS "Appending -O2 flag for ${_source}")
endforeach()
```

5. To make sure source properties were set, we loop once again and print the COMPILE_FLAGS property on each of the sources:

```
message(STATUS "Querying sources properties using plain syntax:")
foreach(_source ${sources_with_lower_optimization})
  get_source_file_property(_flags ${_source} COMPILE_FLAGS)
  message(STATUS "Source ${_source} has the following extra
COMPILE_FLAGS: ${_flags}")
endforeach()
```

6. Finally, we add the compute-areas executable target and link it against the geometry library:

```
add_executable(compute-areas compute-areas.cpp)

target_link_libraries(compute-areas geometry)
```

7. Let us verify that the flags were correctly set at the configure step:

```
$ mkdir -p build
$ cd build
$ cmake ..

...
-- Setting source properties using IN LISTS syntax:
-- Appending -O2 flag for geometry_circle.cpp
-- Appending -O2 flag for geometry_rhombus.cpp
-- Querying sources properties using plain syntax:
-- Source geometry_circle.cpp has the following extra
COMPILE_FLAGS: -O2
-- Source geometry_rhombus.cpp has the following extra
COMPILE_FLAGS: -O2
```

8. Finally, also check the build step with VERBOSE=1. You will see that the -O2 flag gets appended to the -O3 flag but the last optimization level flag (in this case -O2) "wins":

```
$ cmake --build . -- VERBOSE=1
```

How it works

The foreach-endforeach syntax can be used to express the repetition of certain tasks over a list of variables. In our case, we used it to manipulate, set, and get the compiler flags of specific files in the project. This CMake snippet introduced two additional new commands:

- set_source_files_properties(file PROPERTIES property value), which sets the property to the passed value for the given file. Much like targets, files also have properties in CMake. This allows for extremely fine-grained control over the build system generation. The list of available properties for source files can be found here: https://cmake.org/cmake/help/v3.5/manual/cmake-properties.7.html#source-file-properties.

- get_source_file_property(VAR file property), which retrieves the value of the desired property for the given file and stores it in the CMake VAR variable.

> In CMake, lists are semicolon-separated groups of strings. A list can be created either by the list or the set commands. For example, both set(var a b c d e) and list(APPEND a b c d e) create the list a;b;c;d;e.

> TIP
>
> To lower optimization for a set of files, it would probably be cleaner to collect them into a separate target (library) and set the optimization level explicitly for this target instead of appending a flag, but in this recipe our focus was on foreach-endforeach.

There is more

The `foreach()` construct can be used in four different ways:

- `foreach(loop_var arg1 arg2 ...)`: Where a loop variable and an explicit list of items are provided. This form was used when printing the compiler flag sets for the items in `sources_with_lower_optimization`. Note that if the list of items is in a variable, it has to be explicitly expanded; that is, `${sources_with_lower_optimization}` has to be passed as an argument.

- As a loop over integer numbers by specifying a range, such as `foreach(loop_var RANGE total)` or alternatively `foreach(loop_var RANGE start stop [step])`.

- As a loop over list-valued variables, such as `foreach(loop_var IN LISTS [list1 [...]])`. The arguments are interpreted as lists and their contents automatically expanded accordingly.

- As a loop over items, such as `foreach(loop_var IN ITEMS [item1 [...]])`. The contents of the arguments are not expanded.

Detecting the Environment 2

In this chapter, we will cover the following recipes:

- Discovering the operating system
- Dealing with platform-dependent source code
- Dealing with compiler-dependent source code
- Discovering the host processor architecture
- Discovering the host processor instruction set
- Enabling vectorization for the Eigen library

Introduction

Although CMake is cross-platform and in our projects we strive for the source code to be portable across platforms, operating systems, and compilers, sometimes the source code is not fully portable; for example, when using vendor-dependent extensions, we may find it necessary to configure and/or build code slightly differently depending on the platform. This is particularly relevant for legacy code or when cross-compiling, a topic we will return to in *Chapter 13*, *Alternative Generators and Cross-compilation*. It can also be advantageous to know the processor instruction set to optimize performance for a specific target platform. This chapter presents recipes to detect such environments and provides recommendations for how to implement such solutions.

Discovering the operating system

The code for this recipe is available at `https://github.com/dev-cafe/cmake-cookbook/tree/v1.0/chapter-02/recipe-01`. The recipe is valid with CMake version 3.5 (and higher) and has been tested on GNU/Linux, macOS, and Windows.

CMake is a set of cross-platform tools. Nevertheless, it can be very useful to know on which operating system (OS) the configuration or build step is executed. Such OS discovery can be used either to tweak CMake code for a particular OS, to enable conditional compilation depending on the OS, or to use compiler-specific extensions if available or necessary. In this recipe, we will demonstrate how to use CMake to detect the OS with an example that does not require compilation of any source code. For simplicity, we will only consider the configuration step.

How to do it

We will demonstrate OS discovery with a very simple CMakeLists.txt:

1. We first define the minimum CMake version and project name. Note that our language requirement is NONE:

```
cmake_minimum_required(VERSION 3.5 FATAL_ERROR)

project(recipe-01 LANGUAGES NONE)
```

2. Then we wish to print a custom message depending on the detected OS:

```
if(CMAKE_SYSTEM_NAME STREQUAL "Linux")
  message(STATUS "Configuring on/for Linux")
elseif(CMAKE_SYSTEM_NAME STREQUAL "Darwin")
  message(STATUS "Configuring on/for macOS")
elseif(CMAKE_SYSTEM_NAME STREQUAL "Windows")
  message(STATUS "Configuring on/for Windows")
elseif(CMAKE_SYSTEM_NAME STREQUAL "AIX")
  message(STATUS "Configuring on/for IBM AIX")
else()
  message(STATUS "Configuring on/for ${CMAKE_SYSTEM_NAME}")
endif()
```

Before testing it out, first examine the preceding code block and consider what behavior you expect on your system.

3. Now we are ready to test it out and configure the project:

```
$ mkdir -p build
$ cd build
$ cmake ..
```

4. Of the CMake output, one line is interesting here – on a Linux system, this is the line of interest (on other systems, the output will hopefully be different):

```
-- Configuring on/for Linux
```

How it works

CMake correctly defines `CMAKE_SYSTEM_NAME` for the target OS and therefore there is typically no need to use custom commands, tools, or scripts to query this information. The value of this variable can then be used to implement OS-specific conditionals and workarounds. On systems that have the `uname` command, this variable is set to the output of `uname -s`. The variable is set to "Darwin" on macOS. On Linux and Windows, it evaluates to "Linux" and "Windows", respectively. We now know how to execute a specific CMake code on a certain OS if we need to. Of course, we should try to minimize such customization in order to simplify migration to new platforms.

> **TIP**
>
> To minimize trouble when moving from one platform to another, you should avoid using Shell commands directly and also avoid explicit path delimiters (forward slashes on Linux and macOS and backward slashes on Windows). Only use forward slashes in CMake code as path delimiters and CMake will automatically translate them for the OS environment in question.

Dealing with platform-dependent source code

> The code for this recipe is available at `https://github.com/dev-cafe/cmake-cookbook/tree/v1.0/chapter-02/recipe-02` and has a C++ example. The recipe is valid with CMake version 3.5 (and higher) and has been tested on GNU/Linux, macOS, and Windows.

Ideally, we should avoid platform-dependent source code, but sometimes we have no choice – particularly when we are given code to configure and compile that we have not written ourselves. In this recipe, we will demonstrate how to use CMake to conditionally compile source code depending on the OS.

Getting ready

For this example, we will modify the `hello-world.cpp` example code from *Chapter 1, From a Simple Executable to Libraries, Recipe 1, Compiling a single source file into an executable*:

```
#include <cstdlib>
#include <iostream>
#include <string>

std::string say_hello() {
#ifdef IS_WINDOWS
  return std::string("Hello from Windows!");
#elif IS_LINUX
  return std::string("Hello from Linux!");
#elif IS_MACOS
  return std::string("Hello from macOS!");
#else
  return std::string("Hello from an unknown system!");
#endif
}

int main() {
  std::cout << say_hello() << std::endl;
  return EXIT_SUCCESS;
}
```

How to do it

Let us build a corresponding `CMakeLists.txt` instance, which will enable us to conditionally compile the source code based on the target OS:

1. We first set the minimum CMake version, project name, and supported language:

   ```
   cmake_minimum_required(VERSION 3.5 FATAL_ERROR)

   project(recipe-02 LANGUAGES CXX)
   ```

2. Then we define the executable and its corresponding source file:

   ```
   add_executable(hello-world hello-world.cpp)
   ```

3. Then we let the preprocessor know the system name by defining the following target compile definitions:

```
if(CMAKE_SYSTEM_NAME STREQUAL "Linux")
  target_compile_definitions(hello-world PUBLIC "IS_LINUX")
endif()
if(CMAKE_SYSTEM_NAME STREQUAL "Darwin")
  target_compile_definitions(hello-world PUBLIC "IS_MACOS")
endif()
if(CMAKE_SYSTEM_NAME STREQUAL "Windows")
  target_compile_definitions(hello-world PUBLIC "IS_WINDOWS")
endif()
```

Before continuing, first examine the preceding expressions and consider what behavior you expect on your system.

4. Now we are ready to test it out and to configure the project:

```
$ mkdir -p build
$ cd build
$ cmake ..
$ cmake --build .
$ ./hello-world

Hello from Linux!
```

On a Windows system, you will see `Hello from Windows!`; other operating systems will yield different outputs.

How it works

The interesting part in the `hello-world.cpp` example is the conditional compilation based on the preprocessor definitions IS_WINDOWS, IS_LINUX, or IS_MACOS:

```
std::string say_hello() {
#ifdef IS_WINDOWS
  return std::string("Hello from Windows!");
#elif IS_LINUX
  return std::string("Hello from Linux!");
#elif IS_MACOS
```

```
   return std::string("Hello from macOS!");
#else
   return std::string("Hello from an unknown system!");
#endif
}
```

These definitions are defined at configure time by CMake in `CMakeLists.txt` by using `target_compile_definitions` before being passed on to the preprocessor. We could have achieved a more compact expression without repeating `if-endif` statements and we will demonstrate this refactoring in the next recipe. We could also have joined the `if-endif` statements into one `if-elseif-elseif-endif` statement.

At this stage, we should point out that we could have set the definitions using `add_definitions(-DIS_LINUX)` (of course, adjusting the definition according to the platform in question) instead of using `target_compile_definitions`. The disadvantage of using `add_definitions` is that it modifies compile definitions for the entire project, whereas `target_compile_definitions` gives us the possibility to restrict both the scope of the definitions to a specific target, as well as to restrict visibility of these definitions by using the `PRIVATE`, `PUBLIC`, or `INTERFACE` qualifiers. These qualifiers have the same meaning they had for compiler flags, as we have seen already in *Chapter 1, From a Simple Executable to Libraries, Recipe 8, Controlling compiler flags*:

- With the `PRIVATE` qualifier, compile definitions will only be applied to the given target and not by other targets consuming it.
- With the `INTERFACE` qualifier, compile definitions on a given target will only be applied to targets consuming it.
- With the `PUBLIC` qualifier, compile definitions will be applied to the given target and all other targets consuming it.

> Minimize platform-dependent source code in your project to make porting easier.

Dealing with compiler-dependent source code

The code for this recipe is available at `https://github.com/dev-cafe/cmake-cookbook/tree/v1.0/chapter-02/recipe-03` and has a C++ and a Fortran example. The recipe is valid with CMake version 3.5 (and higher) and has been tested on GNU/Linux, macOS, and Windows.

This recipe is similar to the previous one in the sense that we will use CMake to accommodate the compilation of conditional source code that is dependent on the environment: in this case, it will be dependent on the chosen compiler. Again, for the sake of portability, this is a situation that we try to avoid when writing new code, but it is also a situation that we are almost guaranteed to meet sooner or later, especially when using legacy code or when dealing with compiler-dependent tooling, such as sanitizers. From the recipes of this and the previous chapter, we have all the ingredients to achieve this. Nevertheless, it will be useful to discuss the problem of dealing with compiler-dependent source code since we will have the chance to introduce some new aspects of CMake.

Getting ready

In this recipe, we will start out with an example in C++, and later we will demonstrate a Fortran example and attempt to refactor and simplify the CMake code.

Let us consider the following `hello-world.cpp` source code:

```
#include <cstdlib>
#include <iostream>
#include <string>

std::string say_hello() {
#ifdef IS_INTEL_CXX_COMPILER
  // only compiled when Intel compiler is selected
  // such compiler will not compile the other branches
  return std::string("Hello Intel compiler!");
#elif IS_GNU_CXX_COMPILER
  // only compiled when GNU compiler is selected
  // such compiler will not compile the other branches
  return std::string("Hello GNU compiler!");
#elif IS_PGI_CXX_COMPILER
```

```
    // etc.
    return std::string("Hello PGI compiler!");
#elif IS_XL_CXX_COMPILER
    return std::string("Hello XL compiler!");
#else
    return std::string("Hello unknown compiler - have we met before?");
#endif
}

int main() {
    std::cout << say_hello() << std::endl;
    std::cout << "compiler name is " COMPILER_NAME << std::endl;
    return EXIT_SUCCESS;
}
```

We will also use a corresponding Fortran example (`hello-world.F90`):

```
program hello
  implicit none

#ifdef IS_Intel_FORTRAN_COMPILER
  print *, 'Hello Intel compiler!'
#elif IS_GNU_FORTRAN_COMPILER
  print *, 'Hello GNU compiler!'
#elif IS_PGI_FORTRAN_COMPILER
  print *, 'Hello PGI compiler!'
#elif IS_XL_FORTRAN_COMPILER
  print *, 'Hello XL compiler!'
#else
  print *, 'Hello unknown compiler - have we met before?'
#endif

end program
```

How to do it

We shall start out with the C++ example before moving on to the Fortran example:

1. In the CMakeLists.txt file, we define the now familiar minimum version, project name, and supported language:

   ```
   cmake_minimum_required(VERSION 3.5 FATAL_ERROR)

   project(recipe-03 LANGUAGES CXX)
   ```

2. We then define the executable target and its corresponding source file:

```
add_executable(hello-world hello-world.cpp)
```

3. Then we let the preprocessor know about the compiler name and vendor by defining the following target compile definitions:

```
target_compile_definitions(hello-world PUBLIC
"COMPILER_NAME=\"${CMAKE_CXX_COMPILER_ID}\"")

if(CMAKE_CXX_COMPILER_ID MATCHES Intel)
    target_compile_definitions(hello-world PUBLIC
"IS_INTEL_CXX_COMPILER")
endif()
if(CMAKE_CXX_COMPILER_ID MATCHES GNU)
    target_compile_definitions(hello-world PUBLIC
"IS_GNU_CXX_COMPILER")
endif()
if(CMAKE_CXX_COMPILER_ID MATCHES PGI)
    target_compile_definitions(hello-world PUBLIC
"IS_PGI_CXX_COMPILER")
endif()
if(CMAKE_CXX_COMPILER_ID MATCHES XL)
    target_compile_definitions(hello-world PUBLIC
"IS_XL_CXX_COMPILER")
endif()
```

The previous recipes have trained our eyes and now we can already anticipate the result:

```
$ mkdir -p build
$ cd build
$ cmake ..
$ cmake --build .
$ ./hello-world

Hello GNU compiler!
```

If you use a different compiler vendor, then this example code will provide a different greeting.

The `if` statements in the `CMakeLists.txt` file in the preceding example and the previous recipe seem repetitive, and as programmers, we do not like to repeat ourselves. Can we express this more compactly? Indeed we can! For this, let us turn to the Fortran example.

In the `CMakeLists.txt` file of the Fortran example, we need to do the following:

1. We need to adapt the language to Fortran:

```
project(recipe-03 LANGUAGES Fortran)
```

2. Then we define the executable and its corresponding source file; in this case, with an uppercase `.F90` suffix:

```
add_executable(hello-world hello-world.F90)
```

3. Then we let the preprocessor know very compactly about the compiler vendor by defining the following target compile definition:

```
target_compile_definitions(hello-world
  PUBLIC "IS_${CMAKE_Fortran_COMPILER_ID}_FORTRAN_COMPILER"
)
```

The remaining behavior of the Fortran example is the same as in the C++ example.

How it works

The preprocessor definitions are defined at configure time by CMake in `CMakeLists.txt` and are passed on to the preprocessor. The Fortran example contains a very compact expression where we use the `CMAKE_Fortran_COMPILER_ID` variable to construct the preprocessor definition using `target_compile_definitions`. To accommodate this, we had to change the case of "Intel" from `IS_INTEL_CXX_COMPILER` to `IS_Intel_FORTRAN_COMPILER`. We could achieve the same for C or C++ by using the corresponding `CMAKE_C_COMPILER_ID` and `CMAKE_CXX_COMPILER_ID` variables. Please do note, however, that `CMAKE_<LANG>_COMPILER_ID` *is not guaranteed* to be defined for all compilers or languages.

> Use the `.F90` suffix for Fortran code that is supposed to be preprocessed and use the `.f90` suffix for code that is not to be preprocessed.

Discovering the host processor architecture

The code for this recipe is available at `https://github.com/dev-cafe/cmake-cookbook/tree/v1.0/chapter-02/recipe-04` and has a C++ example. The recipe is valid with CMake version 3.5 (and higher) and has been tested on GNU/Linux, macOS, and Windows.

The advent of 64-bit integer arithmetic in 1970s supercomputing and 64-bit addressing in the early 2000s for personal computers has widened the memory-addressing range, and significant resources have been invested into porting code that was hardcoded for 32-bit architectures to enable 64-bit addressing. A number of blog posts, such as `https://www.viva64.com/en/a/0004/`, are devoted to discussing typical issues and solutions in porting C++ code to 64-bit platforms. It is very much advisable to program in a way that avoids explicitly hardcoded limits, but you may be in a situation where you need to accommodate hardcoded limits in a code configured with CMake, and in this recipe, we wish to discuss options for detecting the host processor architecture.

Getting ready

We will use the following `arch-dependent.cpp` example source:

```cpp
#include <cstdlib>
#include <iostream>
#include <string>

#define STRINGIFY(x) #x
#define TOSTRING(x) STRINGIFY(x)

std::string say_hello() {
  std::string arch_info(TOSTRING(ARCHITECTURE));
  arch_info += std::string(" architecture. ");
#ifdef IS_32_BIT_ARCH
  return arch_info + std::string("Compiled on a 32 bit host processor.");
#elif IS_64_BIT_ARCH
  return arch_info + std::string("Compiled on a 64 bit host processor.");
#else
  return arch_info + std::string("Neither 32 nor 64 bit, puzzling ...");
#endif
}
```

```
int main() {
  std::cout << say_hello() << std::endl;
  return EXIT_SUCCESS;
}
```

How to do it

Now let us turn to the CMake side. In the `CMakeLists.txt` file, we need to apply the following:

1. We first define the executable and its source file dependency:

   ```
   cmake_minimum_required(VERSION 3.5 FATAL_ERROR)

   project(recipe-04 LANGUAGES CXX)

   add_executable(arch-dependent arch-dependent.cpp)
   ```

2. We check for the size of the `void` pointer type. This is defined in the `CMAKE_SIZEOF_VOID_P` CMake variable and will tell us whether the CPU is 32 or 64 bits. We let the user know about the detected size with a status message and set a preprocessor definition:

   ```
   if(CMAKE_SIZEOF_VOID_P EQUAL 8)
     target_compile_definitions(arch-dependent PUBLIC
   "IS_64_BIT_ARCH")
     message(STATUS "Target is 64 bits")
   else()
     target_compile_definitions(arch-dependent PUBLIC
   "IS_32_BIT_ARCH")
     message(STATUS "Target is 32 bits")
   endif()
   ```

3. Then we let the preprocessor know about the host processor architecture by defining the following target compile definitions, at the same time printing status messages during configuration:

   ```
   if(CMAKE_HOST_SYSTEM_PROCESSOR MATCHES "i386")
     message(STATUS "i386 architecture detected")
   elseif(CMAKE_HOST_SYSTEM_PROCESSOR MATCHES "i686")
     message(STATUS "i686 architecture detected")
   elseif(CMAKE_HOST_SYSTEM_PROCESSOR MATCHES "x86_64")
     message(STATUS "x86_64 architecture detected")
   else()
   ```

```
message(STATUS "host processor architecture is unknown")
endif()

target_compile_definitions(arch-dependent
  PUBLIC "ARCHITECTURE=${CMAKE_HOST_SYSTEM_PROCESSOR}"
  )
```

4. We configure the project and note the status message (the precise message may of course change):

```
$ mkdir -p build
$ cd build
$ cmake ..


. . .
-- Target is 64 bits
-- x86_64 architecture detected
. . .
```

5. Finally, we build and execute the code (the actual output will depend on the host processor architecture):

```
$ cmake --build .
$ ./arch-dependent

x86_64 architecture. Compiled on a 64 bit host processor.
```

How it works

CMake defines the CMAKE_HOST_SYSTEM_PROCESSOR variable to contain the name of the processor it is currently running on. This can be set to "i386", "i686", "x86_64", "AMD64", and such like, depending, of course, on the CPU at hand. CMAKE_SIZEOF_VOID_P is defined to hold the size of a pointer to the void type. We can query both at the CMake level in order to modify targets or target compile definitions. Using preprocessor definitions, we can branch source code compilation based on the detected host processor architecture. As discussed in previous recipes, such customization should be avoided when writing new code, but sometimes it is useful when working with legacy code or when cross-compiling, which is the subject of *Chapter 13, Alternative Generators and Cross-compilation*.

> Using CMAKE_SIZEOF_VOID_P is the only truly portable way of checking whether the CPU at hand has a 32- or 64-bit architecture.

There is more

In addition to `CMAKE_HOST_SYSTEM_PROCESSOR`, CMake also defines the `CMAKE_SYSTEM_PROCESSOR` variable. Whereas the former contains the name of the CPU CMake is **currently running on**, the latter will contain the name of the CPU we are **currently building for**. This is a subtle difference that plays a very fundamental role when cross-compiling. We will see more about cross-compilation in *Chapter 13, Alternative Generators and Cross-compilation.*

An alternative to letting CMake detect the host processor architecture is to use symbols defined within C or C++ and use CMake's `try_run` function to build and attempt to execute the source code (see *Chapter 5, Configure-time and Build-time Operations, Recipe 8, Probing execution*) that is branched by the preprocessor symbols. This returns well-defined errors that can be caught on the CMake side (this strategy is inspired by `https://github.com/axr/solar-cmake/blob/master/TargetArch.cmake`):

```
#if defined(__i386) || defined(__i386__) || defined(_M_IX86)
    #error cmake_arch i386
#elif defined(__x86_64) || defined(__x86_64__) || defined(__amd64) ||
defined(_M_X64)
    #error cmake_arch x86_64
#endif
```

This strategy is also the recommended one for detecting the target processor architecture, where CMake does not seem to offer a portable intrinsic solution.

Yet another alternative exists. It will only use CMake, doing away entirely with the preprocessor, at the expense of having a different source file for each case, which would then be set as the source file for the executable target `arch-dependent` using the `target_sources` CMake command:

```
add_executable(arch-dependent "")

if(CMAKE_HOST_SYSTEM_PROCESSOR MATCHES "i386")
  message(STATUS "i386 architecture detected")
  target_sources(arch-dependent
    PRIVATE
      arch-dependent-i386.cpp
    )
```

```
  elseif(CMAKE_HOST_SYSTEM_PROCESSOR MATCHES "i686")
    message(STATUS "i686 architecture detected")
    target_sources(arch-dependent
      PRIVATE
        arch-dependent-i686.cpp
      )
  elseif(CMAKE_HOST_SYSTEM_PROCESSOR MATCHES "x86_64")
    message(STATUS "x86_64 architecture detected")
    target_sources(arch-dependent
      PRIVATE
        arch-dependent-x86_64.cpp
      )
  else()
    message(STATUS "host processor architecture is unknown")
  endif()
```

This approach will clearly require more work for an existing project, since the source files will need to be separated. Moreover, code duplication between the different source files might certainly become a problem.

Discovering the host processor instruction set

The code for this recipe is available at `https://github.com/dev-cafe/cmake-cookbook/tree/v1.0/chapter-02/recipe-05` and has a C++ example. The recipe is valid with CMake version 3.10 (and higher) and has been tested on GNU/Linux, macOS, and Windows.

In this recipe, we will discuss how to discover the host processor instruction set with the help of CMake. This functionality has been added to CMake relatively recently and requires CMake 3.10 or later. The detected host system information can be used to either set corresponding compiler flags or to implement optional compilation of sources or source code generation depending on the host system. In this recipe, our goal will be to detect the host system information, pass it to the C++ source code using preprocessor definitions, and print the information to the output.

Getting ready

Our example C++ source file (processor-info.cpp) consists of the following:

```cpp
#include "config.h"

#include <cstdlib>
#include <iostream>

int main() {
  std::cout << "Number of logical cores: "
            << NUMBER_OF_LOGICAL_CORES << std::endl;
  std::cout << "Number of physical cores: "
            << NUMBER_OF_PHYSICAL_CORES << std::endl;

  std::cout << "Total virtual memory in megabytes: "
            << TOTAL_VIRTUAL_MEMORY << std::endl;
  std::cout << "Available virtual memory in megabytes: "
            << AVAILABLE_VIRTUAL_MEMORY << std::endl;
  std::cout << "Total physical memory in megabytes: "
            << TOTAL_PHYSICAL_MEMORY << std::endl;
  std::cout << "Available physical memory in megabytes: "
            << AVAILABLE_PHYSICAL_MEMORY << std::endl;

  std::cout << "Processor is 64Bit: "
            << IS_64BIT << std::endl;
  std::cout << "Processor has floating point unit: "
            << HAS_FPU << std::endl;
  std::cout << "Processor supports MMX instructions: "
            << HAS_MMX << std::endl;
  std::cout << "Processor supports Ext. MMX instructions: "
            << HAS_MMX_PLUS << std::endl;
  std::cout << "Processor supports SSE instructions: "
            << HAS_SSE << std::endl;
  std::cout << "Processor supports SSE2 instructions: "
            << HAS_SSE2 << std::endl;
  std::cout << "Processor supports SSE FP instructions: "
            << HAS_SSE_FP << std::endl;
  std::cout << "Processor supports SSE MMX instructions: "
            << HAS_SSE_MMX << std::endl;
  std::cout << "Processor supports 3DNow instructions: "
            << HAS_AMD_3DNOW << std::endl;
```

```
    std::cout << "Processor supports 3DNow+ instructions: "
              << HAS_AMD_3DNOW_PLUS << std::endl;
    std::cout << "IA64 processor emulating x86 : "
              << HAS_IA64 << std::endl;

    std::cout << "OS name: "
              << OS_NAME << std::endl;
    std::cout << "OS sub-type: "
              << OS_RELEASE << std::endl;
    std::cout << "OS build ID: "
              << OS_VERSION << std::endl;
    std::cout << "OS platform: "
              << OS_PLATFORM << std::endl;

    return EXIT_SUCCESS;
}
```

This file includes `config.h`, which we will generate from `config.h.in`, given here:

```
#pragma once
#define NUMBER_OF_LOGICAL_CORES @_NUMBER_OF_LOGICAL_CORES@
#define NUMBER_OF_PHYSICAL_CORES @_NUMBER_OF_PHYSICAL_CORES@
#define TOTAL_VIRTUAL_MEMORY @_TOTAL_VIRTUAL_MEMORY@
#define AVAILABLE_VIRTUAL_MEMORY @_AVAILABLE_VIRTUAL_MEMORY@
#define TOTAL_PHYSICAL_MEMORY @_TOTAL_PHYSICAL_MEMORY@
#define AVAILABLE_PHYSICAL_MEMORY @_AVAILABLE_PHYSICAL_MEMORY@
#define IS_64BIT @_IS_64BIT@
#define HAS_FPU @_HAS_FPU@
#define HAS_MMX @_HAS_MMX@
#define HAS_MMX_PLUS @_HAS_MMX_PLUS@
#define HAS_SSE @_HAS_SSE@
#define HAS_SSE2 @_HAS_SSE2@
#define HAS_SSE_FP @_HAS_SSE_FP@
#define HAS_SSE_MMX @_HAS_SSE_MMX@
#define HAS_AMD_3DNOW @_HAS_AMD_3DNOW@
#define HAS_AMD_3DNOW_PLUS @_HAS_AMD_3DNOW_PLUS@
#define HAS_IA64 @_HAS_IA64@
#define OS_NAME "@_OS_NAME@"
#define OS_RELEASE "@_OS_RELEASE@"
#define OS_VERSION "@_OS_VERSION@"
#define OS_PLATFORM "@_OS_PLATFORM@"
```

How to do it

We will use CMake to fill the definitions in `config.h` with sensible values for our platform and to compile our sample source file into an executable:

1. First, we define the minimum CMake version, project name, and project language:

```
cmake_minimum_required(VERSION 3.10 FATAL_ERROR)

project(recipe-05 CXX)
```

2. We then define the target executable, its source file, and include directories:

```
add_executable(processor-info "")

target_sources(processor-info
  PRIVATE
    processor-info.cpp
  )

target_include_directories(processor-info
  PRIVATE
    ${PROJECT_BINARY_DIR}
  )
```

3. We then go on to query the host system information for a number of keys:

```
foreach(key
  IN ITEMS
    NUMBER_OF_LOGICAL_CORES
    NUMBER_OF_PHYSICAL_CORES
    TOTAL_VIRTUAL_MEMORY
    AVAILABLE_VIRTUAL_MEMORY
    TOTAL_PHYSICAL_MEMORY
    AVAILABLE_PHYSICAL_MEMORY
    IS_64BIT
    HAS_FPU
    HAS_MMX
    HAS_MMX_PLUS
    HAS_SSE
    HAS_SSE2
    HAS_SSE_FP
    HAS_SSE_MMX
    HAS_AMD_3DNOW
```

```
            HAS_AMD_3DNOW_PLUS
            HAS_IA64
            OS_NAME
            OS_RELEASE
            OS_VERSION
            OS_PLATFORM
        )
        cmake_host_system_information(RESULT _${key} QUERY ${key})
    endforeach()
```

4. Having defined the corresponding variables, we configure `config.h`:

```
        configure_file(config.h.in config.h @ONLY)
```

5. Now we are ready to configure, build, and test the project:

```
        $ mkdir -p build
        $ cd build
        $ cmake ..
        $ cmake --build .
        $ ./processor-info

        Number of logical cores: 4
        Number of physical cores: 2
        Total virtual memory in megabytes: 15258
        Available virtual memory in megabytes: 14678
        Total physical memory in megabytes: 7858
        Available physical memory in megabytes: 4072
        Processor is 64Bit: 1
        Processor has floating point unit: 1
        Processor supports MMX instructions: 1
        Processor supports Ext. MMX instructions: 0
        Processor supports SSE instructions: 1
        Processor supports SSE2 instructions: 1
        Processor supports SSE FP instructions: 0
        Processor supports SSE MMX instructions: 0
        Processor supports 3DNow instructions: 0
        Processor supports 3DNow+ instructions: 0
        IA64 processor emulating x86 : 0
        OS name: Linux
        OS sub-type: 4.16.7-1-ARCH
        OS build ID: #1 SMP PREEMPT Wed May 2 21:12:36 UTC 2018
        OS platform: x86_64
```

6. The output will of course vary depending on the processor.

How it works

The `foreach` loop in `CMakeLists.txt` queries values for a number of keys and defines corresponding variables. The core function of this recipe is `cmake_host_system_information`, which queries system information of the host system on which CMake runs. This function can be invoked with multiple keys in one function call, but in this case, we have used one function call per key. We then use these variables to configure the placeholders in `config.h.in` and generate `config.h`. This configuration is done with the `configure_file` command. Finally, `config.h` is included in `processor-info.cpp`, and once compiled, it will print the values to the screen. We will revisit this approach in *Chapter 5, Configure-time and Build-time Operations*, and *Chapter 6, Generating Source Code*.

There is more

For a more fine-grained processor instruction set detection, consider this module: `https://github.com/VcDevel/Vc/blob/master/cmake/OptimizeForArchitecture.cmake`. We would also like to note that, sometimes, the host building the code may not be the same as the host running the code. This is often the case on compute clusters where the login node architecture may differ from the architecture found on compute nodes. One way to solve this is to submit the configuration and compilation as a computation step and deploy it to the compute nodes.

> We have not used all keys available in `cmake_host_system_information`. For this, please consult `https://cmake.org/cmake/help/latest/command/cmake_host_system_information.html`.

Enabling vectorization for the Eigen library

> The code for this recipe is available at `https://github.com/dev-cafe/cmake-cookbook/tree/v1.0/chapter-02/recipe-06` and has a C++ example. The recipe is valid with CMake version 3.5 (and higher) and has been tested on GNU/Linux, macOS, and Windows.

The vector capabilities of modern processor architectures can dramatically enhance the performance of your code. This is particularly the case for certain classes of operations, and linear algebra is foremost among these. This recipe will show how to enable vectorization to speed up a simple executable using the Eigen C++ library for linear algebra.

Getting ready

We will use the Eigen C++ template library for linear algebra and show how to set up compiler flags to enable vectorization. The source code for this recipe the linear-algebra.cpp file:

```cpp
#include <chrono>
#include <iostream>

#include <Eigen/Dense>

EIGEN_DONT_INLINE
double simple_function(Eigen::VectorXd &va, Eigen::VectorXd &vb) {
  // this simple function computes the dot product of two vectors
  // of course it could be expressed more compactly
  double d = va.dot(vb);
  return d;
}

int main() {
  int len = 1000000;
  int num_repetitions = 100;

  // generate two random vectors
  Eigen::VectorXd va = Eigen::VectorXd::Random(len);
  Eigen::VectorXd vb = Eigen::VectorXd::Random(len);

  double result;
  auto start = std::chrono::system_clock::now();
  for (auto i = 0; i < num_repetitions; i++) {
    result = simple_function(va, vb);
  }
  auto end = std::chrono::system_clock::now();
  auto elapsed_seconds = end - start;

  std::cout << "result: " << result << std::endl;
  std::cout << "elapsed seconds: " << elapsed_seconds.count() << std::endl;
}
```

We expect vectorization to speed up the execution of the dot product operation in `simple_function`.

How to do it

According to the documentation of the Eigen library, it is sufficient to set the appropriate compiler flag to enable the generation of vectorized code. Let us look at `CMakeLists.txt`:

1. We declare a C++11 project:

```
cmake_minimum_required(VERSION 3.5 FATAL_ERROR)
project(recipe-06 LANGUAGES CXX)

set(CMAKE_CXX_STANDARD 11)
set(CMAKE_CXX_EXTENSIONS OFF)
set(CMAKE_CXX_STANDARD_REQUIRED ON)
```

2. Since we wish to use the Eigen library, we need to find its header files on the system:

```
find_package(Eigen3 3.3 REQUIRED CONFIG)
```

3. We include the `CheckCXXCompilerFlag.cmake` standard module file:

```
include(CheckCXXCompilerFlag)
```

4. We check that the `-march=native` compiler flag works:

```
check_cxx_compiler_flag("-march=native" _march_native_works)
```

5. The alternative `-xHost` compiler flag is also checked:

```
check_cxx_compiler_flag("-xHost" _xhost_works)
```

6. We set an empty variable, `_CXX_FLAGS`, to hold the one compiler flag that was found to work among the two we just checked. If we see `_march_native_works`, we set `_CXX_FLAGS` to `-march=native`. If we see `_xhost_works`, we set `_CXX_FLAGS` to `-xHost`. If none of them worked, we will leave `_CXX_FLAGS` empty and vectorization will be disabled:

```
set(_CXX_FLAGS)
if(_march_native_works)
  message(STATUS "Using processor's vector instructions (-
```

```
march=native compiler flag set)")
  set(_CXX_FLAGS "-march=native")
elseif(_xhost_works)
  message(STATUS "Using processor's vector instructions (-xHost
compiler flag set)")
  set(_CXX_FLAGS "-xHost")
else()
  message(STATUS "No suitable compiler flag found for
vectorization")
endif()
```

7. For comparison, we also define an executable target for the unoptimized version where we do not use the preceding optimization flags:

```
add_executable(linear-algebra-unoptimized linear-algebra.cpp)

target_link_libraries(linear-algebra-unoptimized
  PRIVATE
    Eigen3::Eigen
  )
```

8. In addition, we define an optimized version:

```
add_executable(linear-algebra linear-algebra.cpp)

target_compile_options(linear-algebra
  PRIVATE
    ${_CXX_FLAGS}
  )

target_link_libraries(linear-algebra
  PRIVATE
    Eigen3::Eigen
  )
```

9. Let us compare the two executables—first we configure (in this case, -march=native_works):

```
$ mkdir -p build
$ cd build
$ cmake ..

...
-- Performing Test _march_native_works
-- Performing Test _march_native_works - Success
```

```
-- Performing Test _xhost_works
-- Performing Test _xhost_works - Failed
-- Using processor's vector instructions (-march=native compiler
flag set)
...
```

10. Finally, let us compile and compare timings:

```
$ cmake --build .
```

```
$ ./linear-algebra-unoptimized
```

```
result: -261.505
elapsed seconds: 1.97964
```

```
$ ./linear-algebra
```

```
result: -261.505
elapsed seconds: 1.05048
```

How it works

Most modern processors provide vector instruction sets. Carefully crafted code can exploit these and achieve enhanced performance with respect to non-vectorized code. The Eigen library has been written with vectorization explicitly in mind since linear algebra operations can greatly benefit from it. All we need to do is instruct the compiler to inspect the processor for us and generate the native set of instructions for the current architecture. Different compiler vendors use different flags to achieve this: the GNU compiler implements this by means of the -march=native flag, whereas the Intel compiler uses the -xHost flag. We then use the check_cxx_compiler_flag function offered by the CheckCXXCompilerFlag.cmake module:

```
check_cxx_compiler_flag("-march=native" _march_native_works)
```

This function accepts two arguments: the first one is the compiler flag to check, the second is a variable for storing the result, true or false, of the check. If the check is positive, we add the working flag to the _CXX_FLAGS variable, which will then be used to set the compiler flags for our executable target.

There is more

This recipe could be combined with the previous recipe; processor capabilities could be queried using `cmake_host_system_information`.

3
Detecting External Libraries and Programs

In this chapter, we will cover the following recipes:

- Detecting the Python interpreter
- Detecting the Python library
- Detecting Python modules and packages
- Detecting the BLAS and LAPACK math libraries
- Detecting the OpenMP parallel environment
- Detecting the MPI parallel environment
- Detecting the Eigen library
- Detecting the Boost libraries
- Detecting external libraries: I. Using `pkg-config`
- Detecting external libraries: II. Writing a find-module

Introduction

Projects often depend on other projects and libraries. This chapter demonstrates how to detect external libraries, frameworks, and projects and how to link to these. CMake has a rather extensive set of prepackaged modules to detect the most commonly used libraries and programs, such as Python and Boost, for example. You can get a list of existing modules using `cmake --help-module-list`. However, not all libraries and programs are covered and from time to time you will have to provide your own detection scripts. In this chapter, we will discuss the necessary tools and discover the find family of CMake commands:

- `find_file` to find a full path to a named file
- `find_library` to find a library

- `find_package` to find and load settings from an external project
- `find_path` to find a directory containing the named file
- `find_program` to find a program

> **TIP**
>
> You can use the `--help-command` command-line switch to print the documentation for any of the CMake built-in commands to screen.

Detecting the Python interpreter

> **i**
>
> The code for this recipe is available at `https://github.com/dev-cafe/cmake-cookbook/tree/v1.0/chapter-03/recipe-01`. The recipe is valid with CMake version 3.5 (and higher) and has been tested on GNU/Linux, macOS, and Windows.

Python is a very popular dynamic language. Many projects package tools written in Python together with their main programs and libraries, or use Python scripts in the configuration or build process. In such cases, it is important to ensure that the runtime dependency on the Python interpreter is also satisfied. This recipe will show how to detect and use the Python interpreter at the configuration step. We will introduce the `find_package` command, which will be used throughout this chapter.

How to do it

We will build up the `CMakeLists.txt` file step by step:

1. We start out by defining the minimum CMake version and project name. Note that for this example we will not need any language support:

   ```
   cmake_minimum_required(VERSION 3.5 FATAL_ERROR)

   project(recipe-01 LANGUAGES NONE)
   ```

2. Then, we use the `find_package` command to find the Python interpreter:

   ```
   find_package(PythonInterp REQUIRED)
   ```

3. Then, we execute a Python command and capture its output and return value:

```
execute_process(
  COMMAND
    ${PYTHON_EXECUTABLE} "-c" "print('Hello, world!')"
  RESULT_VARIABLE _status
  OUTPUT_VARIABLE _hello_world
  ERROR_QUIET
  OUTPUT_STRIP_TRAILING_WHITESPACE
  )
```

4. Finally, we print the return value and the output of the Python command:

```
message(STATUS "RESULT_VARIABLE is: ${_status}")
message(STATUS "OUTPUT_VARIABLE is: ${_hello_world}")
```

5. Now, we can examine the output of the configuration step:

```
$ mkdir -p build
$ cd build
$ cmake ..

-- Found PythonInterp: /usr/bin/python (found version "3.6.5")
-- RESULT_VARIABLE is: 0
-- OUTPUT_VARIABLE is: Hello, world!
-- Configuring done
-- Generating done
-- Build files have been written to: /home/user/cmake-
cookbook/chapter-03/recipe-01/example/build
```

How it works

`find_package` is a wrapper command for CMake modules written for discovering and setting up packages. These modules contain CMake commands to identify packages in standard locations on the system. The files for the CMake modules are called `Find<name>.cmake` and the commands they contain will be run internally when a call to `find_package(<name>)` is issued.

In addition to actually discovering the requested package on your system, find modules also set up a handful of useful variables, reflecting what was actually found, which you can use in your own CMakeLists.txt. In the case of the Python interpreter, the relevant module is FindPythonInterp.cmake, which is shipped with CMake, and sets the following variables:

- PYTHONINTERP_FOUND, a Boolean signaling whether the interpreter was found
- PYTHON_EXECUTABLE, the path to the executable for the Python interpreter
- PYTHON_VERSION_STRING, the full version of the Python interpreter
- PYTHON_VERSION_MAJOR, the major version of the Python interpreter
- PYTHON_VERSION_MINOR, the minor version of the Python interpreter
- PYTHON_VERSION_PATCH, the patch number of the Python interpreter

It is possible to force CMake to look for specific versions of a package. For example, use this to request any version of the Python interpreter greater or equal to 2.7:

```
find_package(PythonInterp 2.7)
```

It is also possible to enforce that dependencies are satisfied:

```
find_package(PythonInterp REQUIRED)
```

In this case, CMake will abort configuration if no suitable executable for the Python interpreter is found in the usual lookup locations.

> CMake has modules for finding many widespread software packages. We recommend to always search the CMake online documentation for existing Find<package>.cmake modules and to read their documentation before using them. The documentation for the find_package command can be found at https://cmake.org/cmake/help/v3.5/command/find_package.html. A good alternative to online documentation is to browse CMake module sources in https://github.com/Kitware/CMake/tree/master/Modules - their headers document the variables that a module uses, as well as the variables set by the module that can be used in your CMakeLists.txt.

There is more

Sometimes, packages are not installed in standard locations and CMake might fail to locate them correctly. It is possible to tell CMake to look into certain specific locations to find certain software using the CLI switch -D to pass the appropriate option. In the case of the Python interpreter, you may configure with the following:

```
$ cmake -D PYTHON_EXECUTABLE=/custom/location/python ..
```

This will correctly identify the Python executable in the non-standard /custom/location/python installation directory.

> Every package is different and the Find<package>.cmake modules try to take that into account and offer a unified interface for detection. When a package that is installed on the system cannot be found by CMake, we recommend you read the documentation for the corresponding detection module to understand how to instruct CMake correctly. You can browse the documentation directly in the terminal, in this case using cmake --help-module FindPythonInterp.

Independently of detecting packages, we would like to mention a handy helper module for printing variables. In this recipe, we have used the following:

```
message(STATUS "RESULT_VARIABLE is: ${_status}")
message(STATUS "OUTPUT_VARIABLE is: ${_hello_world}")
```

A handy alternative for debugging is to use the following:

```
include(CMakePrintHelpers)
cmake_print_variables(_status _hello_world)
```

This produces the following output:

```
-- _status="0" ; _hello_world="Hello, world!"
```

For more documentation on convenience macros for printing properties and variables, see https://cmake.org/cmake/help/v3.5/module/CMakePrintHelpers.html.

Detecting the Python library

The code for this recipe is available at `https://github.com/dev-cafe/cmake-cookbook/tree/v1.0/chapter-03/recipe-02` and has a C example. The recipe is valid with CMake version 3.5 (and higher) and has been tested on GNU/Linux, macOS, and Windows.

The use of Python tools to analyze and manipulate output from compiled programs is nowadays widespread. However, there are also other, more powerful ways of combining an interpreted language such as Python with compiled languages such as C or C++. One way is to *extend* Python by providing new types and new functionalities on these types *via* C or C++ modules, compiled into shared libraries. This will be the topic of recipes in *Chapter 9, Mixed-language Projects*. Another approach is to *embed* the Python interpreter into a C or C++ program. Both approaches require the following:

- A working version of the Python interpreter
- The availability of the Python header file `Python.h`
- The Python runtime library `libpython`

All three components have to be pinned to the exact same version. We have demonstrated how to find the Python interpreter; in this recipe, we will show how to find the two missing ingredients for a successful embedding.

Getting ready

We will use a simple example of Python embedding into a C program that can be found on the Python documentation pages. The source file is called `hello-embedded-python.c`:

```
#include <Python.h>
int main(int argc, char *argv[]) {
  Py_SetProgramName(argv[0]); /* optional but recommended */
  Py_Initialize();
  PyRun_SimpleString("from time import time,ctime\n"
                     "print 'Today is',ctime(time())\n");
  Py_Finalize();
  return 0;
}
```

This code samples will initialize an instance of the Python interpreter within the program and print the date using the `time` Python module.

> The embedding sample code can be found online in the Python documentation pages at `https://docs.python.org/2/extending/embedding.html` and `https://docs.python.org/3/extending/embedding.html`.

How to do it

These are the steps to follow in our `CMakeLists.txt`:

1. The first block contains the minimum CMake version, project name, and required language:

```
cmake_minimum_required(VERSION 3.5 FATAL_ERROR)

project(recipe-02 LANGUAGES C)
```

2. In this recipe we enforce the use of the C99 standard for C. This is not strictly required for linking with Python, but is something you might want to have in place:

```
set(CMAKE_C_STANDARD 99)
set(CMAKE_C_EXTENSIONS OFF)
set(CMAKE_C_STANDARD_REQUIRED ON)
```

3. Find the Python interpreter. This is now a required dependency:

```
find_package(PythonInterp REQUIRED)
```

4. Find the Python header and library. The appropriate module is called `FindPythonLibs.cmake`:

```
find_package(PythonLibs
${PYTHON_VERSION_MAJOR}.${PYTHON_VERSION_MINOR} EXACT REQUIRED)
```

5. We add an executable target which uses the `hello-embedded-python.c` source file:

```
add_executable(hello-embedded-python hello-embedded-python.c)
```

6. The executable includes the `Python.h` header file. Thus, the include directories for this target have to include the Python include directory, accessible from the `PYTHON_INCLUDE_DIRS` variable:

```
target_include_directories(hello-embedded-python
  PRIVATE
```

```
      ${PYTHON_INCLUDE_DIRS}
    )
```

7. Finally, we link the executable to the Python library, accessible *via* the `PYTHON_LIBRARIES` variable:

```
target_link_libraries(hello-embedded-python
  PRIVATE
    ${PYTHON_LIBRARIES}
  )
```

8. Now, we are ready to run the configuration step:

```
$ mkdir -p build
$ cd build
$ cmake ..

...
-- Found PythonInterp: /usr/bin/python (found version "3.6.5")
-- Found PythonLibs: /usr/lib/libpython3.6m.so (found suitable
exact version "3.6.5")
```

9. Finally, we execute the build step and run the executable:

```
$ cmake --build .
$ ./hello-embedded-python

Today is Thu Jun 7 22:26:02 2018
```

How it works

The `FindPythonLibs.cmake` module will look in standard locations for the Python header and library. Since these are required dependencies of our project, configuration will stop with an error if these are not found.

Notice that we explicitly asked CMake to detect the installation of the Python executable. This is to ensure that executable, header, and library all have a matching version. This is paramount to ensure that there are no mismatches between versions that could cause crashes at runtime. We have achieved this by using `PYTHON_VERSION_MAJOR` and `PYTHON_VERSION_MINOR`, defined in `FindPythonInterp.cmake`:

```
find_package(PythonInterp REQUIRED)
find_package(PythonLibs ${PYTHON_VERSION_MAJOR}.${PYTHON_VERSION_MINOR}
EXACT REQUIRED)
```

Using the EXACT keyword, we have constrained CMake to detect a particular, and in this case matching, version of the Python include files and libraries. For an even closer match, we could have used the precise PYTHON_VERSION_STRING:

```
find_package(PythonInterp REQUIRED)
find_package(PythonLibs ${PYTHON_VERSION_STRING} EXACT REQUIRED)
```

There is more

How do we make sure that the Python header and libraries are correctly located even when they are not in a standard installation directory? For the Python interpreter, it is possible to force CMake to look in specific directories by passing the PYTHON_LIBRARY and PYTHON_INCLUDE_DIR options *via* the -D option to the CLI. These options specify the following:

- PYTHON_LIBRARY, the path to the Python library
- PYTHON_INCLUDE_DIR, the path to where Python.h is located

This ensures that the desired version of Python will be picked up.

> Sometimes it is necessary to pass -D PYTHON_EXECUTABLE, -D PYTHON_LIBRARY, and -D PYTHON_INCLUDE_DIR to the CMake CLI in order to locate all necessary components and pin them down to the exact same version.

See also

It might be very difficult to exactly pin the Python interpreter and its development components to be of the exact same version. This is especially true for those cases where they are installed in non-standard locations or there is more than one version of each installed on your system. New Python detection modules have been added to CMake in its version 3.12 that are aimed at solving this vexing problem. The detection portion of our CMakeLists.txt would also be greatly simplified to:

```
find_package(Python COMPONENTS Interpreter Development REQUIRED)
```

We encourage you to read the documentation for the new module at: https://cmake.org/cmake/help/v3.12/module/FindPython.html

Detecting Python modules and packages

The code for this recipe is available at `https://github.com/dev-cafe/cmake-cookbook/tree/v1.0/chapter-03/recipe-03` and has a C++ example. The recipe is valid with CMake version 3.5 (and higher) and has been tested on GNU/Linux, macOS, and Windows.

In the previous recipe, we showed how to detect the Python interpreter and how to compile a simple C program, embedding the Python interpreter. Both are fundamental tasks to get you off the ground when combining Python and a compiled language. Often, your code will depend on specific Python modules, be they Python tools, compiled programs embedding Python, or libraries extending it. For example, NumPy has become very popular in the scientific community for problems involving matrix algebra. In projects that depend on Python modules or packages, it is important to make sure that the dependency on these Python modules is satisfied. This recipe will show how to probe the user's environment to find specific Python modules and packages.

Getting ready

We will try a slightly more involved embedding example in a C++ program. The example is again taken from the Python online documentation (`https://docs.python.org/3.5/extending/embedding.html#pure-embedding`) and shows how to execute functions from a user-defined Python module by calling the compiled C++ executable.

The Python 3 example code (`Py3-pure-embedding.cpp`) contains the following source code (see `https://docs.python.org/2/extending/embedding.html#pure-embedding` for the corresponding Python 2 equivalent):

```
#include <Python.h>

int main(int argc, char *argv[]) {
  PyObject *pName, *pModule, *pDict, *pFunc;
  PyObject *pArgs, *pValue;
  int i;

  if (argc < 3) {
    fprintf(stderr, "Usage: pure-embedding pythonfile funcname [args]\n");
    return 1;
  }

  Py_Initialize();
```

```
PyRun_SimpleString("import sys");
PyRun_SimpleString("sys.path.append(\".\")");

pName = PyUnicode_DecodeFSDefault(argv[1]);
/* Error checking of pName left out */

pModule = PyImport_Import(pName);
Py_DECREF(pName);

if (pModule != NULL) {
  pFunc = PyObject_GetAttrString(pModule, argv[2]);
  /* pFunc is a new reference */

  if (pFunc && PyCallable_Check(pFunc)) {
    pArgs = PyTuple_New(argc - 3);
    for (i = 0; i < argc - 3; ++i) {
      pValue = PyLong_FromLong(atoi(argv[i + 3]));
      if (!pValue) {
        Py_DECREF(pArgs);
        Py_DECREF(pModule);
        fprintf(stderr, "Cannot convert argument\n");
        return 1;
      }
      /* pValue reference stolen here: */
      PyTuple_SetItem(pArgs, i, pValue);
    }
    pValue = PyObject_CallObject(pFunc, pArgs);
    Py_DECREF(pArgs);
    if (pValue != NULL) {
      printf("Result of call: %ld\n", PyLong_AsLong(pValue));
      Py_DECREF(pValue);
    } else {
      Py_DECREF(pFunc);
      Py_DECREF(pModule);
      PyErr_Print();
      fprintf(stderr, "Call failed\n");
      return 1;
    }
  } else {
    if (PyErr_Occurred())
      PyErr_Print();
    fprintf(stderr, "Cannot find function \"%s\"\n", argv[2]);
  }
  Py_XDECREF(pFunc);
  Py_DECREF(pModule);
} else {
  PyErr_Print();
  fprintf(stderr, "Failed to load \"%s\"\n", argv[1]);
```

```
    return 1;
  }
  Py_Finalize();
  return 0;
}
```

The Python code that we wish to embed (`use_numpy.py`) uses NumPy to set up a matrix with all matrix elements set to 1.0:

```
import numpy as np


def print_ones(rows, cols):

    A = np.ones(shape=(rows, cols), dtype=float)
    print(A)

    # we return the number of elements to verify
    # that the C++ code is able to receive return values
    num_elements = rows*cols
    return(num_elements)
```

How to do it

In the following code, we wish to be able to check whether NumPy is available using CMake. We will first need to make sure that the Python interpreter, headers, and libraries are all available on our system. We will then move on to make sure that NumPy is available:

1. First, we define the minimum CMake version, project name, language, and C++ standard:

```
cmake_minimum_required(VERSION 3.5 FATAL_ERROR)

project(recipe-03 LANGUAGES CXX)

set(CMAKE_CXX_STANDARD 11)
set(CMAKE_CXX_EXTENSIONS OFF)
set(CMAKE_CXX_STANDARD_REQUIRED ON)
```

2. Finding the interpreter, headers, and libraries is achieved exactly as in the previous recipe:

```
find_package(PythonInterp REQUIRED)
find_package(PythonLibs
${PYTHON_VERSION_MAJOR}.${PYTHON_VERSION_MINOR} EXACT REQUIRED)
```

3. Properly packaged Python modules are aware of their installation location and version. This can be probed by executing a minimal Python script. We can execute this step *within* our CMakeLists.txt:

```
execute_process(
  COMMAND
    ${PYTHON_EXECUTABLE} "-c" "import re, numpy;
print(re.compile('/__init__.py.*').sub('',numpy.__file__))"
  RESULT_VARIABLE _numpy_status
  OUTPUT_VARIABLE _numpy_location
  ERROR_QUIET
  OUTPUT_STRIP_TRAILING_WHITESPACE
  )
```

4. The _numpy_status variable will be an integer if NumPy was found or a string with some error message otherwise, whereas _numpy_location will contain the path to the NumPy module. If NumPy is found, we save its location to a new variable simply called NumPy. Notice that the new variable is cached; this means that CMake creates a persistent variable that can be later modified by the user:

```
if(NOT _numpy_status)
  set(NumPy ${_numpy_location} CACHE STRING "Location of NumPy")
endif()
```

5. The next step is to check the version of the module. Once again, we deploy some Python magic in our CMakeLists.txt, saving the version into a _numpy_version variable:

```
execute_process(
  COMMAND
    ${PYTHON_EXECUTABLE} "-c" "import numpy;
print(numpy.__version__)"
  OUTPUT_VARIABLE _numpy_version
  ERROR_QUIET
  OUTPUT_STRIP_TRAILING_WHITESPACE
  )
```

6. Finally, we let the FindPackageHandleStandardArgs CMake package set up the NumPy_FOUND variable and output status information in the correct format:

```
include(FindPackageHandleStandardArgs)
find_package_handle_standard_args(NumPy
  FOUND_VAR NumPy_FOUND
  REQUIRED_VARS NumPy
  VERSION_VAR _numpy_version
  )
```

7. Once all dependencies have been correctly found, we can compile the executable and link it to the Python libraries:

```
add_executable(pure-embedding "")

target_sources(pure-embedding
  PRIVATE
    Py${PYTHON_VERSION_MAJOR}-pure-embedding.cpp
  )

target_include_directories(pure-embedding
  PRIVATE
    ${PYTHON_INCLUDE_DIRS}
  )

target_link_libraries(pure-embedding
  PRIVATE
    ${PYTHON_LIBRARIES}
  )
```

8. We also have to make sure that `use_numpy.py` is available in the build directory:

```
add_custom_command(
  OUTPUT
    ${CMAKE_CURRENT_BINARY_DIR}/use_numpy.py
  COMMAND
    ${CMAKE_COMMAND} -E copy_if_different
${CMAKE_CURRENT_SOURCE_DIR}/use_numpy.py
${CMAKE_CURRENT_BINARY_DIR}/use_numpy.py
  DEPENDS
    ${CMAKE_CURRENT_SOURCE_DIR}/use_numpy.py
  )

# make sure building pure-embedding triggers the above custom
command
target_sources(pure-embedding
  PRIVATE
    ${CMAKE_CURRENT_BINARY_DIR}/use_numpy.py
  )
```

9. Now, we can test the detection and embedding of the code:

```
$ mkdir -p build
$ cd build
$ cmake ..

-- ...
-- Found PythonInterp: /usr/bin/python (found version "3.6.5")
```

```
-- Found PythonLibs: /usr/lib/libpython3.6m.so (found suitable
exact version "3.6.5")
-- Found NumPy: /usr/lib/python3.6/site-packages/numpy (found
version "1.14.3")

$ cmake --build .
$ ./pure-embedding use_numpy print_ones 2 3

[[1. 1. 1.]
 [1. 1. 1.]]
Result of call: 6
```

How it works

There are three new CMake commands in this recipe: `execute_process`
and `add_custom_command`, which are always available,
and `find_package_handle_standard_args`, which requires
`include(FindPackageHandleStandardArgs)`.

The `execute_process` command will execute one or more commands as child processes
to the currently issued CMake command. The return value for the last child process will be
saved into the variable passed as an argument to `RESULT_VARIABLE`, while the contents of
the standard output and standard error pipes will be saved into the variables passed as
arguments to `OUTPUT_VARIABLE` and `ERROR_VARIABLE`. `execute_process` allows us to
execute arbitrary commands and use their results to infer the configuration of our system.
In our case, we first use it to make sure that NumPy is available and then to obtain the
version of the module.

The `find_package_handle_standard_args` command provides the standard tool for
handling common operations related to finding programs and libraries installed on a given
system. The version-related options, `REQUIRED` and `EXACT`, are all correctly handled
without further CMake code when referring to this command. The additional options
`QUIET` and `COMPONENTS`, which we will meet shortly, are also handled under the hood by
this CMake command. In this recipe, we have used the following:

```
include(FindPackageHandleStandardArgs)
find_package_handle_standard_args(NumPy
  FOUND_VAR NumPy_FOUND
  REQUIRED_VARS NumPy
  VERSION_VAR _numpy_version
  )
```

The command will set the variable to signal that the module was found (NumPy_FOUND) when all required variables are set to valid file paths (NumPy). It will also set the version to the passed version variable (_numpy_version) and print out status messages for the user:

```
-- Found NumPy: /usr/lib/python3.6/site-packages/numpy (found version
"1.14.3")
```

In the present recipe, we have not used these variables further. What we could have done is to stop the configuration if NumPy_FOUND was returned as FALSE.

Finally, we should comment on the section of the code that copies use_numpy.py to the build directory:

```
add_custom_command(
  OUTPUT
    ${CMAKE_CURRENT_BINARY_DIR}/use_numpy.py
  COMMAND
    ${CMAKE_COMMAND} -E copy_if_different
${CMAKE_CURRENT_SOURCE_DIR}/use_numpy.py
${CMAKE_CURRENT_BINARY_DIR}/use_numpy.py
  DEPENDS
    ${CMAKE_CURRENT_SOURCE_DIR}/use_numpy.py
  )

target_sources(pure-embedding
  PRIVATE
    ${CMAKE_CURRENT_BINARY_DIR}/use_numpy.py
  )
```

We could have achieved the copying with a file(COPY ...) command. Here, we opted to use add_custom_command to make sure that the file gets copied every time it changes, not only the first time we run the configuration. We will return to add_custom_command in more detail in *Chapter 5, Configure-time and Build-time Operations*. Note also the target_sources command, which adds the dependency to ${CMAKE_CURRENT_BINARY_DIR}/use_numpy.py; this was done to make sure that building the pure-embedding target triggers the preceding custom command.

Detecting the BLAS and LAPACK math libraries

The code for this recipe is available at `https://github.com/dev-cafe/cmake-cookbook/tree/v1.0/chapter-03/recipe-04` and has a C++ example. The recipe is valid with CMake version 3.5 (and higher) and has been tested on GNU/Linux, macOS, and Windows.

Many numerical codes rely heavily on matrix and vector operations. Think for example of matrix-vector and matrix-matrix products, the solution of linear system of equations, the calculation of eigenvalues and eigenvectors or singular-value decompositions. These operations might be so ubiquitous in the code base or might have to be run on such large data sets that the availability of efficient implementations becomes an absolute necessity in your code. Fortunately, there are libraries just for that: the basic linear algebra subprograms (BLAS) and the linear algebra package (LAPACK) offer *standard* APIs for many tasks involving linear algebraic manipulations. Different vendors provide different implementations, but all of them share the same API. While the actual programming languages for the underlying implementation of the math libraries varied over time (Fortran, C, Assembly), the remaining historical trace is the Fortran calling convention. Our task in this recipe will be to link against these libraries and show how to seamlessly work with a library written in a different language, considering the above-mentioned calling convention.

Getting ready

To demonstrate the detection and linking of math libraries, we wish to compile a C++ program that takes the dimension of a matrix as command-line input, generates a random square matrix **A**, a random vector **b** and solves the ensuing linear systems of equations: $\mathbf{Ax} = \mathbf{b}$. In addition, we will scale the random vector **b** by a random factor. The subroutines we need to use are DSCAL from BLAS, to perform the scaling and DGESV from LAPACK to find the solution of the linear system of equations. The listing for the example C++ code contains (`linear-algebra.cpp`):

```
#include "CxxBLAS.hpp"
#include "CxxLAPACK.hpp"

#include <iostream>
#include <random>
#include <vector>
```

```
int main(int argc, char **argv) {
  if (argc != 2) {
    std::cout << "Usage: ./linear-algebra dim" << std::endl;
    return EXIT_FAILURE;
  }

  // Generate a uniform distribution of real number between -1.0 and 1.0
  std::random_device rd;
  std::mt19937 mt(rd());
  std::uniform_real_distribution<double> dist(-1.0, 1.0);

  // Allocate matrices and right-hand side vector
  int dim = std::atoi(argv[1]);
  std::vector<double> A(dim * dim);
  std::vector<double> b(dim);
  std::vector<int> ipiv(dim);
  // Fill matrix and RHS with random numbers between -1.0 and 1.0
  for (int r = 0; r < dim; r++) {
    for (int c = 0; c < dim; c++) {
      A[r + c * dim] = dist(mt);
    }
    b[r] = dist(mt);
  }

  // Scale RHS vector by a random number between -1.0 and 1.0
  C_DSCAL(dim, dist(mt), b.data(), 1);
  std::cout << "C_DSCAL done" << std::endl;

  // Save matrix and RHS
  std::vector<double> A1(A);
  std::vector<double> b1(b);

  int info;
  info = C_DGESV(dim, 1, A.data(), dim, ipiv.data(), b.data(), dim);
  std::cout << "C_DGESV done" << std::endl;
  std::cout << "info is " << info << std::endl;

  double eps = 0.0;
  for (int i = 0; i < dim; ++i) {
    double sum = 0.0;
    for (int j = 0; j < dim; ++j)
      sum += A1[i + j * dim] * b[j];
    eps += std::abs(b1[i] - sum);
  }
  std::cout << "check is " << eps << std::endl;

  return 0;
}
```

We are using the random library, introduced in C++11, to generate a random distribution between -1.0 and 1.0. C_DSCAL and C_DGESV are interfaces to the BLAS and LAPACK libraries, respectively, taking care of the name mangling in order to call these functions from a different programming language. This is done in the following interface files in combination with a CMake module which we will discuss further below.

The file CxxBLAS.hpp wraps the BLAS routine with extern "C" linkage:

```
#pragma once

#include "fc_mangle.h"

#include <cstddef>

#ifdef __cplusplus
extern "C" {
#endif

extern void DSCAL(int *n, double *alpha, double *vec, int *inc);

#ifdef __cplusplus
}
#endif

void C_DSCAL(size_t length, double alpha, double *vec, int inc);
```

The corresponding implementation file CxxBLAS.cpp contains:

```
#include "CxxBLAS.hpp"

#include <climits>

// see http://www.netlib.no/netlib/blas/dscal.f
void C_DSCAL(size_t length, double alpha, double *vec, int inc) {
  int big_blocks = (int)(length / INT_MAX);
  int small_size = (int)(length % INT_MAX);
  for (int block = 0; block <= big_blocks; block++) {
    double *vec_s = &vec[block * inc * (size_t)INT_MAX];
    signed int length_s = (block == big_blocks) ? small_size : INT_MAX;
    ::DSCAL(&length_s, &alpha, vec_s, &inc);
  }
}
```

The files CxxLAPACK.hpp and CxxLAPACK.cpp perform corresponding translations for the LAPACK calls.

How to do it

The corresponding `CMakeLists.txt` contains the following building blocks:

1. We define the minimum CMake version, the project name and supported languages:

   ```
   cmake_minimum_required(VERSION 3.5 FATAL_ERROR)

   project(recipe-04 LANGUAGES CXX C Fortran)
   ```

2. We require the C++11 standard:

   ```
   set(CMAKE_CXX_STANDARD 11)
   set(CMAKE_CXX_EXTENSIONS OFF)
   set(CMAKE_CXX_STANDARD_REQUIRED ON)
   ```

3. Further, we verify whether Fortran and C/C++ compilers work together and generate the header file which will take care of name mangling. Both functions are provided by the `FortranCInterface` module:

   ```
   include(FortranCInterface)

   FortranCInterface_VERIFY(CXX)

   FortranCInterface_HEADER(
    fc_mangle.h
    MACRO_NAMESPACE "FC_"
    SYMBOLS DSCAL DGESV
    )
   ```

4. We then ask CMake to find BLAS and LAPACK. These are required dependencies:

   ```
   find_package(BLAS REQUIRED)
   find_package(LAPACK REQUIRED)
   ```

5. Next, we add a library with our sources for the BLAS and LAPACK wrappers and link against `LAPACK_LIBRARIES` which brings in also `BLAS_LIBRARIES`:

   ```
   add_library(math "")

   target_sources(math
     PRIVATE
       CxxBLAS.cpp
       CxxLAPACK.cpp
     )
   ```

```
target_include_directories(math
  PUBLIC
    ${CMAKE_CURRENT_SOURCE_DIR}
    ${CMAKE_CURRENT_BINARY_DIR}
  )

target_link_libraries(math
  PUBLIC
    ${LAPACK_LIBRARIES}
  )
```

6. Notice that the include directories and link libraries for this target are declared as PUBLIC and therefore any additional target depending on the math library will also set these directories in its include directories.

7. Finally, we add an executable target and link to math:

```
add_executable(linear-algebra "")

target_sources(linear-algebra
  PRIVATE
    linear-algebra.cpp
  )

target_link_libraries(linear-algebra
  PRIVATE
    math
  )
```

8. In the configuration step we can focus on the relevant output:

```
$ mkdir -p build
$ cd build
$ cmake ..

...
-- Detecting Fortran/C Interface
-- Detecting Fortran/C Interface - Found GLOBAL and MODULE mangling
-- Verifying Fortran/C Compiler Compatibility
-- Verifying Fortran/C Compiler Compatibility - Success
...
-- Found BLAS: /usr/lib/libblas.so
...
-- A library with LAPACK API found.
...
```

9. Finally, we build and test the executable:

```
$ cmake --build .
$ ./linear-algebra 1000

C_DSCAL done
C_DGESV done
info is 0
check is 1.54284e-10
```

How it works

`FindBLAS.cmake` and `FindLAPACK.cmake` will look in standard locations for libraries offering the standard BLAS and LAPACK APIs. For the former, the module will look for the Fortran implementation of the SGEMM function, for single-precision matrix-matrix products for general matrices. For the latter, the module searches for the Fortran implementation of the CHEEV function, for the calculation of eigenvalues and eigenvectors of complex, Hermitian matrices. These lookups are carried out internally by compiling a small program calling these functions and trying to link against the candidate libraries. If that fails, it signals that a compliant library is not available on the system.

Every compiler performs name-mangling of symbols when generating machine code and unfortunately conventions for this operation are not universal, but compiler-dependent. To overcome this difficulty, we have used the `FortranCInterface` module (https://cmake.org/cmake/help/v3.5/module/FortranCInterface.html) to both verify that the Fortran and C/C++ compilers work together and to generate a Fortran-C interface header `fc_mangle.h` which is compatible with the compiler in question. The generated `fc_mangle.h` must then be included in the interface header files `CxxBLAS.hpp` and `CxxLAPACK.hpp`. We had to add C and Fortran support to the list of LANGUAGES in order to use `FortranCInterface`. Of course we could have defined own preprocessor definitions instead, however at the price of limited portability.

We will discuss the interoperability of Fortran and C more closely in *Chapter 9, Mixed-language Projects*.

> Nowadays, many implementations of BLAS and LAPACK already ship with a thin C layer wrapper around the Fortran subroutines. These wrappers have been standardized over the years and are called CBLAS and LAPACKE.

There is more

Many numerical codes rely heavily on matrix algebra operations and it is important to correctly link against high-performance implementations of the BLAS and LAPACK APIs. There is a large variability in the way vendors package their libraries for different architectures and parallel environments. `FindBLAS.cmake` and `FindLAPACK.cmake` will most likely not be able to locate an existing library in all possible cases. If that happens, you can explicitly set the libraries from the CLI *via* the `-D` option.

Detecting the OpenMP parallel environment

The code for this recipe is available at `https://github.com/dev-cafe/cmake-cookbook/tree/v1.0/chapter-03/recipe-05` and has a C++ and Fortran example. The recipe is valid with CMake version 3.9 (and higher) and has been tested on GNU/Linux, macOS, and Windows. In `https://github.com/dev-cafe/cmake-cookbook/tree/v1.0/chapter-03/recipe-05`, we also provide examples compatible with CMake 3.5.

Today, basically any computer on the market is a multi-core machine and for programs focusing on performance, we may have to focus on these multi-core CPUs and use concurrency in our programming models. OpenMP is the standard for shared-memory parallelism on multi-core CPUs. Existing programs often do not need to be radically modified or rewritten in order to benefit from OpenMP parallelization. Once the performance-critical sections in the code are identified, for example using a profiling tool, the programmer can add preprocessor directives that will instruct the compiler to generate parallel code for those regions.

In this recipe, we will show how to compile a program containing OpenMP directives, provided we use an OpenMP-aware compiler. Many Fortran, C, and C++ compilers exist that can take advantage of OpenMP parallelism. CMake provides very good support for OpenMP in combination with C, C++, or Fortran for relatively recent versions of CMake. This recipe will show you how to detect and link to OpenMP using imported targets for simple C++ and Fortran programs when using CMake 3.9 or above.

Depending on the Linux distribution, the Clang compiler may not have OpenMP support in its default version. This recipe **will not work** on macOS unless a separate libomp installation (`https://iscinumpy.gitlab.io/post/omp-on-high-sierra/`) or a non-Apple version of Clang (e.g., provided by Conda) or the GNU compilers are used.

Getting ready

C and C++ programs can access OpenMP functionality by including the `omp.h` header file and by linking to the correct library. The compiler will generate parallel code according to preprocessor directives preceding the performance-critical sections. In this recipe, we will build the following example source code (`example.cpp`). This code sums integers from 1 to N, where N is given as a command-line argument:

```cpp
#include <iostream>
#include <omp.h>
#include <string>

int main(int argc, char *argv[]) {
  std::cout << "number of available processors: " << omp_get_num_procs()
            << std::endl;
  std::cout << "number of threads: " << omp_get_max_threads() << std::endl;

  auto n = std::stol(argv[1]);
  std::cout << "we will form sum of numbers from 1 to " << n << std::endl;

  // start timer
  auto t0 = omp_get_wtime();

  auto s = 0LL;
#pragma omp parallel for reduction(+ : s)
  for (auto i = 1; i <= n; i++) {
    s += i;
  }

  // stop timer
  auto t1 = omp_get_wtime();

  std::cout << "sum: " << s << std::endl;
  std::cout << "elapsed wall clock time: " << t1 - t0 << " seconds" <<
std::endl;

  return 0;
}
```

In Fortran, one needs to use the `omp_lib` module and link to the correct library. Use of parallel directives is once again possible in code comments preceding the performance-critical sections. The corresponding `example.F90` contains the following:

```fortran
program example
  use omp_lib

  implicit none
```

```fortran
  integer(8) :: i, n, s
  character(len=32) :: arg
  real(8) :: t0, t1

  print *, "number of available processors:", omp_get_num_procs()
  print *, "number of threads:", omp_get_max_threads()

  call get_command_argument(1, arg)
  read(arg , *) n

  print *, "we will form sum of numbers from 1 to", n

  ! start timer
  t0 = omp_get_wtime()

  s = 0
!$omp parallel do reduction(+:s)
  do i = 1, n
    s = s + i
  end do

  ! stop timer
  t1 = omp_get_wtime()

  print *, "sum:", s
  print *, "elapsed wall clock time (seconds):", t1 - t0

end program
```

How to do it

Our `CMakeLists.txt` for the C++ and Fortran examples will follow a template that is largely similar between the two languages:

1. Both define a minimum CMake version, project name, and language (CXX or Fortran; we will show the C++ version):

   ```cmake
   cmake_minimum_required(VERSION 3.9 FATAL_ERROR)

   project(recipe-05 LANGUAGES CXX)
   ```

2. For the C++ example, we require the C++11 standard:

   ```cmake
   set(CMAKE_CXX_STANDARD 11)
   set(CMAKE_CXX_EXTENSIONS OFF)
   set(CMAKE_CXX_STANDARD_REQUIRED ON)
   ```

3. Both call `find_package` to search for OpenMP:

```
find_package(OpenMP REQUIRED)
```

4. Finally, we define the executable target and link to the imported target provided by the `FindOpenMP` module (in the Fortran case, we link against `OpenMP::OpenMP_Fortran`):

```
add_executable(example example.cpp)

target_link_libraries(example
  PUBLIC
    OpenMP::OpenMP_CXX
  )
```

5. Now, we can configure and build the code:

```
$ mkdir -p build
$ cd build
$ cmake ..
$ cmake --build .
```

6. Let us first test it out in parallel (in this example using four cores):

```
$ ./example 1000000000

number of available processors: 4
number of threads: 4
we will form sum of numbers from 1 to 1000000000
sum: 500000000500000000
elapsed wall clock time: 1.08343 seconds
```

7. For comparison, we can rerun the example with the number of OpenMP threads set to 1:

```
$ env OMP_NUM_THREADS=1 ./example 1000000000

number of available processors: 4
number of threads: 1
we will form sum of numbers from 1 to 1000000000
sum: 500000000500000000
elapsed wall clock time: 2.96427 seconds
```

How it works

Our simple example seems to work: the code compiled and linked, and we observe a speed-up when running on multiple cores. The fact that the speed-up is not a perfect multiple of OMP_NUM_THREADS is not our concern in this recipe, since we focus on the CMake aspect of a project which requires OpenMP. We have found linking to OpenMP to be extremely compact thanks to imported targets provided by a reasonably modern FindOpenMP module:

```
target_link_libraries(example
  PUBLIC
    OpenMP::OpenMP_CXX
  )
```

We did not have to worry about compile flags or about include directories - these settings and dependencies are encoded in the definition of the library OpenMP::OpenMP_CXX which is of the IMPORTED type. As we mentioned in *Recipe 3, Building and linking static and shared libraries*, in *Chapter 1, From a Simple Executable to Libraries*, IMPORTED libraries are pseudo-targets that fully encode usage requirements for dependencies outside our own project. To use OpenMP one needs to set compiler flags, include directories, and link libraries. All of these are set as properties on the OpenMP::OpenMP_CXX target and transitively applied to our example target simply by using the target_link_libraries command. This makes using libraries within our CMake scripts exceedingly easy. We can print the properties of interface with the cmake_print_properties command, offered by the CMakePrintHelpers.cmake standard module:

```
include(CMakePrintHelpers)
cmake_print_properties(
  TARGETS
    OpenMP::OpenMP_CXX
  PROPERTIES
    INTERFACE_COMPILE_OPTIONS
    INTERFACE_INCLUDE_DIRECTORIES
    INTERFACE_LINK_LIBRARIES
  )
```

Note that all properties of interest have the prefix INTERFACE_, because these properties usage requirements for any target wanting to *interface* and use the OpenMP target.

For CMake versions below 3.9, we would have to do a bit more work:

```
add_executable(example example.cpp)

target_compile_options(example
  PUBLIC
    ${OpenMP_CXX_FLAGS}
  )

set_target_properties(example
  PROPERTIES
    LINK_FLAGS ${OpenMP_CXX_FLAGS}
  )
```

For CMake versions below 3.5, we might need to explicitly define compile flags for a Fortran project.

In this recipe, we have discussed C++ and Fortran, but the arguments and approach are valid also for a C project.

Detecting the MPI parallel environment

The code for this recipe is available at `https://github.com/dev-cafe/cmake-cookbook/tree/v1.0/chapter-03/recipe-06` and has a C++ and C example. The recipe is valid with CMake version 3.9 (and higher) and has been tested on GNU/Linux, macOS, and Windows. In `https://github.com/dev-cafe/cmake-cookbook/tree/v1.0/chapter-03/recipe-06`, we also provide a C example compatible with CMake 3.5.

An alternative and often complementary approach to OpenMP shared-memory parallelism is the Message Passing Interface (MPI), which has become the *de facto* standard for modeling a program executing in parallel on a distributed memory system. Although modern MPI implementations allow shared-memory parallelism as well, a typical approach in high-performance computing is to use OpenMP within a compute node combined with MPI across compute nodes. The implementation of the MPI standard consists of the following:

1. Runtime libraries.
2. Header files and Fortran 90 modules.

3. Compiler wrappers, which invoke the compiler that was used to build the MPI library with additional command-line arguments to take care of include directories and libraries. Usually, the available compiler wrappers are `mpic++`/`mpiCC`/`mpicxx` for C++, `mpicc` for C, and `mpifort` for Fortran.

4. MPI launcher: This is the program you should call to launch a parallel execution of your compiled code. Its name is implementation-dependent and it is usually one of the following: `mpirun`, `mpiexec`, or `orterun`.

This recipe will show how to find a suitable MPI implementation on your system in order to compile a simple MPI "Hello, World" program.

Getting ready

The example code (`hello-mpi.cpp`, downloaded from `http://www.mpitutorial.com`), which we will compile in this recipe, will initialize the MPI library, have every process print its name, and eventually finalize the library:

```cpp
#include <iostream>

#include <mpi.h>

int main(int argc, char **argv) {
  // Initialize the MPI environment. The two arguments to MPI Init are not
  // currently used by MPI implementations, but are there in case future
  // implementations might need the arguments.
  MPI_Init(NULL, NULL);

  // Get the number of processes
  int world_size;
  MPI_Comm_size(MPI_COMM_WORLD, &world_size);

  // Get the rank of the process
  int world_rank;
  MPI_Comm_rank(MPI_COMM_WORLD, &world_rank);

  // Get the name of the processor
  char processor_name[MPI_MAX_PROCESSOR_NAME];
  int name_len;
  MPI_Get_processor_name(processor_name, &name_len);

  // Print off a hello world message
  std::cout << "Hello world from processor " << processor_name << ", rank "
            << world_rank << " out of " << world_size << " processors" <<
std::endl;
```

```
// Finalize the MPI environment. No more MPI calls can be made after this
MPI_Finalize();
}
```

How to do it

In this recipe, we set out to find the MPI implementation: library, header files, compiler wrappers, and launcher. To do so, we will leverage the `FindMPI.cmake` standard CMake module:

1. First, we define the minimum CMake version, project name, supported language, and language standard:

```
cmake_minimum_required(VERSION 3.9 FATAL_ERROR)

project(recipe-06 LANGUAGES CXX)

set(CMAKE_CXX_STANDARD 11)
set(CMAKE_CXX_EXTENSIONS OFF)
set(CMAKE_CXX_STANDARD_REQUIRED ON)
```

2. We then call `find_package` to locate the MPI implementation:

```
find_package(MPI REQUIRED)
```

3. We define the executable name and, source, and similarly to the previous recipe, link against the imported target:

```
add_executable(hello-mpi hello-mpi.cpp)

target_link_libraries(hello-mpi
  PUBLIC
    MPI::MPI_CXX
  )
```

4. Let us configure and build the executable:

```
$ mkdir -p build
$ cd build
$ cmake -D CMAKE_CXX_COMPILER=mpicxx ..

-- ...
-- Found MPI_CXX: /usr/lib/openmpi/libmpi_cxx.so (found version
"3.1")
```

```
-- Found MPI: TRUE (found version "3.1")
-- ...
```

```
$ cmake --build .
```

5. To execute this program in parallel, we use the `mpirun` launcher (in this case, using two tasks):

```
$ mpirun -np 2 ./hello-mpi
```

```
Hello world from processor larry, rank 1 out of 2 processors
Hello world from processor larry, rank 0 out of 2 processors
```

How it works

Remember that the compiler wrapper is a thin layer around the compiler used to build the MPI library. Under the hood, it will call the same compiler and augment it with additional arguments, such as include paths and libraries, needed to successfully build a parallel program.

Which flags does the wrapper actually apply when compiling and linking a source file? We can probe this using the `--showme` option to the compiler wrapper. To find out the compiler flags we can use:

```
$ mpicxx --showme:compile
```

```
-pthread
```

Whereas to find out the linker flags we use the following:

```
$ mpicxx --showme:link
```

```
-pthread -Wl,-rpath -Wl,/usr/lib/openmpi -Wl,--enable-new-dtags -
L/usr/lib/openmpi -lmpi_cxx -lmpi
```

Similarly to the previous OpenMP recipe, we have found the linking to MPI to be extremely compact thanks to the imported targets provided by a reasonably modern `FindMPI` module:

```
target_link_libraries(hello-mpi
  PUBLIC
    MPI::MPI_CXX
  )
```

We did not have to worry about compile flags or about include directories - these settings and dependencies are already encoded as INTERFACE-type properties in the IMPORTED target provided by CMake.

And as discussed in the previous recipe, for CMake versions below 3.9, we would have to do a bit more work:

```
add_executable(hello-mpi hello-mpi.c)

target_compile_options(hello-mpi
  PUBLIC
    ${MPI_CXX_COMPILE_FLAGS}
  )

target_include_directories(hello-mpi
  PUBLIC
    ${MPI_CXX_INCLUDE_PATH}
  )

target_link_libraries(hello-mpi
  PUBLIC
    ${MPI_CXX_LIBRARIES}
  )
```

In this recipe, we have discussed C++, but the arguments and approach are equally valid for a C or Fortran project.

Detecting the Eigen library

The code for this recipe is available at https://github.com/dev-cafe/cmake-cookbook/tree/v1.0/chapter-03/recipe-07 and has a C++ example. The recipe is valid with CMake version 3.9 (and higher) and has been tested on GNU/Linux, macOS, and Windows. In https://github.com/dev-cafe/cmake-cookbook/tree/v1.0/chapter-03/recipe-07, we also provide a C++ example compatible with CMake 3.5.

The BLAS library offers a standardized interface for common operations involving matrices and vectors. This interface was however standardized with the Fortran language in mind. While we have shown how these libraries can be used more or less directly from C++, it may be desirable to have a higher-level interface in modern C++ programs.

The header-only Eigen library uses template programming to offer such an interface. Its matrix and vector types are intuitive to use and even provide type checking at compile time, to ensure that incompatible matrix dimensions are not mixed. Dense and sparse matrix operations, such as matrix-matrix products, solvers for linear systems, and eigenvalue problems, are also implemented using expression templates for efficiency. From version 3.3, Eigen can be linked to the BLAS and LAPACK libraries, which provides the flexibility to offload certain operations to the implementation given in these libraries for additional performance.

This recipe will show how to find the Eigen library and to instruct it to use OpenMP parallelization and offload some of the work to the BLAS library.

Getting ready

In this example, we will compile a program that allocates a random square matrix and vector of dimension passed from the command line. We will then solve the linear system **Ax=b** using LU decomposition. We will use the following source code (`linear-algebra.cpp`):

```
#include <chrono>
#include <cmath>
#include <cstdlib>
#include <iomanip>
#include <iostream>
#include <vector>

#include <Eigen/Dense>

int main(int argc, char **argv) {
  if (argc != 2) {
    std::cout << "Usage: ./linear-algebra dim" << std::endl;
    return EXIT_FAILURE;
  }

  std::chrono::time_point<std::chrono::system_clock> start, end;
  std::chrono::duration<double> elapsed_seconds;
  std::time_t end_time;

  std::cout << "Number of threads used by Eigen: " << Eigen::nbThreads()
            << std::endl;

  // Allocate matrices and right-hand side vector
  start = std::chrono::system_clock::now();
  int dim = std::atoi(argv[1]);
```

```
    Eigen::MatrixXd A = Eigen::MatrixXd::Random(dim, dim);
    Eigen::VectorXd b = Eigen::VectorXd::Random(dim);
    end = std::chrono::system_clock::now();

    // Report times
    elapsed_seconds = end - start;
    end_time = std::chrono::system_clock::to_time_t(end);
    std::cout << "matrices allocated and initialized "
            << std::put_time(std::localtime(&end_time), "%a %b %d %Y
%r\n")
            << "elapsed time: " << elapsed_seconds.count() << "s\n";

    start = std::chrono::system_clock::now();
    // Save matrix and RHS
    Eigen::MatrixXd A1 = A;
    Eigen::VectorXd b1 = b;
    end = std::chrono::system_clock::now();
    end_time = std::chrono::system_clock::to_time_t(end);
    std::cout << "Scaling done, A and b saved "
            << std::put_time(std::localtime(&end_time), "%a %b %d %Y %r\n")
            << "elapsed time: " << elapsed_seconds.count() << "s\n";

    start = std::chrono::system_clock::now();
    Eigen::VectorXd x = A.lu().solve(b);
    end = std::chrono::system_clock::now();

    // Report times
    elapsed_seconds = end - start;
    end_time = std::chrono::system_clock::to_time_t(end);

    double relative_error = (A * x - b).norm() / b.norm();

    std::cout << "Linear system solver done "
            << std::put_time(std::localtime(&end_time), "%a %b %d %Y %r\n")
            << "elapsed time: " << elapsed_seconds.count() << "s\n";
    std::cout << "relative error is " << relative_error << std::endl;

    return 0;
}
```

Matrix-vector multiplications and LU decompositions are implemented in Eigen, but can optionally be offloaded to the BLAS and LAPACK libraries. In this recipe, we only consider offloading to the BLAS library.

How to do it

In this project, we will find the Eigen and BLAS libraries, as well as OpenMP, and instruct Eigen to use OpenMP parallelization and to offload part of the linear algebra work to the BLAS library:

1. We first declare the minimum CMake version, project name, and use of the C++11 language:

```
cmake_minimum_required(VERSION 3.9 FATAL_ERROR)

project(recipe-07 LANGUAGES CXX)

set(CMAKE_CXX_STANDARD 11)
set(CMAKE_CXX_EXTENSIONS OFF)
set(CMAKE_CXX_STANDARD_REQUIRED ON)
```

2. We also ask for OpenMP, since Eigen can make use of shared-memory parallelism for dense operations:

```
find_package(OpenMP REQUIRED)
```

3. We search for Eigen by calling `find_package` in `CONFIG` mode (we will discuss this in the next section):

```
find_package(Eigen3 3.3 REQUIRED CONFIG)
```

4. If Eigen was found, we print out a helpful status message. Notice that we are using the `Eigen3::Eigen` target. As we have learnt in the previous two recipes, this is an `IMPORTED` target, offered by the native CMake scripts distributed with Eigen:

```
if(TARGET Eigen3::Eigen)
  message(STATUS "Eigen3 v${EIGEN3_VERSION_STRING} found in ${EIGEN3_INCLUDE_DIR}")
endif()
```

5. Next, we declare an executable target for our source file:

```
add_executable(linear-algebra linear-algebra.cpp)
```

6. We then find BLAS. Notice that the dependency is now not required:

```
find_package(BLAS)
```

7. If BLAS is found, we set the corresponding compile definition and link libraries for the executable target:

```
if(BLAS_FOUND)
  message(STATUS "Eigen will use some subroutines from BLAS.")
  message(STATUS "See:
http://eigen.tuxfamily.org/dox-devel/TopicUsingBlasLapack.html")
  target_compile_definitions(linear-algebra
    PRIVATE
      EIGEN_USE_BLAS
    )
  target_link_libraries(linear-algebra
    PUBLIC
      ${BLAS_LIBRARIES}
    )
else()
  message(STATUS "BLAS not found. Using Eigen own functions")
endif()
```

8. Finally, we link to the imported `Eigen3::Eigen` and `OpenMP::OpenMP_CXX` targets. This is enough to set all the necessary compile and link flags:

```
target_link_libraries(linear-algebra
  PUBLIC
    Eigen3::Eigen
    OpenMP::OpenMP_CXX
  )
```

9. We are now ready to configure the project:

```
$ mkdir -p build
$ cd build
$ cmake ..

-- ...
-- Found OpenMP_CXX: -fopenmp (found version "4.5")
-- Found OpenMP: TRUE (found version "4.5")
-- Eigen3 v3.3.4 found in /usr/include/eigen3
-- ...
-- Found BLAS: /usr/lib/libblas.so
-- Eigen will use some subroutines from BLAS.
-- See:
http://eigen.tuxfamily.org/dox-devel/TopicUsingBlasLapack.html
```

10. Finally, we compile and test the code. Observe that the binary uses, in this case, four available threads:

```
$ cmake --build .
$ ./linear-algebra 1000

Number of threads used by Eigen: 4
matrices allocated and initialized Sun Jun 17 2018 11:04:20 AM
elapsed time: 0.0492328s
Scaling done, A and b saved Sun Jun 17 2018 11:04:20 AM
elapsed time: 0.0492328s
Linear system solver done Sun Jun 17 2018 11:04:20 AM
elapsed time: 0.483142s
relative error is 4.21946e-13
```

How it works

Eigen provides native CMake support, which makes it easy to set up a C++ project using it. Starting from version 3.3, Eigen ships CMake modules that export the appropriate target, `Eigen3::Eigen`, which we have used here.

You will have noticed the `CONFIG` option to the `find_package` command. This signals to CMake that the package search will not proceed through a `FindEigen3.cmake` module, but rather through the `Eigen3Config.cmake`, `Eigen3ConfigVersion.cmake`, and `Eigen3Targets.cmake` files provided by the Eigen3 package in the standard location, `<installation-prefix>/share/eigen3/cmake`. This package location mode is called "Config" mode and is more versatile than the `Find<package>.cmake` approach we have been using so far. For more information about "Module" mode versus "Config" mode, please consult the official documentation at `https://cmake.org/cmake/help/v3.5/command/find_package.html`.

Also note that while the Eigen3, BLAS, and OpenMP dependencies were declared as `PUBLIC` dependencies, the `EIGEN_USE_BLAS` compile definition was declared as `PRIVATE`. Instead of linking the executable directly, we could collect the library dependencies in a separate library target. Using the `PUBLIC`/`PRIVATE` keywords, we can then adjust the visibility of the corresponding flags and definitions to dependents of the library target.

There is more

CMake will look for config modules in a predefined hierarchy of locations. First off is CMAKE_PREFIX_PATH, while <package>_DIR is the next search path. Thus, if Eigen3 was installed in a non-standard location, we can use two alternatives to tell CMake where to look for it:

1. By passing the installation prefix for Eigen3 as CMAKE_PREFIX_PATH:

   ```
   $ cmake -D CMAKE_PREFIX_PATH=<installation-prefix> ..
   ```

2. By passing the location of the configuration files as Eigen3_DIR:

   ```
   $ cmake -D Eigen3_DIR=<installation-prefix>/share/eigen3/cmake/
   ```

Detecting the Boost libraries

The code for this recipe is available at https://github.com/dev-cafe/cmake-cookbook/tree/v1.0/chapter-03/recipe-08 and has a C++ example. The recipe is valid with CMake version 3.5 (and higher) and has been tested on GNU/Linux, macOS, and Windows.

The Boost libraries are a collection of general-purpose C++ libraries. These libraries provide a lot of functionality that may be indispensable in a modern C++ project, but which is not yet available through the C++ standard. For example, Boost provides components for metaprogramming, handling optional arguments, and filesystem manipulations, among others. Many of these libraries have later been adopted by the C++11, C++14, and C++17 standards, but many Boost components are still the libraries of choice for code bases that have to keep compatibility with older compilers.

This recipe will show you how to detect and link against some components of the Boost libraries.

Getting ready

The source code we will compile is one of the examples for the filesystem library provided by Boost to interact with the filesystem. This library is conveniently cross-platform and abstracts the differences between operating systems and filesystems into a coherent, high-level API. The following example code (path-info.cpp) will accept a path as an argument and print a report about its components to the screen:

```cpp
#include <iostream>

#include <boost/filesystem.hpp>

using namespace std;
using namespace boost::filesystem;

const char *say_what(bool b) { return b ? "true" : "false"; }

int main(int argc, char *argv[]) {
  if (argc < 2) {
    cout
        << "Usage: path_info path-element [path-element...]\n"
           "Composes a path via operator/= from one or more path-element
arguments\n"
           "Example: path_info foo/bar baz\n"
#ifdef BOOST_POSIX_API
           " would report info about the composed path foo/bar/baz\n";
#else // BOOST_WINDOWS_API
           " would report info about the composed path foo/bar\\baz\n";
#endif
    return 1;
  }

  path p;
  for (; argc > 1; --argc, ++argv)
    p /= argv[1]; // compose path p from the command line arguments

  cout << "\ncomposed path:\n";
  cout << " operator<<()---------: " << p << "\n";
  cout << " make_preferred()-----: " << p.make_preferred() << "\n";

  cout << "\nelements:\n";
  for (auto element : p)
    cout << " " << element << '\n';

  cout << "\nobservers, native format:" << endl;
#ifdef BOOST_POSIX_API
  cout << " native()-------------: " << p.native() << endl;
```

```
      cout << " c_str()-------------: " << p.c_str() << endl;
#else // BOOST_WINDOWS_API
  wcout << L" native()------------: " << p.native() << endl;
  wcout << L" c_str()-------------: " << p.c_str() << endl;
#endif
    cout << " string()------------: " << p.string() << endl;
  wcout << L" wstring()-----------: " << p.wstring() << endl;

    cout << "\nobservers, generic format:\n";
    cout << " generic_string()-----: " << p.generic_string() << endl;
  wcout << L" generic_wstring()----: " << p.generic_wstring() << endl;

    cout << "\ndecomposition:\n";
    cout << " root_name()----------: " << p.root_name() << '\n';
    cout << " root_directory()-----: " << p.root_directory() << '\n';
    cout << " root_path()----------: " << p.root_path() << '\n';
    cout << " relative_path()------: " << p.relative_path() << '\n';
    cout << " parent_path()--------: " << p.parent_path() << '\n';
    cout << " filename()-----------: " << p.filename() << '\n';
    cout << " stem()---------------: " << p.stem() << '\n';
    cout << " extension()----------: " << p.extension() << '\n';

    cout << "\nquery:\n";
    cout << " empty()--------------: " << say_what(p.empty()) << '\n';
    cout << " is_absolute()--------: " << say_what(p.is_absolute()) <<
    '\n';
    cout << " has_root_name()------: " << say_what(p.has_root_name()) <<
    '\n';
    cout << " has_root_directory()-: " << say_what(p.has_root_directory()) <<
'\n';
    cout << " has_root_path()------: " << say_what(p.has_root_path()) <<
    '\n';
    cout << " has_relative_path()--: " << say_what(p.has_relative_path()) <<
'\n';
    cout << " has_parent_path()----: " << say_what(p.has_parent_path()) <<
'\n';
    cout << " has_filename()-------: " << say_what(p.has_filename()) <<
    '\n';
    cout << " has_stem()-----------: " << say_what(p.has_stem()) << '\n';
    cout << " has_extension()------: " << say_what(p.has_extension()) <<
    '\n';

    return 0;
}
```

How to do it

Boost consists of many different libraries and these can be used almost independently from each other. Internally, CMake represents this library collection as a collection of components. The `FindBoost.cmake` module can search not only for the full installation of the library collection but also for particular components and their dependencies within the collection, if any. We will build up the corresponding `CMakeLists.txt` step by step:

1. We first declare the minimum CMake version, project name, language, and enforce the use of the C++11 standard:

```
cmake_minimum_required(VERSION 3.5 FATAL_ERROR)

project(recipe-08 LANGUAGES CXX)

set(CMAKE_CXX_STANDARD 11)
set(CMAKE_CXX_EXTENSIONS OFF)
set(CMAKE_CXX_STANDARD_REQUIRED ON)
```

2. Then, we use `find_package` to search for Boost. The dependency on Boost is mandatory, hence the `REQUIRED` argument. Since we only need the filesystem component in this example, we pass that as an argument after the `COMPONENTS` keyword to `find_package`:

```
find_package(Boost 1.54 REQUIRED COMPONENTS filesystem)
```

3. We add an executable target, to compile the example source file:

```
add_executable(path-info path-info.cpp)
```

4. Finally, we link the target to the Boost library component. Since the dependency is declared `PUBLIC`, targets depending on our target will pick up the dependency automatically:

```
target_link_libraries(path-info
  PUBLIC
    Boost::filesystem
  )
```

How it works

The `FindBoost.cmake` module, which is used in this recipe, will try to locate the Boost libraries in standard system installation directories. Since we link to the imported `Boost::filesystem` target, CMake will automatically set the include directories and adjust the compile and link flags. In case the Boost libraries are installed in a non-standard location, one can pass the root of the Boost installation at configuration time using the `BOOST_ROOT` variable in order to point CMake to also search the non-standard path:

```
$ cmake -D BOOST_ROOT=/custom/boost/
```

Alternatively, one can pass both the `BOOST_INCLUDEDIR` and `BOOST_LIBRARYDIR` variables for the directories containing headers and libraries:

```
$ cmake -D BOOST_INCLUDEDIR=/custom/boost/include -D
BOOST_LIBRARYDIR=/custom/boost/lib
```

Detecting external libraries: I. Using pkg-config

The code for this recipe is available at `https://github.com/dev-cafe/cmake-cookbook/tree/v1.0/chapter-03/recipe-09` and has a C example. The recipe is valid with CMake version 3.6 (and higher) and has been tested on GNU/Linux, macOS, and Windows (using MSYS Makefiles). In `https://github.com/dev-cafe/cmake-cookbook/tree/v1.0/chapter-03/recipe-09`, we also provide an example compatible with CMake 3.5.

We have so far discussed two ways of detecting external dependencies:

- Using find-modules shipped with CMake. This is generally reliable and well tested. However, not all packages have a find-module in the official release of CMake.
- Using `<package>Config.cmake`, `<package>ConfigVersion.cmake`, and `<package>Targets.cmake` files provided by the package vendor and installed alongside the package itself in standard locations.

What if a certain dependency provides neither a find-module nor vendor-packaged CMake files? In this case, we are left with two options:

- Rely on the `pkg-config` utility to discover packages on the system. This relies on the package vendors distributing metadata about their packages in `.pc` configuration files.
- Write our own find-package module for the dependency.

In this recipe, we will show how to leverage `pkg-config` from within CMake to locate the ZeroMQ messaging library. The next recipe, *Detecting external libraries: II. Writing a find-module*, will show how to write your own basic find-module for ZeroMQ.

Getting ready

The code we will build is an example from the ZeroMQ manual at `http://zguide.zeromq.org/page:all`. It consists of two source files, `hwserver.c`, and `hwclient.c`, which will be built into two separate executables. When executed, they will print the familiar "Hello, World" message.

How to do it

This is a C project and we will use the C99 standard. We will build the `CMakeLists.txt` file step by step:

1. We declare a C project and enforce compliance with the C99 standard:

```
cmake_minimum_required(VERSION 3.6 FATAL_ERROR)
project(recipe-09 LANGUAGES C)

set(CMAKE_C_STANDARD 99)
set(CMAKE_C_EXTENSIONS OFF)
set(CMAKE_C_STANDARD_REQUIRED ON)
```

2. We look for `pkg-config`, using its find-module shipped with CMake. Notice the `QUIET` argument passed to `find_package`. CMake will print messages only if the required `pkg-config` is not found:

```
find_package(PkgConfig REQUIRED QUIET)
```

3. When `pkg-config` is found, we will have access to the `pkg_search_module` function to search for any library or program that ships a package configuration `.pc` file. In our case, we look for the ZeroMQ library:

```
pkg_search_module(
  ZeroMQ
  REQUIRED
    libzeromq libzmq lib0mq
  IMPORTED_TARGET
  )
```

4. A status message is printed, in case the ZeroMQ library was found:

```
if(TARGET PkgConfig::ZeroMQ)
  message(STATUS "Found ZeroMQ")
endif()
```

5. We can then add the two executable targets and link against the `IMPORTED` target for ZeroMQ. This will set include directories and link libraries automatically:

```
add_executable(hwserver hwserver.c)

target_link_libraries(hwserver PkgConfig::ZeroMQ)

add_executable(hwclient hwclient.c)

target_link_libraries(hwclient PkgConfig::ZeroMQ)
```

6. Now, we can configure and build the example:

```
$ mkdir -p build
$ cd build
$ cmake ..
$ cmake --build .
```

7. In one terminal, start the server, which will respond with a message similar to this example:

```
Current 0MQ version is 4.2.2
```

8. Then, in another terminal start the client, which will print the following:

```
Connecting to hello world server...
Sending Hello 0...
Received World 0
Sending Hello 1...
Received World 1
Sending Hello 2...
. . .
```

How it works

Once `pkg-config` is found, CMake will provide two functions to wrap the functionality offered by this program:

- `pkg_check_modules`, to find all modules (libraries and/or programs) in the passed list
- `pkg_search_module`, to find the first working module in the passed list

These functions accept the `REQUIRED` and `QUIET` arguments, as `find_package` does. In more detail, our call to `pkg_search_module` is the following:

```
pkg_search_module(
  ZeroMQ
  REQUIRED
    libzeromq libzmq lib0mq
  IMPORTED_TARGET
  )
```

Here, the first argument is the prefix that will be used to name the target that is storing the result of the search for the ZeroMQ library: `PkgConfig::ZeroMQ`. Notice that we need to pass different options for the names of the library on the system: `libzeromq`, `libzmq`, and `lib0mq`. This is due to the fact that different operating systems and package managers can choose different names for the same package.

> The `pkg_check_modules` and `pkg_search_module` functions gained the `IMPORTED_TARGET` option and the functionality to also define an imported target in CMake 3.6. Prior to this version of CMake, only the variables `ZeroMQ_INCLUDE_DIRS`, for the include directories, and `ZeroMQ_LIBRARIES`, for the link libraries, would have been defined for later use.

Detecting external libraries: II. Writing a find-module

The code for this recipe is available at `https://github.com/dev-cafe/cmake-cookbook/tree/v1.0/chapter-03/recipe-10` and has a C example. The recipe is valid with CMake version 3.5 (and higher) and has been tested on GNU/Linux, macOS, and Windows.

This recipe complements the previous recipe, *Detecting external libraries: I. Using pkg-config*. We will show how to write a basic find-module to locate the ZeroMQ messaging library on your system so that the detection of the library can be made to work on non-Unix operating systems. We will reuse the same server-client sample code.

How to do it

This is a C project and we will use the C99 standard. We will build the `CMakeLists.txt` file step by step:

1. We declare a C project and enforce compliance with the C99 standard:

    ```
    cmake_minimum_required(VERSION 3.5 FATAL_ERROR)
    project(recipe-10 LANGUAGES C)

    set(CMAKE_C_STANDARD 99)
    set(CMAKE_C_EXTENSIONS OFF)
    set(CMAKE_C_STANDARD_REQUIRED ON)
    ```

2. We append the current source directory, `CMAKE_CURRENT_SOURCE_DIR`, to the list of paths where CMake will look for modules, `CMAKE_MODULE_PATH`. This is where our own `FindZeroMQ.cmake` module is located:

    ```
    list(APPEND CMAKE_MODULE_PATH ${CMAKE_CURRENT_SOURCE_DIR})
    ```

3. We will discuss `FindZeroMQ.cmake` later, but now that the `FindZeroMQ.cmake` module is available, we search for the library. This is a required dependency for our project. Since we did not use the `QUIET` option to `find_package`, status messages will be printed automatically when the library is found:

    ```
    find_package(ZeroMQ REQUIRED)
    ```

4. We proceed to add the `hwserver` executable target. The include directories and link libraries are specified using the `ZeroMQ_INCLUDE_DIRS` and `ZeroMQ_LIBRARIES` variables set by the successful `find_package` command:

```
add_executable(hwserver hwserver.c)

target_include_directories(hwserver
  PRIVATE
    ${ZeroMQ_INCLUDE_DIRS}
  )

target_link_libraries(hwserver
  PRIVATE
    ${ZeroMQ_LIBRARIES}
  )
```

5. Finally, we do the same for the `hwclient` executable target:

```
add_executable(hwclient hwclient.c)

target_include_directories(hwclient
  PRIVATE
    ${ZeroMQ_INCLUDE_DIRS}
  )

target_link_libraries(hwclient
  PRIVATE
    ${ZeroMQ_LIBRARIES}
  )
```

The main `CMakeLists.txt` for this recipe differs from the one used in the previous recipe in the use of the `FindZeroMQ.cmake` module. This module searches for the ZeroMQ header files and libraries using the `find_path` and `find_library` CMake built-in commands and sets relevant variables using the `find_package_handle_standard_args`, as we did in *Recipe 3, Detecting Python modules and packages*.

1. In `FindZeroMQ.cmake`, we first check whether the `ZeroMQ_ROOT` CMake variable was set by the user. This variable can be used to guide detection of the ZeroMQ library to a non-standard installation directory. The user might have set `ZeroMQ_ROOT` as an environment variable and we also check for that:

```
if(NOT ZeroMQ_ROOT)
  set(ZeroMQ_ROOT "$ENV{ZeroMQ_ROOT}")
endif()
```

2. We then search for the location of the `zmq.h` header file on the system. This is based on the `_ZeroMQ_ROOT` variable and uses the `find_path` CMake command:

```
if(NOT ZeroMQ_ROOT)
  find_path(_ZeroMQ_ROOT NAMES include/zmq.h)
else()
  set(_ZeroMQ_ROOT "${ZeroMQ_ROOT}")
endif()

find_path(ZeroMQ_INCLUDE_DIRS NAMES zmq.h HINTS
${_ZeroMQ_ROOT}/include)
```

3. If the header file was successfully found, `ZeroMQ_INCLUDE_DIRS` is set to its location. We proceed to find the version of the ZeroMQ library available, using string manipulations and regular expressions:

```
set(_ZeroMQ_H ${ZeroMQ_INCLUDE_DIRS}/zmq.h)

function(_zmqver_EXTRACT _ZeroMQ_VER_COMPONENT _ZeroMQ_VER_OUTPUT)
  set(CMAKE_MATCH_1 "0")
  set(_ZeroMQ_expr "^[ \\t]*#define[ \\t]+${_ZeroMQ_VER_COMPONENT}[
\\t]+([0-9]+)$")
  file(STRINGS "${_ZeroMQ_H}" _ZeroMQ_ver REGEX "${_ZeroMQ_expr}")
  string(REGEX MATCH "${_ZeroMQ_expr}" ZeroMQ_ver "${_ZeroMQ_ver}")
  set(${_ZeroMQ_VER_OUTPUT} "${CMAKE_MATCH_1}" PARENT_SCOPE)
endfunction()

_zmqver_EXTRACT("ZMQ_VERSION_MAJOR" ZeroMQ_VERSION_MAJOR)
_zmqver_EXTRACT("ZMQ_VERSION_MINOR" ZeroMQ_VERSION_MINOR)
_zmqver_EXTRACT("ZMQ_VERSION_PATCH" ZeroMQ_VERSION_PATCH)
```

4. We then prepare the `ZeroMQ_VERSION` variable for the `find_package_handle_standard_args` command:

```
if(ZeroMQ_FIND_VERSION_COUNT GREATER 2)
  set(ZeroMQ_VERSION
"${ZeroMQ_VERSION_MAJOR}.${ZeroMQ_VERSION_MINOR}.${ZeroMQ_VERSION_P
ATCH}")
else()
  set(ZeroMQ_VERSION
"${ZeroMQ_VERSION_MAJOR}.${ZeroMQ_VERSION_MINOR}")
endif()
```

5. We use the `find_library` command to search for the `ZeroMQ` library. Here, we need to make a distinction between Unix-based and Windows platforms, since the naming conventions for libraries are different:

```
if(NOT ${CMAKE_C_PLATFORM_ID} STREQUAL "Windows")
  find_library(ZeroMQ_LIBRARIES
      NAMES
        zmq
      HINTS
        ${_ZeroMQ_ROOT}/lib
        ${_ZeroMQ_ROOT}/lib/x86_64-linux-gnu
      )
else()
  find_library(ZeroMQ_LIBRARIES
      NAMES
        libzmq
        "libzmq-mt-
${ZeroMQ_VERSION_MAJOR}_${ZeroMQ_VERSION_MINOR}_${ZeroMQ_VERSION_PA
TCH}"
        "libzmq-${CMAKE_VS_PLATFORM_TOOLSET}-mt-
${ZeroMQ_VERSION_MAJOR}_${ZeroMQ_VERSION_MINOR}_${ZeroMQ_VERSION_PA
TCH}"
        libzmq_d
        "libzmq-mt-gd-
${ZeroMQ_VERSION_MAJOR}_${ZeroMQ_VERSION_MINOR}_${ZeroMQ_VERSION_PA
TCH}"
        "libzmq-${CMAKE_VS_PLATFORM_TOOLSET}-mt-gd-
${ZeroMQ_VERSION_MAJOR}_${ZeroMQ_VERSION_MINOR}_${ZeroMQ_VERSION_PA
TCH}"
      HINTS
        ${_ZeroMQ_ROOT}/lib
      )
endif()
```

6. Finally, we include the standard `FindPackageHandleStandardArgs.cmake` module and invoke the corresponding CMake command. If all required variables are found and the version matches, then the `ZeroMQ_FOUND` variable is set to TRUE:

```
include(FindPackageHandleStandardArgs)

find_package_handle_standard_args(ZeroMQ
  FOUND_VAR
    ZeroMQ_FOUND
  REQUIRED_VARS
```

```
        ZeroMQ_INCLUDE_DIRS
        ZeroMQ_LIBRARIES
    VERSION_VAR
        ZeroMQ_VERSION
    )
```

> The `FindZeroMQ.cmake` module we just described has been adapted from `https://github.com/zeromq/azmq/blob/master/config/FindZeroMQ.cmake`.

How it works

Find-modules typically follow a specific pattern:

1. Check whether the user provided a custom location for the desired package.
2. Use commands from the `find_` family to search for known required components of the required package, that is, header files, libraries, executables, and so forth. We have used `find_path` to find the full path to a header file and `find_library` to find a library. CMake also offers `find_file`, `find_program`, and `find_package`. These commands have the following general signature:

   ```
   find_path(<VAR> NAMES name PATHS paths)
   ```

3. Here, `<VAR>` will hold the result of the search, if successful, or `<VAR>-NOTFOUND` if unsuccessful. `NAMES` and `PATHS` are names for the file CMake should look for and paths where the search should be directed, respectively.
4. From the results of this preliminary search, a version number is extracted. In our example, the ZeroMQ header file contains the library version, which can be extracted with string operations and regular expressions.
5. Finally, the `find_package_handle_standard_args` command is invoked. This will handle the standard `REQUIRED`, `QUIET`, and version arguments to the `find_package` command, additionally setting the `ZeroMQ_FOUND` variable.

The full documentation for any CMake command can be obtained from the command line. For example, `cmake --help-command find_file` will output the manual page for the `find_file` command. For the manual page of CMake standard modules, use the `--help-module` CLI switch. For example, `cmake --help-module FindPackageHandleStandardArgs` will output to screen the manual page for the `FindPackageHandleStandardArgs.cmake` module.

There is more

To summarize, when discovering packages there are four available routes:

1. Use the CMake files `<package>Config.cmake`, `<package>ConfigVersion.cmake`, and `<package>Targets.cmake` provided by the package vendor and installed alongside the package itself in standard locations.
2. Use a find-module for the desired package, whether shipped by CMake or a third party.
3. Resort to `pkg-config`, as shown in this recipe.
4. If none of these are viable, write your own find-module.

The four alternative routes have been ranked by relevance, but each approach has its challenges.

Not all package vendors provide CMake discovery files, but it is becoming more common. This is due to the fact that exporting CMake targets makes it very easy for third-party code to consume additional dependencies imposed by libraries and/or programs that it depends on.

Find-modules have been the workhorse of dependency location in CMake since the very beginning. However, most of them still rely on setting variables consumed by the dependent, such as `Boost_INCLUDE_DIRS`, `PYTHON_INTERPRETER`, and so forth. This approach makes it difficult to redistribute your own package for third-parties and ensure that your dependencies are consistently met.

The approach using `pkg-config` can work very well since it has become a *de facto* standard for Unix-based systems. For this reason, however, it is not a fully cross-platform approach. Moreover, as the CMake documentation states, in some cases, the user can accidentally override package detection and lead `pkg-config` to supply incorrect information.

The very last resort is then to write your own find-module CMake script, as we have done in this recipe. This is doable and relies on the `FindPackageHandleStandardArgs.cmake` module we briefly discussed. However, writing a fully comprehensive find-module is far from trivial; there are many corner cases that are hard to discover, and we have shown an example of that when looking for the ZeroMQ library files on Unix and Windows platforms.

These concerns and difficulties are very well-known to all software developers, as witnessed by the lively discussions on the CMake mailing list: `https://cmake.org/pipermail/cmake/2018-May/067556.html`. `pkg-config` is accepted among Unix package developers, but it cannot be easily ported to not-Unix platforms. CMake configuration files are powerful, but not all software developers are familiar with the CMake syntax. The Common Package Specification project is a very recent attempt at unifying the `pkg-config` and CMake configuration files approaches for package discovery. You can find more information on the project's website: `https://mwoehlke.github.io/cps/`

In *Chapter 10, Writing an Installer*, we will discuss how to make your own package discoverable to third-party applications by using the first route outlined in the previous discussion: providing your own CMake discovery files alongside your project.

4
Creating and Running Tests

In this chapter, we will cover the following recipes:

- Creating a simple unit test
- Defining a unit test using the Catch2 library
- Defining a unit test and linking against Google Test
- Defining a unit test and linking against Boost test
- Using dynamic analysis to detect memory defects
- Testing expected failures
- Using timeouts for long tests
- Running tests in parallel
- Running a subset of tests
- Using test fixtures

Introduction

Testing is a core component of the code development toolbox. Performing automated testing by using unit and integration tests not only helps the developer to detect functionality regressions early, but can also serve as a starting point for developers joining the project. It can help new developers to submit changes to the code project, with assurance that the expected functionality is preserved. For users of the code, automated tests can be essential when verifying that the installation preserves the functionality of the code. A nice byproduct of employing tests for units, modules, or libraries right from the start is that it can guide the programmer towards more modular and less complex code structures, using a pure, functional style, that minimizes and localizes global variables and the global state.

In this chapter, we will demonstrate how to integrate testing into the CMake build structure, using popular testing libraries and frameworks, with the following goals in mind:

- Making it easy for users, developers, and continuous integration services to run the test set. When using Unix Makefiles, it should be as simple as typing `make test`.

- Running tests efficiently by minimizing the total test time, in order to maximize the probability that tests are run often-ideally, with each code change.

Creating a simple unit test

The code for this recipe is available at `https://github.com/dev-cafe/cmake-cookbook/tree/v1.0/chapter-04/recipe-01`, and includes a C++ example. The recipe is valid with CMake version 3.5 (and higher), and has been tested on GNU/Linux, macOS, and Windows.

In this recipe, we will introduce unit tests using CTest, the testing tool distributed as a part of CMake. In order to keep the focus on the CMake/CTest aspect and to minimize the cognitive load, we wish to keep the code that is to be tested as simple as possible. Our plan is to write and test code that can sum up integers, and nothing more. Just like in primary school, when we learned multiplication and division after learning how to add, at this point, our example code will only add and will only understand integers; it will not need to deal with floating point numbers. And, just as the young Carl Friedrich Gauss was tested by his teacher to sum all natural numbers from 1 to 100, we will ask our code to do the same-albeit without using the clever grouping trick employed by Gauss. To show that CMake does not impose any restrictions on the language to implement the actual tests, we will test our code using not only a C++ executable, but also using a Python script and a shell script. For simplicity, we will do this without using any testing libraries, but we will introduce C++ testing frameworks in later recipes in this chapter.

Getting ready

Our code example consists of three files. The implementation source file, `sum_integers.cpp`, does the work of summing up over a vector of integers, and returns the sum:

```
#include "sum_integers.hpp"
#include <vector>
```

```
int sum_integers(const std::vector<int> integers) {
  auto sum = 0;
  for (auto i : integers) {
    sum += i;
  }
  return sum;
}
```

For this example, it does not matter whether this is the most elegant implementation of a sum over a vector. The interface is exported to our example library in sum_integers.hpp, as follows:

```
#pragma once
#include <vector>

int sum_integers(const std::vector<int> integers);
```

Finally, the main function is defined in main.cpp, which collects the command-line arguments from argv[], converts them into a vector of integers, calls the sum_integers function, and prints the result to the output:

```
#include "sum_integers.hpp"
#include <iostream>
#include <string>
#include <vector>

// we assume all arguments are integers and we sum them up
// for simplicity we do not verify the type of arguments
int main(int argc, char *argv[]) {

  std::vector<int> integers;
  for (auto i = 1; i < argc; i++) {
    integers.push_back(std::stoi(argv[i]));
  }
  auto sum = sum_integers(integers);

  std::cout << sum << std::endl;
}
```

Our goal is to test this code using a C++ executable (test.cpp), a Bash shell script (test.sh), and a Python script (test.py), to demonstrate that CMake does not really mind which programming or scripting language we prefer, as long as the implementation can return a zero or non-zero value that CMake can interpret as a success or failure, respectively.

In the C++ example (`test.cpp`), we verify that $1 + 2 + 3 + 4 + 5$ equals 15, by calling `sum_integers`:

```cpp
#include "sum_integers.hpp"
#include <vector>

int main() {
  auto integers = {1, 2, 3, 4, 5};

  if (sum_integers(integers) == 15) {
    return 0;
  } else {
    return 1;
  }
}
```

The Bash shell script test example calls the executable, which is received as a positional argument:

```bash
#!/usr/bin/env bash
EXECUTABLE=$1

OUTPUT=$($EXECUTABLE 1 2 3 4)

if [ "$OUTPUT" = "10" ]
then
    exit 0
else
    exit 1
fi
```

Also, the Python test script calls the executable (passed using the `--executable` command-line argument) directly, and allows it to be executed with the `--short` command-line argument:

```python
import subprocess
import argparse

# test script expects the executable as argument
parser = argparse.ArgumentParser()
parser.add_argument('--executable',
                    help='full path to executable')
parser.add_argument('--short',
                    default=False,
                    action='store_true',
                    help='run a shorter test')
args = parser.parse_args()
```

```python
def execute_cpp_code(integers):
    result = subprocess.check_output([args.executable] + integers)
    return int(result)


if args.short:
    # we collect [1, 2, ..., 100] as a list of strings
    result = execute_cpp_code([str(i) for i in range(1, 101)])
    assert result == 5050, 'summing up to 100 failed'
else:
    # we collect [1, 2, ..., 1000] as a list of strings
    result = execute_cpp_code([str(i) for i in range(1, 1001)])
    assert result == 500500, 'summing up to 1000 failed'
```

How to do it

We will now describe, step by step, how to set up testing for our project, as follows:

1. For this example, we require C++11 support, a working Python interpreter, and the Bash shell:

```cmake
cmake_minimum_required(VERSION 3.5 FATAL_ERROR)

project(recipe-01 LANGUAGES CXX)

set(CMAKE_CXX_STANDARD 11)
set(CMAKE_CXX_EXTENSIONS OFF)
set(CMAKE_CXX_STANDARD_REQUIRED ON)

find_package(PythonInterp REQUIRED)
find_program(BASH_EXECUTABLE NAMES bash REQUIRED)
```

2. We then define the library, the dependencies of the main executable, and the testing executable:

```cmake
# example library
add_library(sum_integers sum_integers.cpp)

# main code
add_executable(sum_up main.cpp)
target_link_libraries(sum_up sum_integers)
```

```
# testing binary
add_executable(cpp_test test.cpp)
target_link_libraries(cpp_test sum_integers)
```

3. Finally, we turn on the testing functionality and define four tests. The last two tests call the same Python script; first without any command-line argument, and then with `--short`:

```
enable_testing()

add_test(
  NAME bash_test
  COMMAND ${BASH_EXECUTABLE} ${CMAKE_CURRENT_SOURCE_DIR}/test.sh
$<TARGET_FILE:sum_up>
  )

add_test(
  NAME cpp_test
  COMMAND $<TARGET_FILE:cpp_test>
  )

add_test(
  NAME python_test_long
  COMMAND ${PYTHON_EXECUTABLE} ${CMAKE_CURRENT_SOURCE_DIR}/test.py
--executable $<TARGET_FILE:sum_up>
  )

add_test(
  NAME python_test_short
  COMMAND ${PYTHON_EXECUTABLE} ${CMAKE_CURRENT_SOURCE_DIR}/test.py
--short --executable $<TARGET_FILE:sum_up>
  )
```

4. We are now ready to configure and build the code. First, we test it manually:

```
$ mkdir -p build
$ cd build
$ cmake ..
$ cmake --build .
$ ./sum_up 1 2 3 4 5
```

15

5. Then, we can run the test set with `ctest`:

```
$ ctest
```

```
Test project /home/user/cmake-recipes/chapter-04/recipe-01/cxx-
example/build
    Start 1: bash_test
1/4 Test #1: bash_test ..................... Passed 0.01 sec
    Start 2: cpp_test
2/4 Test #2: cpp_test ...................... Passed 0.00 sec
    Start 3: python_test_long
3/4 Test #3: python_test_long .............. Passed 0.06 sec
    Start 4: python_test_short
4/4 Test #4: python_test_short ............. Passed 0.05 sec

100% tests passed, 0 tests failed out of 4

Total Test time (real) = 0.12 sec
```

6. You should also try to break the implementation, to verify whether the test set catches the change.

How it works

The two key commands here are `enable_testing()`, which enables testing for this directory and all subfolders within it (in this case, the entire project, since we place it in the main `CMakeLists.txt`), and `add_test()`, which defines a new test and sets the test name and the command to run; an example is as follows:

```
add_test(
  NAME cpp_test
  COMMAND $<TARGET_FILE:cpp_test>
  )
```

In the preceding example, we employed a generator expression: `$<TARGET_FILE:cpp_test>`. Generator expressions are expressions that are evaluated at **build system generation time**. We will return to generator expressions in more detail in *Chapter 5, Configure-time and Build-time Operations, Recipe 9, Fine-tuning configuration and compilation with generator expressions*. At this point, we can state that `$<TARGET_FILE:cpp_test>` will be replaced by the full path to the `cpp_test` executable target.

Generator expressions are extremely convenient in the context of defining tests, because we do not have to explicitly hardcode the locations and names of the executables into the test definitions. It would be very tedious to achieve this in a portable way, since both the location of the executable and the executable suffix (for example, the .exe suffix on Windows) can vary between operating systems, build types, and generators. Using the generator expression, we do not have to explicitly know the location and name.

It is also possible to pass arguments to the test command to run; for example:

```
add_test(
  NAME python_test_short
  COMMAND ${PYTHON_EXECUTABLE} ${CMAKE_CURRENT_SOURCE_DIR}/test.py --short
--executable $<TARGET_FILE:sum_up>
  )
```

In this example, we run the tests sequentially (*Recipe 8, Running tests in parallel*, will show you how to shorten the total test time by executing tests in parallel), and the tests are executed in the same order that they are defined (*Recipe 9, Running a subset of tests*, will show you how to change the order or run a subset of tests). It is up to the programmer to define the actual test command, which can be programmed in any language supported by the operating system environment running the test set. The only thing that CTest cares about, in order to decide whether a test has passed or failed, is the return code of the test command. CTest follows the standard convention that a zero return code means success, and a non-zero return code means failure. Any script that can return zero or non-zero can be used to implement a test case.

Now that we know how to define and execute tests, it is also important that we know how to diagnose test failures. For this, we can introduce a bug into our code and let all of the tests fail:

```
    Start 1: bash_test
1/4 Test #1: bash_test ........................***Failed 0.01 sec
    Start 2: cpp_test
2/4 Test #2: cpp_test .........................***Failed 0.00 sec
    Start 3: python_test_long
3/4 Test #3: python_test_long .................***Failed 0.06 sec
    Start 4: python_test_short
4/4 Test #4: python_test_short ................***Failed 0.06 sec

0% tests passed, 4 tests failed out of 4

Total Test time (real) = 0.13 sec
```

```
The following tests FAILED:
    1 - bash_test (Failed)
    2 - cpp_test (Failed)
    3 - python_test_long (Failed)
    4 - python_test_short (Failed)
Errors while running CTest
```

If we then wish to learn more, we can inspect the file
`Testing/Temporary/LastTestsFailed.log`. This file contains the full output of the test
commands, and is the first place to look during a postmortem analysis. It is possible to
obtain more verbose test output from CTest by using the following CLI switches:

- `--output-on-failure`: Will print to the screen anything that the test program
  produces, in case the test fails.
- `-V`: Will enable verbose output from tests.
- `-VV`: Enables even more verbose output from tests.

CTest offers a very handy shortcut to rerun only the tests that have previously failed; the
CLI switch to use is `--rerun-failed`, and it proves extremely useful during debugging.

There is more

Consider the following definition:

```
add_test(
  NAME python_test_long
  COMMAND ${PYTHON_EXECUTABLE} ${CMAKE_CURRENT_SOURCE_DIR}/test.py --
executable $<TARGET_FILE:sum_up>
  )
```

The preceding definition can be re-expressed by explicitly specifying
the `WORKING_DIRECTORY` in which the script will be run, as follows:

```
add_test(
  NAME python_test_long
  COMMAND ${PYTHON_EXECUTABLE} test.py --executable $<TARGET_FILE:sum_up>
  WORKING_DIRECTORY ${CMAKE_CURRENT_SOURCE_DIR}
  )
```

We will also mention that test names can contain the / character, which may be useful when organizing related tests by name; for example:

```
add_test(
  NAME python/long
  COMMAND ${PYTHON_EXECUTABLE} test.py --executable $<TARGET_FILE:sum_up>
  WORKING_DIRECTORY ${CMAKE_CURRENT_SOURCE_DIR}
  )
```

Sometimes, we need to set environment variables for a test script. This can be achieved with set_tests_properties:

```
set_tests_properties(python_test
  PROPERTIES
    ENVIRONMENT
      ACCOUNT_MODULE_PATH=${CMAKE_CURRENT_SOURCE_DIR}
      ACCOUNT_HEADER_FILE=${CMAKE_CURRENT_SOURCE_DIR}/account/account.h
      ACCOUNT_LIBRARY_FILE=$<TARGET_FILE:account>
  )
```

This approach might not always be robust across different platforms, but CMake offers a way around this potential lack of robustness. The following snippet is equivalent to the one given above and invokes CMake, *via* CMAKE_COMMAND, to prepend environment variables before executing the actual Python test script:

```
add_test(
  NAME
    python_test
  COMMAND
    ${CMAKE_COMMAND} -E env ACCOUNT_MODULE_PATH=${CMAKE_CURRENT_SOURCE_DIR}
ACCOUNT_HEADER_FILE=${CMAKE_CURRENT_SOURCE_DIR}/account/account.h
                          ACCOUNT_LIBRARY_FILE=$<TARGET_FILE:account>
    ${PYTHON_EXECUTABLE} ${CMAKE_CURRENT_SOURCE_DIR}/account/test.py
  )
```

Once again, note the use of the generator expression $<TARGET_FILE:account> to pass the location of the library file without explicitly hardcoding paths.

We have executed the test set using the ctest command, but CMake will also create targets for the generator in question (make test for Unix Makefile generators, ninja test for the Ninja tool, or RUN_TESTS for Visual Studio). This means that there is yet another (almost) portable way to run the test step:

```
$ cmake --build . --target test
```

Unfortunately, this fails when using the Visual Studio generator where we have to use RUN_TESTS instead:

```
$ cmake --build . --target RUN_TESTS
```

> The command `ctest` offers a wealth of command-line arguments. Some of these will be explored in later recipes. For a full list, try `ctest --help`. The command `cmake --help-manual ctest` will output the full CTest manual to the screen.

Defining a unit test using the Catch2 library

> The code for this recipe is available at `https://github.com/dev-cafe/cmake-cookbook/tree/v1.0/chapter-04/recipe-02`, and has a C++ example. The recipe is valid with CMake version 3.5 (and higher), and has been tested on GNU/Linux, macOS, and Windows.

In the previous recipe, we used an integer return code to signal success or failure in `test.cpp`. This is fine for simple tests, but typically, we would like to use a testing framework that offers an infrastructure to run more sophisticated tests with fixtures, comparisons with numerical tolerance, and better error reporting if a test fails. A modern and popular test library is Catch2 (`https://github.com/catchorg/Catch2`). One nice feature of this test framework is the fact that it can be included in your project as a single-header library, which makes compilation and updating the framework particularly easy. In this recipe, we will use CMake in combination with Catch2, to test the summation code introduced in the previous recipe.

Getting ready

We will keep the `main.cpp`, `sum_integers.cpp`, and `sum_integers.hpp` unchanged from the previous recipe, but will update the `test.cpp`:

```cpp
#include "sum_integers.hpp"
// this tells catch to provide a main()
// only do this in one cpp file
#define CATCH_CONFIG_MAIN
#include "catch.hpp"

#include <vector>

TEST_CASE("Sum of integers for a short vector", "[short]") {
```

```
    auto integers = {1, 2, 3, 4, 5};
    REQUIRE(sum_integers(integers) == 15);
  }

  TEST_CASE("Sum of integers for a longer vector", "[long]") {
    std::vector<int> integers;
    for (int i = 1; i < 1001; ++i) {
      integers.push_back(i);
    }
    REQUIRE(sum_integers(integers) == 500500);
  }
```

We also need the `catch.hpp` header, which we can download from `https://github.com/catchorg/Catch2` (we have used version 2.0.1) and place in the root of our project, alongside `test.cpp`.

How to do it

To use the Catch2 library, we will modify `CMakeLists.txt` from the previous recipe, to perform the following steps:

1. We can keep most of `CMakeLists.txt` unchanged:

    ```
    # set minimum cmake version
    cmake_minimum_required(VERSION 3.5 FATAL_ERROR)

    # project name and language
    project(recipe-02 LANGUAGES CXX)

    # require C++11
    set(CMAKE_CXX_STANDARD 11)
    set(CMAKE_CXX_EXTENSIONS OFF)
    set(CMAKE_CXX_STANDARD_REQUIRED ON)

    # example library
    add_library(sum_integers sum_integers.cpp)

    # main code
    add_executable(sum_up main.cpp)
    target_link_libraries(sum_up sum_integers)

    # testing binary
    add_executable(cpp_test test.cpp)
    target_link_libraries(cpp_test sum_integers)
    ```

2. The only change, with respect to the previous recipe, is to remove all of the tests except for one, and rename it (to make clear what we have changed). Note that we pass the `--success` option to our unit tests executable. This is a Catch2 option, and will produce output from tests, even upon success:

```
enable_testing()

add_test(
  NAME catch_test
  COMMAND $<TARGET_FILE:cpp_test> --success
  )
```

3. That's it! Let us configure, build, and test. The tests will be run using the `-VV` option in CTest, to get output from the unit tests executable:

```
$ mkdir -p build
$ cd build
$ cmake ..
$ cmake --build .
$ ctest -V

UpdateCTestConfiguration from :/home/user/cmake-
cookbook/chapter-04/recipe-02/cxx-
example/build/DartConfiguration.tcl
UpdateCTestConfiguration from :/home/user/cmake-
cookbook/chapter-04/recipe-02/cxx-
example/build/DartConfiguration.tcl
Test project /home/user/cmake-cookbook/chapter-04/recipe-02/cxx-
example/build
Constructing a list of tests
Done constructing a list of tests
Updating test list for fixtures
Added 0 tests to meet fixture requirements
Checking test dependency graph...
Checking test dependency graph end
test 1
  Start 1: catch_test

1: Test command: /home/user/cmake-
cookbook/chapter-04/recipe-02/cxx-example/build/cpp_test "--
success"
1: Test timeout computed to be: 10000000
1:
1:
~~~~~~~~~~~~~~~~~~~~~~~~~~~~~~~~~~~~~~~~~~~~~~~~~~~~~~~~~~~~~~~~~~~~~~~~
1: cpp_test is a Catch v2.0.1 host application.
1: Run with -? for options
```

```
1:
1: -------------------------------------------------------------
1: Sum of integers for a short vector
1: -------------------------------------------------------------
1: /home/user/cmake-cookbook/chapter-04/recipe-02/cxx-
example/test.cpp:10
1:
.............................................................
1:
1: /home/user/cmake-cookbook/chapter-04/recipe-02/cxx-
example/test.cpp:12:
1: PASSED:
1: REQUIRE( sum_integers(integers) == 15 )
1: with expansion:
1: 15 == 15
1:
1: -------------------------------------------------------------
1: Sum of integers for a longer vector
1: -------------------------------------------------------------
1: /home/user/cmake-cookbook/chapter-04/recipe-02/cxx-
example/test.cpp:15
1:
.............................................................
1:
1: /home/user/cmake-cookbook/chapter-04/recipe-02/cxx-
example/test.cpp:20:
1: PASSED:
1: REQUIRE( sum_integers(integers) == 500500 )
1: with expansion:
1: 500500 (0x7a314) == 500500 (0x7a314)
1:
1:
===============================================================
1: All tests passed (2 assertions in 2 test cases)
1:
1/1 Test #1: catch_test ..................... Passed 0.00 s

100% tests passed, 0 tests failed out of 1

Total Test time (real) = 0.00 sec
```

4. We can also try the `cpp_test` binary directly, and can see output directly from Catch2:

```
$ ./cpp_test --success

~~~~~~~~~~~~~~~~~~~~~~~~~~~~~~~~~~~~~~~~~~~~~~~~~~~~~~~~~~~~~~~~~~~~~~~~
cpp_test is a Catch v2.0.1 host application.
Run with -? for options

-------------------------------------------------------------------
Sum of integers for a short vector
-------------------------------------------------------------------
/home/user/cmake-cookbook/chapter-04/recipe-02/cxx-
example/test.cpp:10
...................................................................

/home/user/cmake-cookbook/chapter-04/recipe-02/cxx-
example/test.cpp:12:
PASSED:
  REQUIRE( sum_integers(integers) == 15 )
with expansion:
  15 == 15


-------------------------------------------------------------------
Sum of integers for a longer vector
-------------------------------------------------------------------
/home/user/cmake-cookbook/chapter-04/recipe-02/cxx-
example/test.cpp:15
...................................................................

/home/user/cmake-cookbook/chapter-04/recipe-02/cxx-
example/test.cpp:20:
PASSED:
  REQUIRE( sum_integers(integers) == 500500 )
with expansion:
  500500 (0x7a314) == 500500 (0x7a314)


===================================================================
All tests passed (2 assertions in 2 test cases)
```

5. Catch will generate an executable with a command-line interface. We invite you to also try to execute the following command to explore the options offered by the unit testing framework:

```
$ ./cpp_test --help
```

How it works

Since Catch2 is a single-header framework, no additional targets have to be defined and built. We only have to make sure that CMake can find `catch.hpp`, to build `test.cpp`. For convenience, we placed it in the same directory as `test.cpp`, but we could have chosen a different location and indicated that location by using `target_include_directories`. Yet another approach would be to wrap the header into an `INTERFACE` library. This can be done as illustrated in the Catch2 documentation (`https://github.com/catchorg/Catch2/blob/master/docs/build-systems.md#cmake`):

```
# Prepare "Catch" library for other executables
set(CATCH_INCLUDE_DIR ${CMAKE_CURRENT_SOURCE_DIR}/catch)
add_library(Catch INTERFACE)
target_include_directories(Catch INTERFACE ${CATCH_INCLUDE_DIR})
```

We would have then linked against the library as follows:

```
target_link_libraries(cpp_test Catch)
```

We recall from the discussion in *Recipe 3*, *Building and linking static and shared libraries*, in *Chapter 1*, *From a Simple Executable to Libraries* that `INTERFACE` libraries are pseudo-targets offered by CMake that are useful to specify usage requirements for targets outside our project.

There is more

This was a simple example, with a focus on CMake. Catch2 offers much more, of course. For a full documentation of the Catch2 framework, visit `https://github.com/catchorg/Catch2`.

See also

The Catch2 code repository contains a contributed CMake function to parse Catch tests and automatically create CMake tests, without explicitly typing `add_test()` functions; see `https://github.com/catchorg/Catch2/blob/master/contrib/ParseAndAddCatchTests.cmake`.

Defining a unit test and linking against Google Test

The code for this recipe is available at `https://github.com/dev-cafe/cmake-cookbook/tree/v1.0/chapter-04/recipe-03`, and has a C++ example. The recipe is valid with CMake version 3.11 (and higher), and has been tested on GNU/Linux, macOS, and Windows. The code repository also contains an example compatible with CMake 3.5.

In this recipe, we will demonstrate how to implement unit testing using the Google Test framework, with the help of CMake. In contrast to the previous recipe, the Google Test framework is more than a header file; it is a library containing a couple of files that need to be built and linked against. We could place these alongside our code project, but to make the code project more lightweight, we will choose to download a well-defined version of the Google Test sources at configure time, and then build the framework and link against it. We will use the relatively new `FetchContent` module (available since CMake version 3.11). We will revisit `FetchContent` in *Chapter 8, The Superbuild Pattern*, where we will discuss how the module works under the hood, and where we will also illustrate how to emulate it by using `ExternalProject_Add`. This recipe is inspired by (and adapted from) the example at `https://cmake.org/cmake/help/v3.11/module/FetchContent.html`.

Getting ready

We will keep `main.cpp`, `sum_integers.cpp`, and `sum_integers.hpp` unchanged from the previous recipes, but will update the `test.cpp` source code, as follows:

```
#include "sum_integers.hpp"
#include "gtest/gtest.h"

#include <vector>

int main(int argc, char **argv) {
```

```
    ::testing::InitGoogleTest(&argc, argv);
    return RUN_ALL_TESTS();
}

TEST(example, sum_zero) {
  auto integers = {1, -1, 2, -2, 3, -3};
  auto result = sum_integers(integers);
  ASSERT_EQ(result, 0);
}

TEST(example, sum_five) {
  auto integers = {1, 2, 3, 4, 5};
  auto result = sum_integers(integers);
  ASSERT_EQ(result, 15);
}
```

As indicated in the preceding code, we chose to explicitly place neither gtest.h nor other Google Test sources in our code project repository, but will download them at configure time by using the FetchContent module.

How to do it

The following steps describe how you can set up a CMakeLists.txt step by step, to compile the executable and its corresponding test using GTest:

1. The beginning of CMakeLists.txt is mostly unchanged, as compared to the previous two recipes, except that we require CMake 3.11 to have access to the FetchContent module:

```
# set minimum cmake version
cmake_minimum_required(VERSION 3.11 FATAL_ERROR)

# project name and language
project(recipe-03 LANGUAGES CXX)

# require C++11
set(CMAKE_CXX_STANDARD 11)
set(CMAKE_CXX_EXTENSIONS OFF)
set(CMAKE_CXX_STANDARD_REQUIRED ON)

set(CMAKE_WINDOWS_EXPORT_ALL_SYMBOLS ON)

# example library
add_library(sum_integers sum_integers.cpp)
```

```
# main code
add_executable(sum_up main.cpp)
target_link_libraries(sum_up sum_integers)
```

2. We then introduce an if-clause, checking for ENABLE_UNIT_TESTS. By default, it is ON, but we want to have the possibility to turn it OFF, in case we do not have any network to download the Google Test sources:

```
option(ENABLE_UNIT_TESTS "Enable unit tests" ON)
message(STATUS "Enable testing: ${ENABLE_UNIT_TESTS}")

if(ENABLE_UNIT_TESTS)
   # all the remaining CMake code will be placed here
endif()
```

3. Inside of the if-clause, we first include the FetchContent module, declare a new content to fetch, and query its properties:

```
include(FetchContent)

FetchContent_Declare(
  googletest
  GIT_REPOSITORY https://github.com/google/googletest.git
  GIT_TAG release-1.8.0
)

FetchContent_GetProperties(googletest)
```

4. If the content is not yet populated (fetched), we fetch and configure it. This will add a couple of targets that we can link against. In this example, we are interested in gtest_main. The example also contains some workarounds, for compilation using Visual Studio:

```
if(NOT googletest_POPULATED)
  FetchContent_Populate(googletest)

  # Prevent GoogleTest from overriding our compiler/linker options
  # when building with Visual Studio
  set(gtest_force_shared_crt ON CACHE BOOL "" FORCE)
  # Prevent GoogleTest from using PThreads
  set(gtest_disable_pthreads ON CACHE BOOL "" FORCE)

  # adds the targers: gtest, gtest_main, gmock, gmock_main
  add_subdirectory(
    ${googletest_SOURCE_DIR}
    ${googletest_BINARY_DIR}
    )
```

```
    # Silence std::tr1 warning on MSVC
    if(MSVC)
      foreach(_tgt gtest gtest_main gmock gmock_main)
        target_compile_definitions(${_tgt}
          PRIVATE
            "_SILENCE_TR1_NAMESPACE_DEPRECATION_WARNING"
          )
      endforeach()
    endif()
endif()
```

5. We then define the `cpp_test` executable target and specify its sources, using the `target_sources` command and its link libraries, using the `target_link_libraries` command:

```
add_executable(cpp_test "")

target_sources(cpp_test
  PRIVATE
    test.cpp
  )

target_link_libraries(cpp_test
  PRIVATE
    sum_integers
    gtest_main
  )
```

6. Finally, we use the now familiar `enable_testing` and `add_test` commands to define the unit test:

```
enable_testing()

add_test(
  NAME google_test
  COMMAND $<TARGET_FILE:cpp_test>
  )
```

7. Now, we are ready to configure, build, and test the project:

```
$ mkdir -p build
$ cd build
$ cmake ..
$ cmake --build .
$ ctest
```

```
Test project /home/user/cmake-cookbook/chapter-04/recipe-03/cxx-
example/build
```

```
          Start 1: google_test
1/1 Test #1: google_test ..................... Passed 0.00 sec

100% tests passed, 0 tests failed out of 1

Total Test time (real) = 0.00 sec
```

8. We can also try to run `cpp_test` directly, as follows:

$ ./cpp_test

```
[==========] Running 2 tests from 1 test case.
[----------] Global test environment set-up.
[----------] 2 tests from example
[ RUN      ] example.sum_zero
[       OK ] example.sum_zero (0 ms)
[ RUN      ] example.sum_five
[       OK ] example.sum_five (0 ms)
[----------] 2 tests from example (0 ms total)

[----------] Global test environment tear-down
[==========] 2 tests from 1 test case ran. (0 ms total)
[  PASSED  ] 2 tests.
```

How it works

The `FetchContent` module enables populating content at configure time, *via* any method supported by the `ExternalProject` module, and has become a standard part of CMake in its 3.11 version. Whereas `ExternalProject_Add()` downloads at build time (as seen in *Chapter 8, The Superbuild Pattern*), the `FetchContent` module makes content available immediately, such that the main project and the fetched external project (in this case, the Google Test) can be processed when CMake is first invoked, and can be nested using `add_subdirectory`.

To fetch Google Test sources, we have first declared the external content:

```
include(FetchContent)

FetchContent_Declare(
  googletest
  GIT_REPOSITORY https://github.com/google/googletest.git
  GIT_TAG release-1.8.0
)
```

In this case, we fetched a Git repository with a specific tag (`release-1.8.0`), but we could also fetch an external project from a Subversion, Mercurial, or HTTP(S) source. For available options, consult the options of the corresponding `ExternalProject_Add` command at `https://cmake.org/cmake/help/v3.11/module/ExternalProject.html`.

We checked whether content population was already processed with the `FetchContent_GetProperties()` command, before calling `FetchContent_Populate()`; otherwise, `FetchContent_Populate()` would have thrown an error if it was called more than once.

The command `FetchContent_Populate(googletest)` populates the sources and defines `googletest_SOURCE_DIR` and `googletest_BINARY_DIR`, which we can use to process the Google Test project (using `add_subdirectory()`, since it happens to be a CMake project, as well):

```
add_subdirectory(
  ${googletest_SOURCE_DIR}
  ${googletest_BINARY_DIR}
  )
```

The preceding defines the following targets: `gtest`, `gtest_main`, `gmock`, and `gmock_main`. In this recipe, we were only interested in the `gtest_main` target, as a library dependency for the unit test example:

```
target_link_libraries(cpp_test
  PRIVATE
    sum_integers
    gtest_main
  )
```

When building our code, we can see how it correctly triggers the configure and build steps for Google Test. One day, we will wish to upgrade to a later Google Test release, and the only line that we will probably need to change is the one detailing the `GIT_TAG`.

There is more

We have scraped the surface of `FetchContent` and its build-time cousin, `ExternalProject_Add`, and we will revisit these commands in *Chapter 8, The Superbuild Pattern*. For a detailed discussion of the available options, please consult `https://cmake.org/cmake/help/v3.11/module/FetchContent.html`.

In this recipe, we fetched the sources at configure time, but we could have also installed them on the system environment and used the `FindGTest` module to detect the library and header files (`https://cmake.org/cmake/help/v3.5/module/FindGTest.html`). From version 3.9, CMake also offers a `GoogleTest` module (`https://cmake.org/cmake/help/v3.9/module/GoogleTest.html`), which provides a `gtest_add_tests` function. This function can be used to automatically add tests, by scanning the source code for Google Test macros.

See also

Obviously, Google Test has a myriad of features that are outside the scope of this recipe, as listed at `https://github.com/google/googletest`.

Defining a unit test and linking against Boost test

> The code for this recipe is available at `https://github.com/dev-cafe/cmake-cookbook/tree/v1.0/chapter-04/recipe-04`, and has a C++ example. The recipe is valid with CMake version 3.5 (and higher), and has been tested on GNU/Linux, macOS, and Windows.

Boost test is another very popular unit testing framework in the C++ community, and in this example, we will demonstrate how to unit test our familiar summing example code using Boost test.

Getting ready

We will keep the `main.cpp`, `sum_integers.cpp`, and `sum_integers.hpp` unchanged from the previous recipes, but we will update `test.cpp` as a minimal example of a unit test using the Boost test library:

```
#include "sum_integers.hpp"
#include <vector>

#define BOOST_TEST_MODULE example_test_suite
#include <boost/test/unit_test.hpp>

BOOST_AUTO_TEST_CASE(add_example) {
```

```
    auto integers = {1, 2, 3, 4, 5};
    auto result = sum_integers(integers);
    BOOST_REQUIRE(result == 15);
}
```

How to do it

These are the steps to follow to build our project using Boost test:

1. We start out with the now familiar CMakeLists.txt structure:

```
# set minimum cmake version
cmake_minimum_required(VERSION 3.5 FATAL_ERROR)

# project name and language
project(recipe-04 LANGUAGES CXX)

# require C++11
set(CMAKE_CXX_STANDARD 11)
set(CMAKE_CXX_EXTENSIONS OFF)
set(CMAKE_CXX_STANDARD_REQUIRED ON)

# example library
add_library(sum_integers sum_integers.cpp)

# main code
add_executable(sum_up main.cpp)
target_link_libraries(sum_up sum_integers)
```

2. We detect the Boost library and link cpp_test against it:

```
find_package(Boost 1.54 REQUIRED COMPONENTS unit_test_framework)

add_executable(cpp_test test.cpp)

target_link_libraries(cpp_test
  PRIVATE
    sum_integers
    Boost::unit_test_framework
  )

# avoid undefined reference to "main" in test.cpp
target_compile_definitions(cpp_test
  PRIVATE
    BOOST_TEST_DYN_LINK
  )
```

3. Finally, we define the unit test:

```
enable_testing()

add_test(
  NAME boost_test
  COMMAND $<TARGET_FILE:cpp_test>
  )
```

4. The following is everything we need to configure, build, and test the code:

```
$ mkdir -p build
$ cd build
$ cmake ..
$ cmake --build .
$ ctest

Test project /home/user/cmake-recipes/chapter-04/recipe-04/cxx-
example/build
    Start 1: boost_test
1/1 Test #1: boost_test ...................... Passed 0.01 sec

100% tests passed, 0 tests failed out of 1

Total Test time (real) = 0.01 sec

$ ./cpp_test

Running 1 test case...

*** No errors detected
```

How it works

We have used `find_package` to detect the `unit_test_framework` component of Boost (see *Chapter 3*, *Detecting External Libraries and Programs*, *Recipe 8*, *Detecting the Boost libraries*). We have insisted that this component is `REQUIRED`, and the configuration will stop if it cannot be found in the system environment. The `cpp_test` target needs to know where to find Boost header files, and needs to be linked against the corresponding libraries; these are both provided by the `IMPORTED` library target, `Boost::unit_test_framework`, set by a successful call to `find_package`. We recall from the discussion in *Recipe 3*, *Building and linking static and shared libraries*, in *Chapter 1*, *From a Simple Executable to Libraries* that `IMPORTED` libraries are pseudo-targets offered by CMake to represent pre-existing dependencies and their usage requirements.

There is more

In this recipe, we assumed that Boost was installed on the system. Alternatively, we could have fetched and built the Boost dependency at compile-time (see *Chapter 8, The Superbuild Pattern, Recipe 2, Managing dependencies with a superbuild: I. The Boost libraries*). However, Boost is not a lightweight dependency. In our example code, we used only the most basic infrastructure, but Boost offers a wealth of features and options, and we will refer the interested reader to `http://www.boost.org/doc/libs/1_65_1/libs/test/doc/html/index.html`.

Using dynamic analysis to detect memory defects

The code for this recipe is available at `https://github.com/dev-cafe/cmake-cookbook/tree/v1.0/chapter-04/recipe-05`, and has a C++ example. The recipe is valid with CMake version 3.5 (and higher), and has been tested on GNU/Linux, macOS, and Windows.

Memory defects, such as writing to or reading from memory beyond allocated bounds, or memory leaks (memory that is allocated, but never released), can create nasty bugs that are difficult to track down, and it is useful to detect them early. Valgrind (`http://valgrind.org`) is a popular and versatile tool to detect memory defects and memory leaks, and in this recipe, we will use Valgrind to alert us about memory problems when running tests using CMake/CTest (see *Chapter 14, Testing Dashboards*, for a discussion of the related `AddressSanitizer` and `ThreadSanitizer`).

Getting ready

For this recipe, we require three files. The first is the implementation that we wish to test (we can call the file `leaky_implementation.cpp`):

```
#include "leaky_implementation.hpp"

int do_some_work() {

  // we allocate an array
  double *my_array = new double[1000];

  // do some work
```

```
  // ...

  // we forget to deallocate it
  // delete[] my_array;

  return 0;
}
```

We also need the corresponding header file (`leaky_implementation.hpp`):

```
#pragma once

int do_some_work();
```

And, we need the test file (`test.cpp`):

```
#include "leaky_implementation.hpp"

int main() {
  int return_code = do_some_work();

  return return_code;
}
```

We expect the test to pass, since the `return_code` is hardcoded to 0. However, we also hope to detect a memory leak, since we forgot to de-allocate `my_array`.

How to do it

The following shows how to set up `CMakeLists.txt` to perform the dynamic analysis of the code:

1. We first define the minimum CMake version, project name, language, targets, and dependencies:

```
cmake_minimum_required(VERSION 3.5 FATAL_ERROR)

project(recipe-05 LANGUAGES CXX)

set(CMAKE_CXX_STANDARD 11)
set(CMAKE_CXX_EXTENSIONS OFF)
set(CMAKE_CXX_STANDARD_REQUIRED ON)

add_library(example_library leaky_implementation.cpp)
```

```
add_executable(cpp_test test.cpp)
target_link_libraries(cpp_test example_library)
```

2. Then, we define not only the test, but also the MEMORYCHECK_COMMAND:

```
find_program(MEMORYCHECK_COMMAND NAMES valgrind)
set(MEMORYCHECK_COMMAND_OPTIONS "--trace-children=yes --leak-
check=full")

# add memcheck test action
include(CTest)

enable_testing()

add_test(
  NAME cpp_test
  COMMAND $<TARGET_FILE:cpp_test>
  )
```

3. Running the test set reports that the test is passing, as follows:

$ ctest

```
Test project /home/user/cmake-recipes/chapter-04/recipe-05/cxx-
example/build
    Start 1: cpp_test
1/1 Test #1: cpp_test ........................ Passed 0.00 sec

100% tests passed, 0 tests failed out of 1

Total Test time (real) = 0.00 sec
```

4. Now, we wish to check for memory defects, and can observe that the memory leak is detected:

$ ctest -T memcheck

```
   Site: myhost
   Build name: Linux-c++
Create new tag: 20171127-1717 - Experimental
Memory check project /home/user/cmake-
recipes/chapter-04/recipe-05/cxx-example/build
    Start 1: cpp_test
1/1 MemCheck #1: cpp_test ........................ Passed 0.40 sec

100% tests passed, 0 tests failed out of 1

Total Test time (real) = 0.40 sec
```

```
-- Processing memory checking output:
1/1 MemCheck: #1: cpp_test ........................ Defects: 1
MemCheck log files can be found here: ( * corresponds to test
number)
/home/user/cmake-recipes/chapter-04/recipe-05/cxx-
example/build/Testing/Temporary/MemoryChecker.*.log
Memory checking results:
Memory Leak - 1
```

5. As a final step, you should try to fix the memory leak and verify that `ctest -T memcheck` reports no errors.

How it works

We used `find_program(MEMORYCHECK_COMMAND NAMES valgrind)` to find Valgrind and set `MEMORYCHECK_COMMAND` to its full path. We also needed to explicitly include the `CTest` module to enable the `memcheck` test action, which we can employ by using `ctest -T memcheck`. Also, observe that we were able to pass options to Valgrind using `set(MEMORYCHECK_COMMAND_OPTIONS "--trace-children=yes --leak-check=full")`. The memory checking step creates a log file, which can be used to inspect the memory defect in detail.

> Some tools, like code coverage and static analysis tools, can be set up similarly. The use of some of these tools is, however, more complicated, since specialized builds and toolchains are required. Sanitizers are one such example. For more information, see `https://github.com/arsenm/sanitizers-cmake`. Also, check out *Chapter 14, Testing Dashboards*, for a discussion of the `AddressSanitizer` and `ThreadSanitizer`.

There is more

This recipe can be used to report memory defects to a nightly testing dashboard, but we demonstrated here that this functionality can also be used independent of a testing dashboard. We will revisit discuss usage in conjunction with CDash in *Chapter 14, Testing Dashboards*.

See also

For documentation on Valgrind and its features and options, see `http://valgrind.org`.

Testing expected failures

The code for this recipe is available at `https://github.com/dev-cafe/cmake-cookbook/tree/v1.0/chapter-04/recipe-06`. The recipe is valid with CMake version 3.5 (and higher), and has been tested on GNU/Linux, macOS, and Windows.

Ideally, we want all of our tests to always pass on every platform. However, we may want to test whether an expected failure or exception will occur in a controlled setting, and in that case, we would define the expected failure as a successful outcome. We believe that typically, this is a task that should be given to the test framework (such as Catch2 or Google Test), which should check for the expected failure and report successes to CMake. But, there may be situations where you wish to define a non-zero return code from a test as success; in other words, you may want to invert the definitions of success and failure. In this recipe, we will demonstrate such a situation.

Getting ready

The ingredient for this recipe will be a tiny Python script (`test.py`) that always returns 1, which CMake interprets as a failure:

```
import sys

# simulate a failing test
sys.exit(1)
```

How to do it

Step by step, this is how to write `CMakeLists.txt` to accomplish our task:

1. In this recipe, we will not require any language support from CMake, but we will need to locate a working Python interpreter:

```
cmake_minimum_required(VERSION 3.5 FATAL_ERROR)

project(recipe-06 LANGUAGES NONE)

find_package(PythonInterp REQUIRED)
```

2. We then define the test and tell CMake that we expect it to fail:

```
enable_testing()

add_test(example ${PYTHON_EXECUTABLE}
${CMAKE_CURRENT_SOURCE_DIR}/test.py)

set_tests_properties(example PROPERTIES WILL_FAIL true)
```

3. Finally, we verify that it is reported as a successful test, as follows:

```
$ mkdir -p build
$ cd build
$ cmake ..
$ cmake --build .
$ ctest

Test project /home/user/cmake-
recipes/chapter-04/recipe-06/example/build
    Start 1: example
1/1 Test #1: example ........................ Passed 0.00 sec

100% tests passed, 0 tests failed out of 1

Total Test time (real) = 0.01 sec
```

How it works

Using `set_tests_properties(example PROPERTIES WILL_FAIL true)`, we set the property `WILL_FAIL` to `true`, which inverts success/failure. However, this feature should not be used to temporarily fix broken tests.

There is more

If you need more flexibility, you can use the test properties `PASS_REGULAR_EXPRESSION` and `FAIL_REGULAR_EXPRESSION` in combination with `set_tests_properties`. If these are set, the test output will be checked against a list of regular expressions given as arguments, and, if at least one of the regular expressions matches, the test either passes or fails, respectively. Many other properties can be set on tests. A full list of available properties can be found at https://cmake.org/cmake/help/v3.5/manual/cmake-properties.7.html#properties-on-tests.

Using timeouts for long tests

The code for this recipe is available at `https://github.com/dev-cafe/cmake-cookbook/tree/v1.0/chapter-04/recipe-07`. The recipe is valid with CMake version 3.5 (and higher), and has been tested on GNU/Linux, macOS, and Windows.

Ideally, the test set should take only a short time, in order to motivate developers to run the test set often, and to make it possible (or easier) to test every commit (changeset). However, some tests might take longer or get stuck (for instance, due to a high file I/O load), and we may need to implement timeouts to terminate tests that go overtime, before they pile up and delay the entire test and deploy pipeline. In this recipe, we will demonstrate one way of implementing timeouts, which can be adjusted separately for each test.

Getting ready

The ingredient for this recipe will be a tiny Python script (`test.py`) that always returns 0. To keep it super simple and to maintain focus on the CMake aspect, the test script does nothing other than wait for two seconds; but, we can imagine that in real life, this test script would perform more meaningful work:

```
import sys
import time

# wait for 2 seconds
time.sleep(2)

# report success
sys.exit(0)
```

How to do it

We need to inform CTest that tests need to be terminated if they go into overtime, as follows:

1. We define the project name, enable testing, and define the test:

```
# set minimum cmake version
cmake_minimum_required(VERSION 3.5 FATAL_ERROR)

# project name
```

```
project(recipe-07 LANGUAGES NONE)

# detect python
find_package(PythonInterp REQUIRED)

# define tests
enable_testing()

# we expect this test to run for 2 seconds
add_test(example ${PYTHON_EXECUTABLE}
${CMAKE_CURRENT_SOURCE_DIR}/test.py)
```

2. In addition, we specify a TIMEOUT for the test, and set it to 10 seconds:

```
set_tests_properties(example PROPERTIES TIMEOUT 10)
```

3. We know how to configure and build, and we expect the test to pass:

$ ctest

```
Test project /home/user/cmake-
recipes/chapter-04/recipe-07/example/build
    Start 1: example
1/1 Test #1: example ......................... Passed 2.01 sec

100% tests passed, 0 tests failed out of 1

Total Test time (real) = 2.01 sec
```

4. Now, to verify that the TIMEOUT works, we increase the sleep command in test.py to 11 seconds, and rerun the test:

$ ctest

```
Test project /home/user/cmake-
recipes/chapter-04/recipe-07/example/build
    Start 1: example
1/1 Test #1: example .........................***Timeout 10.01 sec

0% tests passed, 1 tests failed out of 1

Total Test time (real) = 10.01 sec

The following tests FAILED:
          1 - example (Timeout)
Errors while running CTest
```

How it works

TIMEOUT is a handy property that can be used to specify a timeout for individual tests, by using set_tests_properties. If the test goes past that time, for whatever reason (the test has stalled or the machine is too slow), the test is terminated and marked as failed.

Running tests in parallel

> The code for this recipe is available at https://github.com/dev-cafe/cmake-cookbook/tree/v1.0/chapter-04/recipe-08. The recipe is valid with CMake version 3.5 (and higher), and has been tested on GNU/Linux, macOS, and Windows.

Most modern computers have four or more CPU cores. One fantastic feature of CTest is its ability to run tests in parallel, if you have more than one core available. This can significantly reduce the total time to test, and reducing the total test time is what really counts, to motivate developers to test frequently. In this recipe, we will demonstrate this feature and discuss how you can optimize the definition of your tests for maximum performance.

Getting ready

Let us assume that our test set contains tests labeled *a, b, ..., j*, each with a specific time duration:

Tests	Duration (in time units)
a, b, c, d	0.5
e, f, g	1.5
h	2.5
i	3.5
j	4.5

The time units can be minutes, but to keep it simple and short, we will use seconds. For simplicity, we can represent test *a*, which consumes 0.5 time units, with a Python script:

```
import sys
import time

# wait for 0.5 seconds
time.sleep(0.5)
```

```
# finally report success
sys.exit(0)
```

The other tests can be represented accordingly. We will place these scripts one directory below CMakeLists.txt, in a directory called test.

How to do it

For this recipe, we need to declare a list of tests, as follows:

1. CMakeLists.txt is very brief:

```
# set minimum cmake version
cmake_minimum_required(VERSION 3.5 FATAL_ERROR)

# project name
project(recipe-08 LANGUAGES NONE)

# detect python
find_package(PythonInterp REQUIRED)

# define tests
enable_testing()

add_test(a ${PYTHON_EXECUTABLE}
${CMAKE_CURRENT_SOURCE_DIR}/test/a.py)
add_test(b ${PYTHON_EXECUTABLE}
${CMAKE_CURRENT_SOURCE_DIR}/test/b.py)
add_test(c ${PYTHON_EXECUTABLE}
${CMAKE_CURRENT_SOURCE_DIR}/test/c.py)
add_test(d ${PYTHON_EXECUTABLE}
${CMAKE_CURRENT_SOURCE_DIR}/test/d.py)
add_test(e ${PYTHON_EXECUTABLE}
${CMAKE_CURRENT_SOURCE_DIR}/test/e.py)
add_test(f ${PYTHON_EXECUTABLE}
${CMAKE_CURRENT_SOURCE_DIR}/test/f.py)
add_test(g ${PYTHON_EXECUTABLE}
${CMAKE_CURRENT_SOURCE_DIR}/test/g.py)
add_test(h ${PYTHON_EXECUTABLE}
${CMAKE_CURRENT_SOURCE_DIR}/test/h.py)
add_test(i ${PYTHON_EXECUTABLE}
${CMAKE_CURRENT_SOURCE_DIR}/test/i.py)
add_test(j ${PYTHON_EXECUTABLE}
${CMAKE_CURRENT_SOURCE_DIR}/test/j.py)
```

2. We can configure the project and run the tests using `ctest`, which takes 17 seconds in total:

```
$ mkdir -p build
$ cd build
$ cmake ..
$ ctest

        Start 1: a
 1/10 Test #1: a .............................. Passed 0.51 sec
        Start 2: b
 2/10 Test #2: b .............................. Passed 0.51 sec
        Start 3: c
 3/10 Test #3: c .............................. Passed 0.51 sec
        Start 4: d
 4/10 Test #4: d .............................. Passed 0.51 sec
        Start 5: e
 5/10 Test #5: e .............................. Passed 1.51 sec
        Start 6: f
 6/10 Test #6: f .............................. Passed 1.51 sec
        Start 7: g
 7/10 Test #7: g .............................. Passed 1.51 sec
        Start 8: h
 8/10 Test #8: h .............................. Passed 2.51 sec
        Start 9: i
 9/10 Test #9: i .............................. Passed 3.51 sec
        Start 10: j
10/10 Test #10: j .............................. Passed 4.51 sec

100% tests passed, 0 tests failed out of 10
Total Test time (real) = 17.11 sec
```

3. Now, if we happen to have four cores available, we can run the test set on four cores in less than five seconds:

```
$ ctest --parallel 4

        Start 10: j
        Start 9: i
        Start 8: h
        Start 5: e
 1/10 Test #5: e .............................. Passed 1.51 sec
        Start 7: g
 2/10 Test #8: h .............................. Passed 2.51 sec
        Start 6: f
 3/10 Test #7: g .............................. Passed 1.51 sec
        Start 3: c
 4/10 Test #9: i .............................. Passed 3.63 sec
```

```
 5/10 Test #3: c ............................. Passed 0.60 sec
      Start 2: b
      Start 4: d
 6/10 Test #6: f ............................. Passed 1.51 sec
 7/10 Test #4: d ............................. Passed 0.59 sec
 8/10 Test #2: b ............................. Passed 0.59 sec
      Start 1: a
 9/10 Test #10: j ............................ Passed 4.51 sec
10/10 Test #1: a ............................. Passed 0.51 sec

100% tests passed, 0 tests failed out of 10

Total Test time (real) = 4.74 sec
```

How it works

We can see that in the parallel case, tests *j, i, h,* and *e* started at the same time. The reduction in total test time when running in parallel can be significant. Looking at the output from `ctest --parallel 4`, we can see that the parallel test run started with the longest tests, and ran the shortest tests at the end. Starting with the longest tests is a very good strategy. It is like packing moving boxes: we start with larger items, and fill in the gaps with smaller items. Comparing the stacking of the *a-j* tests on four cores, when starting with the longest, looks as follows:

```
         --> time
core 1: jjjjjjjjj
core 2: iiiiiiibd
core 3: hhhhhggg
core 4: eeefffac
```

Running tests in the order in which they are defined looks as follows:

```
         --> time
core 1: aeeeiiiiiii
core 2: bfffjjjjjjjjj
core 3: cggg
core 4: dhhhhh
```

Running the tests in the order in which they are defined takes more time overall, since it leaves two cores idle for most of the time (here, cores 3 and 4). How did CMake know which tests would take the longest? CMake knew the time cost for each test because we ran the test sequentially first, and this recorded the cost data for each test in the file `Testing/Temporary/CTestCostData.txt`, which looks as follows:

```
a 1 0.506776
b 1 0.507882
c 1 0.508175
d 1 0.504618
e 1 1.51006
f 1 1.50975
g 1 1.50648
h 1 2.51032
i 1 3.50475
j 1 4.51111
```

If we had started with the parallel test right after configuring the project, it would run the tests in the order in which they were defined, and on four cores, the total test time would be noticeably longer. What does this mean for us? Does it mean that we should order tests according to decreasing time costs? This is an option, but it turns out that there is another way; we can indicate the time cost for each test by ourselves:

```
add_test(a ${PYTHON_EXECUTABLE} ${CMAKE_CURRENT_SOURCE_DIR}/test/a.py)
add_test(b ${PYTHON_EXECUTABLE} ${CMAKE_CURRENT_SOURCE_DIR}/test/b.py)
add_test(c ${PYTHON_EXECUTABLE} ${CMAKE_CURRENT_SOURCE_DIR}/test/c.py)
add_test(d ${PYTHON_EXECUTABLE} ${CMAKE_CURRENT_SOURCE_DIR}/test/d.py)
set_tests_properties(a b c d PROPERTIES COST 0.5)

add_test(e ${PYTHON_EXECUTABLE} ${CMAKE_CURRENT_SOURCE_DIR}/test/e.py)
add_test(f ${PYTHON_EXECUTABLE} ${CMAKE_CURRENT_SOURCE_DIR}/test/f.py)
add_test(g ${PYTHON_EXECUTABLE} ${CMAKE_CURRENT_SOURCE_DIR}/test/g.py)
set_tests_properties(e f g PROPERTIES COST 1.5)

add_test(h ${PYTHON_EXECUTABLE} ${CMAKE_CURRENT_SOURCE_DIR}/test/h.py)
set_tests_properties(h PROPERTIES COST 2.5)

add_test(i ${PYTHON_EXECUTABLE} ${CMAKE_CURRENT_SOURCE_DIR}/test/i.py)
set_tests_properties(i PROPERTIES COST 3.5)

add_test(j ${PYTHON_EXECUTABLE} ${CMAKE_CURRENT_SOURCE_DIR}/test/j.py)
set_tests_properties(j PROPERTIES COST 4.5)
```

The COST parameter can be either an estimate or extracted from `Testing/Temporary/CTestCostData.txt`.

There is more

Instead of using `ctest --parallel N`, you can also use the environment variable `CTEST_PARALLEL_LEVEL`, and set it to the desired level.

Running a subset of tests

The code for this recipe is available at `https://github.com/dev-cafe/cmake-cookbook/tree/v1.0/chapter-04/recipe-09`. The recipe is valid with CMake version 3.5 (and higher), and has been tested on GNU/Linux, macOS, and Windows.

In the previous recipe, we learned how to run tests in parallel with the help of CMake, and we discussed that it is advantageous to start with the longest tests. While this strategy minimizes the total test time, during the code development of a particular feature, or during debugging, we may not wish to run the entire test set. We may prefer to start with the longest tests, especially while debugging functionality that is exercised by a short test. For debugging and code development, we need the ability to only run a selected subset of tests. In this recipe, we will present strategies to accomplish that.

Getting ready

In this example, we assume that we have six tests in total; the first three tests are shorter, and have the names `feature-a`, `feature-b`, and `feature-c`. We also have three longer tests, with the names `feature-d`, `benchmark-a`, and `benchmark-b`. In this recipe, we can represent these tests with Python scripts, where we can adjust the sleep time:

```
import sys
import time

# wait for 0.1 seconds
time.sleep(0.1)

# finally report success
sys.exit(0)
```

How to do it

The following is a detailed breakdown of the contents of our CMakeLists.txt:

1. We start out with a relatively compact CMakeLists.txt, which defines the six tests:

```
cmake_minimum_required(VERSION 3.5 FATAL_ERROR)

# project name
project(recipe-09 LANGUAGES NONE)

# detect python
find_package(PythonInterp REQUIRED)

# define tests
enable_testing()

add_test(
  NAME feature-a
  COMMAND ${PYTHON_EXECUTABLE}
${CMAKE_CURRENT_SOURCE_DIR}/test/feature-a.py
  )
add_test(
  NAME feature-b
  COMMAND ${PYTHON_EXECUTABLE}
${CMAKE_CURRENT_SOURCE_DIR}/test/feature-b.py
  )
add_test(
  NAME feature-c
  COMMAND ${PYTHON_EXECUTABLE}
${CMAKE_CURRENT_SOURCE_DIR}/test/feature-c.py
  )
add_test(
  NAME feature-d
  COMMAND ${PYTHON_EXECUTABLE}
${CMAKE_CURRENT_SOURCE_DIR}/test/feature-d.py
  )

add_test(
  NAME benchmark-a
  COMMAND ${PYTHON_EXECUTABLE}
${CMAKE_CURRENT_SOURCE_DIR}/test/benchmark-a.py
  )
```

```
add_test(
  NAME benchmark-b
  COMMAND ${PYTHON_EXECUTABLE}
${CMAKE_CURRENT_SOURCE_DIR}/test/benchmark-b.py
  )
```

2. In addition, we give the shorter tests the label "quick" and the longer tests the label "long":

```
set_tests_properties(
  feature-a
  feature-b
  feature-c
  PROPERTIES
    LABELS "quick"
  )

set_tests_properties(
  feature-d
  benchmark-a
  benchmark-b
  PROPERTIES
    LABELS "long"
  )
```

3. We are now ready to run the test set, as follows:

```
$ mkdir -p build
$ cd build
$ cmake ..
$ ctest

    Start 1: feature-a
1/6 Test #1: feature-a ...................... Passed 0.11 sec
    Start 2: feature-b
2/6 Test #2: feature-b ...................... Passed 0.11 sec
    Start 3: feature-c
3/6 Test #3: feature-c ...................... Passed 0.11 sec
    Start 4: feature-d
4/6 Test #4: feature-d ...................... Passed 0.51 sec
    Start 5: benchmark-a
5/6 Test #5: benchmark-a ..................... Passed 0.51 sec
    Start 6: benchmark-b
6/6 Test #6: benchmark-b ..................... Passed 0.51 sec
```

```
100% tests passed, 0 tests failed out of 6

Label Time Summary:
long = 1.54 sec*proc (3 tests)
quick = 0.33 sec*proc (3 tests)

Total Test time (real) = 1.87 sec
```

How it works

Each test now has a name and a label. In CMake, all tests are numbered, so they also carry a unique number. Having defined the test label, we can now either run the entire set or run tests by their names (using regular expressions), their labels, or their numbers.

Running tests by their names (here, we run all tests with names matching `feature`) looks as follows:

$ ctest -R feature

```
    Start 1: feature-a
1/4 Test #1: feature-a ........................ Passed 0.11 sec
    Start 2: feature-b
2/4 Test #2: feature-b ........................ Passed 0.11 sec
    Start 3: feature-c
3/4 Test #3: feature-c ........................ Passed 0.11 sec
    Start 4: feature-d
4/4 Test #4: feature-d ........................ Passed 0.51 sec

100% tests passed, 0 tests failed out of 4
```

Running tests by their labels (here, we run all `long` tests) produces:

$ ctest -L long

```
    Start 4: feature-d
1/3 Test #4: feature-d ........................ Passed 0.51 sec
    Start 5: benchmark-a
2/3 Test #5: benchmark-a ...................... Passed 0.51 sec
    Start 6: benchmark-b
3/3 Test #6: benchmark-b ...................... Passed 0.51 sec

100% tests passed, 0 tests failed out of 3
```

Running tests by their numbers (here, we run tests 2 to 4) yields:

```
$ ctest -I 2,4

    Start 2: feature-b
1/3 Test #2: feature-b ...................... Passed 0.11 sec
    Start 3: feature-c
2/3 Test #3: feature-c ...................... Passed 0.11 sec
    Start 4: feature-d
3/3 Test #4: feature-d ...................... Passed 0.51 sec

100% tests passed, 0 tests failed out of 3
```

There is more

Try using **$ ctest --help**, and you will see a wealth of options to choose from to customize your testing.

Using test fixtures

> The code for this recipe is available at https://github.com/dev-cafe/cmake-cookbook/tree/v1.0/chapter-04/recipe-10. The recipe is valid with CMake version 3.5 (and higher), and has been tested on GNU/Linux, macOS, and Windows.

This recipe was inspired by the work of Craig Scott, and we recommend the reader to also consult the corresponding blog post for more background, at https://crascit.com/2016/10/18/test-fixtures-with-cmake-ctest/. The motivation for this recipe was to demonstrate how to employ test fixtures. These are useful for more sophisticated tests that require setup actions before the test is run, and cleanup actions after it has completed (such as creating an example database, setting up a connection, disconnecting, cleaning up the test database, and so on). We want to make sure that running a test that requires a setup or cleanup action automatically triggers these steps in a predictable and robust way, without introducing code repetition. These setup and cleanup steps can be delegated to the testing framework, such as Google Test or Catch2, but here, we demonstrate how to implement test fixtures at the CMake level.

Getting ready

We will prepare four tiny Python scripts, and place them under the `test` directory: `setup.py`, `feature-a.py`, `feature-b.py`, and `cleanup.py`.

How to do it

We start with a familiar `CMakeLists.txt` structure, with some additional steps, as follows:

1. We prepare the now familiar infrastructure:

```
# set minimum cmake version
cmake_minimum_required(VERSION 3.5 FATAL_ERROR)

# project name
project(recipe-10 LANGUAGES NONE)

# detect python
find_package(PythonInterp REQUIRED)

# define tests
enable_testing()
```

2. Then, we define the four test steps and bind them with a fixture:

```
add_test(
  NAME setup
  COMMAND ${PYTHON_EXECUTABLE}
${CMAKE_CURRENT_SOURCE_DIR}/test/setup.py
  )
set_tests_properties(
  setup
  PROPERTIES
    FIXTURES_SETUP my-fixture
  )

add_test(
  NAME feature-a
  COMMAND ${PYTHON_EXECUTABLE}
${CMAKE_CURRENT_SOURCE_DIR}/test/feature-a.py
  )
add_test(
  NAME feature-b
  COMMAND ${PYTHON_EXECUTABLE}
${CMAKE_CURRENT_SOURCE_DIR}/test/feature-b.py
  )
```

```
set_tests_properties(
  feature-a
  feature-b
  PROPERTIES
    FIXTURES_REQUIRED my-fixture
  )

add_test(
  NAME cleanup
  COMMAND ${PYTHON_EXECUTABLE}
${CMAKE_CURRENT_SOURCE_DIR}/test/cleanup.py
  )
set_tests_properties(
  cleanup
  PROPERTIES
    FIXTURES_CLEANUP my-fixture
  )
```

3. Running the entire set brings no surprises, as shown in the following output:

```
$ mkdir -p build
$ cd build
$ cmake ..
$ ctest

    Start 1: setup
1/4 Test #1: setup ........................... Passed 0.01 sec
    Start 2: feature-a
2/4 Test #2: feature-a ....................... Passed 0.01 sec
    Start 3: feature-b
3/4 Test #3: feature-b ....................... Passed 0.00 sec
    Start 4: cleanup
4/4 Test #4: cleanup ......................... Passed 0.01 sec

100% tests passed, 0 tests failed out of 4
```

4. However, the interesting part is when we try to run the test feature-a alone. It correctly invokes both the setup step and the cleanup step:

```
$ ctest -R feature-a

  Start 1: setup
1/3 Test #1: setup ........................... Passed 0.01 sec
  Start 2: feature-a
```

```
2/3 Test #2: feature-a ....................... Passed 0.00 sec
  Start 4: cleanup
3/3 Test #4: cleanup ......................... Passed 0.01 sec

100% tests passed, 0 tests failed out of 3
```

How it works

In this example, we defined a text fixture and called it my-fixture. We gave the setup test the FIXTURES_SETUP property and the cleanup test the FIXTURES_CLEANUP property, and, using FIXTURES_REQUIRED, we made sure that the tests feature-a and feature-b both required the setup and cleanup steps in order to be run. Binding these together ensures that we always enter and leave steps in a well-defined state.

There is more

For more background and an excellent motivation for using this technique for fixtures see https://crascit.com/2016/10/18/test-fixtures-with-cmake-ctest/.

5
Configure-time and Build-time Operations

In this chapter, we will cover the following recipes:

- Using platform-independent file operations
- Running a custom command at configure time
- Running a custom command at build time: I. Using `add_custom_command`
- Running a custom command at build time: II. Using `add_custom_target`
- Running custom commands for specific targets at build time
- Probing compilation and linking
- Probing compiler flags
- Probing execution
- Fine-tuning configuration and compilation with generator expressions

Introduction

In this chapter, we will learn how to perform custom operations at configure time and build time. Let us briefly recall the notion of *times* as related to the workflow of a project managed by CMake:

1. **CMake time** or **configure time**: This is when CMake is running and processing the `CMakeLists.txt` files in your project.
2. **Generation time**: This is when the files for the native build tool, such as Makefiles or Visual Studio project files, are generated.
3. **Build time**: This is when the native build tools are invoked on the platform- and tool-native build scripts previously generated by CMake. At this point, the compiler will be invoked and the targets (executables and libraries) will be built in a specific build directory.

4. **CTest time** or **test time**: When we run the test suite to check whether the targets perform as intended.
5. **CDash time** or **report time:** When the results of testing the project are uploaded to a dashboard to be shared with other developers.
6. **Install-time**: When the targets, source files, executables, and libraries are installed from the build directory to an install location.
7. **CPack time** or **packaging time**: When we package our project for distribution, either as source code or binary.
8. **Package install time**: When the newly minted package is installed system-wide.

The complete workflow and the corresponding times are depicted in the following figure:

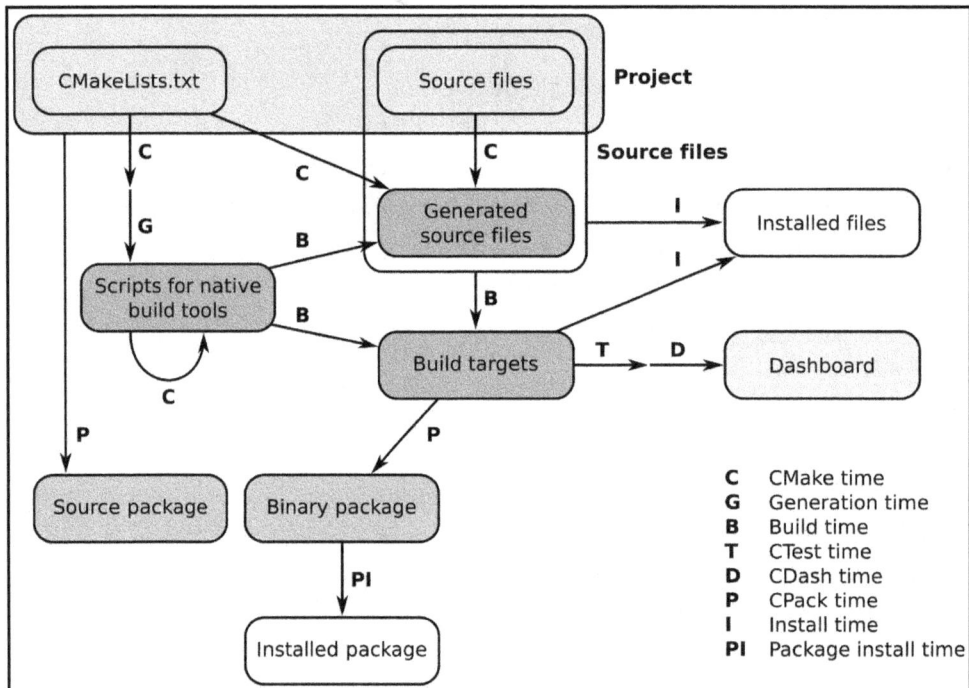

This chapter is concerned with customizing the behavior at configure time and build time. We will learn how to use these commands:

- `execute_process` to execute arbitrary processes from within CMake and retrieve their outputs

- `add_custom_target` to create targets that will execute custom commands
- `add_custom_command` to specify commands that have to be executed to generate files or at specific build events of other targets

Using platform-independent file operations

The code for this recipe is available at `https://github.com/dev-cafe/cmake-cookbook/tree/v1.0/chapter-05/recipe-01` and has a C++ example. The recipe is valid with CMake version 3.5 (and higher) and has been tested on GNU/Linux, macOS, and Windows.

When building some projects, we may need to interact with the host platform filesystem. The interaction with the files might be simply checking whether a file exists, creating a new file to store temporary information, creating or extracting an archive, and so forth. With CMake, we are not only able to generate the build system on different platforms, we are also able to perform these operations without complicated logic to abstract away the different operating systems. This recipe will show how to extract a previously downloaded archive in a portable way.

Getting ready

We will show how to extract the archive bundling the Eigen library and use the extracted source files to compile our project. In this recipe, we will reuse the linear algebra example `linear-algebra.cpp` from *Chapter 3, Detecting External Libraries and Programs, Recipe 7, Detecting the Eigen library*. The recipe also assumes that the archive containing the source code for Eigen has been downloaded in the same directory as the project itself.

How to do it

The project needs to unpack the Eigen archive and set the include directories for the target accordingly:

1. Let us first declare a C++11 project:

```
cmake_minimum_required(VERSION 3.5 FATAL_ERROR)

project(recipe-01 LANGUAGES CXX)

set(CMAKE_CXX_STANDARD 11)
```

```
set(CMAKE_CXX_EXTENSIONS OFF)
set(CMAKE_CXX_STANDARD_REQUIRED ON)
```

2. We add a custom target to our build system. The custom target will extract the archive inside the build directory:

```
add_custom_target(unpack-eigen
  ALL
  COMMAND
    ${CMAKE_COMMAND} -E tar xzf ${CMAKE_CURRENT_SOURCE_DIR}/eigen-
eigen-5a0156e40feb.tar.gz
  COMMAND
    ${CMAKE_COMMAND} -E rename eigen-eigen-5a0156e40feb eigen-3.3.4
  WORKING_DIRECTORY
    ${CMAKE_CURRENT_BINARY_DIR}
  COMMENT
    "Unpacking Eigen3 in ${CMAKE_CURRENT_BINARY_DIR}/eigen-3.3.4"
  )
```

3. We add an executable target for our source file:

```
add_executable(linear-algebra linear-algebra.cpp)
```

4. Since the compilation of our source file depends on the Eigen header files, we need to explicitly specify the dependency of the executable target on the custom target:

```
add_dependencies(linear-algebra unpack-eigen)
```

5. Finally, we can specify which include directories we need to compile our source file:

```
target_include_directories(linear-algebra
  PRIVATE
    ${CMAKE_CURRENT_BINARY_DIR}/eigen-3.3.4
  )
```

How it works

Let us take a closer look at the invocation of add_custom_target:

```
add_custom_target(unpack-eigen
  ALL
  COMMAND
    ${CMAKE_COMMAND} -E tar xzf ${CMAKE_CURRENT_SOURCE_DIR}/eigen-
eigen-5a0156e40feb.tar.gz
```

```
COMMAND
  ${CMAKE_COMMAND} -E rename eigen-eigen-5a0156e40feb eigen-3.3.4
WORKING_DIRECTORY
  ${CMAKE_CURRENT_BINARY_DIR}
COMMENT
  "Unpacking Eigen3 in ${CMAKE_CURRENT_BINARY_DIR}/eigen-3.3.4"
)
```

We are introducing a target called `unpack-eigen` into our build system. The target will always be executed since we passed the `ALL` argument. The `COMMAND` argument lets you specify what commands to execute. In this example, we wish to extract the archive and rename the extracted directory to `eigen-3.3.4`. This is achieved with these two commands:

1. `${CMAKE_COMMAND} -E tar xzf ${CMAKE_CURRENT_SOURCE_DIR}/eigen-eigen-5a0156e40feb.tar.gz`
2. `${CMAKE_COMMAND} -E rename eigen-eigen-5a0156e40feb eigen-3.3.4`

Notice how we are calling the CMake command itself, with the `-E` flag, to execute the actual work. For many common operations, CMake implements an interface common to all the operating systems it runs on. This allows the build system generation to be largely independent of the specific platform. The next argument in the `add_custom_target` command is the working directory, which in our example corresponds to the build directory: `CMAKE_CURRENT_BINARY_DIR`. The last argument, `COMMENT`, is used to specify what message CMake should print out when executing the custom target.

There is more

The command `add_custom_target` can be used whenever a series of custom commands with no output has to be executed during the build. As we have shown in this recipe, the custom target can be specified as a dependency of other targets in the project. Moreover, custom targets can also depend on other targets, thus offering the possibility to set up the order of execution in our build.

Using the `-E` flag to CMake, we can run many common operations in an operating system-agnostic fashion. The full list on the specific operating system can be obtained by running `cmake -E` or `cmake -E help`. For example, this is the summary of commands on a Linux system:

```
Usage: cmake -E <command> [arguments...]
Available commands:
  capabilities - Report capabilities built into cmake in JSON format
```

```
  chdir dir cmd [args...] - run command in a given directory
  compare_files file1 file2 - check if file1 is same as file2
  copy <file>... destination - copy files to destination (either file or
directory)
  copy_directory <dir>... destination - copy content of <dir>...
directories to 'destination' directory
  copy_if_different <file>... destination - copy files if it has changed
  echo [<string>...] - displays arguments as text
  echo_append [<string>...] - displays arguments as text but no new line
  env [--unset=NAME]... [NAME=VALUE]... COMMAND [ARG]...
                             - run command in a modified environment
  environment - display the current environment
  make_directory <dir>... - create parent and <dir> directories
  md5sum <file>... - create MD5 checksum of files
  remove [-f] <file>... - remove the file(s), use -f to force it
  remove_directory dir - remove a directory and its contents
  rename oldname newname - rename a file or directory (on one volume)
  server - start cmake in server mode
  sleep <number>... - sleep for given number of seconds
  tar [cxt][vf][zjJ] file.tar [file/dir1 file/dir2 ...]
                             - create or extract a tar or zip archive
  time command [args...] - run command and return elapsed time
  touch file - touch a file.
  touch_nocreate file - touch a file but do not create it.
Available on UNIX only:
  create_symlink old new - create a symbolic link new -> old
```

Running a custom command at configure time

The code for this recipe is available at `https://github.com/dev-cafe/cmake-cookbook/tree/v1.0/chapter-05/recipe-02`. The recipe is valid with CMake version 3.5 (and higher) and has been tested on GNU/Linux, macOS, and Windows.

Running CMake generates the build system, thus specifying what commands the native build tools will have to execute to get your project built, and in which order. We have already seen how CMake runs many subtasks at configure time in order to find out the working compiler and necessary dependencies. In this recipe, we will discuss how to run custom commands at configure time by using the `execute_process` command.

How to do it

We have already shown the use of `execute_process` when trying to find the NumPy Python module in *Chapter 3, Detecting External Libraries and Programs, Recipe 3, Detecting Python modules and packages*. In this example, we will use the `execute_process` command to find out whether a particular Python module (in this case, Python CFFI) is present, and if it is, we will discover its version:

1. For this simple example, we will not require any language support:

```
cmake_minimum_required(VERSION 3.5 FATAL_ERROR)
project(recipe-02 LANGUAGES NONE)
```

2. We will require the Python interpreter to execute a short Python snippet, and for this we discover the interpreter using `find_package`:

```
find_package(PythonInterp REQUIRED)
```

3. We then invoke `execute_process` to run a short Python snippet; we will discuss this command in more detail in the next section:

```
# this is set as variable to prepare
# for abstraction using loops or functions
set(_module_name "cffi")

execute_process(
  COMMAND
    ${PYTHON_EXECUTABLE} "-c" "import ${_module_name};
print(${_module_name}.__version__)"
  OUTPUT_VARIABLE _stdout
  ERROR_VARIABLE _stderr
  OUTPUT_STRIP_TRAILING_WHITESPACE
  ERROR_STRIP_TRAILING_WHITESPACE
  )
```

4. Then, we print the result:

```
if(_stderr MATCHES "ModuleNotFoundError")
  message(STATUS "Module ${_module_name} not found")
else()
  message(STATUS "Found module ${_module_name} v${_stdout}")
endif()
```

5. An example configuration yields the following (assuming the Python CFFI package is installed in the corresponding Python environment):

```
$ mkdir -p build
$ cd build
$ cmake ..

-- Found PythonInterp: /home/user/cmake-
cookbook/chapter-05/recipe-02/example/venv/bin/python (found
version "3.6.5")
-- Found module cffi v1.11.5
```

How it works

The `execute_process` command will spawn one or more child processes from within the currently executing CMake process, thus providing a powerful and convenient way of running arbitrary commands when configuring your project. It is possible to execute more than one command within one invocation of `execute_process`. Notice, however, that the output of each command will be piped into the next. The command accepts a number of arguments:

- `WORKING_DIRECTORY` lets you specify in which directory the commands should be executed.
- `RESULT_VARIABLE` will contain the result of running the processes. This is either an integer to signal successful execution or a string with the error condition incurred.
- `OUTPUT_VARIABLE` and `ERROR_VARIABLE` will contain the standard output and standard error of the executed commands. Keep in mind that since the outputs of commands are piped, only the standard output of the last command will be saved into `OUTPUT_VARIABLE`.
- `INPUT_FILE`, `OUTPUT_FILE`, and `ERROR_FILE` specify filenames for the standard input and standard output of the last command, and the standard error for all commands.
- By setting `OUTPUT_QUIET` and `ERROR_QUIET`, CMake will silently ignore the standard output and the standard error, respectively.
- Any trailing whitespace in the standard output and standard error for the running commands can be stripped by setting `OUTPUT_STRIP_TRAILING_WHITESPACE` and `ERROR_STRIP_TRAILING_WHITESPACE`, respectively.

With these explanations, we can return to our example:

```
set(_module_name "cffi")

execute_process(
  COMMAND
    ${PYTHON_EXECUTABLE} "-c" "import ${_module_name};
print(${_module_name}.__version__)"
  OUTPUT_VARIABLE _stdout
  ERROR_VARIABLE _stderr
  OUTPUT_STRIP_TRAILING_WHITESPACE
  ERROR_STRIP_TRAILING_WHITESPACE
  )

if(_stderr MATCHES "ModuleNotFoundError")
  message(STATUS "Module ${_module_name} not found")
else()
  message(STATUS "Found module ${_module_name} v${_stdout}")
endif()
```

The command checks the output of `python -c "import cffi;
print(cffi.__version__)"`. If the module is not found, `_stderr` will
contain `ModuleNotFoundError`, which we check for in the if-statement, and in this case we
would print `Module cffi not found`. If the import is successful, the Python code will
print the version of the module, which is piped into `_stdout` so that we can print the
following:

```
message(STATUS "Found module ${_module_name} v${_stdout}")
```

There is more

In this example, we have only printed the result, but in a real project we could warn, abort
the configuration, or set variables that could be queried to toggle certain configuration
options.

It would be an interesting exercise to extend the code example to multiple Python modules,
such as Cython, avoiding code repetition. One option could be to loop over the module
names using `foreach`; another approach could be to abstract the code into a function or
macro. We will discuss such abstractions in *Chapter 7, Structuring Projects*.

In *Chapter 9, Mixed-language Projects*, we will use Python CFFI and Cython, and the present
recipe can serve as a useful and reusable code snippet to detect whether these packages are
present.

Running a custom command at build time: I. Using add_custom_command

The code for this recipe is available at `https://github.com/dev-cafe/cmake-cookbook/tree/v1.0/chapter-05/recipe-03` and has a C++ example. The recipe is valid with CMake version 3.5 (and higher) and has been tested on GNU/Linux, macOS, and Windows.

Build targets for your projects might depend on the results of commands that can only be executed at build time, after the build system generation has been completed. CMake offers three options to execute custom commands at build time:

1. Using `add_custom_command` to generate output files to be compiled within a target.
2. Using `add_custom_target` to execute commands with no output.
3. Using `add_custom_command` to execute commands with no output, before or after a target has been built.

These three options enforce specific semantics and are not interchangeable. The next three recipes will clarify their use cases.

Getting ready

We will reuse the C++ example from *Chapter 3*, *Detecting External Libraries and Programs*, *Recipe 4*, *Detecting the BLAS and LAPACK math libraries*, to illustrate the use of the first variant of `add_custom_command`. In that code sample, we probed for existing BLAS and LAPACK libraries and compiled a tiny C++ wrapper library to call the Fortran implementation of the linear algebra routines we needed.

We will split the code into two portions. The source file for `linear-algebra.cpp` is unchanged compared to *Chapter 3*, *Detecting External Libraries and Programs*, *Recipe 4*, *Detecting the BLAS and LAPACK math libraries*, and will include headers from the linear algebra wrappers library and link against the compiled library. The sources of the library will, however, be packaged into a zipped tar archive shipped alongside the example project. The archive will be extracted at build time and the linear algebra wrapper library compiled before the executable.

How to do it

Our `CMakeLists.txt` will have to contain a custom command to extract the sources for the linear algebra wrapper library. Let us look at it in detail:

1. We start with a familiar definition of the minimum CMake version, project name, and supported language:

```
cmake_minimum_required(VERSION 3.5 FATAL_ERROR)

project(recipe-03 LANGUAGES CXX Fortran)
```

2. We pick the C++11 standard, as usual:

```
set(CMAKE_CXX_STANDARD 11)
set(CMAKE_CXX_EXTENSIONS OFF)
set(CMAKE_CXX_STANDARD_REQUIRED ON)
```

3. It is then time to look for the BLAS and LAPACK libraries on our system:

```
find_package(BLAS REQUIRED)
find_package(LAPACK REQUIRED)
```

4. We declare a variable, `wrap_BLAS_LAPACK_sources`, to hold the names of the source files contained in the `wrap_BLAS_LAPACK.tar.gz` archive:

```
set(wrap_BLAS_LAPACK_sources
  ${CMAKE_CURRENT_BINARY_DIR}/wrap_BLAS_LAPACK/CxxBLAS.hpp
  ${CMAKE_CURRENT_BINARY_DIR}/wrap_BLAS_LAPACK/CxxBLAS.cpp
  ${CMAKE_CURRENT_BINARY_DIR}/wrap_BLAS_LAPACK/CxxLAPACK.hpp
  ${CMAKE_CURRENT_BINARY_DIR}/wrap_BLAS_LAPACK/CxxLAPACK.cpp
  )
```

5. We declare the custom command to extract the `wrap_BLAS_LAPACK.tar.gz` archive and update the timestamps of the extracted files. Notice that the contents of the `wrap_BLAS_LAPACK_sources` variable are the expected outputs of the custom command:

```
add_custom_command(
  OUTPUT
    ${wrap_BLAS_LAPACK_sources}
  COMMAND
    ${CMAKE_COMMAND} -E tar xzf
${CMAKE_CURRENT_SOURCE_DIR}/wrap_BLAS_LAPACK.tar.gz
  COMMAND
```

```
    ${CMAKE_COMMAND} -E touch ${wrap_BLAS_LAPACK_sources}
  WORKING_DIRECTORY
    ${CMAKE_CURRENT_BINARY_DIR}
  DEPENDS
    ${CMAKE_CURRENT_SOURCE_DIR}/wrap_BLAS_LAPACK.tar.gz
  COMMENT
    "Unpacking C++ wrappers for BLAS/LAPACK"
  VERBATIM
  )
```

6. Next, we add a library target whose sources are the freshly extracted files:

```
add_library(math "")

target_sources(math
  PRIVATE
    ${CMAKE_CURRENT_BINARY_DIR}/wrap_BLAS_LAPACK/CxxBLAS.cpp
    ${CMAKE_CURRENT_BINARY_DIR}/wrap_BLAS_LAPACK/CxxLAPACK.cpp
  PUBLIC
    ${CMAKE_CURRENT_BINARY_DIR}/wrap_BLAS_LAPACK/CxxBLAS.hpp
    ${CMAKE_CURRENT_BINARY_DIR}/wrap_BLAS_LAPACK/CxxLAPACK.hpp
  )

target_include_directories(math
  INTERFACE
    ${CMAKE_CURRENT_BINARY_DIR}/wrap_BLAS_LAPACK
  )

target_link_libraries(math
  PUBLIC
    ${LAPACK_LIBRARIES}
  )
```

7. Finally, the linear-algebra executable target is added. This executable target links against the wrapper library:

```
add_executable(linear-algebra linear-algebra.cpp)

target_link_libraries(linear-algebra
  PRIVATE
    math
  )
```

8. With this, we can configure, build, and execute the example:

```
$ mkdir -p build
$ cd build
$ cmake ..
$ cmake --build .
$ ./linear-algebra 1000

C_DSCAL done
C_DGESV done
info is 0
check is 4.35597e-10
```

How it works

Let us have a closer look at the invocation of add_custom_command:

```
add_custom_command(
  OUTPUT
    ${wrap_BLAS_LAPACK_sources}
  COMMAND
    ${CMAKE_COMMAND} -E tar xzf
${CMAKE_CURRENT_SOURCE_DIR}/wrap_BLAS_LAPACK.tar.gz
  COMMAND
    ${CMAKE_COMMAND} -E touch ${wrap_BLAS_LAPACK_sources}
  WORKING_DIRECTORY
    ${CMAKE_CURRENT_BINARY_DIR}
  DEPENDS
    ${CMAKE_CURRENT_SOURCE_DIR}/wrap_BLAS_LAPACK.tar.gz
  COMMENT
    "Unpacking C++ wrappers for BLAS/LAPACK"
  VERBATIM
  )
```

add_custom_command adds rules to targets so that they know how to generate the output by executing the commands. *Any target* declared within the same directory of add_custom_command, that is, in the same CMakeLists.txt, and that uses *any file* in the output as its source file, will be given a rule to generate those files at build time. Dependencies between targets and custom commands are thus automatically handled at build system generation, while the actual generation of source files happens at build time.

In our specific case, the outputs are the sources contained in the zipped tar archive. To retrieve and use those files, the archive will have to be extracted at build time. This is achieved by using the CMake command itself with the -E flag, to achieve platform independence. The next command updates the timestamps of the extracted files. We do this to make sure we are not dealing with stale source files. WORKING_DIRECTORY specifies where to execute the commands. In our case, this is CMAKE_CURRENT_BINARY_DIR, which is the build directory currently being processed. The argument to the DEPENDS keyword lists dependencies to the custom command. In our case, the zipped tar archive is a dependency. The COMMENT field will be used by CMake to print status messages at build time. Finally, VERBATIM tells CMake to generate the right command for the specific generator and platform, thus ensuring full platform independence.

Let us also have a closer look at the way the library with the wrappers is created:

```
add_library(math "")

target_sources(math
  PRIVATE
    ${CMAKE_CURRENT_BINARY_DIR}/wrap_BLAS_LAPACK/CxxBLAS.cpp
    ${CMAKE_CURRENT_BINARY_DIR}/wrap_BLAS_LAPACK/CxxLAPACK.cpp
  PUBLIC
    ${CMAKE_CURRENT_BINARY_DIR}/wrap_BLAS_LAPACK/CxxBLAS.hpp
    ${CMAKE_CURRENT_BINARY_DIR}/wrap_BLAS_LAPACK/CxxLAPACK.hpp
  )

target_include_directories(math
  INTERFACE
    ${CMAKE_CURRENT_BINARY_DIR}/wrap_BLAS_LAPACK
  )

target_link_libraries(math
  PUBLIC
    ${LAPACK_LIBRARIES}
  )
```

We declare a library target with no sources. This is because we then use target_sources to populate the sources of the target. This achieves the very important task of letting dependents on this target know what include directories and header files they need, in order to successfully use the library. The C++ source files are PRIVATE to the target, and hence only used in building the library. The header files are PUBLIC because both the target and its dependents will need to use them to successfully compile. The include directories are specified using target_include_directories with wrap_BLAS_LAPACK declared as INTERFACE, since only dependents on the math target will need it.

This form of the `add_custom_command` has two limitations:

- It will only be valid if all of the targets depending on its output are specified in the same `CMakeLists.txt`.
- Using the same output as `add_custom_command` for different, independent targets might re-execute the custom commands rule. This may cause conflicts and should be avoided.

The second limitation can be avoided by carefully introducing dependencies with `add_dependencies`, but the proper approach to circumvent both would be to use the `add_custom_target` command, as we will detail in the next recipe.

Running a custom command at build time: II. Using add_custom_target

The code for this recipe is available at `https://github.com/dev-cafe/cmake-cookbook/tree/v1.0/chapter-05/recipe-04` and has a C++ example. The recipe is valid with CMake version 3.5 (and higher) and has been tested on GNU/Linux, macOS, and Windows.

As we discussed in the previous recipe, `add_custom_command` has some limitations that can be circumvented by using `add_custom_target`. This CMake command will introduce new targets in the build system. These targets, in turn, execute commands that do not return an output, in contrast to `add_custom_command`. The commands `add_custom_target` and `add_custom_command` can be combined. With this, the custom target can be specified in a directory different than the one where its dependents are, and this can be very helpful when designing a modular CMake infrastructure for your project.

Getting ready

For this recipe, we will reuse the source code sample from the previous recipe. We will, however, modify the layout of the sources slightly. In particular, instead of storing the zipped tar archive in the top-level directory, we will place it inside a subdirectory called `deps`. This subdirectory contains its own `CMakeLists.txt`, which will be included by the main `CMakeLists.txt`.

How to do it

We will start with the main `CMakeLists.txt` and later move to `deps/CMakeLists.txt`:

1. As before, we declare a C++11 project:

```
cmake_minimum_required(VERSION 3.5 FATAL_ERROR)
project(recipe-04 LANGUAGES CXX Fortran)

set(CMAKE_CXX_STANDARD 11)
set(CMAKE_CXX_EXTENSIONS OFF)
set(CMAKE_CXX_STANDARD_REQUIRED ON)
```

2. At this point, we move on to `deps/CMakeLists.txt`. This is achieved with the `add_subdirectory` command:

```
add_subdirectory(deps)
```

3. Inside `deps/CMakeLists.txt`, we first locate the necessary libraries (BLAS and LAPACK):

```
find_package(BLAS REQUIRED)
find_package(LAPACK REQUIRED)
```

4. Then, we collect the contents of the tarball archive into a variable, `MATH_SRCS`:

```
set(MATH_SRCS
  ${CMAKE_CURRENT_BINARY_DIR}/wrap_BLAS_LAPACK/CxxBLAS.cpp
  ${CMAKE_CURRENT_BINARY_DIR}/wrap_BLAS_LAPACK/CxxLAPACK.cpp
  ${CMAKE_CURRENT_BINARY_DIR}/wrap_BLAS_LAPACK/CxxBLAS.hpp
  ${CMAKE_CURRENT_BINARY_DIR}/wrap_BLAS_LAPACK/CxxLAPACK.hpp
  )
```

5. Having listed the sources that are to be extracted, we define a custom target and a custom command. This combination extracts the archive in `${CMAKE_CURRENT_BINARY_DIR}`. However, here we are in a different scope and refer to `deps/CMakeLists.txt`, and therefore the tarball will be extracted into a `deps` subdirectory below the main project build directory:

```
add_custom_target(BLAS_LAPACK_wrappers
  WORKING_DIRECTORY
    ${CMAKE_CURRENT_BINARY_DIR}
  DEPENDS
    ${MATH_SRCS}
  COMMENT
    "Intermediate BLAS_LAPACK_wrappers target"
  VERBATIM
```

```
  )

add_custom_command(
  OUTPUT
    ${MATH_SRCS}
  COMMAND
    ${CMAKE_COMMAND} -E tar xzf
${CMAKE_CURRENT_SOURCE_DIR}/wrap_BLAS_LAPACK.tar.gz
  WORKING_DIRECTORY
    ${CMAKE_CURRENT_BINARY_DIR}
  DEPENDS
    ${CMAKE_CURRENT_SOURCE_DIR}/wrap_BLAS_LAPACK.tar.gz
  COMMENT
    "Unpacking C++ wrappers for BLAS/LAPACK"
  )
```

6. Then, we add our math library as a target and specify corresponding sources, include directories, and link libraries:

```
add_library(math "")

target_sources(math
  PRIVATE
    ${MATH_SRCS}
  )

target_include_directories(math
  INTERFACE
    ${CMAKE_CURRENT_BINARY_DIR}/wrap_BLAS_LAPACK
  )

# BLAS_LIBRARIES are included in LAPACK_LIBRARIES
target_link_libraries(math
  PUBLIC
    ${LAPACK_LIBRARIES}
  )
```

7. Once the execution of the commands in deps/CMakeLists.txt is done, we move back to the parent scope, define the executable target, and link it against the math library that we have defined one directory below:

```
add_executable(linear-algebra linear-algebra.cpp)

target_link_libraries(linear-algebra
  PRIVATE
    math
  )
```

How it works

With `add_custom_target`, users can execute custom commands within targets. This is subtly different from the `add_custom_command` recipe we have discussed previously. The target added by `add_custom_target` has no output and is thus always executed. It is thus possible to introduce a custom target in subdirectories, and still be able to refer to it in the top-level `CMakeLists.txt`.

In this example, we have extracted an archive of source files using a combination of `add_custom_target` and `add_custom_command`. These source files were later used to compile a library that we managed to link against in a different (parent) directory scope. In the construction of the `CMakeLists.txt` files, we briefly commented that the tarball is extracted under `deps`, one subdirectory below the build directory of the project. This is because in CMake, the structure of the build tree mimics the hierarchy of the source tree.

A remarkable detail in this recipe, which we should discuss, is the curious fact that we have marked the math library sources as `PRIVATE`:

```
set (MATH_SRCS
  ${CMAKE_CURRENT_BINARY_DIR}/wrap_BLAS_LAPACK/CxxBLAS.cpp
  ${CMAKE_CURRENT_BINARY_DIR}/wrap_BLAS_LAPACK/CxxLAPACK.cpp
  ${CMAKE_CURRENT_BINARY_DIR}/wrap_BLAS_LAPACK/CxxBLAS.hpp
  ${CMAKE_CURRENT_BINARY_DIR}/wrap_BLAS_LAPACK/CxxLAPACK.hpp
  )

# ...

add_library(math "")

target_sources(math
  PRIVATE
    ${MATH_SRCS}
  )

# ...
```

Although these sources are `PRIVATE`, we compiled `linear-algebra.cpp` in the parent scope and this source code includes `CxxBLAS.hpp` and `CxxLAPACK.hpp`. Why is `PRIVATE` used here, and how was it possible to compile `linear-algebra.cpp` and build the executable? Had we marked the header files as `PUBLIC`, CMake would have stopped at CMake time with an error, "Cannot find source file", since the to-be-generated (extracted) source files do not exist in the file tree yet.

This is a known limitation (see `https://gitlab.kitware.com/cmake/cmake/issues/14633`, as well as a related blog post: `https://samthursfield.wordpress.com/2015/11/21/cmake-dependencies-between-targets-and-files-and-custom-commands`). We have worked around this limitation by declaring the sources `PRIVATE`. By doing this, we did not get any file dependencies on non-existent sources at CMake time. However, the CMake built-in C/C++ file dependency scanner picked them up at build time and the sources compiled and linked.

Running custom commands for specific targets at build time

> The code for this recipe is available at `https://github.com/dev-cafe/cmake-cookbook/tree/v1.0/chapter-05/recipe-05` and has a Fortran example. The recipe is valid with CMake version 3.5 (and higher) and has been tested on GNU/Linux, macOS, and Windows with MSYS Makefiles.

This recipe will show how to use the second signature of `add_custom_command` to perform custom operations without output. This is useful to perform certain operations right before or right after a specific target is built or linked. Since the custom commands are only executed if the target itself has to be built, we achieve target-level control over their execution. We will demonstrate this with an example where we print the link line of a target right before it is built, and then we measure the static size allocation of the compiled executable right after it has been compiled.

Getting ready

In this recipe, we will work with the following example Fortran code (`example.f90`):

```
program example

  implicit none

  real(8) :: array(20000000)
  real(8) :: r
  integer :: i

  do i = 1, size(array)
    call random_number(r)
    array(i) = r
  end do
```

```
    print *, sum(array)

end program
```

The fact that this is Fortran code does not matter much for the discussion that will follow, but we have chosen Fortran since there is a lot of legacy Fortran code out there where static size allocations are an issue.

In this code, we define an array holding 20,000,000 double precision floats, and we expect this array to occupy 160 MB of memory. What we have done here is not recommended programming practice, since in general this memory will be consumed independently of whether it is used in the code. A much better approach would have been to allocate the array dynamically only when it is needed and deallocate it right afterwards.

The example code fills the array with random numbers and computes their sum - this was done to make sure that the array is really used and the compiler does not optimize the allocation away. We will measure the size of static allocation of the example binary with a Python script (`static-size.py`) wrapping around the `size` command:

```
import subprocess
import sys

# for simplicity we do not check number of
# arguments and whether the file really exists
file_path = sys.argv[-1]

try:
    output = subprocess.check_output(['size', file_path]).decode('utf-8')
except FileNotFoundError:
    print('command "size" is not available on this platform')
    sys.exit(0)

size = 0.0
for line in output.split('\n'):
    if file_path in line:
        # we are interested in the 4th number on this line
        size = int(line.split()[3])

print('{0:.3f} MB'.format(size/1.0e6))
```

To print the link line, we will use a second Python helper script (`echo-file.py`) to print the contents of a file:

```
import sys
# for simplicity we do not verify the number and
# type of arguments
file_path = sys.argv[-1]
```

```
try:
    with open(file_path, 'r') as f:
        print(f.read())
except FileNotFoundError:
    print('ERROR: file {0} not found'.format(file_path))
```

How to do it

Let us have a look at our CMakeLists.txt:

1. We first declare a Fortran project:

   ```
   cmake_minimum_required(VERSION 3.5 FATAL_ERROR)

   project(recipe-05 LANGUAGES Fortran)
   ```

2. This example depends on the Python interpreter so that we can execute the helper scripts in a portable fashion:

   ```
   find_package(PythonInterp REQUIRED)
   ```

3. In this example, we default to the "Release" build type so that CMake adds optimization flags so that we have something to print later:

   ```
   if(NOT CMAKE_BUILD_TYPE)
     set(CMAKE_BUILD_TYPE Release CACHE STRING "Build type" FORCE)
   endif()
   ```

4. Now, we define the executable target:

   ```
   add_executable(example "")

   target_sources(example
     PRIVATE
       example.f90
     )
   ```

5. We then define a custom command to print the link line before the example target is linked:

   ```
   add_custom_command(
     TARGET
       example
     PRE_LINK
   ```

```
COMMAND
  ${PYTHON_EXECUTABLE}
    ${CMAKE_CURRENT_SOURCE_DIR}/echo-file.py
    ${CMAKE_CURRENT_BINARY_DIR}/CMakeFiles/example.dir/link.txt
COMMENT
  "link line:"
VERBATIM
)
```

6. Finally, we define a custom command to print the static size of the executable after it has been successfully built:

```
add_custom_command(
  TARGET
    example
  POST_BUILD
  COMMAND
    ${PYTHON_EXECUTABLE}
      ${CMAKE_CURRENT_SOURCE_DIR}/static-size.py
      $<TARGET_FILE:example>
  COMMENT
    "static size of executable:"
  VERBATIM
  )
```

7. Let us test it out. Observe the printed link line and static size of executable:

```
$ mkdir -p build
$ cd build
$ cmake ..
$ cmake --build .

Scanning dependencies of target example
[ 50%] Building Fortran object CMakeFiles/example.dir/example.f90.o
[100%] Linking Fortran executable example
link line:
/usr/bin/f95 -O3 -DNDEBUG -O3 CMakeFiles/example.dir/example.f90.o
-o example

static size of executable:
160.003 MB
[100%] Built target example
```

How it works

Once a library or executable target has been declared, one can latch additional commands onto the target by using `add_custom_command`. As we have seen, these commands will be executed at specific times, contextually to the execution of the target they are attached to. CMake understands the following options for the execution order of custom commands:

- `PRE_BUILD`: For commands to be executed before any other rules pertaining to the target are executed. This is however only supported for Visual Studio 7 or later.
- `PRE_LINK`: With this option, commands are executed after the target has been compiled but before the linker or archiver are invoked. Using `PRE_BUILD` with generators other than Visual Studio 7 or later will be interpreted as `PRE_LINK`.
- `POST_BUILD`: As already explained, the commands will be run after all the rules for the given target have been executed.

In this example, we have bolted on two custom commands to the executable target. The `PRE_LINK` command prints the content of `${CMAKE_CURRENT_BINARY_DIR}/CMakeFiles/example.dir/link.txt` to the screen. This file contains the link command and in our example, the link line turned out to be this:

```
link line:
/usr/bin/f95 -O3 -DNDEBUG -O3 CMakeFiles/example.dir/example.f90.o -o
example
```

We have used a Python wrapper for this to not depend on shell commands, which might not be portable.

In the second step, the `POST_BUILD` custom command called the Python helper script `static-size.py` with the generator expression `$<TARGET_FILE:example>` as argument. CMake will expand the generator expression to the target file path at *generation time*, that is, when the build system is generated. The Python script `static-size.py` in turn uses the size command to obtain the size of static allocation of the executable file, converts it to MB, and prints the result. In our case, we obtained the expected 160 MB:

```
static size of executable:
160.003 MB
```

Probing compilation and linking

The code for this recipe is available at `https://github.com/dev-cafe/` `cmake-cookbook/tree/v1.0/chapter-05/recipe-06` and has a C++ example. The recipe is valid with CMake version 3.9 (and higher) and has been tested on GNU/Linux, macOS, and Windows. The code repository also contains an example compatible with CMake 3.5.

One of the most common operations during build system generation is to assess what kind of system we are trying to build our project on. That means trying to find out which functionality works and which does not, and adapting the compilation of our project accordingly, either by signaling that dependencies are unmet or by enabling proper workarounds in our codebase. The next few recipes will show how to perform these operations with CMake. In particular, we will consider the following:

1. How to make sure that specific code snippets compile successfully into executables.
2. How to make sure that the compiler understands desired flags.
3. How to make sure that specific code snippets compile successfully into *running executables*.

Getting ready

This recipe will show how to use the `check_<lang>_source_compiles` function from the corresponding `Check<LANG>SourceCompiles.cmake` standard module, in order to assess whether the given compiler can compile a predefined code snippet into an executable. The command can help you ascertain whether:

- Your compiler supports desired features.
- The linker works properly and understands specific flags.
- Include directories and libraries found using `find_package` are usable.

In this recipe, we will show how to detect the task loop feature of the OpenMP 4.5 standard for its use in a C++ executable. We will use a sample C++ source file to probe whether the compiler supports such a feature. CMake offers an additional command, `try_compile`, to probe compilation. This recipe will show how to use both approaches.

You can use the CMake command-line interface to get documentation about specific modules (cmake --help-module <module-name>) and commands (cmake --help-command <command-name>). In our example, cmake --help-module CheckCXXSourceCompiles will output the documentation for the check_cxx_source_compiles function to screen, while cmake --help-command try_compile will do the same for the try_compile command.

How to do it

We will use both try_compile and check_cxx_source_compiles and compare how the two commands work:

1. We first create a C++11 project:

```
cmake_minimum_required(VERSION 3.9 FATAL_ERROR)

project(recipe-06 LANGUAGES CXX)

set(CMAKE_CXX_STANDARD 11)
set(CMAKE_CXX_EXTENSIONS OFF)
set(CMAKE_CXX_STANDARD_REQUIRED ON)
```

2. We find OpenMP support for the compiler:

```
find_package(OpenMP)

if(OpenMP_FOUND)
  # ... <- the steps below will be placed here
else()
  message(STATUS "OpenMP not found: no test for taskloop is run")
endif()
```

3. If OpenMP was found, we move forward and probe whether the desired feature is available. To this end, we set a scratch directory. This will be used by try_compile to generate its intermediate files. We place this inside the if-clause introduced in the previous step:

```
set(_scratch_dir ${CMAKE_CURRENT_BINARY_DIR}/omp_try_compile)
```

4. We call `try_compile` to generate a small project to attempt compiling the source file `taskloop.cpp`. Success or failure will be saved into the `omp_taskloop_test_1` variable. We need to set appropriate compiler flags, include directories, and link libraries for this small sample compilation. Since we are using the *imported target* `OpenMP::OpenMP_CXX`, this is simply done by setting the `LINK_LIBRARIES` option to `try_compile`. If compilation succeeds, then the task loop feature is available and we print a message for the user:

```
try_compile(
  omp_taskloop_test_1
  ${_scratch_dir}
  SOURCES
    ${CMAKE_CURRENT_SOURCE_DIR}/taskloop.cpp
  LINK_LIBRARIES
    OpenMP::OpenMP_CXX
  )
message(STATUS "Result of try_compile: ${omp_taskloop_test_1}")
```

5. To use the `check_cxx_source_compiles` function, we need to include the `CheckCXXSourceCompiles.cmake` module file. This is distributed with CMake, alongside similar files for C (`CheckCSourceCompiles.cmake`) and Fortran (`CheckFortranSourceCompiles.cmake`):

```
include(CheckCXXSourceCompiles)
```

6. We copy the contents of the source file we are attempting to compile and link into a CMake variable by reading its contents with the `file(READ ...)` command:

```
file(READ ${CMAKE_CURRENT_SOURCE_DIR}/taskloop.cpp _snippet)
```

7. We set `CMAKE_REQUIRED_LIBRARIES`. This is needed for the correct invocation of the compiler in the next step. Note the use of the *imported* `OpenMP::OpenMP_CXX` target, which will set also the proper compiler flags and include directories:

```
set(CMAKE_REQUIRED_LIBRARIES OpenMP::OpenMP_CXX)
```

8. We invoke the `check_cxx_source_compiles` function with our code snippet. The result of the check will be saved into the `omp_taskloop_test_2` variable:

```
check_cxx_source_compiles("${_snippet}" omp_taskloop_test_2)
```

9. We unset the variables defined before calling `check_cxx_source_compiles` and print a message to the user:

```
unset(CMAKE_REQUIRED_LIBRARIES)
message(STATUS "Result of check_cxx_source_compiles:
${omp_taskloop_test_2}"
```

10. Finally, we test the recipe:

```
$ mkdir -p build
$ cd build
$ cmake ..

-- ...
-- Found OpenMP_CXX: -fopenmp (found version "4.5")
-- Found OpenMP: TRUE (found version "4.5")
-- Result of try_compile: TRUE
-- Performing Test omp_taskloop_test_2
-- Performing Test omp_taskloop_test_2 - Success
-- Result of check_cxx_source_compiles: 1
```

How it works

Both `try_compile` and `check_cxx_source_compiles` will compile and link a source file into an executable. If those operations succeed, then the output variable, `omp_task_loop_test_1` for the former and `omp_task_loop_test_2` for the latter, will be set to TRUE. The way this task is achieved is slightly different between the two commands, however. The `check_<lang>_source_compiles` family of commands is a simplified wrapper to the `try_compile` command. As such, it offers a minimal interface:

1. The code snippet to be compiled has to be passed in as a CMake variable. Most of the time this means that files have to be read in using `file(READ ...)`, as we have done in our example. The snippet is then saved to a file in the `CMakeFiles/CMakeTmp` subdirectory of the build directory.

2. Fine-tuning compilation and linking has to be done by setting the following CMake variables before calling the function:

   - `CMAKE_REQUIRED_FLAGS` to set the compiler flags
   - `CMAKE_REQUIRED_DEFINITIONS` to set preprocessor macros
   - `CMAKE_REQUIRED_INCLUDES` to set the list of include directories
   - `CMAKE_REQUIRED_LIBRARIES` to set the list of libraries to link into the executable

3. These variables have to be manually unset after calling the `check_<lang>_compiles_function`, to guarantee that further uses of the same variables does not have spurious contents.

> OpenMP imported targets were introduced with CMake 3.9, but the current recipe can also be made to work with earlier versions of CMake by manually setting the required flags and libraries for `check_cxx_source_compiles` as: `set(CMAKE_REQUIRED_FLAGS ${OpenMP_CXX_FLAGS})` and `set(CMAKE_REQUIRED_LIBRARIES ${OpenMP_CXX_LIBRARIES})`.

> In the case of Fortran, CMake assumes the sample snippet to be in fixed-form format, which might not always be the case. To overcome false negatives, one needs to set the `-ffree-form` compiler flag for `check_fortran_source_compiles`. This can be achieved with `set(CMAKE_REQUIRED_FLAGS "-ffree-form")`.

This minimal interface reflects the fact that the test compilation is carried out by generating and executing build and link commands directly within the CMake invocation.

The command `try_compile` offers a more complete interface and two different modes of operation:

1. The first one takes a full-fledged CMake project as input and will configure, build, and link it based on its `CMakeLists.txt`. This mode of operation offers more flexibility, since the project to be compiled can be arbitrarily complex.
2. The second one, which we have used, where a source file is provided together with configuration options for include directories, link libraries, and compiler flags.

`try_compile` is thus based on invoking CMake on a project, either one where the `CMakeLists.txt` is already existing (in the first mode of operation) or one where the file is generated on the fly based on the arguments passed to the `try_compile`.

There is more

Checks of the type outlined in this recipe are not always bulletproof and can generate both false positives and false negatives. As an example, you can try to comment out the lines containing `CMAKE_REQUIRED_LIBRARIES` and the example will still report "Success". The reason for this is that OpenMP pragmas will then be ignored by the compiler.

What should you do when you suspect that a wrong result is being returned? The `CMakeOutput.log` and `CMakeError.log` files in the `CMakeFiles` subdirectory of the build directory offer clues as to what went wrong. They report the standard output and standard error for operations run by CMake. If you suspect false positives, you should check the former, by searching for the variable set to hold the result of the compilation check. If you suspect false negatives, you should check the latter.

Debugging `try_compile` will require some care. CMake erases all files generated by that command, even if the check was unsuccessful. Fortunately, `--debug-trycompile` will prevent CMake from cleaning up. If there are multiple calls to `try_compile` in your code, you will only be able to debug them one at a time:

1. Run CMake once, without `--debug-trycompile`. All `try_compile` commands will be run and their execution directories and files cleaned up.

2. Erase the variable holding the result of the check from the CMake cache. The cache is saved into the `CMakeCache.txt` file. To clear the contents of a variable, you can use the `-U` CLI switch followed by the name of the variable, which will be interpreted as a globbing expression and may thus use * and ?:

   ```
   $ cmake -U <variable-name>
   ```

3. Run CMake once more, with `--debug-trycompile`. Only the check for which the cache was cleared up will be rerun. Its execution directories and files will not be cleaned up this time.

> `try_compile` offers more flexibility and a cleaner interface, especially when the code to be compiled is not a short snippet of code. We recommend to use `check_<lang>_source_compiles` whenever a small, self-contained snippet of code that does not need extensive configuration has to be test-compiled. In all other cases, `try_compile` is to be considered a superior alternative.

Probing compiler flags

> The code for this recipe is available at https://github.com/dev-cafe/cmake-cookbook/tree/v1.0/chapter-05/recipe-07 and has a C++ example. The recipe is valid with CMake version 3.5 (and higher) and has been tested on GNU/Linux, macOS, and Windows.

Setting compiler flags is critical to make sure that your code is compiled correctly. Different compiler vendors implement different flags for similar tasks. Even different compiler versions from the same vendor might present slight differences in the available flags. Sometimes, new flags are introduced that are extremely convenient to use for debugging or optimization purposes. In this recipe, we will show how to check that certain flags are available for the selected compiler.

Getting ready

Sanitizers (refer to `https://github.com/google/sanitizers`) have become incredibly useful tools for static and dynamic code analysis. By simply recompiling your code with the appropriate flags and linking against the necessary libraries, you can investigate and debug problems related to memory errors (address sanitizer), uninitialized reads (memory sanitizer), thread safety (thread sanitizer), and undefined behavior (undefined behavior sanitizer). Compared to similar analysis tools, sanitizers typically introduce a much smaller performance penalty and tend to give more detailed information on the problems detected. The drawback is that your code, and possibly parts of your toolchain, need to be recompiled with the additional flags.

In this recipe, we will set up a project to compile code with the different sanitizers activated and show how to check that the correct compiler flags are available.

How to do it

Sanitizers have been available for a while with the Clang compiler and were later also introduced into the GCC toolset. They were designed for use with C and C++ programs, but recent versions of Fortran will understand the same flags and produce correctly instrumented libraries and executables. This recipe will however focus on a C++ example.

1. As usual, we first declare a C++11 project:

```
cmake_minimum_required(VERSION 3.5 FATAL_ERROR)

project(recipe-07 LANGUAGES CXX)

set(CMAKE_CXX_STANDARD 11)
set(CMAKE_CXX_EXTENSIONS OFF)
set(CMAKE_CXX_STANDARD_REQUIRED ON)
```

2. We declare a list, CXX_BASIC_FLAGS, containing the compiler flags to be always used when building the project, -g3 and -O1:

```
list(APPEND CXX_BASIC_FLAGS "-g3" "-O1")
```

3. We include the CMake module CheckCXXCompilerFlag.cmake. A similar module is available also for C (CheckCCompilerFlag.cmake) and Fortran (CheckFortranCompilerFlag.cmake, since CMake 3.3):

```
include(CheckCXXCompilerFlag)
```

4. We declare an ASAN_FLAGS variable, which holds the flags needed to activate the address sanitizer, and set the CMAKE_REQUIRED_FLAGS variable, used internally by the check_cxx_compiler_flag function:

```
set(ASAN_FLAGS "-fsanitize=address -fno-omit-frame-pointer")
set(CMAKE_REQUIRED_FLAGS ${ASAN_FLAGS})
```

5. We call check_cxx_compiler_flag to ensure that the compiler understands the flags in the ASAN_FLAGS variable. After calling the function, we unset CMAKE_REQUIRED_FLAGS:

```
check_cxx_compiler_flag(${ASAN_FLAGS} asan_works)
unset(CMAKE_REQUIRED_FLAGS)
```

6. If the compiler understands the options, we transform the variable into a list by replacing the spaces with semicolons:

```
if(asan_works)
  string(REPLACE " " ";" _asan_flags ${ASAN_FLAGS})
```

7. We add an executable target for our code sample with the address sanitizer:

```
add_executable(asan-example asan-example.cpp)
```

8. We set the compiler flags for the executable to contain the basic and address sanitizer flags:

```
target_compile_options(asan-example
  PUBLIC
    ${CXX_BASIC_FLAGS}
    ${_asan_flags}
  )
```

9. Finally, we add the address sanitizer flags also to the set of flags used by the linker. This closes the `if(asan_works)` block:

```
target_link_libraries(asan-example PUBLIC ${_asan_flags})
endif()
```

The full recipe source code also shows how to compile and link sample executables for the thread, memory, and undefined behavior sanitizers. These are not discussed in detail here, since we use the same pattern for the compiler flag checking.

> A custom CMake module for finding support for sanitizers on your system is available on GitHub: `https://github.com/arsenm/sanitizers-cmake`.

How it works

The `check_<lang>_compiler_flag` functions are simply wrappers around the `check_<lang>_source_compiles` function, which we discussed in the previous recipe. These wrappers provide a shortcut for the common use case where it is not important to check whether a specific code snippet compiles, but whether the compiler understands a set of flags.

Compiler flags for sanitizers are a special case, in that they also need to be passed on to the linker. To achieve this with the `check_<lang>_compiler_flag` functions, we need to set the `CMAKE_REQUIRED_FLAGS` variable prior to the call. The flags passed as the first argument would otherwise only be used in the call to the compiler, resulting in a false negative.

One more point to notice in the current recipe is the use of string variables and lists to set compiler flags. Using string variables with the `target_compile_options` and `target_link_libraries` functions will result in a compiler and/or linker error. CMake will pass these options quoted, resulting in parsing errors. This justifies the need to express these options in terms of lists and the ensuing string manipulations, to replace spaces in string variables with semicolons. We recall, in fact, that lists in CMake are semicolon-separated strings.

See also

We will revisit and generalize the pattern for testing and setting compiler flags in *Chapter 7, Structuring Projects, Recipe 3, Writing a function to test and set compiler flags.*

Probing execution

The code for this recipe is available at `https://github.com/dev-cafe/cmake-cookbook/tree/v1.0/chapter-05/recipe-08` and has a C/C++ example. The recipe is valid with CMake version 3.6 (and higher) and has been tested on GNU/Linux and macOS. The code repository also contains an example compatible with CMake 3.5.

We have so far shown how to check that a given source snippet can be compiled by the chosen compiler and how to make sure that the desired compiler and linker flags are available. This recipe will show how to check whether a code snippet can be compiled, linked, and run on the current system.

Getting ready

The code sample for this recipe is a slight variation of *Chapter 3, Detecting External Libraries and Programs, Recipe 9, Detecting external libraries: I. Using* `pkg-config`. There, we showed how to find the ZeroMQ library on your system and link it into a C program. In this recipe, we will check that a small C program using the system UUID library on GNU/Linux can actually run, before generating the actual C++ program.

How to do it

We wish to check whether the UUID system library on GNU/Linux can be linked against, before embarking on building our own C++ project. This can be achieved with the following series of steps:

1. We start by declaring a mixed C and C++11 program. This is needed since the test code snippet we want to compile and run is in the C language:

```
cmake_minimum_required(VERSION 3.6 FATAL_ERROR)
project(recipe-08 LANGUAGES CXX C)
```

```
set(CMAKE_CXX_STANDARD 11)
set(CMAKE_CXX_EXTENSIONS OFF)
set(CMAKE_CXX_STANDARD_REQUIRED ON)
```

2. We need to find the UUID library on our system. This is achieved by using `pkg-config`. We ask for the search to return a CMake imported target using the `IMPORTED_TARGET` argument:

```
find_package(PkgConfig REQUIRED QUIET)
pkg_search_module(UUID REQUIRED uuid IMPORTED_TARGET)
if(TARGET PkgConfig::UUID)
  message(STATUS "Found libuuid")
endif()
```

3. Next, we include the `CheckCSourceRuns.cmake` module. There is a similar `CheckCXXSourceRuns.cmake` module for C++. No such module is available for the Fortran language as of CMake 3.11, however:

```
include(CheckCSourceRuns)
```

4. We declare an `_test_uuid` variable containing the C code snippet to compile and run:

```
set(_test_uuid
    "
#include <uuid/uuid.h>

int main(int argc, char * argv[]) {
  uuid_t uuid;

  uuid_generate(uuid);

  return 0;
}
    ")
```

5. We declare the `CMAKE_REQUIRED_LIBRARIES` variable to fine-tune the call to the `check_c_source_runs` function. Next, we issue a call to `check_c_source_runs` with the test snippet as the first argument and the `_runs` variable as the second argument, to hold the result of the check performed. We also unset the `CMAKE_REQUIRED_LIBRARIES` variable:

```
set(CMAKE_REQUIRED_LIBRARIES PkgConfig::UUID)
check_c_source_runs("${_test_uuid}" _runs)
unset(CMAKE_REQUIRED_LIBRARIES)
```

6. If the check did not succeed, either because the snippet didn't compile or because it didn't run, we stop the configuration with a fatal error:

```
if(NOT _runs)
  message(FATAL_ERROR "Cannot run a simple C executable using
libuuid!")
endif()
```

7. Otherwise, we move on and add the C++ executable as a target and link against UUID:

```
add_executable(use-uuid use-uuid.cpp)

target_link_libraries(use-uuid
  PUBLIC
    PkgConfig::UUID
  )
```

How it works

The `check_<lang>_source_runs` functions for C and C++ operate with the same general principles as `check_<lang>_source_compiles`, but add an extra step where the produced executable is actually run. As for `check_<lang>_source_compiles`, the execution of `check_<lang>_source_runs` can be directed by the following variables:

- `CMAKE_REQUIRED_FLAGS` to set the compiler flags
- `CMAKE_REQUIRED_DEFINITIONS` to set preprocessor macros
- `CMAKE_REQUIRED_INCLUDES` to set the list of include directories
- `CMAKE_REQUIRED_LIBRARIES` to set the list of libraries to link into the executable

Since we used the imported target as produced by `pkg_search_module`, it was only necessary to set `CMAKE_REQUIRES_LIBRARIES` to `PkgConfig::UUID`, to also get the include directories correctly set.

Just as `check_<lang>_source_compiles` is a wrapper to `try_compile`, `check_<lang>_source_runs` is a wrapper to another, more powerful command in CMake: `try_run`. It is thus possible to write a `CheckFortranSourceRuns.cmake` module that offers the same functionality as the C and C++ modules by appropriately wrapping `try_run`.

pkg_search_module learned how to define imported targets only with CMake 3.6, but the current recipe can be made to work also with earlier versions of CMake by manually setting the required include directories and libraries for check_c_source_runs as follows: set(CMAKE_REQUIRED_INCLUDES ${UUID_INCLUDE_DIRS}) and set(CMAKE_REQUIRED_LIBRARIES ${UUID_LIBRARIES}).

Fine-tuning configuration and compilation with generator expressions

The code for this recipe is available at https://github.com/dev-cafe/cmake-cookbook/tree/v1.0/chapter-05/recipe-09 and has a C++ example. The recipe is valid with CMake version 3.9 (and higher) and has been tested on GNU/Linux, macOS, and Windows.

CMake offers a domain-specific language to describe how to configure and build a project. It is natural that variables describing particular conditions are introduced and conditional statements based on this are included in CMakeLists.txt.

In this recipe, we will revisit generator expressions, which we used throughout *Chapter 4, Creating and Running Tests*, to compactly refer to explicit test executable paths. Generator expressions offer a powerful and compact pattern for logical and informational expressions that are evaluated during build system generation and produce information specific to each build configuration. In other words, generator expressions are useful to refer to information that is only known at generation time, but not known or difficult to know at configure time; this is particularly the case for filenames, file locations, and library file suffixes.

In this example, we will employ generator expressions to conditionally set a preprocessor definition and conditionally link to a message passing interface (MPI) library and allow us to build the same source code either sequentially or using MPI parallelism.

In this example, we will use an imported target to link to MPI, which is only available starting with CMake 3.9. However, the generator expression aspect is transferable to CMake 3.0 or later versions.

Getting ready

We will compile the following example source code (`example.cpp`):

```cpp
#include <iostream>
#ifdef HAVE_MPI
#include <mpi.h>
#endif

int main() {
#ifdef HAVE_MPI
  // initialize MPI
  MPI_Init(NULL, NULL);

  // query and print the rank
  int rank;
  MPI_Comm_rank(MPI_COMM_WORLD, &rank);
  std::cout << "hello from rank " << rank << std::endl;

  // initialize MPI
  MPI_Finalize();
#else
  std::cout << "hello from a sequential binary" << std::endl;
#endif /* HAVE_MPI */
}
```

The code contains preprocessor statements (`#ifdef HAVE_MPI ... #else ... #endif`) so that we can compile either a sequential or a parallel executable with the same source code.

How to do it

When composing the `CMakeLists.txt` file, we will reuse some of the building blocks we encountered in *Chapter 3, Detecting External Libraries and Programs, Recipe 6, Detecting the MPI parallel environment*:

1. We declare a C++11 project:

```cmake
cmake_minimum_required(VERSION 3.9 FATAL_ERROR)

project(recipe-09 LANGUAGES CXX)

set(CMAKE_CXX_STANDARD 11)
set(CMAKE_CXX_EXTENSIONS OFF)
set(CMAKE_CXX_STANDARD_REQUIRED ON)
```

2. Then, we introduce an option, USE_MPI, to select MPI parallelization and set it ON by default. If it is ON, we use find_package to locate the MPI environment:

```
option(USE_MPI "Use MPI parallelization" ON)

if(USE_MPI)
  find_package(MPI REQUIRED)
endif()
```

3. We then define the executable target and conditionally set the corresponding library dependency (MPI::MPI_CXX) and preprocessor definition (HAVE_MPI), which we will explain in a moment:

```
add_executable(example example.cpp)

target_link_libraries(example
  PUBLIC
    $<$<BOOL:${MPI_FOUND}>:MPI::MPI_CXX>
  )

target_compile_definitions(example
  PRIVATE
    $<$<BOOL:${MPI_FOUND}>:HAVE_MPI>
  )
```

4. If MPI is found, we also print the INTERFACE_LINK_LIBRARIES exported by FindMPI.cmake to demonstrate the very handy cmake_print_properties() function:

```
if(MPI_FOUND)
  include(CMakePrintHelpers)
  cmake_print_properties(
    TARGETS MPI::MPI_CXX
    PROPERTIES INTERFACE_LINK_LIBRARIES
    )
endif()
```

5. Let us first configure the code with the default MPI paralellization switched ON. Observe the output from `cmake_print_properties()`:

```
$ mkdir -p build_mpi
$ cd build_mpi
$ cmake ..

-- ...
--
 Properties for TARGET MPI::MPI_CXX:
 MPI::MPI_CXX.INTERFACE_LINK_LIBRARIES = "-Wl,-rpath -
Wl,/usr/lib/openmpi -Wl,--enable-new-dtags -
pthread;/usr/lib/openmpi/libmpi_cxx.so;/usr/lib/openmpi/libmpi.so"
```

6. We compile and run the parallel example:

```
$ cmake --build .
$ mpirun -np 2 ./example

hello from rank 0
hello from rank 1
```

7. Now, let us step one directory up, create a new build directory, and this time build the sequential version:

```
$ mkdir -p build_seq
$ cd build_seq
$ cmake -D USE_MPI=OFF ..
$ cmake --build .
$ ./example

hello from a sequential binary
```

How it works

The build system for a project is generated by CMake in two phases: a configuration phase, where CMakeLists.txt is parsed, and a generation phase, where the build environment is actually generated. Generator expressions are evaluated in this second phase and can be used to tweak the build system with information that can only be known at generation time. Generator expressions are thus particularly useful when cross-compiling, where some of the information is only available after the CMakeLists.txt has been parsed, or in multi-configuration projects, where the build system is generated at once for all the different configurations the project can have, such as Debug and Release.

In our case, we will use generator expressions to conditionally set a link dependency and compile definition. For this, we can focus on these two expressions:

```
target_link_libraries(example
  PUBLIC
    $<$<BOOL:${MPI_FOUND}>:MPI::MPI_CXX>
  )

target_compile_definitions(example
  PRIVATE
    $<$<BOOL:${MPI_FOUND}>:HAVE_MPI>
  )
```

If `MPI_FOUND` is true, then `$<BOOL:${MPI_FOUND}>` will evaluate to 1. In this case, `$<$<BOOL:${MPI_FOUND}>:MPI::MPI_CXX>` will evaluate to `MPI::MPI_CXX` and the second generator expression will evaluate to `HAVE_MPI`. If we set `USE_MPI` to `OFF`, `MPI_FOUND` is false and both generator expressions evaluate to empty strings, and thus no link dependency is introduced and no preprocessor definition is set.

We could have achieved the same effect by introducing an if-statement:

```
if(MPI_FOUND)
  target_link_libraries(example
    PUBLIC
      MPI::MPI_CXX
    )

  target_compile_definitions(example
    PRIVATE
      HAVE_MPI
    )
endif()
```

This solution is a bit less compact but possibly a bit more readable. We can often re-express if-statements using generator expressions and the choice is often a matter of taste. However, generator expressions particularly shine when we need to access or manipulate explicit file paths, since these can be difficult to construct using variables and if-clauses, and in this case we clearly favor generator expressions for readability. This was the case in *Chapter 4, Creating and Running Tests,* where we used generator expressions to resolve the file path of a particular target. We will also appreciate generator expressions in *Chapter 11, Packaging Projects.*

There is more

CMake offers three types of generator expression:

- Logical expressions, with the basic pattern `$<condition:outcome>`. The basic conditions are `0` for false and `1` for true, but any Boolean can be used as a condition, provided that the correct keywords are used.
- Informational expression, with the basic pattern `$<information>` or `$<information:input>`. These expressions evaluate to some build system information, for example, include directories, target properties, and so forth. The input parameter to these expressions might be the name of a target, as in the expression `$<TARGET_PROPERTY:tgt,prop>`, where the information obtained will be the `prop` property on the `tgt` target.
- Output expressions, with the basic pattern `$<operation>` or `$<operation:input>`. These expressions generate an output, possibly based on some input parameters. Their output can be used directly inside CMake commands or combined with other generator expressions. For example, `-I$<JOIN:$<TARGET_PROPERTY:INCLUDE_DIRECTORIES>, -I>` will generate a string containing the include directories for the target being processed, each prependend by `-I`.

See also

For a full list of generator expressions, please consult `https://cmake.org/cmake/help/latest/manual/cmake-generator-expressions.7.html`.

Generating Source Code

6

In this chapter, we will cover the following recipes:

- Generating sources at configure time
- Generating source code at configure time using Python
- Generating source code at build time using Python
- Recording the project version information for reproducibility
- Recording the project version from a file
- Recording the Git hash at configure time
- Recording the Git hash at build time

Introduction

For most projects, the source code is tracked using a version control system; it typically serves as input for the build system, which transforms it into objects, libraries, and executables. In certain cases, we use the build system to generate source code during the configuration or build steps. This can be useful to fine-tune the source code based on information gathered in the configuration step, or to automatize an otherwise error-prone mechanical generation of repetitive code. Another frequent use case for generating source code is to record information about the configuration or compilation for reproducibility. In this chapter, we will illustrate various strategies to generate source code, using the powerful tools provided by CMake.

Generating sources at configure time

The code for this recipe is available at `https://github.com/dev-cafe/cmake-cookbook/tree/v1.0/chapter-06/recipe-01`, including a Fortran/C example. The recipe is valid with CMake version 3.10 (and higher), and has been tested on GNU/Linux, macOS, and Windows with MSYS Makefiles.

The most straightforward code generation happens at configure time. For example, CMake can detect the operating system and available libraries; based on that information, we can tailor what sources are built, to offer maximum performance to the end user of our library or program. In this and some of the following recipes, we will illustrate how to generate a simple source file that defines a function to report the build system configuration.

Getting ready

The code sample for this recipe is in Fortran and C, setting the stage for *Chapter 9, Mixed-language Projects*, where mixed-language programming will be discussed. The main program is a simple Fortran executable that calls a C function, `print_info()`, which will print the configuration information. It is worth noting that with Fortran 2003, the compiler will take care of name mangling (given a proper interface declaration of the C function), as seen in the simple `example.f90` source file that we will use:

```
program hello_world

    implicit none

    interface
        subroutine print_info() bind(c, name="print_info")
        end subroutine
    end interface

    call print_info()

end program
```

The `print_info()` C function is defined in the template file, `print_info.c.in`. The variables starting and ending with @ will be substituted for their actual values at configure time:

```
#include <stdio.h>
#include <unistd.h>
```

```
void print_info(void) {
  printf("\n");
  printf("Configuration and build information\n");
  printf("-----------------------------------\n");
  printf("\n");
  printf("Who compiled | %s\n", "@_user_name@");
  printf("Compilation hostname | %s\n", "@_host_name@");
  printf("Fully qualified domain name | %s\n", "@_fqdn@");
  printf("Operating system | %s\n",
         "@_os_name@, @_os_release@, @_os_version@");
  printf("Platform | %s\n", "@_os_platform@");
  printf("Processor info | %s\n",
         "@_processor_name@, @_processor_description@");
  printf("CMake version | %s\n", "@CMAKE_VERSION@");
  printf("CMake generator | %s\n", "@CMAKE_GENERATOR@");
  printf("Configuration time | %s\n", "@_configuration_time@");
  printf("Fortran compiler | %s\n", "@CMAKE_Fortran_COMPILER@");
  printf("C compiler | %s\n", "@CMAKE_C_COMPILER@");
  printf("\n");

  fflush(stdout);
}
```

How to do it

In our CMakeLists.txt, we first have to collect the configuration options, and can then substitute their values for the corresponding placeholders in print_info.c.in; we compile both the Fortran and C sources into one executable:

1. We create a mixed Fortran-C project, as follows:

   ```
   cmake_minimum_required(VERSION 3.10 FATAL_ERROR)
   project(recipe-01 LANGUAGES Fortran C)
   ```

2. We obtain the username for the user configuring the project by using execute_process:

   ```
   execute_process(
     COMMAND
       whoami
     TIMEOUT
       1
     OUTPUT_VARIABLE
       _user_name
     OUTPUT_STRIP_TRAILING_WHITESPACE
     )
   ```

3. Using the `cmake_host_system_information()` function (which we already encountered in *Chapter 2, Detecting the Environment, Recipe 5, Discovering the host processor instruction set*), we can query for more system information:

```
# host name information
cmake_host_system_information(RESULT _host_name QUERY HOSTNAME)
cmake_host_system_information(RESULT _fqdn QUERY FQDN)

# processor information
cmake_host_system_information(RESULT _processor_name QUERY
PROCESSOR_NAME)
cmake_host_system_information(RESULT _processor_description QUERY
PROCESSOR_DESCRIPTION)

# os information
cmake_host_system_information(RESULT _os_name QUERY OS_NAME)
cmake_host_system_information(RESULT _os_release QUERY OS_RELEASE)
cmake_host_system_information(RESULT _os_version QUERY OS_VERSION)
cmake_host_system_information(RESULT _os_platform QUERY
OS_PLATFORM)
```

4. We also obtain a timestamp for the configuration, by using a string manipulation function:

```
string(TIMESTAMP _configuration_time "%Y-%m-%d %H:%M:%S [UTC]" UTC)
```

5. We are now ready to configure the template file, `print_info.c.in`, by using CMake's own `configure_file` function. Notice that we only require the strings starting and terminating with @ to be substituted:

```
configure_file(print_info.c.in print_info.c @ONLY)
```

6. Finally, we add an executable target and define the target sources, as follows:

```
add_executable(example "")

target_sources(example
  PRIVATE
    example.f90
    ${CMAKE_CURRENT_BINARY_DIR}/print_info.c
  )
```

Chapter 6

7. The following is an example output:

```
$ mkdir -p build
$ cd build
$ cmake ..
$ cmake --build .
$ ./example

Configuration and build information
-----------------------------------

Who compiled              | somebody
Compilation hostname      | laptop
Fully qualified domain name | laptop
Operating system          | Linux, 4.16.13-1-ARCH, #1 SMP PREEMPT
Thu May 31 23:29:29 UTC 2018
Platform                  | x86_64
Processor info            | Unknown P6 family, 2 core Intel(R)
Core(TM) i5-5200U CPU @ 2.20GHz
CMake version             | 3.11.3
CMake generator           | Unix Makefiles
Configuration time        | 2018-06-25 15:38:03 [UTC]
Fortran compiler          | /usr/bin/f95
C compiler                | /usr/bin/cc
```

How it works

The command `configure_file` can copy files and replace their contents with variable values. In our example, we used `configure_file` to both modify the contents of our template file and copy it to a location where it could then be compiled into our executable. Let us look at our invocation of `configure_file`:

```
configure_file(print_info.c.in print_info.c @ONLY)
```

The first argument is the name of the scaffold: `print_info.c.in`. CMake assumes that the input file is located relative to the root directory of the project; that is, in `${CMAKE_CURRENT_SOURCE_DIR}/print_info.c.in`. The second argument is the name of the configured file, which we chose to be `print_info.c`. The output file is assumed to be located relative to the project build directory; that is, in `${CMAKE_CURRENT_BINARY_DIR}/print_info.c`.

When limiting the invocation to just two arguments, the input and output files, CMake will not only configure variables of the form `@VAR@`, but also those of the form `${VAR}`. This can be inconvenient when `${VAR}` is part of the syntax and should not be touched (such as in shell scripts). To instruct CMake in this regard, the option `@ONLY` should be passed to the invocation of `configure_file`, as we illustrated previously.

There is more

Note that the substitution of placeholders with values expects the variable names in CMake to be exactly the same as those used in the to-be configured file, and placed in between @-markers. Any CMake variable defined at the point where `configure_file` is invoked can be used. This includes all built-in CMake variables, such as `CMAKE_VERSION` or `CMAKE_GENERATOR`, in our example. Moreover, whenever the template file is modified, rebuilding the code will trigger a regeneration of the build system. In this way, the configured file will always be up to date.

> A complete list of internal CMake variables can be obtained from the CMake manual by using `cmake --help-variable-list`.

> The command `file(GENERATE ...)` provides an interesting alternative to `configure_file` as it allows generator expressions to be evaluated as part of the configured file. However, `file(GENERATE ...)` updates the output file every time CMake is run which forces a rebuild of all targets which depend on that output. See also `https://crascit.com/2017/04/18/generated-sources-in-cmake-builds/`.

Generating source code at configure time using Python

> The code for this recipe is available at `https://github.com/dev-cafe/cmake-cookbook/tree/v1.0/chapter-06/recipe-02`, including a Fortran/C example. The recipe is valid with CMake version 3.10 (and higher), and has been tested on GNU/Linux, macOS, and Windows with MSYS Makefiles.

In this recipe, we will revisit the previous example, and will again generate print_info.c from the template print_info.c.in. However, this time, we will imagine that the CMake function configure_file() has not been invented yet, and will emulate it with a Python script. The goal of this recipe is to learn how we can generate source code at configure time by using a now familiar example. Of course, we will probably favor configure_file() for a real project, but when faced with the challenge of generating sources using Python at configure time, we will know how to do it.

We should point out that this recipe has a serious limitation and cannot emulate configure_file() fully. The approach that we will present here cannot generate an automatic dependency which would regenerate print_info.c at build time. In other words, if you remove the generated print_info.c after the configure step, this file will not be regenerated and the build step will fail. To properly mimic the behavior of configure_file() we would require add_custom_command() and add_custom_target(), which we will use in the subsequent *Recipe 3*, *Generating source code at build time using Python*, where we will overcome this limitation.

In this recipe, we will use a relatively simple Python script which we will detail below. This script will read in print_info.c.in and replace the placeholders in the file with parameters passed to the Python script from CMake. For more sophisticated templating, we recommend external tools, such as Jinja (see http://jinja.pocoo.org).

Getting ready

The files print_info.c.in and example.f90 are unchanged with respect to the previous recipe. In addition, we will use a Python script, configurator.py, which provides one function:

```python
def configure_file(input_file, output_file, vars_dict):

    with input_file.open('r') as f:
        template = f.read()

    for var in vars_dict:
        template = template.replace('@' + var + '@', vars_dict[var])

    with output_file.open('w') as f:
        f.write(template)
```

This function reads an input file, goes over all of the keys of a `vars_dict` dictionary, replaces the pattern `@key@` with its corresponding value, and writes the results to an output file. The key-value pairs will be provided by CMake.

How to do it

Similar to the previous recipe, we need to configure a template file, but this time, we will emulate the `configure_file()` function with a Python script. We keep the `CMakeLists.txt` largely unchanged, but we replace `configure_file(print_info.c.in print_info.c @ONLY)` with a set of commands, which we will introduce step by step:

1. First, we construct a variable, `_config_script`, which will hold a Python script that we will execute a moment later:

```
set(_config_script
"
from pathlib import Path
source_dir = Path('${CMAKE_CURRENT_SOURCE_DIR}')
binary_dir = Path('${CMAKE_CURRENT_BINARY_DIR}')
input_file = source_dir / 'print_info.c.in'
output_file = binary_dir / 'print_info.c'

import sys
sys.path.insert(0, str(source_dir))

from configurator import configure_file
vars_dict = {
    '_user_name':            '${_user_name}',
    '_host_name':            '${_host_name}',
    '_fqdn':                 '${_fqdn}',
    '_processor_name':       '${_processor_name}',
    '_processor_description': '${_processor_description}',
    '_os_name':              '${_os_name}',
    '_os_release':           '${_os_release}',
    '_os_version':           '${_os_version}',
    '_os_platform':          '${_os_platform}',
    '_configuration_time':   '${_configuration_time}',
    'CMAKE_VERSION':         '${CMAKE_VERSION}',
    'CMAKE_GENERATOR':       '${CMAKE_GENERATOR}',
    'CMAKE_Fortran_COMPILER': '${CMAKE_Fortran_COMPILER}',
    'CMAKE_C_COMPILER':      '${CMAKE_C_COMPILER}',
}
configure_file(input_file, output_file, vars_dict)
")
```

2. We then use `find_package` to ensure that the Python interpreter is available for CMake to use:

```
find_package(PythonInterp QUIET REQUIRED)
```

3. If the Python interpreter was found, we can execute `_config_script` from within CMake, to generate the `print_info.c` file:

```
execute_process(
  COMMAND
    ${PYTHON_EXECUTABLE} "-c" ${_config_script}
  )
```

4. After that, we define the executable target and dependencies, but this is unchanged from the previous recipe. Also, the obtained output is unchanged.

How it works

Let us examine the changes that we applied to `CMakeLists.txt`, by discussing them backwards.

We executed a Python script that generates `print_info.c`. To run the Python script, we first had to detect Python and construct the Python script. The Python script imports the `configure_file` function, which we defined in `configurator.py`. It requires that we provide it with file locations for reading and writing, as well as a dictionary holding CMake variables and their values as key-value pairs.

This recipe has shown an alternative way of generating a configuration report that can be compiled into an executable, or even a library target, by delegating the generation of sources to an external script. The first approach that we discussed in the previous recipe was cleaner and simpler, but with the approach that we have presented in this recipe, we have the flexibility to implement, in principle, any configure-time step that Python (or another language) allows. Using the present approach, we can perform actions that go *beyond* what `cmake_host_system_information()` currently provides.

However, we need to remember the limitation of this approach which cannot generate an automatic dependency which would regenerate `print_info.c` at build time. In the next recipe we will overcome this limitation.

There is more

It is possible to express this recipe more compactly. Instead of explicitly constructing `vars_dict`, which felt a bit repetitive, we could have used `get_cmake_property(_vars VARIABLES)` to obtain a list of *all* variables defined at this particular time, and could have looped over all elements of `_vars` to access their values:

```
get_cmake_property(_vars VARIABLES)
foreach(_var IN ITEMS ${_vars})
  message("variable ${_var} has the value ${${_var}}")
endforeach()
```

Using this approach, it is possible to build `vars_dict` implicitly. However, care has to be taken to escape values that contain characters such as ";", which Python interprets as terminating an instruction.

Generating source code at build time using Python

> The code for this recipe is available at `https://github.com/dev-cafe/cmake-cookbook/tree/v1.0/chapter-06/recipe-03`, including a C++ example. The recipe is valid with CMake version 3.5 (and higher), and has been tested on GNU/Linux, macOS, and Windows.

Being able to generate source code at build time is a powerful feature in the toolbox of the pragmatic developer who wishes to generate possibly lengthy and repetitive code based on some rules, while at the same time avoiding tracking the generated code explicitly in the source code repository. We can, for instance, imagine generating different source code, based on the detected platform or architecture. Or, we can use the simplicity of Python to generate explicit and efficient C++ code at build time, based on the input that we gathered during the configuration step. Other relevant examples are parser generators, such as Flex (`https://github.com/westes/flex`) and Bison (`https://www.gnu.org/software/bison/`), meta-object compilers, such as Qt moc (`http://doc.qt.io/qt-5/moc.html`), and serialization frameworks, such as Google protobuf (`https://developers.google.com/protocol-buffers/`).

Getting ready

To provide a concrete example, we imagine that we need to write a code to verify whether a number is prime. Many algorithms exist, and we can, for instance, use the sieve of Eratosthenes to separate prime numbers from non-primes. If we have to verify many numbers, we will not want to run the sieve of Eratosthenes algorithm for every single one of them. What we would like to do instead is tabulate all prime numbers once, up to a certain limit, and use a table lookup to verify a large set of numbers.

In this example, we will generate the C++ code for the lookup table (a vector of prime numbers) by using Python at compile time. Of course, to solve this particular programming problem, we could also generate the lookup table using C++, and we could do it at runtime instead.

Let us start out with the following Python script, called `generate.py`. This script takes two command-line arguments - an integer that will limit the search, and an output filename:

```
"""
Generates C++ vector of prime numbers up to max_number
using sieve of Eratosthenes.
"""
import pathlib
import sys

# for simplicity we do not verify argument list
max_number = int(sys.argv[-2])
output_file_name = pathlib.Path(sys.argv[-1])

numbers = range(2, max_number + 1)
is_prime = {number: True for number in numbers}

for number in numbers:
    current_position = number
    if is_prime[current_position]:
        while current_position <= max_number:
            current_position += number
            is_prime[current_position] = False

primes = (number for number in numbers if is_prime[number])
code = """#pragma once

#include <vector>

const std::size_t max_number = {max_number};

std::vector<int> & primes() {{
```

```
    static std::vector<int> primes;

{push_back}

    return primes;
}}
"""
push_back = '\n'.join(['  primes.push_back({:d});'.format(x) for x in
primes])
output_file_name.write_text(
    code.format(max_number=max_number, push_back=push_back))
```

Our goal is to generate a header file, `primes.hpp`, at compile time, and include it in the following example code:

```
#include "primes.hpp"
#include <iostream>
#include <vector>

int main() {
  std::cout << "all prime numbers up to " << max_number << ":";

  for (auto prime : primes())
    std::cout << " " << prime;

  std::cout << std::endl;

  return 0;
}
```

How to do it

The following is a breakdown of the commands in `CMakeLists.txt`:

1. First, we need to define the project and detect the Python interpreter, as follows:

```
cmake_minimum_required(VERSION 3.5 FATAL_ERROR)
project(recipe-03 LANGUAGES CXX)

set(CMAKE_CXX_STANDARD 11)
set(CMAKE_CXX_EXTENSIONS OFF)
set(CMAKE_CXX_STANDARD_REQUIRED ON)

find_package(PythonInterp QUIET REQUIRED)
```

2. We decided to place the to-be-generated code under `${CMAKE_CURRENT_BINARY_DIR}/generated`, and we need to instruct CMake to create this directory:

```
file(MAKE_DIRECTORY ${CMAKE_CURRENT_BINARY_DIR}/generated)
```

3. The Python script expects an upper bound for the prime numbers, and, with the following command, we can set a default:

```
set(MAX_NUMBER "100" CACHE STRING "Upper bound for primes")
```

4. Next, we define a custom command to generate the header file:

```
add_custom_command(
  OUTPUT
    ${CMAKE_CURRENT_BINARY_DIR}/generated/primes.hpp
  COMMAND
    ${PYTHON_EXECUTABLE} generate.py ${MAX_NUMBER}
${CMAKE_CURRENT_BINARY_DIR}/generated/primes.hpp
  WORKING_DIRECTORY
    ${CMAKE_CURRENT_SOURCE_DIR}
  DEPENDS
    generate.py
  )
```

5. Finally, we define the executable and its target, including the directory and dependency:

```
add_executable(example "")

target_sources(example
  PRIVATE
    example.cpp
    ${CMAKE_CURRENT_BINARY_DIR}/generated/primes.hpp
  )

target_include_directories(example
  PRIVATE
    ${CMAKE_CURRENT_BINARY_DIR}/generated
  )
```

6. We are now ready to test the implementation, as follows:

```
$ mkdir -p build
$ cd build
$ cmake ..
$ cmake --build .
$ ./example

all prime numbers up to 100: 2 3 5 7 11 13 17 19 23 29 31 37 41 43
47 53 59 61 67 71 73 79 83 89 97
```

How it works

To generate the header file, we defined a custom command that executes the `generate.py` script and takes `${MAX_NUMBER}` and the file path (`${CMAKE_CURRENT_BINARY_DIR}/generated/primes.hpp`) as arguments:

```
add_custom_command(
  OUTPUT
    ${CMAKE_CURRENT_BINARY_DIR}/generated/primes.hpp
  COMMAND
    ${PYTHON_EXECUTABLE} generate.py ${MAX_NUMBER}
${CMAKE_CURRENT_BINARY_DIR}/generated/primes.hpp
  WORKING_DIRECTORY
    ${CMAKE_CURRENT_SOURCE_DIR}
  DEPENDS
    generate.py
  )
```

In order to trigger the source code generation, we need to add it as a source code dependency in the definition of the executable, a task easily achieved with `target_sources`:

```
target_sources(example
  PRIVATE
    example.cpp
    ${CMAKE_CURRENT_BINARY_DIR}/generated/primes.hpp
  )
```

In the preceding code, we do not have to define a new custom target. The header file will be generated as a dependency of `example`, and will be rebuilt every time the `generate.py` script changes. If the code generation script produces several source files, it is important that all generated files are listed as dependencies of some target.

There is more

We mentioned that all generated files should be listed as dependencies of some target. However, we might be in a situation where we do not know this list of files, since it is determined by the scripts generating the files, depending on input that we provide to the configuration. In this case, we might be tempted to use `file(GLOB ...)` to collect generated files into a list (see `https://cmake.org/cmake/help/v3.5/command/file.html`).

However, remember that `file(GLOB ...)` is executed at configure time, whereas code generation happens at build time. Therefore, we may need an additional level of indirection, where we place the `file(GLOB ...)` command in a separate CMake script which we execute at using `${CMAKE_COMMAND} -P`, in order to get the list of generated files at build time.

Recording the project version information for reproducibility

The code for this recipe is available at `https://github.com/dev-cafe/cmake-cookbook/tree/v1.0/chapter-06/recipe-04`, including C and Fortran examples. The recipe is valid with CMake version 3.5 (and higher), and has been tested on GNU/Linux, macOS, and Windows.

Code versions matter, not only for reproducibility but also to document API capabilities or simplify support requests and bug reporting. The source code is typically under some version control, and additional semantic version numbers (see e.g. `https://semver.org`) can be attached using Git tags, for example. However, not only does the source code need to be versioned, but the executable needs to record the project version so that it can be printed to the code output or user interface.

In this example, we will define the version number inside of the CMake sources. Our goal is to record the program version to a header file at the moment when we configure the project. The generated header file can then be included in the code at the right place and time, to print the code version to the output file(s) or screen.

Getting ready

We will use the following C file (`example.c`) to print the version information:

```c
#include "version.h"

#include <stdio.h>

int main() {
  printf("This is output from code %s\n", PROJECT_VERSION);
  printf("Major version number: %i\n", PROJECT_VERSION_MAJOR);
  printf("Minor version number: %i\n", PROJECT_VERSION_MINOR);

  printf("Hello CMake world!\n");
}
```

Here, we assume that `PROJECT_VERSION_MAJOR`, `PROJECT_VERSION_MINOR`, and `PROJECT_VERSION` are defined in `version.h`. Our goal is to generate `version.h` from the following scaffold, `version.h.in`:

```
#pragma once

#define PROJECT_VERSION_MAJOR @PROJECT_VERSION_MAJOR@
#define PROJECT_VERSION_MINOR @PROJECT_VERSION_MINOR@
#define PROJECT_VERSION_PATCH @PROJECT_VERSION_PATCH@

#define PROJECT_VERSION "v@PROJECT_VERSION@"
```

We will use preprocessor definitions, but we could also employ string or integer constants for more type safety (and we will demonstrate that later). From the CMake perspective, the approach is the same.

How to do it

We will follow these steps to register the version in our template header file:

1. To track the code version, we can define the project version when invoking the CMake `project` command in `CMakeLists.txt`:

```
cmake_minimum_required(VERSION 3.5 FATAL_ERROR)

project(recipe-04 VERSION 2.0.1 LANGUAGES C)
```

2. We then configure `version.h`, based on `version.h.in`:

```
configure_file(
  version.h.in
  generated/version.h
  @ONLY
  )
```

3. Finally, we define the executable and provide the target include path:

```
add_executable(example example.c)

target_include_directories(example
  PRIVATE
    ${CMAKE_CURRENT_BINARY_DIR}/generated
  )
```

How it works

When invoking the CMake `project` command with a VERSION argument, CMake will set the PROJECT_VERSION_MAJOR, PROJECT_VERSION_MINOR, and PROJECT_VERSION_PATCH for our project. The key command in this recipe is `configure_file`, which takes an input file (in this case, `version.h.in`) and generates an output file (in this case, `generated/version.h`) by expanding all placeholders between @ to their corresponding CMake variables. It replaces @PROJECT_VERSION_MAJOR@ with 2, and so on. With the keyword @ONLY, we limit `configure_file` to only expand @variables@, but to not touch ${variables}. The latter form is not used in `version.h.in`, but they frequently appear when configuring a shell script using CMake.

The generated header file can be included in our example code, and the version information is available to be printed:

```
$ mkdir -p build
$ cd build
$ cmake ..
$ cmake --build .
$ ./example

This is output from code v2.0.1
Major version number: 2
Minor version number: 0
Hello CMake world!
```

CMake understands version numbers given in the format `X.Y.Z.t`, and will set the variables `PROJECT_VERSION` and `<project-name>_VERSION` to the passed value. In addition, the `PROJECT_VERSION_MAJOR` (`<project-name>_VERSION_MAJOR`), `PROJECT_VERSION_MINOR` (`<project-name>_VERSION_MINOR`), `PROJECT_VERSION_PATCH` (`<project-name>_VERSION_PATCH`), and `PROJECT_VERSION_TWEAK` (`<project-name>_VERSION_TWEAK`), will be set to `X`, `Y`, `Z`, and `t`, respectively.

There is more

To make sure that the preprocessor variables are only defined if the CMake variable is considered a true constant, one can employ `#cmakedefine` instead of `#define` in the header files that are about to be configured, by using `configure_file`.

Depending on whether the CMake variable is defined and evaluates to a true constant, `#cmakedefine YOUR_VARIABLE` will then be replaced with either `#define YOUR_VARIABLE ...` or `/* #undef YOUR_VARIABLE */`. There is also `#cmakedefine01`, which will set a variable to either `0` or `1`, depending on whether the variable is defined.

Recording the project version from a file

The code for this recipe is available at `https://github.com/dev-cafe/cmake-cookbook/tree/v1.0/chapter-06/recipe-05`, including a C++ example. The recipe is valid with CMake version 3.5 (and higher), and has been tested on GNU/Linux, macOS, and Windows.

The goal of this recipe is similar to the previous one, but the starting point is different; our plan is to read the version information from a file, rather than setting it inside of `CMakeLists.txt`. The motivation for keeping the version in a separate file, outside of CMake sources, is to allow other build frameworks or development tools to use the information, independent of CMake, without duplicating the information in several files. One example of a build framework that you might like to employ in parallel to CMake is the Sphinx documentation framework, generating documentation and deploying it to the Read the Docs service to serve your code documentation online.

Getting ready

We will start with a file called VERSION, containing the following:

```
2.0.1-rc-2
```

This time, we will choose to go for more type safety, and will define PROGRAM_VERSION as a string constant in version.hpp.in:

```
#pragma once
#include <string>

const std::string PROGRAM_VERSION = "@PROGRAM_VERSION@";
```

We will include the generated version.hpp in the following example source code (example.cpp):

```cpp
// provides PROGRAM_VERSION
#include "version.hpp"

#include <iostream>

int main() {
  std::cout << "This is output from code v" << PROGRAM_VERSION
                                            << std::endl;

  std::cout << "Hello CMake world!" << std::endl;
}
```

How to do it

The following shows how to accomplish our task, step by step:

1. CMakeLists.txt defines the minimum version, project name, language, and standard:

```cmake
cmake_minimum_required(VERSION 3.5 FATAL_ERROR)

project(recipe-05 LANGUAGES CXX)

set(CMAKE_CXX_STANDARD 11)
set(CMAKE_CXX_EXTENSIONS OFF)
set(CMAKE_CXX_STANDARD_REQUIRED ON)
```

2. We read the version information from the file, as follows:

```
if(EXISTS "${CMAKE_CURRENT_SOURCE_DIR}/VERSION")
  file(READ "${CMAKE_CURRENT_SOURCE_DIR}/VERSION" PROGRAM_VERSION)
  string(STRIP "${PROGRAM_VERSION}" PROGRAM_VERSION)
else()
  message(FATAL_ERROR "File ${CMAKE_CURRENT_SOURCE_DIR}/VERSION not
found")
endif()
```

3. We then configure the header file:

```
configure_file(
  version.hpp.in
  generated/version.hpp
  @ONLY
  )
```

4. Finally, we define the executable and its dependencies:

```
add_executable(example example.cpp)

target_include_directories(example
  PRIVATE
    ${CMAKE_CURRENT_BINARY_DIR}/generated
  )
```

5. We are then ready to test it out:

```
$ mkdir -p build
$ cd build
$ cmake ..
$ cmake --build .
$ ./example

This is output from code v2.0.1-rc-2
Hello CMake world!
```

How it works

We used the following construct to read the version string from a file called VERSION:

```
if(EXISTS "${CMAKE_CURRENT_SOURCE_DIR}/VERSION")
  file(READ "${CMAKE_CURRENT_SOURCE_DIR}/VERSION" PROGRAM_VERSION)
  string(STRIP "${PROGRAM_VERSION}" PROGRAM_VERSION)
```

```
else()
  message(FATAL_ERROR "File ${CMAKE_CURRENT_SOURCE_DIR}/VERSION not found")
endif()
```

Here, we first check that this file exists, and issue an error message if it does not. If it exists, we read its contents into a variable called `PROGRAM_VERSION`, which we strip of any trailing whitespace. Once the variable `PROGRAM_VERSION` is set, it can be used to configure `version.hpp.in` to generate `generated/version.hpp`, as follows:

```
configure_file(
  version.hpp.in
  generated/version.hpp
  @ONLY
  )
```

Recording the Git hash at configure time

The code for this recipe is available at `https://github.com/dev-cafe/cmake-cookbook/tree/v1.0/chapter-06/recipe-06`, including a C++ example. The recipe is valid with CMake version 3.5 (and higher), and has been tested on GNU/Linux, macOS, and Windows.

Most modern source code repositories are tracked using Git as version control system, a fact that can be attributed to the huge popularity of the repository hosting platform GitHub. We will, therefore, use Git in this recipe; the motivation and implementation will, however, translate to other version control systems. If we look at Git as an example, the Git hash of a commit uniquely determines the state of the source code. Therefore, to uniquely brand the executable, we will try to burn the Git hash into the executable by recording the hash string in a header file that can be included and used at the right place in the code.

Getting ready

We will need two source files, both very similar to the previous recipe. One will be configured with the recorded hash (`version.hpp.in`), as follows:

```
#pragma once
#include <string>

const std::string GIT_HASH = "@GIT_HASH@";
```

We will also need an example source file (`example.cpp`), which will print the hash to the screen:

```
#include "version.hpp"

#include <iostream>

int main() {
  std::cout << "This code has been configured from version " << GIT_HASH
            << std::endl;
}
```

This recipe also assumes that we are in a Git repository with at least one commit. So, initialize this example with `git init`, and create commits with `git add <filename>`, followed by `git commit`, in order to get a meaningful example.

How to do it

The following illustrates the steps to record versioning information from Git:

1. In `CMakeLists.txt`, we first define the project and language support:

    ```
    cmake_minimum_required(VERSION 3.5 FATAL_ERROR)

    project(recipe-06 LANGUAGES CXX)

    set(CMAKE_CXX_STANDARD 11)
    set(CMAKE_CXX_EXTENSIONS OFF)
    set(CMAKE_CXX_STANDARD_REQUIRED ON)
    ```

2. We then use the following code snippet to define a variable, `GIT_HASH`:

    ```
    # in case Git is not available, we default to "unknown"
    set(GIT_HASH "unknown")

    # find Git and if available set GIT_HASH variable
    find_package(Git QUIET)
    if(GIT_FOUND)
      execute_process(
        COMMAND ${GIT_EXECUTABLE} log -1 --pretty=format:%h
        OUTPUT_VARIABLE GIT_HASH
        OUTPUT_STRIP_TRAILING_WHITESPACE
        ERROR_QUIET
        WORKING_DIRECTORY
          ${CMAKE_CURRENT_SOURCE_DIR}
        )
    ```

```
endif()

message(STATUS "Git hash is ${GIT_HASH}")
```

3. The rest of CMakeLists.txt is similar to the one in the previous recipes:

```
# generate file version.hpp based on version.hpp.in
configure_file(
  version.hpp.in
  generated/version.hpp
  @ONLY
  )

# example code
add_executable(example example.cpp)

# needs to find the generated header file
target_include_directories(example
  PRIVATE
    ${CMAKE_CURRENT_BINARY_DIR}/generated
  )
```

4. We can verify the output as follows (the hash will differ):

```
$ mkdir -p build
$ cd build
$ cmake ..
$ cmake --build .
$ ./example

This code has been configured from version d58c64f
```

How it works

We use find_package(Git QUIET) to detect whether Git is available on the system. If it is (if GIT_FOUND is true), we run a Git command: ${GIT_EXECUTABLE} log -1 --pretty=format:%h. This command gives us the short version of the current commit hash. Of course, we have full flexibility to run another Git command, instead. We ask the execute_process command to place the result of the command into a variable called GIT_HASH, which we subsequently strip of any trailing whitespace. With ERROR_QUIET, we ask the command to not stop the configuration if the Git command fails for some reason.

Since the Git command might fail (the source code might have been distributed outside of the Git repository) or Git might not even be available on the system, we wish to set a default for the variable, as follows:

```
set(GIT_HASH "unknown")
```

One problem with this recipe is that the Git hash is recorded at configure time, not at build time. In the next recipe, we will demonstrate how to implement the latter approach.

Recording the Git hash at build time

The code for this recipe is available at `https://github.com/dev-cafe/cmake-cookbook/tree/v1.0/chapter-06/recipe-07`, including a C++ example. The recipe is valid with CMake version 3.5 (and higher), and has been tested on GNU/Linux, macOS, and Windows.

In the previous recipe, we recorded the state of the code repository (Git hash) at configure time, and it is very useful to have the state of the repository recorded in the executable. However, one unsatisfactory aspect of the previous approach is that if we changed branches or committed changes after having configured the code, the version record included in our source code could point to the wrong Git hash. In this recipe, we wish to go a step further and demonstrate how to record the Git hash (or, generally, perform other actions) at build time, to make sure that these actions are run every time we build the code, since we may configure only once but build several times.

Getting ready

We will use the same `version.hpp.in` as in the previous recipe, and will modify the `example.cpp` file only minimally, to make it clear that it prints a build-time Git hash:

```cpp
#include "version.hpp"

#include <iostream>

int main() {
  std::cout << "This code has been built from version " << GIT_HASH << std::endl;
}
```

How to do it

Saving the Git information to the version.hpp header file at build time will require the following operations:

1. We will move most of the code from the CMakeLists.txt of the previous recipe to a separate file, and will call the file git-hash.cmake:

```
# in case Git is not available, we default to "unknown"
set(GIT_HASH "unknown")

# find Git and if available set GIT_HASH variable
find_package(Git QUIET)
if(GIT_FOUND)
  execute_process(
    COMMAND ${GIT_EXECUTABLE} log -1 --pretty=format:%h
    OUTPUT_VARIABLE GIT_HASH
    OUTPUT_STRIP_TRAILING_WHITESPACE
    ERROR_QUIET
    )
endif()

message(STATUS "Git hash is ${GIT_HASH}")

# generate file version.hpp based on version.hpp.in
configure_file(
  ${CMAKE_CURRENT_LIST_DIR}/version.hpp.in
  ${TARGET_DIR}/generated/version.hpp
  @ONLY
  )
```

2. The CMakeLists.txt is now left with a part that we recognize very well:

```
# set minimum cmake version
cmake_minimum_required(VERSION 3.5 FATAL_ERROR)

# project name and language
project(recipe-07 LANGUAGES CXX)

# require C++11
set(CMAKE_CXX_STANDARD 11)
set(CMAKE_CXX_EXTENSIONS OFF)
set(CMAKE_CXX_STANDARD_REQUIRED ON)

# example code
add_executable(example example.cpp)
```

```
    # needs to find the generated header file
    target_include_directories(example
      PRIVATE
        ${CMAKE_CURRENT_BINARY_DIR}/generated
      )
```

3. The remaining part of CMakeLists.txt records the Git hash every time we build the code, as follows:

```
add_custom_command(
  OUTPUT
    ${CMAKE_CURRENT_BINARY_DIR}/generated/version.hpp
    ALL
  COMMAND
    ${CMAKE_COMMAND} -D TARGET_DIR=${CMAKE_CURRENT_BINARY_DIR} -P
${CMAKE_CURRENT_SOURCE_DIR}/git-hash.cmake
  WORKING_DIRECTORY
    ${CMAKE_CURRENT_SOURCE_DIR}
  )

# rebuild version.hpp every time
add_custom_target(
  get_git_hash
  ALL
  DEPENDS
    ${CMAKE_CURRENT_BINARY_DIR}/generated/version.hpp
  )

# version.hpp has to be generated
# before we start building example
add_dependencies(example get_git_hash)
```

How it works

In this recipe, we achieved the execution of CMake code at build time. For this, we defined a custom command:

```
add_custom_command(
  OUTPUT
    ${CMAKE_CURRENT_BINARY_DIR}/generated/version.hpp
    ALL
  COMMAND
    ${CMAKE_COMMAND} -D TARGET_DIR=${CMAKE_CURRENT_BINARY_DIR} -P
${CMAKE_CURRENT_SOURCE_DIR}/git-hash.cmake
```

```
WORKING_DIRECTORY
  ${CMAKE_CURRENT_SOURCE_DIR}
)
```

We also defined a custom target, as follows:

```
add_custom_target(
  get_git_hash
  ALL
  DEPENDS
    ${CMAKE_CURRENT_BINARY_DIR}/generated/version.hpp
)
```

The custom command invokes CMake to execute the `git-hash.cmake` CMake script. This is achieved by using the `-P` CLI switch, to pass the location of the script. Notice that we can pass options with the `-D` CLI switch, as we usually would. The `git-hash.cmake` script generates `${TARGET_DIR}/generated/version.hpp`. The custom target is added to the `ALL` target, and depends on the output of the custom command. In other words, when we build the default target, we make sure that the custom command is run. Also, observe that the custom command has the `ALL` target as output. With that, we make sure that `version.hpp` is generated every time.

There is more

We could enhance the recipe in order to include extra information in addition to the recorded Git hash. It is not unusual to detect whether the build environment is "dirty", that is, whether it contains uncommitted changes and untracked files, or "clean". This information could be detected using `git describe --abbrev=7 --long --always --dirty --tags`. Depending on the ambition for reproducibility one could even record the full output of `git status` into a header file but we leave these enhancements as an exercise.

Structuring Projects

7

In this chapter, we will cover the following recipes:

- Code reuse with functions and macros
- Splitting CMake sources into modules
- Writing a function to test and set compiler flags
- Defining a function or macro with named arguments
- Redefining functions and macros
- Deprecating functions, macros, and variables
- Limiting scope with `add_subdirectory`
- Avoiding global variables using `target_sources`
- Organizing Fortran projects

Introduction

In the previous chapters, we have discovered a number of building blocks to create projects configured and built using CMake. In this chapter, we will discuss how to combine these building blocks and introduce abstractions to avoid huge `CMakeLists.txt` files and minimize code repetition, global variables, global state, and explicit ordering. Our goal will be to present patterns for a modular CMake code structure and for limiting the scope of variables. We will discuss strategies that will also help us control CMake code complexity for medium to large code projects.

Code reuse with functions and macros

The code for this recipe is available at `https://github.com/dev-cafe/cmake-cookbook/tree/v1.0/chapter-07/recipe-01` and has a C++ example. The recipe is valid with CMake version 3.5 (and higher) and has been tested on GNU/Linux, macOS, and Windows.

In any programming language, functions allow us to abstract (hide) details and avoid code repetition, and CMake is no exception. In this recipe, we will discuss macros and functions as an example, and we will introduce a macro to make it more convenient for us to define tests and set the ordering of tests. Instead of calling `add_test`
and `set_tests_properties` to define each set and to set the expected COST of each test (*Chapter 4, Creating and Running Tests, Recipe 8, Running tests in parallel*), our goal is to define a macro that will be able to take care of both in one go.

Getting ready

We will start with the example presented in *Chapter 4, Creating and Running Tests, Recipe 2, Defining a unit test using the Catch2 library*. The `main.cpp`, `sum_integers.cpp`, and `sum_integers.hpp` files are unchanged and can be used to compute the sum of integers provided as command line arguments. The source code for the unit tests (`test.cpp`) is used unchanged, as well. We also require the Catch2 header file, `catch.hpp`. In contrast to *Chapter 4, Creating and Running Tests, Recipe 2, Defining a unit test using the Catch2 library*, we will structure the source files into subdirectories and form the following file tree (we will discuss the CMake code later):

```
.
├── CMakeLists.txt
├── src
│   ├── CMakeLists.txt
│   ├── main.cpp
│   ├── sum_integers.cpp
│   └── sum_integers.hpp
└── tests
    ├── catch.hpp
    ├── CMakeLists.txt
    └── test.cpp
```

How to do it

Let us follow the required steps:

1. The top-level CMakeLists.txt defines the minimum CMake version, project name, and supported language, and requires the C++11 standard:

```
cmake_minimum_required(VERSION 3.5 FATAL_ERROR)
project(recipe-01 LANGUAGES CXX)

set(CMAKE_CXX_STANDARD 11)
set(CMAKE_CXX_EXTENSIONS OFF)
set(CMAKE_CXX_STANDARD_REQUIRED ON)
```

2. We further define binary and library paths according to GNU standards:

```
include(GNUInstallDirs)

set(CMAKE_ARCHIVE_OUTPUT_DIRECTORY
  ${CMAKE_BINARY_DIR}/${CMAKE_INSTALL_LIBDIR})
set(CMAKE_LIBRARY_OUTPUT_DIRECTORY
  ${CMAKE_BINARY_DIR}/${CMAKE_INSTALL_LIBDIR})
set(CMAKE_RUNTIME_OUTPUT_DIRECTORY
  ${CMAKE_BINARY_DIR}/${CMAKE_INSTALL_BINDIR})
```

3. And finally, we use add_subdirectory calls to structure our CMake code into src/CMakeLists.txt and tests/CMakeLists.txt parts. We also enable testing:

```
add_subdirectory(src)

enable_testing()
add_subdirectory(tests)
```

4. The src/CMakeLists.txt file defines the source code targets:

```
set(CMAKE_INCLUDE_CURRENT_DIR_IN_INTERFACE ON)
add_library(sum_integers sum_integers.cpp)

add_executable(sum_up main.cpp)

target_link_libraries(sum_up sum_integers)
```

5. In tests/CMakeLists.txt, we first build and link the cpp_test executable:

```
add_executable(cpp_test test.cpp)
target_link_libraries(cpp_test sum_integers)
```

6. We then define a new macro, `add_catch_test`, which we will discuss later:

```
macro(add_catch_test _name _cost)
  math(EXPR num_macro_calls "${num_macro_calls} + 1")
  message(STATUS "add_catch_test called with ${ARGC} arguments:
${ARGV}")

  set(_argn "${ARGN}")
  if(_argn)
    message(STATUS "oops - macro received argument(s) we did not
expect: ${ARGN}")
  endif()

  add_test(
    NAME
      ${_name}
    COMMAND
      $<TARGET_FILE:cpp_test>
      [${_name}] --success --out
      ${PROJECT_BINARY_DIR}/tests/${_name}.log --durations yes
    WORKING_DIRECTORY
      ${CMAKE_CURRENT_BINARY_DIR}
    )

  set_tests_properties(
    ${_name}
    PROPERTIES
      COST ${_cost}
    )
endmacro()
```

7. Finally, we define two tests using `add_catch_test` and in addition, we set and print the value of a variable:

```
set(num_macro_calls 0)

add_catch_test(short 1.5)
add_catch_test(long 2.5 extra_argument)

message(STATUS "in total there were ${num_macro_calls} calls to
add_catch_test")
```

8. Now, we are ready to test it out. First, we configure the project (the interesting output lines are shown):

```
$ mkdir -p build
$ cd build
$ cmake ..
```

```
-- ...
-- add_catch_test called with 2 arguments: short;1.5
-- add_catch_test called with 3 arguments: long;2.5;extra_argument
-- oops - macro received argument(s) we did not expect:
extra_argument
-- in total there were 2 calls to add_catch_test
-- ...
```

9. Finally, we build and run the tests:

```
$ cmake --build .
$ ctest
```

10. Observe that the long test is started first:

```
      Start 2: long
1/2 Test #2: long ........................... Passed 0.00 sec
      Start 1: short
2/2 Test #1: short .......................... Passed 0.00 sec

100% tests passed, 0 tests failed out of 2
```

How it works

The new feature in this recipe is the add_catch_test macro. The macro expects two arguments, _name and _cost, and we can use these arguments inside the macro to call add_test and set_tests_properties. The leading underscores are our choice, but with this we indicate to the reader that these arguments have local scope and can only be accessed within the macro. Also, note that the macro automatically populates ${ARGC} (number of arguments) and ${ARGV} (list of arguments), and we verified this in the output:

```
-- add_catch_test called with 2 arguments: short;1.5
-- add_catch_test called with 3 arguments: long;2.5;extra_argument
```

The macro also defines ${ARGN}, which holds the list of arguments past the last expected argument. In addition, we can also address arguments with ${ARGV0}, ${ARGV1}, and so on. Observe how we caught the unexpected argument (extra_argument) in this call:

```
add_catch_test(long 2.5 extra_argument)
```

We have done that using the following:

```
set(_argn "${ARGN}")
if(_argn)
  message(STATUS "oops - macro received argument(s) we did not expect:
${ARGN}")
endif()
```

In this if-check, we had to introduce a new variable and could not query `ARGN` directly since it is not a variable in the usual CMake sense. With this macro, we were not only able to define tests by their name and command but also indicate the expected cost, which led to the "long" test being started before the "short" test thanks to the `COST` property.

We could have implemented this using a function instead of a macro with the same syntax:

```
function(add_catch_test _name _cost)
  ...
endfunction()
```

The difference between macros and functions is their variable scope. Macros are executed in the scope of the caller whereas functions have own variable scope. In other words, if we need to set or modify variables that should be available to the caller, we typically use a macro. If no output variables are set or modified, we preferably use a function. We remark that it is possible to modify parent scope variables also in a function, but this has to be explicitly indicated using `PARENT_SCOPE`:

```
set(variable_visible_outside "some value" PARENT_SCOPE)
```

To demonstrate the scope, we have written the following call after the definition of the macro:

```
set(num_macro_calls 0)

add_catch_test(short 1.5)
add_catch_test(long 2.5 extra_argument)

message(STATUS "in total there were ${num_macro_calls} calls to
add_catch_test")
```

Inside the macro, we increase `num_macro_calls` by 1:

```
math(EXPR num_macro_calls "${num_macro_calls} + 1")
```

And this is the output produced:

```
-- in total there were 2 calls to add_catch_test
```

If we changed the macro to a function, the tests would still work but `num_macro_calls` would remain 0 throughout the calls in the parent scope. It is useful to imagine CMake macros as being like functions, which are substituted directly into the place where they are called (inlined in the C language sense). It is useful to imagine CMake functions as black boxes where nothing comes back unless you explicitly define it as `PARENT_SCOPE`. Functions in CMake do not have return values.

There is more

It is possible to nest function calls in macros and macro calls in functions, but we need to carefully consider the scope of the variables. If a feature can be implemented using a function, then this is probably preferable to a macro since it gives more default control over the parent scope state.

We should also mention the use of `CMAKE_INCLUDE_CURRENT_DIR_IN_INTERFACE` in `src/CMakeLists.txt`:

```
set(CMAKE_INCLUDE_CURRENT_DIR_IN_INTERFACE ON)
```

This command adds the current directory to the `INTERFACE_INCLUDE_DIRECTORIES` property for all targets defined in this `CMakeLists.txt` file. In other words, we did not have to use `target_include_directories` to indicate the header file location for `cpp_test`.

Splitting CMake sources into modules

The code for this recipe is available at `https://github.com/dev-cafe/cmake-cookbook/tree/v1.0/chapter-07/recipe-02`. The recipe is valid with CMake version 3.5 (and higher) and has been tested on GNU/Linux, macOS, and Windows.

Projects typically start with a single `CMakeLists.txt` file, but over time this file grows and in this recipe we will demonstrate one mechanism for splitting `CMakeLists.txt` up into smaller units. There are several motivations for splitting up `CMakeLists.txt` into modules that can be included in the main `CMakeLists.txt` or other modules:

- The main `CMakeLists.txt` is easier to read.
- CMake modules can be reused in other projects.
- In combination with functions, modules can help us limit the scope of variables.

In this recipe, we will demonstrate how to define and include a macro that allows us to get colored CMake output (for important status messages or warnings).

Getting ready

In this example, we will use two files, the main CMakeLists.txt and cmake/colors.cmake:

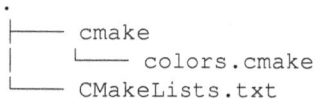

```
.
├──── cmake
│     └──── colors.cmake
└──── CMakeLists.txt
```

The cmake/colors.cmake file contains definitions for colored output:

```cmake
# colorize CMake output

# code adapted from stackoverflow: http://stackoverflow.com/a/19578320
# from post authored by https://stackoverflow.com/users/2556117/fraser

macro(define_colors)
  if(WIN32)
    # has no effect on WIN32
    set(ColourReset "")
    set(ColourBold "")
    set(Red "")
    set(Green "")
    set(Yellow "")
    set(Blue "")
    set(Magenta "")
    set(Cyan "")
    set(White "")
    set(BoldRed "")
    set(BoldGreen "")
    set(BoldYellow "")
    set(BoldBlue "")
    set(BoldMagenta "")
    set(BoldCyan "")
    set(BoldWhite "")
  else()
    string(ASCII 27 Esc)
    set(ColourReset "${Esc}[m")
    set(ColourBold "${Esc}[1m")
```

```
        set(Red "${Esc}[31m")
        set(Green "${Esc}[32m")
        set(Yellow "${Esc}[33m")
        set(Blue "${Esc}[34m")
        set(Magenta "${Esc}[35m")
        set(Cyan "${Esc}[36m")
        set(White "${Esc}[37m")
        set(BoldRed "${Esc}[1;31m")
        set(BoldGreen "${Esc}[1;32m")
        set(BoldYellow "${Esc}[1;33m")
        set(BoldBlue "${Esc}[1;34m")
        set(BoldMagenta "${Esc}[1;35m")
        set(BoldCyan "${Esc}[1;36m")
        set(BoldWhite "${Esc}[1;37m")
    endif()
endmacro()
```

How to do it

This is how we can use the color definitions to generate colored status messages:

1. We start out with a familiar preamble:

```
cmake_minimum_required(VERSION 3.5 FATAL_ERROR)
project(recipe-02 LANGUAGES NONE)
```

2. Then, we append the cmake subdirectory to the list of module paths that CMake will search:

```
list(APPEND CMAKE_MODULE_PATH "${CMAKE_CURRENT_SOURCE_DIR}/cmake")
```

3. We then include the colors.cmake module and call the macro defined within:

```
include(colors)
define_colors()
```

4. Finally, we print a couple of messages in different colors:

```
message(STATUS "This is a normal message")
message(STATUS "${Red}This is a red${ColourReset}")
message(STATUS "${BoldRed}This is a bold red${ColourReset}")
message(STATUS "${Green}This is a green${ColourReset}")
message(STATUS "${BoldMagenta}This is bold${ColourReset}")
```

5. Let us test it out (this output should appear colored on your screen if you use macOS or Linux):

```
-- This is a normal message
-- This is a red
-- This is a bold red
-- This is a green
-- This is bold
-- Configuring done
-- Generating done
-- Build files have been written to: /home/roberto/Workspace/robertodr/cmake-cookbook/chapter-07/recipe-02/example/build
```

How it works

This is an example where no code is compiled and no language support is required, and we have indicated this by LANGUAGES NONE:

```
project(recipe-02 LANGUAGES NONE)
```

We defined the define_colors macro and placed it in cmake/colors.cmake. We chose to use a macro and not a function since we also wish to use the variables defined inside the macro in the scope of the call to change colors in the messages. We have included the macro and called define_colors using the following lines:

```
include(colors)
define_colors()
```

However, we also need to tell CMake where to look for the macro:

```
list(APPEND CMAKE_MODULE_PATH "${CMAKE_CURRENT_SOURCE_DIR}/cmake")
```

The include(colors) command instructs CMake to search ${CMAKE_MODULE_PATH} for a module with the name colors.cmake.

Instead of writing the following:

```
list(APPEND CMAKE_MODULE_PATH "${CMAKE_CURRENT_SOURCE_DIR}/cmake")

include(colors)
```

We could have used an explicit include as follows:

```
include(cmake/colors.cmake)
```

There is more

The recommended practice is to define macros or functions in modules and then call the macro or function. It is not good practice to use module includes as function calls. Including a module should not do more than defining functions and macros and discovering programs, libraries, and paths. The actual include command should not define or modify variables and the reason for this is that a repeated include, which may be accidental, should not introduce any unwanted side effects. In *Recipe 5, Redefining functions and macros*, we will create a guard against accidental includes.

Writing a function to test and set compiler flags

The code for this recipe is available at https://github.com/dev-cafe/
cmake-cookbook/tree/v1.0/chapter-07/recipe-03 and has a C/C++
example. The recipe is valid with CMake version 3.5 (and higher) and has
been tested on GNU/Linux, macOS, and Windows.

In the previous two recipes, we used macros; in this recipe, we will use a function to abstract away details and avoid code repetition. In the example, we will implement a function that accepts a list of compiler flags. The function will try to compile a test code with these flags, one by one, and return the first flag that was understood by the compiler. By doing so, we will learn a couple of new features: functions, list manipulations, string manipulations, and checking whether compiler flags are supported by the compiler.

Getting ready

Following the recommended practice of the previous recipe, we will define the function in a module (`set_compiler_flag.cmake`), include the module, and then call the function. The module contains the following code, which we will discuss later:

```
include(CheckCCompilerFlag)
include(CheckCXXCompilerFlag)
include(CheckFortranCompilerFlag)
function(set_compiler_flag _result _lang)
  # build a list of flags from the arguments
  set(_list_of_flags)
```

```
    # also figure out whether the function
    # is required to find a flag
    set(_flag_is_required FALSE)
    foreach(_arg IN ITEMS ${ARGN})
      string(TOUPPER "${_arg}" _arg_uppercase)
      if(_arg_uppercase STREQUAL "REQUIRED")
        set(_flag_is_required TRUE)
      else()
        list(APPEND _list_of_flags "${_arg}")
      endif()
    endforeach()

    set(_flag_found FALSE)
    # loop over all flags, try to find the first which works
    foreach(flag IN ITEMS ${_list_of_flags})

      unset(_flag_works CACHE)
      if(_lang STREQUAL "C")
        check_c_compiler_flag("${flag}" _flag_works)
      elseif(_lang STREQUAL "CXX")
        check_cxx_compiler_flag("${flag}" _flag_works)
      elseif(_lang STREQUAL "Fortran")
        check_Fortran_compiler_flag("${flag}" _flag_works)
      else()
        message(FATAL_ERROR "Unknown language in set_compiler_flag:
${_lang}")
      endif()

      # if the flag works, use it, and exit
      # otherwise try next flag
      if(_flag_works)
        set(${_result} "${flag}" PARENT_SCOPE)
        set(_flag_found TRUE)
        break()
      endif()
    endforeach()

    # raise an error if no flag was found
    if(_flag_is_required AND NOT _flag_found)
      message(FATAL_ERROR "None of the required flags were supported")
    endif()
endfunction()
```

How to do it

This is how we can use the `set_compiler_flag` function in our `CMakeLists.txt`:

1. In the preamble, we define the minimum CMake version, project name, and supported languages (in this case, C and C++):

```
cmake_minimum_required(VERSION 3.5 FATAL_ERROR)
project(recipe-03 LANGUAGES C CXX)
```

2. Then, we include `set_compiler_flag.cmake`, in this case explicitly:

```
include(set_compiler_flag.cmake)
```

3. Then, we try a list of C flags:

```
set_compiler_flag(
  working_compile_flag C REQUIRED
  "-foo"             # this should fail
  "-wrong"           # this should fail
  "-wrong"           # this should fail
  "-Wall"            # this should work with GNU
  "-warn all"        # this should work with Intel
  "-Minform=inform"  # this should work with PGI
  "-nope"            # this should fail
  )

message(STATUS "working C compile flag: ${working_compile_flag}")
```

4. And we try a list of C++ flags:

```
set_compiler_flag(
  working_compile_flag CXX REQUIRED
  "-foo"   # this should fail
  "-g"     # this should work with GNU, Intel, PGI
  "/RTCcsu" # this should work with MSVC
  )

message(STATUS "working CXX compile flag: ${working_compile_flag}")
```

5. Now, we can configure the project and verify the output. Only the relevant output is shown and the output may differ depending on the compiler:

```
$ mkdir -p build
$ cd build
$ cmake ..
```

```
-- ...
-- Performing Test _flag_works
-- Performing Test _flag_works - Failed
-- Performing Test _flag_works
-- Performing Test _flag_works - Failed
-- Performing Test _flag_works
-- Performing Test _flag_works - Failed
-- Performing Test _flag_works
-- Performing Test _flag_works - Success
-- working C compile flag: -Wall
-- Performing Test _flag_works
-- Performing Test _flag_works - Failed
-- Performing Test _flag_works
-- Performing Test _flag_works - Success
-- working CXX compile flag: -g
-- ...
```

How it works

The pattern that we have used here is:

1. Define a function or macro and place it in a module
2. Include the module
3. Call the function or macro

From the output, we can see that the code checks each flag in the list and as soon as the check is successful, it prints the successful compile flag. Let us look inside the `set_compiler_flag.cmake` module. This module, in turn, includes three modules:

```
include(CheckCCompilerFlag)
include(CheckCXXCompilerFlag)
include(CheckFortranCompilerFlag)
```

These are standard CMake modules and CMake will locate them in `${CMAKE_MODULE_PATH}`. These modules provide the `check_c_compiler_flag`, `check_cxx_compiler_flag`, and `check_fortran_compiler_flag` macros, respectively. Then comes the function definition:

```
function(set_compiler_flag _result _lang)
  ...
endfunction()
```

The `set_compiler_flag` function expects two arguments and we call them `_result` (this will hold the successful compile flag or the empty string "") and `_lang` (which specifies the language: C, C++, or Fortran).

We would like to be able to call the function like this:

```
set_compiler_flag(working_compile_flag C REQUIRED "-Wall" "-warn all")
```

This call has five arguments, but the function header only expects two. This means that `REQUIRED`, `"-Wall"`, and `"-warn all"` will be placed in `${ARGN}`. From `${ARGN}`, we first build a list of flags using `foreach`. At the same time, we filter out `REQUIRED` from the list of flags and use it to set `_flag_is_required`:

```
# build a list of flags from the arguments
set(_list_of_flags)
# also figure out whether the function
# is required to find a flag
set(_flag_is_required FALSE)
foreach(_arg IN ITEMS ${ARGN})
  string(TOUPPER "${_arg}" _arg_uppercase)
  if(_arg_uppercase STREQUAL "REQUIRED")
    set(_flag_is_required TRUE)
  else()
    list(APPEND _list_of_flags "${_arg}")
  endif()
endforeach()
```

Now, we will loop over `${_list_of_flags}`, try each flag, and if `_flag_works` is set to TRUE, we set `_flag_found` to TRUE and abort a further search:

```
set(_flag_found FALSE)
# loop over all flags, try to find the first which works
foreach(flag IN ITEMS ${_list_of_flags})

  unset(_flag_works CACHE)
  if(_lang STREQUAL "C")
    check_c_compiler_flag("${flag}" _flag_works)
  elseif(_lang STREQUAL "CXX")
    check_cxx_compiler_flag("${flag}" _flag_works)
  elseif(_lang STREQUAL "Fortran")
    check_Fortran_compiler_flag("${flag}" _flag_works)
  else()
    message(FATAL_ERROR "Unknown language in set_compiler_flag: ${_lang}")
  endif()
```

```
   # if the flag works, use it, and exit
   # otherwise try next flag
   if(_flag_works)
     set(${_result} "${flag}" PARENT_SCOPE)
     set(_flag_found TRUE)
     break()
   endif()
 endforeach()
```

The `unset(_flag_works CACHE)` line is there to make sure that the result of `check_*_compiler_flag` is not cached between calls using the same `_flag_works` result variable.

If a flag is found and `_flag_works` set to `TRUE`, we define the variable mapped to by `_result`:

```
   set(${_result} "${flag}" PARENT_SCOPE)
```

This needs to be done with `PARENT_SCOPE` since we are modifying a variable that we wish to print and use outside the function body. Note, in addition, how we dereferenced the variable `_result` passed from parent scope using the `${_result}` syntax. This is necessary to ensure that the working flag is set as value of the variable passed from parent scope when invoking the function, regardless of its name. If no flag is found and the `REQUIRED` keyword was provided, we stop the configuration with an error message:

```
   # raise an error if no flag was found
   if(_flag_is_required AND NOT _flag_found)
     message(FATAL_ERROR "None of the required flags were supported")
   endif()
```

There is more

We could have achieved this task with a macro, but with a function, we have more control over the scope. We know that the only variable that can be modified by the function is the result variable.

Also, note that some flags need to be set both at compile and link time by setting `CMAKE_REQUIRED_FLAGS` for the `check_<LANG>_compiler_flag` function to report success correctly. This was the case for the sanitizers, as we discussed in *Chapter 5, Configure-time and Build-time Operations, Recipe 7, Probing compiler flags*.

Defining a function or macro with named arguments

The code for this recipe is available at `https://github.com/dev-cafe/cmake-cookbook/tree/v1.0/chapter-07/recipe-04` and has a C++ example. The recipe is valid with CMake version 3.5 (and higher) and has been tested on GNU/Linux, macOS, and Windows.

In the previous recipes, we explored functions and macros and used positional arguments. In this recipe, we will define a function with named arguments. We will enhance the example from *Recipe 1, Code reuse with functions and macros* and instead of defining tests using the following:

```
add_catch_test(short 1.5)
```

We will be able to call the following:

```
add_catch_test(
  NAME
    short
  LABELS
    short
    cpp_test
  COST
    1.5
  )
```

Getting ready

We will use the example from *Recipe 1, Code reuse with functions and macros* and keep the C++ sources unchanged and the file tree essentially the same:

```
.
├── cmake
│   └── testing.cmake
├── CMakeLists.txt
├── src
│   ├── CMakeLists.txt
│   ├── main.cpp
│   ├── sum_integers.cpp
│   └── sum_integers.hpp
```

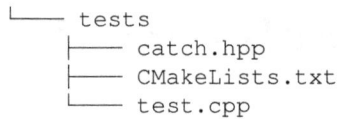

```
└──── tests
    ├──── catch.hpp
    ├──── CMakeLists.txt
    └──── test.cpp
```

How to do it

We will introduce small modifications in the CMake code, as shown here:

1. Only one additional line is added in the top-level CMakeLists.txt, since we will include a module located under cmake:

   ```
   list(APPEND CMAKE_MODULE_PATH "${CMAKE_CURRENT_SOURCE_DIR}/cmake")
   ```

2. We keep src/CMakeLists.txt unmodified.
3. In tests/CMakeLists.txt, we move the add_catch_test function definition to cmake/testing.cmake and define two tests:

   ```
   add_executable(cpp_test test.cpp)
   target_link_libraries(cpp_test sum_integers)

   include(testing)

   add_catch_test(
     NAME
       short
     LABELS
       short
       cpp_test
     COST
       1.5
     )

   add_catch_test(
     NAME
       long
     LABELS
       long
       cpp_test
     COST
       2.5
     )
   ```

4. The `add_catch_test` function is now defined in `cmake/testing.cmake`:

```
function(add_catch_test)
  set(options)
  set(oneValueArgs NAME COST)
  set(multiValueArgs LABELS DEPENDS REFERENCE_FILES)
  cmake_parse_arguments(add_catch_test
    "${options}"
    "${oneValueArgs}"
    "${multiValueArgs}"
    ${ARGN}
    )

  message(STATUS "defining a test ...")
  message(STATUS " NAME: ${add_catch_test_NAME}")
  message(STATUS " LABELS: ${add_catch_test_LABELS}")
  message(STATUS " COST: ${add_catch_test_COST}")
  message(STATUS " REFERENCE_FILES:
${add_catch_test_REFERENCE_FILES}")

  add_test(
    NAME
      ${add_catch_test_NAME}
    COMMAND
      $<TARGET_FILE:cpp_test>
      [${add_catch_test_NAME}] --success --out
      ${PROJECT_BINARY_DIR}/tests/${add_catch_test_NAME}.log --
durations yes
    WORKING_DIRECTORY
      ${CMAKE_CURRENT_BINARY_DIR}
    )

  set_tests_properties(${add_catch_test_NAME}
    PROPERTIES
      LABELS "${add_catch_test_LABELS}"
    )

  if(add_catch_test_COST)
    set_tests_properties(${add_catch_test_NAME}
      PROPERTIES
        COST ${add_catch_test_COST}
      )
  endif()

  if(add_catch_test_DEPENDS)
    set_tests_properties(${add_catch_test_NAME}
      PROPERTIES
        DEPENDS ${add_catch_test_DEPENDS}
```

```
      )
    endif()

    if(add_catch_test_REFERENCE_FILES)
      file(
        COPY
          ${add_catch_test_REFERENCE_FILES}
        DESTINATION
          ${CMAKE_CURRENT_BINARY_DIR}
        )
    endif()
endfunction()
```

5. We are ready to test the output. First, we configure the following:

```
$ mkdir -p build
$ cd build
$ cmake ..

-- ...
-- defining a test ...
--      NAME: short
--      LABELS: short;cpp_test
--      COST: 1.5
--      REFERENCE_FILES:
-- defining a test ...
--      NAME: long
--      LABELS: long;cpp_test
--      COST: 2.5
--      REFERENCE_FILES:
-- ...
```

6. Then, compile and test the code:

```
$ cmake --build .
$ ctest
```

How it works

The new aspects in this recipe are the named arguments so we can focus on the cmake/testing.cmake module. CMake provides the cmake_parse_arguments command, which we call with the function name (add_catch_test) options (in our case, none), one-value arguments (here, NAME and COST), and multi-value arguments (here, LABELS, DEPENDS, and REFERENCE_FILES):

```
function(add_catch_test)
  set(options)
  set(oneValueArgs NAME COST)
  set(multiValueArgs LABELS DEPENDS REFERENCE_FILES)
  cmake_parse_arguments(add_catch_test
    "${options}"
    "${oneValueArgs}"
    "${multiValueArgs}"
    ${ARGN}
    )
  ...
endfunction()
```

The `cmake_parse_arguments` command parses options and arguments, and defines the following in our case:

- `add_catch_test_NAME`
- `add_catch_test_COST`
- `add_catch_test_LABELS`
- `add_catch_test_DEPENDS`
- `add_catch_test_REFERENCE_FILES`

We can then query and use these variables inside our function. This approach gives us the chance to implement functions and macros with more robust interfaces and more readable function/macro calls.

There is more

Option keywords (which we have not used in this example) are defined by `cmake_parse_arguments` to either `TRUE` or `FALSE`. A further enhancement of the `add_catch_test` function could be to also provide the test command as a named argument, which we have omitted for the benefit of a more concise example.

> The `cmake_parse_arguments` command was made available within the `CMakeParseArguments.cmake` module prior to the release of CMake 3.5. Thus, this recipe can be made to work with earlier versions of CMake by using the `include(CMakeParseArguments)` command at the top of the `cmake/testing.cmake` module file.

Redefining functions and macros

The code for this recipe is available at `https://github.com/dev-cafe/cmake-cookbook/tree/v1.0/chapter-07/recipe-05`. The recipe is valid with CMake version 3.5 (and higher) and has been tested on GNU/Linux, macOS, and Windows.

We have mentioned that module includes *should not* be used as function calls since modules could be (accidentally) included multiple times. In this recipe, we will program our own simple include guard, which will warn us if we try to include a module multiple times. The built-in `include_guard` command is available in CMake since version 3.10 and behaves like `#pragma once` for C/C++ header files. For this version of CMake, we will discuss and demonstrate how functions and macros can be redefined. We will show how we can check the CMake version and for versions below 3.10, we will use our custom include guard.

Getting ready

In this example, we will use three files:

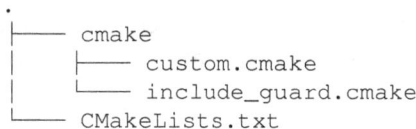

```
.
├── cmake
│   ├── custom.cmake
│   └── include_guard.cmake
└── CMakeLists.txt
```

The custom `custom.cmake` module contains the following code:

```
include_guard(GLOBAL)
message(STATUS "custom.cmake is included and processed")
```

We will discuss `cmake/include_guard.cmake` and `CMakeLists.txt` later.

How to do it

This is a step-by-step breakdown of our three CMake files:

1. In this recipe, we will not compile any code and our language requirement is therefore `NONE`:

```
cmake_minimum_required(VERSION 3.5 FATAL_ERROR)
project(recipe-05 LANGUAGES NONE)
```

2. We then define an `include_guard` macro, which we place in a separate module:

```
# (re)defines include_guard
include(cmake/include_guard.cmake)
```

3. The `cmake/include_guard.cmake` file contains the following (we will discuss it in detail shortly):

```
macro(include_guard)
  if (CMAKE_VERSION VERSION_LESS "3.10")
    # for CMake below 3.10 we define our
    # own include_guard(GLOBAL)
    message(STATUS "calling our custom include_guard")

    # if this macro is called the first time
    # we start with an empty list
    if(NOT DEFINED included_modules)
        set(included_modules)
    endif()

    if ("${CMAKE_CURRENT_LIST_FILE}" IN_LIST included_modules)
      message(WARNING "module ${CMAKE_CURRENT_LIST_FILE} processed
more than once")
    endif()

    list(APPEND included_modules ${CMAKE_CURRENT_LIST_FILE})
  else()
    # for CMake 3.10 or higher we augment
    # the built-in include_guard
    message(STATUS "calling the built-in include_guard")

    _include_guard(${ARGV})
  endif()
endmacro()
```

4. In the main `CMakeLists.txt`, we then simulate including the custom module accidentally twice:

```
include(cmake/custom.cmake)
include(cmake/custom.cmake)
```

5. Finally, we configure with the following commands:

```
$ mkdir -p build
$ cd build
$ cmake ..
```

6. The result using CMake 3.10 and higher is as follows:

```
-- calling the built-in include_guard
-- custom.cmake is included and processed
-- calling the built-in include_guard
```

7. The result using CMake below 3.10 is as follows:

```
-- calling our custom include_guard
-- custom.cmake is included and processed
-- calling our custom include_guard
CMake Warning at cmake/include_guard.cmake:7 (message):
  module
  /home/user/example/cmake/custom.cmake
  processed more than once
Call Stack (most recent call first):
  cmake/custom.cmake:1 (include_guard)
  CMakeLists.txt:12 (include)
```

How it works

Our `include_guard` macro contains two branches, one for CMake below 3.10 and one for CMake 3.10 and higher:

```
macro(include_guard)
  if (CMAKE_VERSION VERSION_LESS "3.10")
    # ...
  else()
    # ...
  endif()
endmacro()
```

If CMake version is below 3.10, we enter the first branch and an intrinsic `include_guard` is not available, so we define our own:

```
message(STATUS "calling our custom include_guard")

# if this macro is called the first time
# we start with an empty list
if(NOT DEFINED included_modules)
    set(included_modules)
endif()

if ("${CMAKE_CURRENT_LIST_FILE}" IN_LIST included_modules)
  message(WARNING "module ${CMAKE_CURRENT_LIST_FILE} processed more than
once")
```

```
endif()

list(APPEND included_modules ${CMAKE_CURRENT_LIST_FILE})
```

If the macro is called the first time, then the `included_modules` variable is not defined so we set it to an empty list. We then check whether `${CMAKE_CURRENT_LIST_FILE}` is an element of the `included_modules` list. If yes, we issue a warning. If no, we append `${CMAKE_CURRENT_LIST_FILE}` to this list. In the CMake output, we can verify that a second include of the custom module indeed leads to the warning.

The situation is different for CMake 3.10 and higher; in this case, an intrinsic `include_guard` exists and we call it with the arguments received by our own macro:

```
macro(include_guard)
  if (CMAKE_VERSION VERSION_LESS "3.10")
    # ...
  else()
    message(STATUS "calling the built-in include_guard")

    _include_guard(${ARGV})
  endif()
endmacro()
```

Here, `_include_guard(${ARGV})` points to the built-in `include_guard`. In this case, we have augmented the built-in command with a custom message ("calling the built-in `include_guard`"). This pattern provides us with a mechanism to redefine own or built-in functions and macros. This can be useful for debugging or logging purposes.

> This pattern can be useful but it should be applied with care since CMake will not warn about the redefinition of macros or functions.

Deprecating functions, macros, and variables

> The code for this recipe is available at `https://github.com/dev-cafe/cmake-cookbook/tree/v1.0/chapter-07/recipe-06`. The recipe is valid with CMake version 3.5 (and higher) and has been tested on GNU/Linux, macOS, and Windows.

Deprecation is an important mechanism in the development of an evolving project to signal to developers that a function or macro or a variable will be removed or replaced at some point in the future. For a certain period, the function, macro, or variable will continue being accessible but signal a warning, which eventually can be elevated to an error.

Getting ready

We will start out with the following CMake project:

```
cmake_minimum_required(VERSION 3.5 FATAL_ERROR)

project(recipe-06 LANGUAGES NONE)

macro(custom_include_guard)
  if(NOT DEFINED included_modules)
    set(included_modules)
  endif()

  if ("${CMAKE_CURRENT_LIST_FILE}" IN_LIST included_modules)
    message(WARNING "module ${CMAKE_CURRENT_LIST_FILE} processed more than
once")
  endif()

  list(APPEND included_modules ${CMAKE_CURRENT_LIST_FILE})
endmacro()

include(cmake/custom.cmake)

message(STATUS "list of all included modules: ${included_modules}")
```

This code defines a custom include guard, includes a custom module (the same module as in the previous recipe), and prints the list of all included modules. For CMake 3.10 and higher, we now know from the previous recipe that there is a built-in `include_guard`. But instead of simply removing `custom_include_guard` and `${included_modules}`, we will deprecate the macro and the variable with a deprecation warning, which at some point we can flip into a `FATAL_ERROR` to make the code stop and force the developers to switch to the built-in command.

How to do it

Deprecating functions, macros, and variables can be done as follows:

1. First, we define a function that we will use to deprecate a variable:

```
function(deprecate_variable _variable _access)
  if(_access STREQUAL "READ_ACCESS")
    message(DEPRECATION "variable ${_variable} is deprecated")
  endif()
endfunction()
```

2. Then, if the version of CMake is greater than 3.9, we redefine `custom_include_guard` and attach `variable_watch` to `included_modules`:

```
if (CMAKE_VERSION VERSION_GREATER "3.9")
  # deprecate custom_include_guard
  macro(custom_include_guard)
    message(DEPRECATION "custom_include_guard is deprecated - use
built-in include_guard instead")
    _custom_include_guard(${ARGV})
  endmacro()

  # deprecate variable included_modules
  variable_watch(included_modules deprecate_variable)
endif()
```

3. Configuring the project on CMake below version 3.10 produces the following:

```
$ mkdir -p build
$ cd build
$ cmake ..

-- custom.cmake is included and processed
-- list of all included modules:
/home/user/example/cmake/custom.cmake
```

4. CMake 3.10 and higher will produce the expected deprecation warnings:

```
CMake Deprecation Warning at CMakeLists.txt:26 (message):
  custom_include_guard is deprecated - use built-in include_guard
instead
Call Stack (most recent call first):
  cmake/custom.cmake:1 (custom_include_guard)
  CMakeLists.txt:34 (include)
```

```
-- custom.cmake is included and processed
CMake Deprecation Warning at CMakeLists.txt:19 (message):
  variable included_modules is deprecated
Call Stack (most recent call first):
  CMakeLists.txt:9999 (deprecate_variable)
  CMakeLists.txt:36 (message)


-- list of all included modules:
/home/user/example/cmake/custom.cmake
```

How it works

Deprecating a function or a macro is equivalent to redefining it, as demonstrated in the previous recipe, and printing a message with DEPRECATION:

```
macro(somemacro)
  message(DEPRECATION "somemacro is deprecated")
  _somemacro(${ARGV})
endmacro()
```

Deprecating a variable can be achieved by first defining the following:

```
function(deprecate_variable _variable _access)
  if(_access STREQUAL "READ_ACCESS")
    message(DEPRECATION "variable ${_variable} is deprecated")
  endif()
endfunction()
```

This function is then attached to the variable that is about to be deprecated:

```
variable_watch(somevariable deprecate_variable)
```

If in this case ${included_modules} is read (READ_ACCESS), then the deprecate_variable function issues the message with DEPRECATION.

Limiting scope with add_subdirectory

The code for this recipe is available at https://github.com/dev-cafe/cmake-cookbook/tree/v1.0/chapter-07/recipe-07 and has a C++ example. The recipe is valid with CMake version 3.5 (and higher) and has been tested on GNU/Linux, macOS, and Windows.

In the remaining recipes of this chapter, we will discuss strategies to structure projects and limit the scope of variables and side effects with the goal to lower code complexity and simplify the maintenance of the project. In this recipe, we will split a project into several `CMakeLists.txt` files with limited scope, which will be processed using the `add_subdirectory` command.

Getting ready

Since we wish to show and discuss how to structure a non-trivial project, we need an example that is more than a "hello world" project. We will develop a relatively simple code that can compute and print elementary cellular automata:

- `https://en.wikipedia.org/wiki/Cellular_automaton#Elementary_cellular_automata`
- `http://mathworld.wolfram.com/ElementaryCellularAutomaton.html`

Our code will be able to compute any of the 256 elementary cellular automata, for instance rule 90 (Wolfram code):

```
$ ./bin/automata 40 15 90

length: 40
number of steps: 15
rule: 90
                        *
                      *   *
                    *       *
                  *   *   *   *
                *               *
              *   *           *   *
            *       *       *       *
          *   *   *   *   *   *   *   *
        *                               *
      *   *                           *   *
    *       *                       *       *
  *   *   *   *                   *   *   *   *
*               *               *               *
  *   *       *   *           *   *       *   *
*       *   *       *       *       *   *       *
  *   *   *   *   *   *   *   *   *   *   *   *
```

The structure of our example code project is as follows:

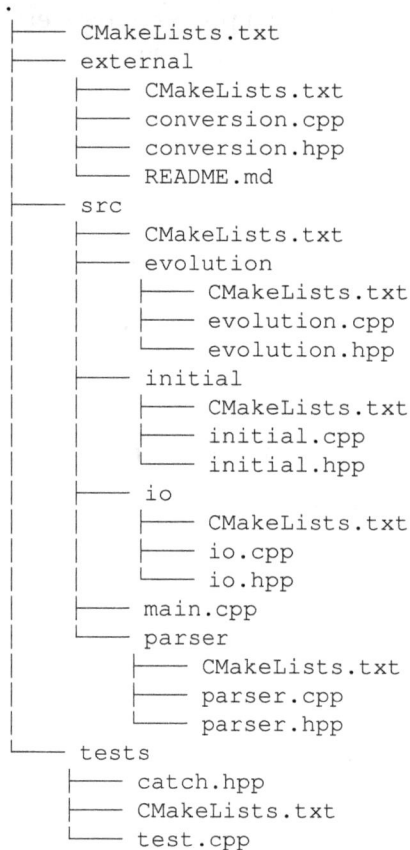

```
.
├── CMakeLists.txt
├── external
│   ├── CMakeLists.txt
│   ├── conversion.cpp
│   ├── conversion.hpp
│   └── README.md
├── src
│   ├── CMakeLists.txt
│   ├── evolution
│   │   ├── CMakeLists.txt
│   │   ├── evolution.cpp
│   │   └── evolution.hpp
│   ├── initial
│   │   ├── CMakeLists.txt
│   │   ├── initial.cpp
│   │   └── initial.hpp
│   ├── io
│   │   ├── CMakeLists.txt
│   │   ├── io.cpp
│   │   └── io.hpp
│   ├── main.cpp
│   └── parser
│       ├── CMakeLists.txt
│       ├── parser.cpp
│       └── parser.hpp
└── tests
    ├── catch.hpp
    ├── CMakeLists.txt
    └── test.cpp
```

Here, we have split the code into many libraries to simulate a real-world medium to large project, where sources can be organized into libraries that are then linked into an executable.

The main function is in `src/main.cpp`:

```cpp
#include "conversion.hpp"
#include "evolution.hpp"
#include "initial.hpp"
#include "io.hpp"
#include "parser.hpp"

#include <iostream>
```

```
int main(int argc, char *argv[]) {

  // parse arguments
  int length, num_steps, rule_decimal;
  std::tie(length, num_steps, rule_decimal) = parse_arguments(argc, argv);

  // print information about parameters
  std::cout << "length: " << length << std::endl;
  std::cout << "number of steps: " << num_steps << std::endl;
  std::cout << "rule: " << rule_decimal << std::endl;

  // obtain binary representation for the rule
  std::string rule_binary = binary_representation(rule_decimal);

  // create initial distribution
  std::vector<int> row = initial_distribution(length);

  // print initial configuration
  print_row(row);

  // the system evolves, print each step
  for (int step = 0; step < num_steps; step++) {
    row = evolve(row, rule_binary);
    print_row(row);
  }
}
```

The `external/conversion.cpp` file contains code to convert from decimal to binary. We simulate here that this code is provided by an "external" library outside of `src`:

```
#include "conversion.hpp"
#include <bitset>
#include <string>

std::string binary_representation(const int decimal) {
  return std::bitset<8>(decimal).to_string();
}
```

The `src/evolution/evolution.cpp` file propagates the system in a time step:

```
#include "evolution.hpp"
#include <string>
#include <vector>

std::vector<int> evolve(const std::vector<int> row, const std::string
rule_binary) {
  std::vector<int> result;
```

```
    for (auto i = 0; i < row.size(); ++i) {

      auto left = (i == 0 ? row.size() : i) - 1;
      auto center = i;
      auto right = (i + 1) % row.size();

      auto ancestors = 4 * row[left] + 2 * row[center] + 1 * row[right];
      ancestors = 7 - ancestors;

      auto new_state = std::stoi(rule_binary.substr(ancestors, 1));

      result.push_back(new_state);
    }

    return result;
}
```

The `src/initial/initial.cpp` file produces the initial state:

```
#include "initial.hpp"
#include <vector>

std::vector<int> initial_distribution(const int length) {

  // we start with a vector which is zeroed out
  std::vector<int> result(length, 0);

  // more or less in the middle we place a living cell
  result[length / 2] = 1;

  return result;
}
```

The `src/io/io.cpp` file contains a function to print a row:

```
#include "io.hpp"
#include <algorithm>
#include <iostream>
#include <vector>

void print_row(const std::vector<int> row) {
  std::for_each(row.begin(), row.end(), [](int const &value) {
    std::cout << (value == 1 ? '*' : ' ');
  });
  std::cout << std::endl;
}
```

The `src/parser/parser.cpp` file parses the command-line input:

```cpp
#include "parser.hpp"
#include <cassert>
#include <string>
#include <tuple>

std::tuple<int, int, int> parse_arguments(int argc, char *argv[]) {
    assert(argc == 4 && "program called with wrong number of arguments");

    auto length = std::stoi(argv[1]);
    auto num_steps = std::stoi(argv[2]);
    auto rule_decimal = std::stoi(argv[3]);

    return std::make_tuple(length, num_steps, rule_decimal);
}
```

And finally, `tests/test.cpp` contains two unit tests using the Catch2 library:

```cpp
#include "evolution.hpp"
// this tells catch to provide a main()
// only do this in one cpp file
#define CATCH_CONFIG_MAIN
#include "catch.hpp"

#include <string>
#include <vector>

TEST_CASE("Apply rule 90", "[rule-90]") {
    std::vector<int> row = {0, 1, 0, 1, 0, 1, 0, 1, 0};
    std::string rule = "01011010";
    std::vector<int> expected_result = {1, 0, 0, 0, 0, 0, 0, 0, 1};
    REQUIRE(evolve(row, rule) == expected_result);
}

TEST_CASE("Apply rule 222", "[rule-222]") {
    std::vector<int> row = {0, 0, 0, 0, 1, 0, 0, 0, 0};
    std::string rule = "11011110";
    std::vector<int> expected_result = {0, 0, 0, 1, 1, 1, 0, 0, 0};
    REQUIRE(evolve(row, rule) == expected_result);
}
```

The corresponding header files contain the function signatures. One could argue that the project contains too many subdirectories for this little code example, but please remember that this is only a simplified example of a project typically containing many source files for each library, ideally organized into separate directories like here.

How to do it

Let us dive into a detailed explanation of the CMake infrastructure needed:

1. The top-level CMakeLists.txt is very similar to *Recipe 1, Code reuse with functions and macros*:

```
cmake_minimum_required(VERSION 3.5 FATAL_ERROR)
project(recipe-07 LANGUAGES CXX)

set(CMAKE_CXX_STANDARD 11)
set(CMAKE_CXX_EXTENSIONS OFF)
set(CMAKE_CXX_STANDARD_REQUIRED ON)

include(GNUInstallDirs)
set(CMAKE_ARCHIVE_OUTPUT_DIRECTORY
  ${CMAKE_BINARY_DIR}/${CMAKE_INSTALL_LIBDIR})
set(CMAKE_LIBRARY_OUTPUT_DIRECTORY
  ${CMAKE_BINARY_DIR}/${CMAKE_INSTALL_LIBDIR})
set(CMAKE_RUNTIME_OUTPUT_DIRECTORY
  ${CMAKE_BINARY_DIR}/${CMAKE_INSTALL_BINDIR})

# defines targets and sources
add_subdirectory(src)

# contains an "external" library we will link to
add_subdirectory(external)

# enable testing and define tests
enable_testing()
add_subdirectory(tests)
```

2. Targets and sources are defined in src/CMakeLists.txt (except the conversion target):

```
add_executable(automata main.cpp)
add_subdirectory(evolution)
add_subdirectory(initial)
add_subdirectory(io)
add_subdirectory(parser)

target_link_libraries(automata
  PRIVATE
    conversion
    evolution
    initial
    io
```

```
        parser
    )
```

3. The conversion library is defined in `external/CMakeLists.txt`:

```
add_library(conversion "")

target_sources(conversion
  PRIVATE
    ${CMAKE_CURRENT_LIST_DIR}/conversion.cpp
  PUBLIC
    ${CMAKE_CURRENT_LIST_DIR}/conversion.hpp
  )

target_include_directories(conversion
  PUBLIC
    ${CMAKE_CURRENT_LIST_DIR}
  )
```

4. The `src/CMakeLists.txt` file adds further subdirectories, which in turn contain `CMakeLists.txt` files. They are all similar in structure; `src/evolution/CMakeLists.txt` contains the following:

```
add_library(evolution "")

target_sources(evolution
  PRIVATE
    evolution.cpp
  PUBLIC
    ${CMAKE_CURRENT_LIST_DIR}/evolution.hpp
  )
target_include_directories(evolution
  PUBLIC
    ${CMAKE_CURRENT_LIST_DIR}
  )
```

5. The unit tests are registered in `tests/CMakeLists.txt`:

```
add_executable(cpp_test test.cpp)

target_link_libraries(cpp_test evolution)

add_test(
  NAME
    test_evolution
  COMMAND
    $<TARGET_FILE:cpp_test>
  )
```

6. Configuring and building the project yields the following output:

```
$ mkdir -p build
$ cd build
$ cmake ..
$ cmake --build .

Scanning dependencies of target conversion
[ 7%] Building CXX object
external/CMakeFiles/conversion.dir/conversion.cpp.o
[ 14%] Linking CXX static library ../lib64/libconversion.a
[ 14%] Built target conversion
Scanning dependencies of target evolution
[ 21%] Building CXX object
src/evolution/CMakeFiles/evolution.dir/evolution.cpp.o
[ 28%] Linking CXX static library ../../lib64/libevolution.a
[ 28%] Built target evolution
Scanning dependencies of target initial
[ 35%] Building CXX object
src/initial/CMakeFiles/initial.dir/initial.cpp.o
[ 42%] Linking CXX static library ../../lib64/libinitial.a
[ 42%] Built target initial
Scanning dependencies of target io
[ 50%] Building CXX object src/io/CMakeFiles/io.dir/io.cpp.o
[ 57%] Linking CXX static library ../../lib64/libio.a
[ 57%] Built target io
Scanning dependencies of target parser
[ 64%] Building CXX object
src/parser/CMakeFiles/parser.dir/parser.cpp.o
[ 71%] Linking CXX static library ../../lib64/libparser.a
[ 71%] Built target parser
Scanning dependencies of target automata
[ 78%] Building CXX object src/CMakeFiles/automata.dir/main.cpp.o
[ 85%] Linking CXX executable ../bin/automata
[ 85%] Built target automata
Scanning dependencies of target cpp_test
[ 92%] Building CXX object tests/CMakeFiles/cpp_test.dir/test.cpp.o
[100%] Linking CXX executable ../bin/cpp_test
[100%] Built target cpp_test
```

7. Finally, we run the unit tests:

```
$ ctest

Running tests...
    Start 1: test_evolution
```

```
1/1 Test #1: test_evolution ................... Passed 0.00 sec

100% tests passed, 0 tests failed out of 1
```

How it works

We could have put all the code into one source file. This would be impractical; every edit would require a full recompilation. Splitting source files into smaller, more manageable units makes sense. We could have equally well compiled all sources into a single library or executable, but in practice, projects prefer to split the compilation of sources into smaller, well-defined libraries. This is done both to localize scope and simplify dependency scanning, but also to simplify code maintenance. This means that building a project out of many libraries as we have done here is a typical situation.

To discuss the CMake structure we can proceed bottom-up from the individual CMakeLists.txt files defining each library, such as src/evolution/CMakeLists.txt:

```
add_library(evolution "")

target_sources(evolution
  PRIVATE
    evolution.cpp
  PUBLIC
    ${CMAKE_CURRENT_LIST_DIR}/evolution.hpp
  )

target_include_directories(evolution
  PUBLIC
    ${CMAKE_CURRENT_LIST_DIR}
  )
```

These individual CMakeLists.txt files define libraries as close as possible to the sources. In this example, we first define the library name with add_library and then define its sources and include directories, as well as their target visibility: the implementation files (here evolution.cpp) are PRIVATE, whereas the interface header file evolution.hpp is defined as PUBLIC since we will access it in main.cpp and test.cpp. The advantage of defining targets as close as possible to the code is that code developers with knowledge of this library and possibly limited knowledge of the CMake framework only need to edit files in this directory; in other words, the library dependencies are encapsulated.

Moving one level up, the libraries are assembled in src/CMakeLists.txt:

```
add_executable(automata main.cpp)
add_subdirectory(evolution)
```

```
add_subdirectory(initial)
add_subdirectory(io)
add_subdirectory(parser)

target_link_libraries(automata
  PRIVATE
    conversion
    evolution
    initial
    io
    parser
  )
```

This file, in turn, is referenced in the top-level CMakeLists.txt. This means that we have built our project from a tree of libraries using a tree of CMakeLists.txt files. This approach is typical for many projects and it scales to large projects without the need to carry lists of source files in global variables across directories. An added bonus of the add_subdirectory approach is that it isolates scopes since variables defined in a subdirectory are not automatically accessible in the parent scope.

There is more

One limitation of building a project using a tree of add_subdirectory calls is that CMake does not allow us to use target_link_libraries with targets that are defined outside of the current directory scope. This was not a problem for the example shown in this recipe. In the next recipe, we will demonstrate an alternative approach where we assemble the different CMakeLists.txt files not using add_subdirectory, but using module includes, which allows us to link to targets defined outside the current directory.

CMake can use the Graphviz graph visualization software (http://www.graphviz.org) to generate the dependency graph of a project:

```
$ cd build
$ cmake --graphviz=example.dot ..
$ dot -T png example.dot -o example.png
```

The generated diagram will show dependencies between targets in different directories:

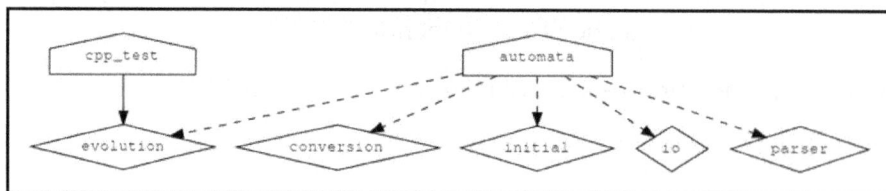

Throughout the book, we have been building the code *out-of-source* to keep the source tree and build tree separate. This is the recommended practice to allow us to configure different builds (sequential or parallel, `Debug` or `Release`) with the same source code, without duplicating the source code and without spilling generated and object files across the source tree. With the following snippet, you can protect your project against in-source builds:

```
if(${PROJECT_SOURCE_DIR} STREQUAL ${PROJECT_BINARY_DIR})
    message(FATAL_ERROR "In-source builds not allowed. Please make a new
directory (called a build directory) and run CMake from there.")
endif()
```

It is useful to recognize that the structure of the build tree mimics the structure of the source tree. In our example here, it is rather instructive to insert the following `message` printout into `src/CMakeLists.txt`:

```
message("current binary dir is ${CMAKE_CURRENT_BINARY_DIR}")
```

When configuring the project to `build`, we will see that the printout refers to `build/src`.

See also

We note that, as of version 3.12 of CMake, `OBJECT` libraries are another viable approach to organizing large projects. The only modification to our example would be in the `CMakeLists.txt` for the libraries. The sources would be compiled into object files: neither archived into a static archive, nor linked into a shared library. For example:

```
add_library(io OBJECT "")

target_sources(io
  PRIVATE
    io.cpp
  PUBLIC
    ${CMAKE_CURRENT_LIST_DIR}/io.hpp
  )

target_include_directories(io
  PUBLIC
    ${CMAKE_CURRENT_LIST_DIR}
  )
```

The top-level `CMakeLists.txt` remains unchanged: the `automata` executable target links these object files into the final executable. Usage requirements, such as include directories, compile flags, and link libraries set on the `OBJECT` libraries will correctly be inherited. For more details on this new feature of `OBJECT` libraries introduced in CMake 3.12 refer to the official documentation: `https://cmake.org/cmake/help/v3.12/manual/cmake-buildsystem.7.html#object-libraries`

Avoiding global variables using target_sources

The code for this recipe is available at `https://github.com/dev-cafe/cmake-cookbook/tree/v1.0/chapter-07/recipe-08` and has a C++ example. The recipe is valid with CMake version 3.5 (and higher) and has been tested on GNU/Linux, macOS, and Windows.

In this recipe, we will discuss an alternative approach to the previous recipe and assemble the different `CMakeLists.txt` files without using `add_subdirectory`, but using module includes. This approach is inspired by `https://crascit.com/2016/01/31/enhanced-source-file-handling-with-target_sources/` and allows us to use `target_link_libraries` to link to targets defined outside of the current directory.

Getting ready

We will use the same source code as in the previous recipe. The only changes will be in `CMakeLists.txt` files and we will discuss these changes in the following sections.

How to do it

Let us look in detail at the various files needed by CMake:

1. The top-level `CMakeLists.txt` contains the following:

    ```
    cmake_minimum_required(VERSION 3.5 FATAL_ERROR)
    project(recipe-08 LANGUAGES CXX)

    set(CMAKE_CXX_STANDARD 11)
    set(CMAKE_CXX_EXTENSIONS OFF)
    set(CMAKE_CXX_STANDARD_REQUIRED ON)
    ```

```
include(GNUInstallDirs)
set(CMAKE_ARCHIVE_OUTPUT_DIRECTORY
  ${CMAKE_BINARY_DIR}/${CMAKE_INSTALL_LIBDIR})
set(CMAKE_LIBRARY_OUTPUT_DIRECTORY
  ${CMAKE_BINARY_DIR}/${CMAKE_INSTALL_LIBDIR})
set(CMAKE_RUNTIME_OUTPUT_DIRECTORY
  ${CMAKE_BINARY_DIR}/${CMAKE_INSTALL_BINDIR})

# defines targets and sources
include(src/CMakeLists.txt)
include(external/CMakeLists.txt)

enable_testing()
add_subdirectory(tests)
```

2. The `external/CMakeLists.txt` file is unchanged compared to the previous recipe.

3. The `src/CMakeLists.txt` file defines two libraries (`automaton` and `evolution`):

```
add_library(automaton "")
add_library(evolution "")

include(${CMAKE_CURRENT_LIST_DIR}/evolution/CMakeLists.txt)
include(${CMAKE_CURRENT_LIST_DIR}/initial/CMakeLists.txt)
include(${CMAKE_CURRENT_LIST_DIR}/io/CMakeLists.txt)
include(${CMAKE_CURRENT_LIST_DIR}/parser/CMakeLists.txt)

add_executable(automata "")

target_sources(automata
  PRIVATE
    ${CMAKE_CURRENT_LIST_DIR}/main.cpp
  )

target_link_libraries(automata
  PRIVATE
    automaton
    conversion
  )
```

4. The `src/evolution/CMakeLists.txt` file contains the following:

```
target_sources(automaton
  PRIVATE
    ${CMAKE_CURRENT_LIST_DIR}/evolution.cpp
```

```
      PUBLIC
        ${CMAKE_CURRENT_LIST_DIR}/evolution.hpp
      )

    target_include_directories(automaton
      PUBLIC
        ${CMAKE_CURRENT_LIST_DIR}
      )

    target_sources(evolution
      PRIVATE
        ${CMAKE_CURRENT_LIST_DIR}/evolution.cpp
      PUBLIC
        ${CMAKE_CURRENT_LIST_DIR}/evolution.hpp
      )

    target_include_directories(evolution
      PUBLIC
        ${CMAKE_CURRENT_LIST_DIR}
      )
```

5. The remaining CMakeLists.txt files are equivalent to src/initial/CMakeLists.txt:

```
    target_sources(automaton
      PRIVATE
        ${CMAKE_CURRENT_LIST_DIR}/initial.cpp
      PUBLIC
        ${CMAKE_CURRENT_LIST_DIR}/initial.hpp
      )

    target_include_directories(automaton
      PUBLIC
        ${CMAKE_CURRENT_LIST_DIR}
      )
```

6. Configuring, building, and testing yields a result equivalent to the previous recipe:

```
$ mkdir -p build
$ cd build
$ cmake ..
$ cmake --build build
$ ctest
```

```
Running tests...
  Start 1: test_evolution
1/1 Test #1: test_evolution .................. Passed 0.00 sec

100% tests passed, 0 tests failed out of 1
```

How it works

In contrast to the previous recipe, we have defined three libraries:

- conversion (defined in external)
- automaton (containing all sources except conversion)
- evolution (defined in src/evolution and linked against by cpp_test)

In this example, we keep all targets available in the parent scope by referencing CMakeLists.txt files using include():

```
include(src/CMakeLists.txt)
include(external/CMakeLists.txt)
```

We can build a tree of includes, remembering that when stepping into subdirectories (src/CMakeLists.txt), we need to use paths relative to the parent scope:

```
include(${CMAKE_CURRENT_LIST_DIR}/evolution/CMakeLists.txt)
include(${CMAKE_CURRENT_LIST_DIR}/initial/CMakeLists.txt)
include(${CMAKE_CURRENT_LIST_DIR}/io/CMakeLists.txt)
include(${CMAKE_CURRENT_LIST_DIR}/parser/CMakeLists.txt)
```

With this, we can define and link to the targets anywhere within the file tree accessed *via* include() statements. However, we should choose to define them at a place that is most intuitive for maintainers and code contributors.

There is more

We can once again use CMake and Graphviz (http://www.graphviz.org/) to generate the dependency graph of this project:

```
$ cd build
$ cmake --graphviz=example.dot ..
$ dot -T png example.dot -o example.png
```

For the current setup, we obtain the following dependency graph:

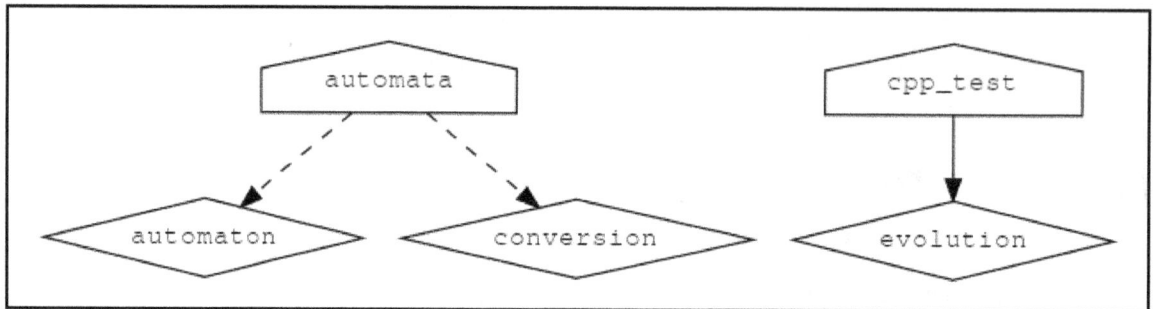

Organizing Fortran projects

The code for this recipe is available at `https://github.com/dev-cafe/cmake-cookbook/tree/v1.0/chapter-07/recipe-09` and has a Fortran example. The recipe is valid with CMake version 3.5 (and higher) and has been tested on GNU/Linux, macOS, and Windows with MSYS Makefiles.

We devote one recipe to the discussion of how to structure and organize Fortran projects for two reasons:

1. There are still many Fortran projects out there, in particular in numerical software (for a more comprehensive list of general purpose Fortran software projects, see `http://fortranwiki.org/fortran/show/Libraries`).
2. Fortran 90 (and later) can be more difficult to build for projects not using CMake, since Fortran module files impose a compilation order. In other words, for manually written Makefiles one typically needs to program a dependency scanner for Fortran module files.

As we will see in this recipe, modern CMake allows us to express the configuration and build process in a very compact and modular way. As an example, we will use the elementary cellular automata from the previous two recipes, now ported to Fortran.

Getting ready

The file tree structure is very similar to the previous two recipes. We have replaced C++ with Fortran sources and in this case, we have no header files:

```
.
├── CMakeLists.txt
├── external
│   ├── CMakeLists.txt
│   ├── conversion.f90
│   └── README.md
├── src
│   ├── CMakeLists.txt
│   ├── evolution
│   │   ├── ancestors.f90
│   │   ├── CMakeLists.txt
│   │   ├── empty.f90
│   │   └── evolution.f90
│   ├── initial
│   │   ├── CMakeLists.txt
│   │   └── initial.f90
│   ├── io
│   │   ├── CMakeLists.txt
│   │   └── io.f90
│   ├── main.f90
│   └── parser
│       ├── CMakeLists.txt
│       └── parser.f90
└── tests
    ├── CMakeLists.txt
    └── test.f90
```

The main program is in `src/main.f90`:

```fortran
program example

    use parser, only: get_arg_as_int
    use conversion, only: binary_representation
    use initial, only: initial_distribution
    use io, only: print_row
    use evolution, only: evolve

    implicit none

    integer :: num_steps
    integer :: length
    integer :: rule_decimal
    integer :: rule_binary(8)
    integer, allocatable :: row(:)
    integer :: step

    ! parse arguments
    num_steps = get_arg_as_int(1)
```

```
    length = get_arg_as_int(2)
    rule_decimal = get_arg_as_int(3)

    ! print information about parameters
    print *, "number of steps: ", num_steps
    print *, "length: ", length
    print *, "rule: ", rule_decimal

    ! obtain binary representation for the rule
    rule_binary = binary_representation(rule_decimal)

    ! create initial distribution
    allocate(row(length))
    call initial_distribution(row)

    ! print initial configuration
    call print_row(row)

    ! the system evolves, print each step
    do step = 1, num_steps
      call evolve(row, rule_binary)
      call print_row(row)
    end do

    deallocate(row)

  end program
```

As in the previous recipe, we have placed the conversion module in external/conversion.f90:

```
  module conversion

    implicit none
    public binary_representation
    private

  contains

    pure function binary_representation(n_decimal)
      integer, intent(in) :: n_decimal
      integer :: binary_representation(8)
      integer :: pos
      integer :: n

      binary_representation = 0
      pos = 8
      n = n_decimal
```

```
      do while (n > 0)
        binary_representation(pos) = mod(n, 2)
        n = (n - binary_representation(pos))/2
        pos = pos - 1
      end do
    end function

end module
```

The evolution library, which implements the time step, is artificially split into three files. The bulk is collected in src/evolution/evolution.f90:

```
module evolution

  implicit none
  public evolve
  private

contains

  subroutine not_visible()
    ! no-op call to demonstrate private/public visibility
    call empty_subroutine_no_interface()
  end subroutine

  pure subroutine evolve(row, rule_binary)
    use ancestors, only: compute_ancestors

    integer, intent(inout) :: row(:)
    integer, intent(in) :: rule_binary(8)
    integer :: i
    integer :: ◄left, center, right
    integer :: ancestry
    integer, allocatable :: new_row(:)

    allocate(new_row(size(row)))

    do i = 1, size(row)
      left = i - 1
      center = i
      right = i + 1

      if (left < 1) left = left + size(row)
      if (right > size(row)) right = right - size(row)

      ancestry = compute_ancestors(row, left, center, right)
      new_row(i) = rule_binary(ancestry)
    end do
```

```
      row = new_row
      deallocate(new_row)

  end subroutine

end module
```

The computation of ancestors is performed in `src/evolution/ancestors.f90`:

```
module ancestors

  implicit none
  public compute_ancestors
  private

contains

  pure integer function compute_ancestors(row, left, center, right)
result(i)
    integer, intent(in) :: row(:)
    integer, intent(in) :: left, center, right

    i = 4*row(left) + 2*row(center) + 1*row(right)
    i = 8 - i
  end function

end module
```

We also have an "empty" module in `src/evolution/empty.f90`:

```
module empty

  implicit none
  public empty_subroutine
  private

contains

  subroutine empty_subroutine()
  end subroutine

end module


subroutine empty_subroutine_no_interface()
  use empty, only: empty_subroutine
  call empty_subroutine()
end subroutine
```

We will explain these choices in the next section.

The code for the starting condition is located in `src/initial/initial.f90`:

```fortran
module initial

  implicit none
  public initial_distribution
  private

contains

  pure subroutine initial_distribution(row)
    integer, intent(out) :: row(:)

    row = 0
    row(size(row)/2) = 1
  end subroutine

end module
```

The `src/io/io.f90` file contains a function to print a row:

```fortran
module io

  implicit none
  public print_row
  private

contains

  subroutine print_row(row)
    integer, intent(in) :: row(:)
    character(size(row)) :: line
    integer :: i

    do i = 1, size(row)
      if (row(i) == 1) then
        line(i:i) = '*'
      else
        line(i:i) = ' '
      end if
    end do

    print *, line
  end subroutine

end module
```

The `src/parser/parser.f90` file parses the command-line arguments:

```
module parser

  implicit none
  public get_arg_as_int
  private

contains

  integer function get_arg_as_int(n) result(i)
    integer, intent(in) :: n
    character(len=32) :: arg

    call get_command_argument(n, arg)
    read(arg , *) i
  end function

end module
```

Finally, we have the test sources in `tests/test.f90`:

```
program test

  use evolution, only: evolve

  implicit none

  integer :: row(9)
  integer :: expected_result(9)
  integer :: rule_binary(8)
  integer :: i

  ! test rule 90
  row = (/0, 1, 0, 1, 0, 1, 0, 1, 0/)
  rule_binary = (/0, 1, 0, 1, 1, 0, 1, 0/)
  call evolve(row, rule_binary)
  expected_result = (/1, 0, 0, 0, 0, 0, 0, 0, 1/)
  do i = 1, 9
    if (row(i) /= expected_result(i)) then
      print *, 'ERROR: test for rule 90 failed'
      call exit(1)
    end if
  end do
```

```fortran
! test rule 222
row = (/0, 0, 0, 0, 1, 0, 0, 0, 0/)
rule_binary = (/1, 1, 0, 1, 1, 1, 1, 0/)
call evolve(row, rule_binary)
expected_result = (/0, 0, 0, 1, 1, 1, 0, 0, 0/)
do i = 1, 9
  if (row(i) /= expected_result(i)) then
    print *, 'ERROR: test for rule 222 failed'
    call exit(1)
  end if
end do

end program
```

How to do it

We will now discuss the corresponding CMake structure:

1. The top-level CMakeLists.txt is similar to *Recipe 7*; we only exchange CXX for Fortran and remove the C++11 requirement:

```cmake
cmake_minimum_required(VERSION 3.5 FATAL_ERROR)

project(recipe-09 LANGUAGES Fortran)

include(GNUInstallDirs)
set(CMAKE_ARCHIVE_OUTPUT_DIRECTORY
  ${CMAKE_BINARY_DIR}/${CMAKE_INSTALL_LIBDIR})
set(CMAKE_LIBRARY_OUTPUT_DIRECTORY
  ${CMAKE_BINARY_DIR}/${CMAKE_INSTALL_LIBDIR})
set(CMAKE_RUNTIME_OUTPUT_DIRECTORY
  ${CMAKE_BINARY_DIR}/${CMAKE_INSTALL_BINDIR})

# defines targets and sources
add_subdirectory(src)

# contains an "external" library we will link to
add_subdirectory(external)

# enable testing and define tests
enable_testing()
add_subdirectory(tests)
```

2. Targets and sources are defined in `src/CMakeLists.txt` (except the `conversion` **target**):

```
add_executable(automata main.f90)
add_subdirectory(evolution)
add_subdirectory(initial)
add_subdirectory(io)
add_subdirectory(parser)

target_link_libraries(automata
  PRIVATE
    conversion
    evolution
    initial
    io
    parser
  )
```

3. The `conversion` library is defined in `external/CMakeLists.txt`:

```
add_library(conversion "")
target_sources(conversion
  PUBLIC
    ${CMAKE_CURRENT_LIST_DIR}/conversion.f90
  )
```

4. The `src/CMakeLists.txt` file adds further subdirectories, which in turn contain `CMakeLists.txt` files. They are all similar in structure; for example, `src/initial/CMakeLists.txt` contains the following:

```
add_library(initial "")
target_sources(initial
  PUBLIC
    ${CMAKE_CURRENT_LIST_DIR}/initial.f90
  )
```

5. The exception is the `evolution` library in `src/evolution/CMakeLists.txt`, which we have split into three source files:

```
add_library(evolution "")
target_sources(evolution
  PRIVATE
    empty.f90
  PUBLIC
    ${CMAKE_CURRENT_LIST_DIR}/ancestors.f90
    ${CMAKE_CURRENT_LIST_DIR}/evolution.f90
  )
```

Chapter 7

6. The unit tests are registered in `tests/CMakeLists.txt`:

```
add_executable(fortran_test test.f90)

target_link_libraries(fortran_test evolution)

add_test(
  NAME
    test_evolution
  COMMAND
    $<TARGET_FILE:fortran_test>
  )
```

7. Configuring and building the project yields the following output:

```
$ mkdir -p build
$ cd build
$ cmake ..
$ cmake --build .

Scanning dependencies of target conversion
[  4%] Building Fortran object
external/CMakeFiles/conversion.dir/conversion.f90.o
[  8%] Linking Fortran static library ../lib64/libconversion.a
[  8%] Built target conversion
Scanning dependencies of target evolution
[ 12%] Building Fortran object
src/evolution/CMakeFiles/evolution.dir/ancestors.f90.o
[ 16%] Building Fortran object
src/evolution/CMakeFiles/evolution.dir/empty.f90.o
[ 20%] Building Fortran object
src/evolution/CMakeFiles/evolution.dir/evolution.f90.o
[ 25%] Linking Fortran static library ../../lib64/libevolution.a
[ 25%] Built target evolution
Scanning dependencies of target initial
[ 29%] Building Fortran object
src/initial/CMakeFiles/initial.dir/initial.f90.o
[ 33%] Linking Fortran static library ../../lib64/libinitial.a
[ 33%] Built target initial
Scanning dependencies of target io
[ 37%] Building Fortran object src/io/CMakeFiles/io.dir/io.f90.o
[ 41%] Linking Fortran static library ../../lib64/libio.a
[ 41%] Built target io
Scanning dependencies of target parser
[ 45%] Building Fortran object
src/parser/CMakeFiles/parser.dir/parser.f90.o
[ 50%] Linking Fortran static library ../../lib64/libparser.a
[ 50%] Built target parser
```

```
Scanning dependencies of target example
[ 54%] Building Fortran object
src/CMakeFiles/example.dir/__/external/conversion.f90.o
[ 58%] Building Fortran object
src/CMakeFiles/example.dir/evolution/ancestors.f90.o
[ 62%] Building Fortran object
src/CMakeFiles/example.dir/evolution/evolution.f90.o
[ 66%] Building Fortran object
src/CMakeFiles/example.dir/initial/initial.f90.o
[ 70%] Building Fortran object
src/CMakeFiles/example.dir/io/io.f90.o
[ 75%] Building Fortran object
src/CMakeFiles/example.dir/parser/parser.f90.o
[ 79%] Building Fortran object
src/CMakeFiles/example.dir/main.f90.o
[ 83%] Linking Fortran executable ../bin/example
[ 83%] Built target example
Scanning dependencies of target fortran_test
[ 87%] Building Fortran object
tests/CMakeFiles/fortran_test.dir/__/src/evolution/ancestors.f90.o
[ 91%] Building Fortran object
tests/CMakeFiles/fortran_test.dir/__/src/evolution/evolution.f90.o
[ 95%] Building Fortran object
tests/CMakeFiles/fortran_test.dir/test.f90.o
[100%] Linking Fortran executable
```

8. Finally, we run the unit tests:

```
$ ctest
```

```
Running tests...
 Start 1: test_evolution
1/1 Test #1: test_evolution ................... Passed 0.00 sec

100% tests passed, 0 tests failed out of 1
```

How it works

Following *Recipe 7, Limiting scope with* add_subdirectory, we will discuss the CMake structure from the bottom up, from the individual CMakeLists.txt files defining each library, such as src/evolution/CMakeLists.txt:

```
add_library(evolution "")

target_sources(evolution
  PRIVATE
```

```
      empty.f90
  PUBLIC
    ${CMAKE_CURRENT_LIST_DIR}/ancestors.f90
    ${CMAKE_CURRENT_LIST_DIR}/evolution.f90
  )
```

These individual CMakeLists.txt files define libraries as close as possible to the sources, following the same reasoning as in previous two recipes: code developers with knowledge of this library and possibly limited knowledge of the CMake framework only need to edit files in this directory: divide and conquer.

We first define the library name with add_library and then define its sources and include directories, as well as their target visibility. In this case, both ancestors.f90 and evolution.f90 are PUBLIC since their module interfaces are accessed outside the library, whereas the module interface of empty.f90 is not accessed outside the file and therefore we mark this source as PRIVATE.

Moving one level up, the libraries are assembled in src/CMakeLists.txt:

```
add_executable(automata main.f90)
add_subdirectory(evolution)
add_subdirectory(initial)
add_subdirectory(io)
add_subdirectory(parser)

target_link_libraries(automata
  PRIVATE
    conversion
    evolution
    initial
    io
    parser
  )
```

This file, in turn, is referenced in the top-level CMakeLists.txt. This means that we have built our project from a tree of libraries using a tree of CMakeLists.txt files, added using add_subdirectory. As discussed in *Recipe 7, Limiting scope with add_subdirectory*, this approach scales to large projects without the need to carry lists of source files in global variables across directories, with the added bonus of isolating scopes and namespaces.

Comparing this Fortran example with the C++ version (*Recipe 7*), we can note that we had to do less CMake work in the Fortran case; we do not have to use `target_include_directories` since there are no header files and interfaces are communicated *via* the generated Fortran module files. Also, observe that we neither have to worry about the order of source files listed in `target_sources`, nor do we have to impose any explicit dependencies between libraries! CMake is able to infer Fortran module dependencies from the source file dependencies. Using `target_sources` in combination with `PRIVATE` and `PUBLIC` allows us to express interfaces in a compact and robust fashion.

There is more

In this recipe, we have not specified a directory where Fortran module files should be placed and we have kept this transparent. The location for module files can be specified by setting the `CMAKE_Fortran_MODULE_DIRECTORY` CMake variable. Note that it is also possible to set this as a target property, `Fortran_MODULE_DIRECTORY`, thus achieving a finer level of control. See `https://cmake.org/cmake/help/v3.5/prop_tgt/Fortran_MODULE_DIRECTORY.html`.

8
The Superbuild Pattern

In this chapter, we will cover the following recipes:

- Using the superbuild pattern
- Managing dependencies with a superbuild: I. The Boost libraries
- Managing dependencies with a superbuild: II. The FFTW library
- Managing dependencies with a superbuild: III. The Google Test framework
- Managing your project as a superbuild

Introduction

Every project has to deal with dependencies and CMake makes it relatively easy to find out whether these dependencies are present on the system where we configure our project. *Chapter 3, Detecting External Libraries and Programs*, showed how to find dependencies installed on the system and we have used that same pattern so far. However, if dependencies are not satisfied, the most we can achieve is fail the configuration and alert the user of the reasons for such a failure. However, with CMake it is possible to organize our projects such that dependencies can be automatically fetched and built if they are not found on the system. This chapter will present and analyze the `ExternalProject.cmake` and `FetchContent.cmake` standard modules and their use in the *superbuild pattern*. The former allows us to retrieve the dependencies of our project at *build time* and has been a part of CMake for a long time. The latter module was added in version 3.11 of CMake and allows us to retrieve dependencies at *configure time*. With the superbuild pattern, we can effectively leverage CMake as an advanced package manager: within your project you will handle dependencies in the same manner, whether already available on the system or whether they need to be built from scratch. The next five recipes will walk you through the pattern and show how it can be used to fetch and build virtually any dependency.

> Both modules are extensively documented online. For
> `ExternalProject.cmake`, we refer the reader to `https://cmake.org/`
> `cmake/help/v3.5/module/ExternalProject.html`. For
> `FetchContent.cmake`, we refer the reader to `https://cmake.org/cmake/`
> `help/v3.11/module/FetchContent.html`.

Using the superbuild pattern

> The code for this recipe is available at `https://github.com/dev-cafe/`
> `cmake-cookbook/tree/v1.0/chapter-08/recipe-01` and has a C++
> example. The recipe is valid with CMake version 3.5 (and higher) and has
> been tested on GNU/Linux, macOS, and Windows.

This recipe will introduce the superbuild pattern with a very simple example. We will show
how to use the `ExternalProject_Add` command to build a simple "Hello, World"
program.

Getting ready

This recipe will build the "Hello, World" executable from the following source code
(`hello-world.cpp`):

```
#include <cstdlib>
#include <iostream>
#include <string>

std::string say_hello() { return std::string("Hello, CMake superbuild
world!"); }

int main() {
  std::cout << say_hello() << std::endl;
  return EXIT_SUCCESS;
}
```

The project is structured as follows, with a root CMakeLists.txt, and a src/CMakeLists.txt file:

```
.
├── CMakeLists.txt
└── src
    ├── CMakeLists.txt
    └── hello-world.cpp
```

How to do it

Let us first look at CMakeLists.txt in the root folder:

1. We declare a C++11 project, with a minimum required CMake version:

   ```
   cmake_minimum_required(VERSION 3.5 FATAL_ERROR)

   project(recipe-01 LANGUAGES CXX)

   set(CMAKE_CXX_STANDARD 11)
   set(CMAKE_CXX_EXTENSIONS OFF)
   set(CMAKE_CXX_STANDARD_REQUIRED ON)
   ```

2. We set the EP_BASE directory property for the current and any underlying directories. This will be discussed shortly:

   ```
   set_property(DIRECTORY PROPERTY EP_BASE
   ${CMAKE_BINARY_DIR}/subprojects)
   ```

3. We include the ExternalProject.cmake standard module. This module provides the ExternalProject_Add function:

   ```
   include(ExternalProject)
   ```

4. The source code for our "Hello, World" example is added as an external project by invoking the ExternalProject_Add function. The name of the external project is recipe-01_core:

   ```
   ExternalProject_Add(${PROJECT_NAME}_core
   ```

5. We set the source directory for the external project using the SOURCE_DIR option:

   ```
   SOURCE_DIR
   ${CMAKE_CURRENT_LIST_DIR}/src
   ```

6. The `src` subdirectory contains a full-fledged CMake project. To configure and build it, we pass the appropriate CMake options to the external project *via* the `CMAKE_ARGS` option. In our case, we only need to pass the C++ compiler and the requirements for the C++ standard:

```
CMAKE_ARGS
  -DCMAKE_CXX_COMPILER=${CMAKE_CXX_COMPILER}
  -DCMAKE_CXX_STANDARD=${CMAKE_CXX_STANDARD}
  -DCMAKE_CXX_EXTENSIONS=${CMAKE_CXX_EXTENSIONS}
  -DCMAKE_CXX_STANDARD_REQUIRED=${CMAKE_CXX_STANDARD_REQUIRED}
```

7. We also set the C++ compiler flags. These are passed using the `CMAKE_CACHE_ARGS` option to the `ExternalProject_Add` command:

```
CMAKE_CACHE_ARGS
  -DCMAKE_CXX_FLAGS:STRING=${CMAKE_CXX_FLAGS}
```

8. We configure the external project so that it is always built:

```
BUILD_ALWAYS
  1
```

9. The install step will not execute any actions (we will revisit installation in *Recipe 4, Installing a superbuild*, in *Chapter 10, Writing an Installer*):

```
INSTALL_COMMAND
  ""
)
```

Let us now move on to `src/CMakeLists.txt`. Since we are adding our "Hello, World" sources as an external project, this is a full-fledged `CMakeLists.txt` file for a standalone project:

1. Also, here we declare a minimum required CMake version:

```
cmake_minimum_required(VERSION 3.5 FATAL_ERROR)
```

2. We declare a C++ project:

```
project(recipe-01_core LANGUAGES CXX)
```

3. Finally, we add an executable target, hello-world, from the hello-world.cpp source file:

```
add_executable(hello-world hello-world.cpp)
```

Configuring and building our project is done as usual:

```
$ mkdir -p build
$ cmake ..
$ cmake --build .
```

The structure of the build directory is now slightly more complex. In particular, we notice the subprojects folder with the following contents:

```
build/subprojects/
├── Build
│   └── recipe-01_core
│       ├── CMakeCache.txt
│       ├── CMakeFiles
│       ├── cmake_install.cmake
│       ├── hello-world
│       └── Makefile
├── Download
│   └── recipe-01_core
├── Install
│   └── recipe-01_core
├── Stamp
│   └── recipe-01_core
│       ├── recipe-01_core-configure
│       ├── recipe-01_core-done
│       ├── recipe-01_core-download
│       ├── recipe-01_core-install
│       ├── recipe-01_core-mkdir
│       ├── recipe-01_core-patch
│       └── recipe-01_core-update
└── tmp
    └── recipe-01_core
        ├── recipe-01_core-cache-.cmake
        ├── recipe-01_core-cfgcmd.txt
        └── recipe-01_core-cfgcmd.txt.in
```

recipe-01_core has been built into a subdirectory of build/subprojects, called Build/recipe-01_core, which is the EP_BASE we have set.

The `hello-world` executable has been created under `Build/recipe-01_core`. The additional subfolders `tmp/recipe-01_core` and `Stamp/recipe-01_core` contain temporary files, such as the CMake cache script `recipe-01_core-cache-.cmake`, and the stamp files for the various steps CMake has performed to build the external project.

How it works

The `ExternalProject_Add` command can be used to add sources from third parties. Our first example, however, shows how to manage our own project as an assembly of different CMake projects. In this example, both the root and the leaf `CMakeLists.txt` declared a CMake project, that is, both of them used the `project` command.

`ExternalProject_Add` has many options that can be used to fine-tune all aspects of the configuration and compilation of external projects. These options can be classified into the following:

- **Directory** options: These are used to tune the structure of the source and build directories for the external project. In our case, we used the `SOURCE_DIR` option to let CMake know that the sources are available in the `${CMAKE_CURRENT_LIST_DIR}/src` folder and thus should not be fetched from somewhere else. The directories for building the project and storing temporary files can also be specified in this class of options or as directory properties. We have followed the latter route by setting the `EP_BASE` directory property. CMake will set up all directories for the various subprojects with the following layout:

```
TMP_DIR      = <EP_BASE>/tmp/<name>
STAMP_DIR    = <EP_BASE>/Stamp/<name>
DOWNLOAD_DIR = <EP_BASE>/Download/<name>
SOURCE_DIR   = <EP_BASE>/Source/<name>
BINARY_DIR   = <EP_BASE>/Build/<name>
INSTALL_DIR  = <EP_BASE>/Install/<name>
```

- **Download** options: The code for the external project might have to be downloaded from an online repository or resource. Options in this class let you control all aspects of this step.
- **Update** and **Patch** options: This class of options can be used to define how to update the sources for the external project or how to apply patches.

- **Configure** options: By default, CMake assumes that the external project is itself configured using CMake. As the following recipes will show, we are however not limited to this case. If the external project is a CMake project, `ExternalProject_Add` will call the CMake executable and pass options to it. For our current example, we passed configuration arguments *via* the `CMAKE_ARGS` and `CMAKE_CACHE_ARGS` options. The former are passed directly as a command line argument, whereas the latter are passed *via* a CMake script file. In our example, the script file is in `build/subprojects/tmp/recipe-01_core/recipe-01_core-cache-.cmake`. The configuration would then look like this example:

```
$ cmake -DCMAKE_CXX_COMPILER=g++ -DCMAKE_CXX_STANDARD=11
-DCMAKE_CXX_EXTENSIONS=OFF -DCMAKE_CXX_STANDARD_REQUIRED=ON
-C/home/roberto/Workspace/robertodr/cmake-
cookbook/chapter-08/recipe-01/cxx-
example/build/subprojects/tmp/recipe-01_core/recipe-01_core-cache-
.cmake "-GUnix Makefiles" /home/roberto/Workspace/robertodr/cmake-
cookbook/chapter-08/recipe-01/cxx-example/src
```

- **Build** options: This class of options can be used to tweak the actual compilation of the external project. Our example used the `BUILD_ALWAYS` option to ensure that the external project is always freshly built.
- **Install** options: These are options to configure how the external project should be installed. Our example left `INSTALL_COMMAND` empty and we will discuss installation with CMake in more detail in *Chapter 10, Writing an Installer*.
- **Test** options: It is always a good idea to run tests for any piece of software that is built from sources. This class of options to `ExternalProject_Add` is here for this purpose. Our example did not use these options, as the "Hello, World" example didn't have any tests, but in *Recipe 5, Managing your project as a superbuild*, we will trigger a test step.

`ExternalProject.cmake` defines the command `ExternalProject_Get_Property` which, as the name suggests, is useful to retrieve properties of external projects. The properties on external projects are set when first invoking the `ExternalProject_Add` command. For example, retrieving the arguments to be passed to CMake when configuring `recipe-01_core` can be achieved with:

```
ExternalProject_Get_Property(${PROJECT_NAME}_core CMAKE_ARGS)
message(STATUS "CMAKE_ARGS of ${PROJECT_NAME}_core ${CMAKE_ARGS}")
```

> The complete list of options to `ExternalProject_Add` can be found in the CMake documentation: `https://cmake.org/cmake/help/v3.5/module/ExternalProject.html#command:externalproject_add`

There is more

We will explore in detail the flexibility of the `ExternalProject_Add` command in the following recipes. Sometimes, however, the external project we want to use might require additional, non-standard steps to be performed. For this reason, the `ExternalProject.cmake` module defines the following additional commands:

1. `ExternalProject_Add_Step`. Once an external project has been added, this command allows to latch additional commands on it as custom steps. See also: `https://cmake.org/cmake/help/v3.5/module/ExternalProject.html#command:externalproject_add_step`

2. `ExternalProject_Add_StepTargets`. Lets you define steps, for example the build and test steps, in any external project as separate targets. This means that one can trigger these steps separately from the full external project and allows fine-grained control over complex dependencies within your project. See also: `https://cmake.org/cmake/help/v3.5/module/ExternalProject.html#command:externalproject_add_steptargets`

3. `ExternalProject_Add_StepDependencies`. Sometimes steps for an external project might depend on targets outside it and this command is designed to take care of these cases. See also: `https://cmake.org/cmake/help/v3.5/module/ExternalProject.html#command:externalproject_add_stepdependencies`

Managing dependencies with a superbuild: I. The Boost libraries

> The code for this recipe is available at `https://github.com/dev-cafe/cmake-cookbook/tree/v1.0/chapter-08/recipe-02` and has a C++ example. The recipe is valid with CMake version 3.5 (and higher) and has been tested on GNU/Linux, macOS, and Windows with MSYS Makefiles and Ninja.

The Boost libraries provide a rich C++ programming infrastructure and are popular among C++ developers. We have already shown how to find the Boost libraries on our system in *Chapter 3*, *Detecting External Libraries and Programs*. Sometimes, however, the version of Boost required by your project might not be available on the system. This recipe will show how to leverage the superbuild pattern to ship your code with the confidence that a missing dependency will not stop the configuration. We will reuse the code example from *Recipe 8*, *Detecting the Boost libraries*, in *Chapter 3*, *Detecting External Libraries and Programs*, but reorganize it in the form of a superbuild. This will be the layout of the project:

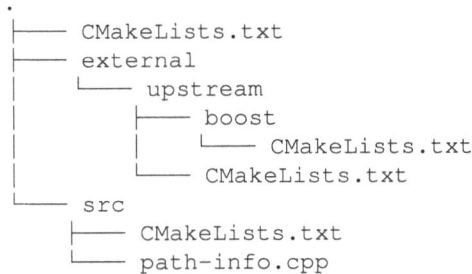

```
.
├── CMakeLists.txt
├── external
│   └── upstream
│       ├── boost
│       │   └── CMakeLists.txt
│       └── CMakeLists.txt
└── src
    ├── CMakeLists.txt
    └── path-info.cpp
```

You will notice that there are four CMakeLists.txt files in the project source tree. The following section will walk you through these.

How to do it

We will begin with the root CMakeLists.txt:

1. We declare a C++11 project as usual:

```
cmake_minimum_required(VERSION 3.5 FATAL_ERROR)

project(recipe-02 LANGUAGES CXX)

set(CMAKE_CXX_STANDARD 11)
set(CMAKE_CXX_EXTENSIONS OFF)
set(CMAKE_CXX_STANDARD_REQUIRED ON)
```

2. We set the EP_BASE directory property:

```
set_property(DIRECTORY PROPERTY EP_BASE
${CMAKE_BINARY_DIR}/subprojects)
```

3. We set the `STAGED_INSTALL_PREFIX` variable. This directory will be used to install the dependencies within our build tree:

```
set(STAGED_INSTALL_PREFIX ${CMAKE_BINARY_DIR}/stage)
message(STATUS "${PROJECT_NAME} staged install:
${STAGED_INSTALL_PREFIX}")
```

4. Our project needs the filesystem and system components of the Boost libraries. We declare a list variable to hold this information and also set the minimum required version of Boost:

```
list(APPEND BOOST_COMPONENTS_REQUIRED filesystem system)
set(Boost_MINIMUM_REQUIRED 1.61)
```

5. We add the `external/upstream` subdirectory, which will in turn add the `external/upstream/boost` subdirectory:

```
add_subdirectory(external/upstream)
```

6. Then, we include the `ExternalProject.cmake` standard CMake module. This defines, among others, the `ExternalProject_Add` command, which is the key to orchestrating superbuilds:

```
include(ExternalProject)
```

7. Our project resides under the `src` subdirectory and we add it as an external project. We pass CMake options using `CMAKE_ARGS` and `CMAKE_CACHE_ARGS`:

```
ExternalProject_Add(${PROJECT_NAME}_core
  DEPENDS
    boost_external
  SOURCE_DIR
    ${CMAKE_CURRENT_LIST_DIR}/src
  CMAKE_ARGS
    -DCMAKE_CXX_COMPILER=${CMAKE_CXX_COMPILER}
    -DCMAKE_CXX_STANDARD=${CMAKE_CXX_STANDARD}
    -DCMAKE_CXX_EXTENSIONS=${CMAKE_CXX_EXTENSIONS}
    -DCMAKE_CXX_STANDARD_REQUIRED=${CMAKE_CXX_STANDARD_REQUIRED}
  CMAKE_CACHE_ARGS
    -DCMAKE_CXX_FLAGS:STRING=${CMAKE_CXX_FLAGS}
    -DCMAKE_INCLUDE_PATH:PATH=${BOOST_INCLUDEDIR}
    -DCMAKE_LIBRARY_PATH:PATH=${BOOST_LIBRARYDIR}
```

```
BUILD_ALWAYS
  1
INSTALL_COMMAND
  ""
)
```

Let us now look at the CMakeLists.txt in external/upstream. This file simply adds the boost folder as an additional directory:

```
add_subdirectory(boost)
```

The CMakeLists.txt in external/upstream/boost describes the operations needed to satisfy the dependency on Boost. Our goal is simple, if the desired version is not installed, download the source archive and build it:

1. First of all, we attempt to find the Boost components needed for the minimum required version:

```
find_package(Boost ${Boost_MINIMUM_REQUIRED} QUIET COMPONENTS
"${BOOST_COMPONENTS_REQUIRED}")
```

2. If these are found, we add an interface library, boost_external. This is a dummy target, needed to properly handle build order in our superbuild:

```
if(Boost_FOUND)
  message(STATUS "Found Boost version
${Boost_MAJOR_VERSION}.${Boost_MINOR_VERSION}.${Boost_SUBMINOR_VERS
ION}")
  add_library(boost_external INTERFACE)
else()
  # ... discussed below
endif()
```

3. If find_package was not successful or we are forcing the superbuild, we need to set up a local build of Boost and for this, we enter the else-section of the previous conditional:

```
else()
  message(STATUS "Boost ${Boost_MINIMUM_REQUIRED} could not be
located, Building Boost 1.61.0 instead.")
```

4. Since these libraries do not use CMake, we need to prepare the arguments for their native build toolchain. First, we set the compiler to be used for Boost:

```
if(CMAKE_CXX_COMPILER_ID MATCHES "GNU")
  if(APPLE)
    set(_toolset "darwin")
  else()
    set(_toolset "gcc")
  endif()
elseif(CMAKE_CXX_COMPILER_ID MATCHES ".*Clang")
  set(_toolset "clang")
elseif(CMAKE_CXX_COMPILER_ID MATCHES "Intel")
  if(APPLE)
    set(_toolset "intel-darwin")
  else()
    set(_toolset "intel-linux")
  endif()
endif()
```

5. We prepare the list of libraries to be built based on the required components. We define some list variables: _build_byproducts, to contain the absolute path to the libraries that will be built; _b2_select_libraries, to contain the list of libraries we want to build; and _bootstrap_select_libraries, which is a string with the same contents in a different format:

```
if(NOT "${BOOST_COMPONENTS_REQUIRED}" STREQUAL "")
    # Replace unit_test_framework (used by CMake's find_package)
with test (understood by Boost build toolchain)
    string(REPLACE "unit_test_framework" "test"
_b2_needed_components "${BOOST_COMPONENTS_REQUIRED}")
    # Generate argument for BUILD_BYPRODUCTS
    set(_build_byproducts)
    set(_b2_select_libraries)
    foreach(_lib IN LISTS _b2_needed_components)
      list(APPEND _build_byproducts
${STAGED_INSTALL_PREFIX}/boost/lib/libboost_${_lib}${CMAKE_SHARED_L
IBRARY_SUFFIX})
      list(APPEND _b2_select_libraries --with-${_lib})
    endforeach()
    # Transform the ;-separated list to a ,-separated list
(digested by the Boost build toolchain!)
    string(REPLACE ";" "," _b2_needed_components
"${_b2_needed_components}")
    set(_bootstrap_select_libraries "--with-
libraries=${_b2_needed_components}")
    string(REPLACE ";" ", " printout
"${BOOST_COMPONENTS_REQUIRED}")
```

```
message(STATUS "  Libraries to be built: ${printout}")
endif()
```

6. We can now add the Boost project as an external project. First of all, we specify the download URL and the checksum in the **Download** options class. `DOWNLOAD_NO_PROGRESS` is set to 1 to suppress printing download progress information:

```
include(ExternalProject)
ExternalProject_Add(boost_external
  URL
https://sourceforge.net/projects/boost/files/boost/1.61.0/boost_1_6
1_0.zip
  URL_HASH
SHA256=02d420e6908016d4ac74dfc712eec7d9616a7fc0da78b0a1b5b937536b2e
01e8
  DOWNLOAD_NO_PROGRESS
    1
```

7. Next, we set **Update/Patch** and **Configure** options:

```
UPDATE_COMMAND
  ""
CONFIGURE_COMMAND
  <SOURCE_DIR>/bootstrap.sh
    --with-toolset=${_toolset}
    --prefix=${STAGED_INSTALL_PREFIX}/boost
    ${_bootstrap_select_libraries}
```

8. The Build options are set using the `BUILD_COMMAND` directive. `BUILD_IN_SOURCE` is set to 1 to signal that building will happen within the source directory. Moreover, we set `LOG_BUILD` to 1 to log ouput from the build script to a file:

```
BUILD_COMMAND
  <SOURCE_DIR>/b2 -q
      link=shared
      threading=multi
      variant=release
      toolset=${_toolset}
      ${_b2_select_libraries}
LOG_BUILD
  1
BUILD_IN_SOURCE
  1
```

9. The Install options are set using the `INSTALL_COMMAND` directive. Note the use of the `LOG_INSTALL` option to also log the install step to file:

```
INSTALL_COMMAND
  <SOURCE_DIR>/b2 -q install
      link=shared
      threading=multi
      variant=release
      toolset=${_toolset}
      ${_b2_select_libraries}
LOG_INSTALL
  1
```

10. Finally, we list our libraries as `BUILD_BYPRODUCTS` and close the `ExternalProject_Add` command:

```
BUILD_BYPRODUCTS
  "${_build_byproducts}"
)
```

11. We set some variables useful for directing the detection of the newly installed Boost:

```
set(
  BOOST_ROOT ${STAGED_INSTALL_PREFIX}/boost
  CACHE PATH "Path to internally built Boost installation root"
  FORCE
  )
set(
  BOOST_INCLUDEDIR ${BOOST_ROOT}/include
  CACHE PATH "Path to internally built Boost include directories"
  FORCE
  )
set(
  BOOST_LIBRARYDIR ${BOOST_ROOT}/lib
  CACHE PATH "Path to internally built Boost library directories"
  FORCE
  )
```

12. The final action performed in the else-branch of the conditional is to unset all internal variables:

```
unset(_toolset)
unset(_b2_needed_components)
unset(_build_byproducts)
unset(_b2_select_libraries)
unset(_boostrap_select_libraries)
```

Finally, let us look at `src/CMakeLists.txt`. This file describes a standalone project:

1. We declare a C++ project:

```
cmake_minimum_required(VERSION 3.5 FATAL_ERROR)

project(recipe-02_core LANGUAGES CXX)
```

2. The project depends on Boost and we invoke `find_package`. The configuration of the project from the root `CMakeLists.txt` guarantees that the dependency is always satisfied, either by using Boost pre-installed on the system or the ones we built as a subproject:

```
find_package(Boost 1.61 REQUIRED COMPONENTS filesystem)
```

3. We add our example executable target, describing its link libraries:

```
add_executable(path-info path-info.cpp)

target_link_libraries(path-info
  PUBLIC
    Boost::filesystem
  )
```

> The use of imported targets, while neat, is not guaranteed to work for arbitrary Boost and CMake version combinations. This is because the CMake `FindBoost.cmake` module creates the imported targets by hand, so if the Boost version was unknown at the time of the CMake release, there will be `Boost_LIBRARIES` and `Boost_INCLUDE_DIRS`, but no imported targets (see also https://stackoverflow.com/questions/42123509/cmake-finds-boost-but-the-imported-targets-not-available-for-boost-version).

How it works

This recipe shows how the superbuild pattern can be harnessed to muster the dependencies of your project. Let us take another look at the layout of the project:

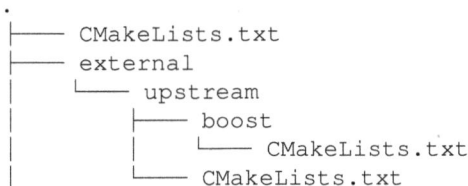

```
.
├── CMakeLists.txt
├── external
│   └── upstream
│       ├── boost
│       │   └── CMakeLists.txt
│       └── CMakeLists.txt
```

```
└── src
    ├── CMakeLists.txt
    └── path-info.cpp
```

We have introduced four CMakeLists.txt files in the project source tree:

1. The root CMakeLists.txt will coordinate the superbuild.
2. The file in external/upstream will lead us to the boost leaf directory.
3. external/upstream/boost/CMakeLists.txt will take care of the Boost dependency.
4. Finally, the CMakeLists.txt under src will build our example code, which depends on Boost.

Let us start start the discussion with the external/upstream/boost/CMakeLists.txt file. Boost uses its own build system and hence we need to be slightly more verbose in our ExternalProject_Add to get everything set up correctly:

1. We keep the default values for the **Directory** options.
2. The **Download** step will download an archive of the desired version of Boost from their online server. We therefore set up the URL and the URL_HASH. The latter is needed to check the integrity of the downloaded archive. Since we do not wish to see a progress report of the download, we also set the DOWNLOAD_NO_PROGRESS option to true.
3. The **Update** step is left blank. If anything needs rebuilding, we do not want to download Boost once again.
4. The **Configure** step will use the native configuration tool provided by Boost in CONFIGURE_COMMAND. Since we want the superbuild to be cross-platform, we use the <SOURCE_DIR> variable to refer to the location for the unpacked sources:

```
CONFIGURE_COMMAND
  <SOURCE_DIR>/bootstrap.sh
  --with-toolset=${_toolset}
  --prefix=${STAGED_INSTALL_PREFIX}/boost
  ${_bootstrap_select_libraries}
```

5. The **Build** options declare an *in-source* build, by setting the BUILD_IN_SOURCE option to true. BUILD_COMMAND uses the Boost native build tool, b2. Since we will be doing an in-source build, we use again the <SOURCE_DIR> variable to refer to the location of the unpacked sources.

6. We then move on to the **Install** options. Boost manages installation using the same native build tool. In fact, the build and installation commands could easily be collapsed into one.

7. The **Output** logging options `LOG_BUILD` and `LOG_INSTALL` direct `ExternalProject_Add` to write log files for the build and installation operations, instead of outputting to screen.

8. Finally, the `BUILD_BYPRODUCTS` option lets `ExternalProject_Add` keep track of the freshly built Boost libraries in subsequent builds, even though their modification times might not get updated.

Once Boost has been built, the `${STAGED_INSTALL_PREFIX}/boost` folder in the build directory will contain our desired libraries. We need to pass this information down to our project, whose build system is generated in `src/CMakeLists.txt`. To achieve this goal, we pass two additional `CMAKE_CACHE_ARGS` in the `ExternalProject_Add` in the root `CMakeLists.txt`:

1. `CMAKE_INCLUDE_PATH`: The path where CMake will look for C/C++ headers
2. `CMAKE_LIBRARY_PATH`: The path where CMake will look for libraries

By setting these variables to our freshly built installation of Boost, we ensure that the dependency will be properly picked up.

> Setting the `CMAKE_DISABLE_FIND_PACKAGE_Boost` to `ON` when configuring the project will skip detection of the Boost libraries and always perform the superbuild. See the documentation: `https://cmake.org/cmake/help/v3.5/variable/CMAKE_DISABLE_FIND_PACKAGE_PackageName.html`

Managing dependencies with a superbuild: II. The FFTW library

> The code for this recipe is available at `https://github.com/dev-cafe/cmake-cookbook/tree/v1.0/chapter-08/recipe-03` and has a C example. The recipe is valid with CMake version 3.5 (and higher) and has been tested on GNU/Linux, macOS, and Windows.

The superbuild pattern can be used to manage fairly complex dependencies, for projects in all the languages supported by CMake. As demonstrated in the previous recipe, it is not necessary for the various subprojects to managed by CMake as well. In contrast to the previous recipe, the external subproject in this recipe will be a CMake project and will show how to download, build, and install the FFTW library using a superbuild. FFTW is a Fast Fourier Transform library, freely available at `http://www.fftw.org`.

Getting ready

The directory layout for this recipe shows the now familiar structure for a superbuild:

```
.
├── CMakeLists.txt
├── external
│   └── upstream
│       ├── CMakeLists.txt
│       └── fftw3
│           └── CMakeLists.txt
└── src
    ├── CMakeLists.txt
    └── fftw_example.c
```

The code for our project, `fftw_example.c`, is located in the `src` subdirectory and will calculate the Fourier transform of a function defined in the source code.

How to do it

Let us start from the root `CMakeLists.txt`. This file puts together the whole superbuild process:

1. We declare a C99 project:

```
cmake_minimum_required(VERSION 3.5 FATAL_ERROR)

project(recipe-03 LANGUAGES C)

set(CMAKE_C_STANDARD 99)
set(CMAKE_C_EXTENSIONS OFF)
set(CMAKE_C_STANDARD_REQUIRED ON)
```

2. As in the previous recipe, we set the `EP_BASE` directory property and the staging installation prefix:

```
set_property(DIRECTORY PROPERTY EP_BASE
${CMAKE_BINARY_DIR}/subprojects)

set(STAGED_INSTALL_PREFIX ${CMAKE_BINARY_DIR}/stage)
message(STATUS "${PROJECT_NAME} staged install:
${STAGED_INSTALL_PREFIX}")
```

3. The dependency on FFTW is checked in the `external/upstream` subdirectory and we proceed to add this subdirectory to the build system:

```
add_subdirectory(external/upstream)
```

4. We include the `ExternalProject.cmake` module:

```
include(ExternalProject)
```

5. We declare the `recipe-03_core` external project. The sources for this project are in the `${CMAKE_CURRENT_LIST_DIR}/src` folder. The project is set up to pick the correct FFTW library using the `FFTW3_DIR` option:

```
ExternalProject_Add(${PROJECT_NAME}_core
  DEPENDS
    fftw3_external
  SOURCE_DIR
    ${CMAKE_CURRENT_LIST_DIR}/src
  CMAKE_ARGS
    -DFFTW3_DIR=${FFTW3_DIR}
    -DCMAKE_C_STANDARD=${CMAKE_C_STANDARD}
    -DCMAKE_C_EXTENSIONS=${CMAKE_C_EXTENSIONS}
    -DCMAKE_C_STANDARD_REQUIRED=${CMAKE_C_STANDARD_REQUIRED}
  CMAKE_CACHE_ARGS
    -DCMAKE_C_FLAGS:STRING=${CMAKE_C_FLAGS}
    -DCMAKE_PREFIX_PATH:PATH=${CMAKE_PREFIX_PATH}
  BUILD_ALWAYS
    1
  INSTALL_COMMAND
    ""
  )
```

The `external/upstream` subdirectory also contains a `CMakeLists.txt`:

1. In this file, we add the `fftw3` folder as another subdirectory in the build system:

    ```
    add_subdirectory(fftw3)
    ```

The `CMakeLists.txt` in `external/upstream/fftw3` takes care of our dependencies:

1. First, we attempt to find the FFTW3 library on the system. Note that we used the `CONFIG` argument to `find_package`:

    ```
    find_package(FFTW3 CONFIG QUIET)
    ```

2. If the library was found we can use the imported target, `FFTW3::fftw3`, to link against it. We print a message to our users showing where the library is located. We add a dummy `INTERFACE` library, `fftw3_external`. This is needed to properly fix dependency trees between subprojects in the superbuild:

    ```
    find_package(FFTW3 CONFIG QUIET)

    if(FFTW3_FOUND)
      get_property(_loc TARGET FFTW3::fftw3 PROPERTY LOCATION)
      message(STATUS "Found FFTW3: ${_loc} (found version
    ${FFTW3_VERSION})")
      add_library(fftw3_external INTERFACE) # dummy
    else()
      # this branch will be discussed below
    endif()
    ```

3. If CMake was unable to locate a pre-installed version of FFTW, we enter the else-branch of the conditional, in which we download, build, and install it using `ExternalProject_Add`. The name of the external project is `fftw3_external`. The `fftw3_external` project will be downloaded from the official online archive. The integrity of the download will be checked using the MD5 checksum:

    ```
    message(STATUS "Suitable FFTW3 could not be located. Downloading
    and building!")

    include(ExternalProject)
    ExternalProject_Add(fftw3_external
      URL
        http://www.fftw.org/fftw-3.3.8.tar.gz
      URL_HASH
        MD5=8aac833c943d8e90d51b697b27d4384d
    ```

4. We disable progress printing for the download and define the update command to be empty:

```
DOWNLOAD_NO_PROGRESS
  1
UPDATE_COMMAND
  " "
```

5. Configuration, building, and installation output will be logged to a file:

```
LOG_CONFIGURE
  1
LOG_BUILD
  1
LOG_INSTALL
  1
```

6. We set the installation prefix for the `fftw3_external` project to the `STAGED_INSTALL_PREFIX` directory previously defined and turn off building the test suite for FFTW3:

```
CMAKE_ARGS
  -DCMAKE_INSTALL_PREFIX=${STAGED_INSTALL_PREFIX}
  -DBUILD_TESTS=OFF
```

7. If we are building on Windows, we set the `WITH_OUR_MALLOC` preprocessor option by means of a generator expression and close the `ExternalProject_Add` command:

```
CMAKE_CACHE_ARGS
  -DCMAKE_C_FLAGS:STRING=$<$<BOOL:WIN32>:-DWITH_OUR_MALLOC>
  )
```

8. Finally, we define the `FFTW3_DIR` variable and cache it. This variable will be used by CMake as a search directory for the exported `FFTW3::fftw3` target:

```
include(GNUInstallDirs)

set(
  FFTW3_DIR
${STAGED_INSTALL_PREFIX}/${CMAKE_INSTALL_LIBDIR}/cmake/fftw3
  CACHE PATH "Path to internally built FFTW3Config.cmake"
  FORCE
  )
```

The `CMakeLists.txt` in the `src` folder is fairly compact:

1. Also in this file, we declare a C project:

```
cmake_minimum_required(VERSION 3.5 FATAL_ERROR)

project(recipe-03_core LANGUAGES C)
```

2. We call `find_package` to detect the FFTW library. Once again, we are using the `CONFIG` detection mode:

```
find_package(FFTW3 CONFIG REQUIRED)
get_property(_loc TARGET FFTW3::fftw3 PROPERTY LOCATION)
message(STATUS "Found FFTW3: ${_loc} (found version
${FFTW3_VERSION})")
```

3. We add the `fftw_example.c` source file to the executable target `fftw_example`:

```
add_executable(fftw_example fftw_example.c)
```

4. We set link libraries for our executable target:

```
target_link_libraries(fftw_example
  PRIVATE
    FFTW3::fftw3
  )
```

How it works

This recipe demonstrated how to download, build, and install an external project whose build system is managed by CMake. In contrast to the previous recipe, where a custom build system had to be used, this superbuild setup is rather compact. It is important to note the use of the `CONFIG` option to the `find_package` command; this tells CMake to first look for a `FFTW3Config.cmake` file in order to locate the FFTW3 library. Such a file exports the library as a target to be picked up by third-party projects. The target contains the version, configuration, and location of the library, that is, complete information on how the target was configured and built. In case the library is not installed on the system, we need to tell CMake where the `FFTW3Config.cmake` file is located. This can be done by setting the `FFTW3_DIR` variable. This was the very last step in the `external/upstream/fftw3/CMakeLists.txt` file, where, by using the `GNUInstallDirs.cmake` module, we set `FFTW3_DIR` as a cache variable to be picked up later on in the superbuild.

Setting the `CMAKE_DISABLE_FIND_PACKAGE_FFTW3` to `ON` when configuring the project will skip detection of the FFTW library and always perform the superbuild. See the documentation: `https://cmake.org/cmake/help/v3.5/variable/CMAKE_DISABLE_FIND_PACKAGE_PackageName.html`

Managing dependencies with a superbuild: III. The Google Test framework

The code for this recipe is available at `https://github.com/dev-cafe/cmake-cookbook/tree/v1.0/chapter-08/recipe-04`, and has a C++ example. The recipe is valid with CMake version 3.11 (and higher), and has been tested on GNU/Linux, macOS, and Windows. The code repository also contains an example compatible with CMake 3.5.

In *Chapter 4*, *Creating and Running Tests*, *Recipe 3*, *Defining a unit test and linking against Google Test*, we implemented unit testing using the Google Test framework and fetched the Google Test sources at configure time using the relatively new `FetchContent` module (available since CMake 3.11). In this chapter, we will revisit this recipe, focus less on the testing aspect, and dive a bit deeper into `FetchContent`, which provides a compact and versatile module to assemble project dependencies at configure time. For additional insight and for CMake below 3.11, we will also discuss how to emulate `FetchContent` using `ExternalProject_Add` *at configure time*.

Getting ready

In this recipe, we will build and test the same source files, `main.cpp`, `sum_integers.cpp`, `sum_integers.hpp`, and `test.cpp`, as in *Chapter 4*, *Creating and Running Tests*, *Recipe 3*, *Defining a unit test and linking against Google Test*. We will download all required Google Test sources at configure time using `FetchContent` or `ExternalProject_Add` and in this recipe only focus on the fetching of dependencies at configure time, not so much on the actual source code and its unit tests.

How to do it

In this recipe, we will only focus on how to fetch the Google Test sources to build the `gtest_main` target. For a discussion on how this target is used to test the example sources, we refer the reader to *Chapter 4, Creating and Running Tests, Recipe 3, Defining a unit test and linking against Google Test*:

1. We first include the `FetchContent` module, which will provide the functions that we will require to declare, query, and populate the dependency:

   ```
   include(FetchContent)
   ```

2. Then, we declare the content - its name, repository location, and the precise version to fetch:

   ```
   FetchContent_Declare(
     googletest
     GIT_REPOSITORY https://github.com/google/googletest.git
     GIT_TAG release-1.8.0
   )
   ```

3. We then query whether the content has already been fetched/populated:

   ```
   FetchContent_GetProperties(googletest)
   ```

4. The previous function call defines `googletest_POPULATED`. If the content is not yet populated, we fetch the content and configure the subproject:

   ```
   if(NOT googletest_POPULATED)
     FetchContent_Populate(googletest)

     # ...

     # adds the targets: gtest, gtest_main, gmock, gmock_main
     add_subdirectory(
       ${googletest_SOURCE_DIR}
       ${googletest_BINARY_DIR}
       )

     # ...

   endif()
   ```

5. Notice how the content is fetched at configure time:

```
$ mkdir -p build
$ cd build
$ cmake ..
```

6. This generates the following build directory tree. The Google Test sources are now in place to be processed by CMake and provide the required target(s):

```
build/
├── ...
├── _deps
│   ├── googletest-build
│   │   ├── ...
│   │   └── ...
│   ├── googletest-src
│   │   ├── ...
│   │   └── ...
│   └── googletest-subbuild
│       ├── ...
│       └── ...
└── ...
```

How it works

The FetchContent module enables populating content at configure time. In our case, we have fetched a Git repository with a well defined Git tag:

```
FetchContent_Declare(
  googletest
  GIT_REPOSITORY https://github.com/google/googletest.git
  GIT_TAG release-1.8.0
)
```

The FetchContent module supports fetching content *via* any method supported by the ExternalProject module - in other words, *via* Subversion, Mercurial, CVS, or HTTP(S). The content name "googletest" was our choice and with this we will be able to reference the content when querying its properties, when populating directories, and later also when configuring the subproject. Before populating the project, we checked whether the content was already fetched, otherwise FetchContent_Populate() would have thrown an error if it was called more than once:

```
if(NOT googletest_POPULATED)
  FetchContent_Populate(googletest)
```

```
  # ...

endif()
```

Only then did we configure the subdirectory, which we can reference with the `googletest_SOURCE_DIR` and `googletest_BINARY_DIR` variables. They were set by `FetchContent_Populate(googletest)` and constructed based on the project name we gave when declaring the content:

```
add_subdirectory(
  ${googletest_SOURCE_DIR}
  ${googletest_BINARY_DIR}
  )
```

The `FetchContent` module has a number of options (see `https://cmake.org/cmake/help/v3.11/module/FetchContent.html`) and here we can show one: how to change the default path into which the external project will be placed. Previously, we saw that by default the content is saved to `${CMAKE_BINARY_DIR}/_deps`. We can change this location by setting `FETCHCONTENT_BASE_DIR`:

```
set(FETCHCONTENT_BASE_DIR ${CMAKE_BINARY_DIR}/custom)

FetchContent_Declare(
  googletest
  GIT_REPOSITORY https://github.com/google/googletest.git
  GIT_TAG release-1.8.0
  )
```

`FetchContent` has become a standard part of CMake in its 3.11 version. In the following code, we will try to emulate `FetchContent` using `ExternalProject_Add` at *configure time*. This will not only be practical for older CMake versions, it will hopefully also give us more insight into what is happening underneath the `FetchContent` layer and provide an interesting alternative to the typical build-time fetching of projects included using `ExternalProject_Add`. Our goal will be to write a `fetch_git_repo` macro and place it in `fetch_git_repo.cmake` so that we can fetch the content like this:

```
include(fetch_git_repo.cmake)

fetch_git_repo(
  googletest
  ${CMAKE_BINARY_DIR}/_deps
  https://github.com/google/googletest.git
  release-1.8.0
  )

  # ...
```

```
# adds the targets: gtest, gtest_main, gmock, gmock_main
add_subdirectory(
  ${googletest_SOURCE_DIR}
  ${googletest_BINARY_DIR}
  )

# ...
```

This feels similar to the use of `FetchContent`. Under the hood, we will
use `ExternalProject_Add`. Let us now lift the hood and inspect the definition of
`fetch_git_repo` in `fetch_git_repo.cmake`:

```
macro(fetch_git_repo _project_name _download_root _git_url _git_tag)

  set(${_project_name}_SOURCE_DIR ${_download_root}/${_project_name}-src)
  set(${_project_name}_BINARY_DIR ${_download_root}/${_project_name}-build)

  # variables used configuring fetch_git_repo_sub.cmake
  set(FETCH_PROJECT_NAME ${_project_name})
  set(FETCH_SOURCE_DIR ${${_project_name}_SOURCE_DIR})
  set(FETCH_BINARY_DIR ${${_project_name}_BINARY_DIR})
  set(FETCH_GIT_REPOSITORY ${_git_url})
  set(FETCH_GIT_TAG ${_git_tag})

  configure_file(
    ${CMAKE_CURRENT_LIST_DIR}/fetch_at_configure_step.in
    ${_download_root}/CMakeLists.txt
    @ONLY
    )

  # undefine them again
  unset(FETCH_PROJECT_NAME)
  unset(FETCH_SOURCE_DIR)
  unset(FETCH_BINARY_DIR)
  unset(FETCH_GIT_REPOSITORY)
  unset(FETCH_GIT_TAG)

  # configure sub-project
  execute_process(
    COMMAND
      "${CMAKE_COMMAND}" -G "${CMAKE_GENERATOR}" .
    WORKING_DIRECTORY
      ${_download_root}
    )
```

The Superbuild Pattern

```
  # build sub-project which triggers ExternalProject_Add
  execute_process(
    COMMAND
      "${CMAKE_COMMAND}" --build .
    WORKING_DIRECTORY
      ${_download_root}
    )
endmacro()
```

The macro receives the project name, download root, Git repository URL, and a Git tag. The macro defines `${_project_name}_SOURCE_DIR` and `${_project_name}_BINARY_DIR`, and we use a macro instead of a function since `${_project_name}_SOURCE_DIR` and `${_project_name}_BINARY_DIR` need to survive the scope of `fetch_git_repo` because we use them later in the main scope to configure the subdirectory:

```
add_subdirectory(
  ${googletest_SOURCE_DIR}
  ${googletest_BINARY_DIR}
  )
```

Inside the `fetch_git_repo` macro, we wish to use `ExternalProject_Add` to fetch the external project at *configure time* and we achieve this with a trick in three steps:

1. First, we configure `fetch_at_configure_step.in`:

```
cmake_minimum_required(VERSION 3.5 FATAL_ERROR)
project(fetch_git_repo_sub LANGUAGES NONE)

include(ExternalProject)

ExternalProject_Add(
  @FETCH_PROJECT_NAME@
  SOURCE_DIR "@FETCH_SOURCE_DIR@"
  BINARY_DIR "@FETCH_BINARY_DIR@"
  GIT_REPOSITORY
    @FETCH_GIT_REPOSITORY@
  GIT_TAG
    @FETCH_GIT_TAG@
  CONFIGURE_COMMAND ""
  BUILD_COMMAND ""
  INSTALL_COMMAND ""
  TEST_COMMAND ""
  )
```

[344]

Using `configure_file`, we generate a `CMakeLists.txt` file in which the previous placeholders are replaced by values defined in `fetch_git_repo.cmake`. Note that the previous `ExternalProject_Add` command is constructed to only fetch, not to configure, build, install, or test.

2. Second, we trigger the `ExternalProject_Add` at configure time (from the perspective of the root project) using a configure step:

```
# configure sub-project
execute_process(
  COMMAND
    "${CMAKE_COMMAND}" -G "${CMAKE_GENERATOR}" .
  WORKING_DIRECTORY
    ${_download_root}
  )
```

3. Third and final trick triggers a configure-time build step in `fetch_git_repo.cmake`:

```
# build sub-project which triggers ExternalProject_Add
execute_process(
  COMMAND
    "${CMAKE_COMMAND}" --build .
  WORKING_DIRECTORY
    ${_download_root}
  )
```

One nice aspect of this solution is that since the external dependency is not configured by `ExternalProject_Add`, we do not need to channel any configuration settings to the project *via* the `ExternalProject_Add` call. We can configure and build the module using `add_subdirectory` as if the external dependency was part of our project source tree. Brilliant disguise!

See also

For a detailed discussion of the available `FetchContent` options, please consult https://cmake.org/cmake/help/v3.11/module/FetchContent.html.

The configure time `ExternalProject_Add` solution is inspired by the work and blog post of Craig Scott: https://crascit.com/2015/07/25/cmake-gtest/.

Managing your project as a superbuild

The code for this recipe is available at `https://github.com/dev-cafe/cmake-cookbook/tree/v1.0/chapter-08/recipe-05` and has a C++ example. The recipe is valid with CMake version 3.6 (and higher) and has been tested on GNU/Linux, macOS, and Windows.

`ExternalProject` and `FetchContent` are two very powerful tools in your CMake arsenal. The previous recipes should have convinced you how versatile the superbuild approach is in managing projects with complex dependencies. We have so far shown how to use `ExternalProject` to handle the following:

- Sources stored within your source tree
- Sources retrieved from archives available on online servers

The previous recipe showed how to use `FetchContent` to handle dependencies available from open source Git repositories. This recipe will show how to use `ExternalProject` to the same effect. This last recipe will introduce an example that will be reused in *Recipe 4, Installing a superbuild*, in *Chapter 10, Writing an Installer*.

Getting ready

The source tree for this superbuild should now feel familiar:

```
.
├── CMakeLists.txt
├── external
│   └── upstream
│       ├── CMakeLists.txt
│       └── message
│           └── CMakeLists.txt
└── src
    ├── CMakeLists.txt
    └── use_message.cpp
```

The root directory has a `CMakeLists.txt`, which we already know will orchestrate the superbuild. The leaf directories `src` and `external` host our own source code and the CMake directives needed to satisfy the dependency on the `message` library, which we will build in this example.

How to do it

The process of setting up a superbuild should by now feel familiar. Let us once again look at the necessary steps, starting with the root `CMakeLists.txt`:

1. We declare a C++11 project with a same default build type:

```
cmake_minimum_required(VERSION 3.6 FATAL_ERROR)

project(recipe-05 LANGUAGES CXX)

set(CMAKE_CXX_STANDARD 11)
set(CMAKE_CXX_EXTENSIONS OFF)
set(CMAKE_CXX_STANDARD_REQUIRED ON)

if(NOT DEFINED CMAKE_BUILD_TYPE OR "${CMAKE_BUILD_TYPE}" STREQUAL
"")
  set(CMAKE_BUILD_TYPE Release CACHE STRING "Build type" FORCE)
endif()

message(STATUS "Build type set to ${CMAKE_BUILD_TYPE}")
```

2. The `EP_BASE` directory property is set. This will fix the layout for all subprojects managed by `ExternalProject`:

```
set_property(DIRECTORY PROPERTY EP_BASE
${CMAKE_BINARY_DIR}/subprojects)
```

3. We set `STAGED_INSTALL_PREFIX`. As before, this location will be used as the installation prefix within the build tree for the dependencies:

```
set(STAGED_INSTALL_PREFIX ${CMAKE_BINARY_DIR}/stage)
message(STATUS "${PROJECT_NAME} staged install:
${STAGED_INSTALL_PREFIX}")
```

4. We add the `external/upstream` subdirectory:

```
add_subdirectory(external/upstream)
```

5. Our own project will also be managed by the superbuild and is hence added with `ExternalProject_Add`:

```
include(ExternalProject)
ExternalProject_Add(${PROJECT_NAME}_core
  DEPENDS
    message_external
  SOURCE_DIR
```

```
            ${CMAKE_CURRENT_SOURCE_DIR}/src
        CMAKE_ARGS
            -DCMAKE_BUILD_TYPE=${CMAKE_BUILD_TYPE}
            -DCMAKE_CXX_COMPILER=${CMAKE_CXX_COMPILER}
            -DCMAKE_CXX_STANDARD=${CMAKE_CXX_STANDARD}
            -DCMAKE_CXX_EXTENSIONS=${CMAKE_CXX_EXTENSIONS}
            -DCMAKE_CXX_STANDARD_REQUIRED=${CMAKE_CXX_STANDARD_REQUIRED}
            -Dmessage_DIR=${message_DIR}
        CMAKE_CACHE_ARGS
            -DCMAKE_CXX_FLAGS:STRING=${CMAKE_CXX_FLAGS}
            -DCMAKE_PREFIX_PATH:PATH=${CMAKE_PREFIX_PATH}
        BUILD_ALWAYS
            1
        INSTALL_COMMAND
            ""
        )
```

The `CMakeLists.txt` in `external/upstream` only contains one command:

```
add_subdirectory(message)
```

Jumping into the `message` folder, we again see the usual commands for managing our dependency on the `message` library:

1. First of all, we call `find_package` to find a suitable version of the library:

```
find_package(message 1 CONFIG QUIET)
```

2. If it is found, we inform the user and add a dummy `INTERFACE` library:

```
get_property(_loc TARGET message::message-shared PROPERTY LOCATION)
message(STATUS "Found message: ${_loc} (found version
${message_VERSION})")
add_library(message_external INTERFACE) # dummy
```

3. If it is not found, we again inform the user and proceed with `ExternalProject_Add`:

```
message(STATUS "Suitable message could not be located, Building
message instead.")
```

4. The project is hosted in a public Git repository and we use the `GIT_TAG` option to specify which branch to download. As before, we leave the `UPDATE_COMMAND` option empty:

```
include(ExternalProject)
ExternalProject_Add(message_external
```

```
GIT_REPOSITORY
  https://github.com/dev-cafe/message.git
GIT_TAG
  master
UPDATE_COMMAND
  ""
```

5. The external project is configured and built using CMake. We pass on all the necessary build options:

```
CMAKE_ARGS
  -DCMAKE_INSTALL_PREFIX=${STAGED_INSTALL_PREFIX}
  -DCMAKE_BUILD_TYPE=${CMAKE_BUILD_TYPE}
  -DCMAKE_CXX_COMPILER=${CMAKE_CXX_COMPILER}
  -DCMAKE_CXX_STANDARD=${CMAKE_CXX_STANDARD}
  -DCMAKE_CXX_EXTENSIONS=${CMAKE_CXX_EXTENSIONS}
  -DCMAKE_CXX_STANDARD_REQUIRED=${CMAKE_CXX_STANDARD_REQUIRED}
CMAKE_CACHE_ARGS
  -DCMAKE_CXX_FLAGS:STRING=${CMAKE_CXX_FLAGS}
```

6. We decide to test the project after it has been installed:

```
TEST_AFTER_INSTALL
  1
```

7. We do not wish to see progress on downloads, nor information on configuring, building, and installing to be reported onscreen, and we close the ExternalProject_Add command:

```
DOWNLOAD_NO_PROGRESS
  1
LOG_CONFIGURE
  1
LOG_BUILD
  1
LOG_INSTALL
  1
)
```

8. To ensure that the subproject is discoverable within the rest of the superbuild, we set the message_DIR directory:

```
if(WIN32 AND NOT CYGWIN)
  set(DEF_message_DIR ${STAGED_INSTALL_PREFIX}/CMake)
else()
  set(DEF_message_DIR ${STAGED_INSTALL_PREFIX}/share/cmake/message)
endif()
```

```
file(TO_NATIVE_PATH "${DEF_message_DIR}" DEF_message_DIR)
set(message_DIR ${DEF_message_DIR}
    CACHE PATH "Path to internally built messageConfig.cmake"
FORCE)
```

Finally, let us look at the `CMakeLists.txt` in the `src` folder:

1. Again, we declare a C++11 project:

```
cmake_minimum_required(VERSION 3.6 FATAL_ERROR)

project(recipe-05_core
  LANGUAGES CXX
  )

set(CMAKE_CXX_STANDARD 11)
set(CMAKE_CXX_EXTENSIONS OFF)
set(CMAKE_CXX_STANDARD_REQUIRED ON)
```

2. This project requires the `message` library:

```
find_package(message 1 CONFIG REQUIRED)
get_property(_loc TARGET message::message-shared PROPERTY LOCATION)
message(STATUS "Found message: ${_loc} (found version
${message_VERSION})")
```

3. We declare an executable target and link it to the `message-shared` library provided by our dependency:

```
add_executable(use_message use_message.cpp)

target_link_libraries(use_message
  PUBLIC
    message::message-shared
  )
```

How it works

This recipe highlighted some new options to the `ExternalProject_Add` command:

1. `GIT_REPOSITORY`: This can be used to specify the URL of the repository containing the sources of our dependency. CMake can also use other version control systems, such as CVS (`CVS_REPOSITORY`), SVN (`SVN_REPOSITORY`), or Mercurial (`HG_REPOSITORY`).

2. GIT_TAG: By default, CMake will check out the default branch of the given repository. However, it is preferable to depend on a well-defined version that is known to be stable. This can be specified with this option, which can accept any identifier recognized by Git as "version" information, such as a Git commit SHA, a Git tag, or just a branch name. Similar options are also available for the other version control systems understood by CMake.

3. TEST_AFTER_INSTALL: Most likely, your dependency has a test suite of its own and you might want to run the test suite to ensure that everything went smoothly during the superbuild. This option will run the tests right after the installation step.

The additional **Test** options understood by ExternalProject_Add are as follows:

- TEST_BEFORE_INSTALL, which will run the test suite *before* the installation step
- TEST_EXCLUDE_FROM_MAIN, with which we can remove the dependency on the main target of the external project from the test suite

These options assume that the external project manages testing using CTest. If the external project does not use CTest to manage testing, we can set the TEST_COMMAND option to execute tests.

Introducing the superbuild pattern even for modules that are part of your own project comes at the cost of introducing an additional layer, re-declaring small CMake projects, and passing configuration settings explicitly through ExternalProject_Add. The benefit of introducing this additional layer is a clear separation of variable and target scopes, which can help to manage complexity, dependencies, and namespaces in projects consisting of several components, where these components can be internal or external, and composed together by CMake.

Mixed-language Projects

9

In this chapter, we will cover the following recipes:

- Building Fortran projects that use C/C++ libraries
- Building C/C++ projects that use Fortran libraries
- Building C++ and Python projects using Cython
- Building C++ and Python projects using Boost.Python
- Building C++ and Python projects using pybind11
- Mixing C, C++, Fortran, and Python using Python CFFI

Introduction

There are plenty of existing libraries that excel at very specific tasks. It's generally a very good idea to reuse such libraries in our own codebases, because we can rely on years of experience from other groups of experts. As computer architectures and compilers evolve, so do programming languages. Whereas years ago most scientific software was written in Fortran, nowadays C, C++, and interpreted languages – first and foremost Python – are taking the center stage. It is indeed more and more common to integrate code written in a compiled language with bindings to an interpreted language, since it affords the following benefits:

- End-users can customize and expand the capabilities offered by the code itself to fully suit their needs.
- One is able to combine the expressiveness of a language such as Python with the performance of a compiled language that is closer "to the metal" in terms of memory addressing, getting the best of both worlds.

As we have consistently shown throughout the previous recipes, the `project` command can be used to set the languages used in the project *via* the LANGUAGES keyword. CMake has support for many – but not all – compiled programming languages. As of CMake 3.5, various flavors of assembly (such as ASM-ATT, ASM, ASM-MASM, and ASM-NASM), C, C++, Fortran, Java, RC (Windows Resource Compiler), and Swift are valid choices. CMake 3.8 added support for two more languages: C# and CUDA (see the release notes here: `https://cmake.org/cmake/help/v3.8/release/3.8.html#languages`).

In this chapter, we will show how to integrate codes written in different compiled (C, C++, and Fortran) and interpreted (Python) languages in a way that is portable and cross-platform. We will show how to leverage CMake and tools intrinsic to the different programming languages we aim to integrate.

Building Fortran projects that use C/C++ libraries

The code for this recipe is available at `https://github.com/dev-cafe/cmake-cookbook/tree/v1.0/chapter-09/recipe-01` and has two examples: one mixing Fortran and C, and the other mixing Fortran and C++. The recipe is valid with CMake version 3.5 (and higher). Both versions of the recipe have been tested on GNU/Linux and macOS.

Fortran has a venerated history as the language of high-performance computing. Many numerical linear algebra libraries are still written primarily in Fortran, as are many big number-crunching packages that need to preserve compatibility with legacy code amassed in the past decades. Whereas Fortran presents a very natural syntax for handling numerical arrays, it is lacking when it comes to interaction with the operating system, primarily because an interoperability layer with C, the *de facto lingua franca* of computer programming, was not mandated until the release of the Fortran 2003 standard. This recipe will show how to interface a Fortran code with both C system libraries and custom C code.

Getting ready

As shown in *Chapter 7*, *Structuring Projects*, we will structure our project as a tree. Each subdirectory has a `CMakeLists.txt` file with instructions pertaining to that directory. This allows us to confine as much information as possible within the leaf directories as in this example:

```
.
├── CMakeLists.txt
└── src
    ├── bt-randomgen-example.f90
    ├── CMakeLists.txt
    ├── interfaces
    │   ├── CMakeLists.txt
    │   ├── interface_backtrace.f90
    │   ├── interface_randomgen.f90
    │   └── randomgen.c
    └── utils
        ├── CMakeLists.txt
        └── util_strings.f90
```

In our case, we have a `src` subdirectory containing the sources, including `bt-randomgen-example.f90`, our executable. Two further subdirectories, `interfaces` and `utils`, contain more source code that will be compiled into libraries.

The source code in the `interfaces` subdirectory shows how to wrap the backtrace C system library. For example, the `interface_backtrace.f90` contains:

```fortran
module interface_backtrace

  implicit none

  interface
    function backtrace(buffer, size) result(bt) bind(C, name="backtrace")
      use, intrinsic :: iso_c_binding, only: c_int, c_ptr
      type(c_ptr) :: buffer
      integer(c_int), value :: size
      integer(c_int) :: bt
    end function

    subroutine backtrace_symbols_fd(buffer, size, fd) bind(C,
name="backtrace_symbols_fd")
      use, intrinsic :: iso_c_binding, only: c_int, c_ptr
      type(c_ptr) :: buffer
      integer(c_int), value :: size, fd
    end subroutine
  end interface

end module
```

The above example shows the use of the following:

- The intrinsic `iso_c_binding` module, which ensures interoperability of Fortran and C types and functions.
- The `interface` declaration, which binds the functions to symbols in a separate library.
- The `bind(C)` attribute, which fixes name-mangling of the declared functions.

This subdirectory contains two more source files:

- `randomgen.c`, which is a C source file that exposes a function, using the C standard `rand` function, to generate random integers within an interval.
- `interface_randomgen.f90`, which wraps the C functions for use within a Fortran executable.

How to do it

We have four `CMakeLists.txt` instances to look at: one root and tree leaves. Let us start with the root `CMakeLists.txt`:

1. We declare a mixed-language Fortran and C project:

   ```
   cmake_minimum_required(VERSION 3.5 FATAL_ERROR)

   project(recipe-01 LANGUAGES Fortran C)
   ```

2. We direct CMake to save static and shared libraries under the `lib` subdirectory of the build directory. Executables will be saved under `bin`, while Fortran compiled module files will be saved under `modules`:

   ```
   set(CMAKE_ARCHIVE_OUTPUT_DIRECTORY ${CMAKE_CURRENT_BINARY_DIR}/lib)
   set(CMAKE_LIBRARY_OUTPUT_DIRECTORY ${CMAKE_CURRENT_BINARY_DIR}/lib)
   set(CMAKE_RUNTIME_OUTPUT_DIRECTORY ${CMAKE_CURRENT_BINARY_DIR}/bin)
   set(CMAKE_Fortran_MODULE_DIRECTORY
     ${CMAKE_CURRENT_BINARY_DIR}/modules)
   ```

3. Next, we move on to the first leaf, `CMakeLists.txt`, by adding the `src` subdirectory:

   ```
   add_subdirectory(src)
   ```

4. The `src/CMakeLists.txt` file adds two more subdirectories:

```
add_subdirectory(interfaces)
add_subdirectory(utils)
```

In the `interfaces` subdirectory, we do the following:

1. We include the `FortranCInterface.cmake` module and verify that the C and Fortran compilers can talk properly to each other:

```
include(FortranCInterface)
FortranCInterface_VERIFY()
```

2. Next, we find the backtrace system library, since we want to use it within our Fortran code:

```
find_package(Backtrace REQUIRED)
```

3. We then create a shared library target with the source files for the backtrace wrapper, the random number generator, and its Fortran wrapper:

```
add_library(bt-randomgen-wrap SHARED "")

target_sources(bt-randomgen-wrap
  PRIVATE
    interface_backtrace.f90
    interface_randomgen.f90
    randomgen.c
  )
```

4. We also set the link libraries for the newly generated library target. We use the `PUBLIC` attribute, so that additional targets linking to our libraries will see dependencies properly:

```
target_link_libraries(bt-randomgen-wrap
  PUBLIC
    ${Backtrace_LIBRARIES}
  )
```

In the `utils` subdirectory, we have one more `CMakeLists.txt`. This is a one-liner: we create a new library target into which the source file in this subdirectory will be compiled. There are no dependencies for this target:

```
add_library(utils SHARED util_strings.f90)
```

Let us return to `src/CMakeLists.txt`:

1. We add an executable target, with `bt-randomgen-example.f90` as source file:

   ```
   add_executable(bt-randomgen-example bt-randomgen-example.f90)
   ```

2. Finally, we link the library targets, generated in the `CMakeLists.txt` leaf, into our executable target:

   ```
   target_link_libraries(bt-randomgen-example
     PRIVATE
       bt-randomgen-wrap
       utils
     )
   ```

How it works

Having identified the correct libraries to link to, we need to make sure that our program can correctly call the functions they define. Every compiler performs name mangling when generating machine code and, unfortunately, conventions for this operation are not universal, but compiler-dependent. `FortranCInterface`, which we have already encountered in *Chapter 3, Detecting External Libraries and Programs, Recipe 4, Detecting the BLAS and LAPACK math libraries,* checks the compatibility of the selected C compiler with the Fortran compiler. For our current purposes, name mangling is not really an issue. The Fortran 2003 standard defines a `bind` attribute for functions and subroutines that accepts an optional `name` argument. If this argument is provided, the compiler will generate symbols for those subroutines and functions using the name fixed by the programmers. For example, the backtrace function can be exposed to Fortran from C, preserving the name, as follows:

```
function backtrace(buffer, size) result(bt) bind(C, name="backtrace")
```

There is more

The CMake code in `interfaces/CMakeLists.txt` also showed that it is possible to create a library from source files in different languages. CMake is evidently able to do the following:

- Discern which compiler to use to get object files from the listed source files.
- Select the linker appropriately to build a library (or executable) from these object files.

How does CMake determine which compiler to use? Specifying the LANGUAGES option to the project command will let CMake check for working compilers for the given languages on your system. When a target is added with lists of source files, CMake will appropriately determine the compiler based on the file extension. Hence, files terminating with .c will be compiled to object files using the C compiler already determined, whereas files terminating with .f90 (or .F90 if they need preprocessing) will be compiled using the working Fortran compiler. Similarly for C++, the .cpp or .cxx extensions will trigger usage of the C++ compiler. We have only listed some of the possible, valid file extensions for the C, C++, and Fortran languages, but CMake can recognize many more. What if the file extensions in your project are, for any reason, not among the ones that are recognized? The LANGUAGE source file property can be used to tell CMake which compiler to use on specific source files, like so:

```
set_source_files_properties(my_source_file.axx
  PROPERTIES
    LANGUAGE CXX
  )
```

Finally, what about the linker? How does CMake determine the linker language for targets? For targets that **do not mix** programming languages, the choice is straightforward: invoke the linker *via* the compiler command that was used to generate the object files. If the targets **do mix** programming languages, as in our example, the linker language is chosen based on that whose preference value is highest among the ones available in the language mix. With our example mixing Fortran and C, the Fortran language has higher preference than the C language and is hence used as linker language. When mixing Fortran and C++, it is the latter to have higher preference and is hence used as the linker language. Much as with the compiler language, we can force CMake to use a specific linker language for our target *via* the corresponding LINKER_LANGUAGE property on targets:

```
set_target_properties(my_target
  PROPERTIES
    LINKER_LANGUAGE Fortran
  )
```

Building C/C++ projects that use Fortran libraries

> The code for this recipe is available at `https://github.com/dev-cafe/cmake-cookbook/tree/v1.0/chapter-09/recipe-02` and has an example mixing C++, C, and Fortran. The recipe is valid with CMake version 3.5 (and higher) and has been tested on GNU/Linux and macOS.

Recipe 4, Detecting the BLAS and LAPACK math libraries, in *Chapter 3, Detecting External Libraries and Programs,* showed how to detect BLAS and LAPACK linear algebra libraries, written in Fortran, and how to use them in C++ code. Here we will revisit this recipe, but this time from a different angle: focusing less on detecting the external libraries but rather discussing the aspect of mixing C++ and Fortran and the name mangling in more depth.

Getting ready

In this recipe, we will reuse the sources from *Chapter 3, Detecting External Libraries and Programs, Recipe 4, Detecting the BLAS and LAPACK math libraries*. Although we will not modify the actual implementation sources or header files, we will modify the project tree structure following the recommendations discussed in *Chapter 7, Structuring Projects,* and arrive at the following source code structure:

```
.
├── CMakeLists.txt
├── README.md
└── src
    ├── CMakeLists.txt
    ├── linear-algebra.cpp
    └── math
        ├── CMakeLists.txt
        ├── CxxBLAS.cpp
        ├── CxxBLAS.hpp
        ├── CxxLAPACK.cpp
        └── CxxLAPACK.hpp
```

Here we have collected all the wrappers to BLAS and LAPACK, which provide the `math` library under `src/math`. The main program is `linear-algebra.cpp`. All sources are thus organized under the `src` subdirectory. To localize the scope, we have also split the CMake code over three `CMakeLists.txt` files, which we will discuss now.

How to do it

This project mixes C++, which is the language of the main program, Fortran, because this is the language the libraries are written in, and C, which is needed to wrap the Fortran subroutines. In the root CMakeLists.txt file, we need to do the following:

1. Declare the project as mixed-language and set the C++ standard:

```
cmake_minimum_required(VERSION 3.5 FATAL_ERROR)

project(recipe-02 LANGUAGES CXX C Fortran)

set(CMAKE_CXX_STANDARD 11)
set(CMAKE_CXX_EXTENSIONS OFF)
set(CMAKE_CXX_STANDARD_REQUIRED ON)
```

2. We use the GNUInstallDirs module to direct CMake to save static and shared libraries and the executable into standard directories. We also instruct CMake to place Fortran compiled module files under modules:

```
include(GNUInstallDirs)
set(CMAKE_ARCHIVE_OUTPUT_DIRECTORY
  ${CMAKE_BINARY_DIR}/${CMAKE_INSTALL_LIBDIR})
set(CMAKE_LIBRARY_OUTPUT_DIRECTORY
  ${CMAKE_BINARY_DIR}/${CMAKE_INSTALL_LIBDIR})
set(CMAKE_RUNTIME_OUTPUT_DIRECTORY
  ${CMAKE_BINARY_DIR}/${CMAKE_INSTALL_BINDIR})
set(CMAKE_Fortran_MODULE_DIRECTORY ${PROJECT_BINARY_DIR}/modules)
```

3. We then move on to the next leaf subdirectory:

```
add_subdirectory(src)
```

The leaf file src/CMakeLists.txt adds yet another subdirectory, math, which contains the linear algebra wrappers. In src/math/CMakeLists.txt, we need to do the following:

1. We invoke find_package to get the location of the BLAS and LAPACK libraries:

```
find_package(BLAS REQUIRED)
find_package(LAPACK REQUIRED)
```

2. We include the `FortranCInterface.cmake` module and verify that the Fortran, C and, C++ compilers are compatible:

```
include(FortranCInterface)
FortranCInterface_VERIFY(CXX)
```

3. We also need to generate preprocessor macros to take care of the name mangling of the BLAS and LAPACK subroutines. Once again, `FortranCInterface` comes to the rescue by generating a header file called `fc_mangle.h` in the current build directory:

```
FortranCInterface_HEADER(
  fc_mangle.h
  MACRO_NAMESPACE "FC_"
  SYMBOLS DSCAL DGESV
  )
```

4. Next, we add a library with our sources for the BLAS and LAPACK wrappers. We also specify the directories where the header files and libraries are to be found. Notice the `PUBLIC` attribute, which will allow other targets depending on `math` to properly get their dependencies:

```
add_library(math "")

target_sources(math
  PRIVATE
    CxxBLAS.cpp
    CxxLAPACK.cpp
  )

target_include_directories(math
  PUBLIC
    ${CMAKE_CURRENT_SOURCE_DIR}
    ${CMAKE_CURRENT_BINARY_DIR}
  )

target_link_libraries(math
  PUBLIC
    ${LAPACK_LIBRARIES}
  )
```

Stepping back to `src/CMakeLists.txt`, we finally add an executable target and link it to our `math` library of BLAS/LAPACK wrappers:

```
add_executable(linear-algebra "")

target_sources(linear-algebra
```

```
  PRIVATE
    linear-algebra.cpp
  )

target_link_libraries(linear-algebra
  PRIVATE
    math
  )
```

How it works

Using `find_package`, we have identified the correct libraries to link to. As in the previous recipe, we need to make sure that our program can correctly call the functions they define. As in *Chapter 3, Detecting External Libraries and Programs, Recipe 4, Detecting the BLAS and LAPACK math libraries,* we face the problem of compiler-dependent name mangling of symbols. We use the `FortranCInterface` CMake module to check the compatibility of the selected C and C++ compilers with the Fortran compiler. We also use the `FortranCInterface_HEADER` function to generate a header file with macros to take care of name mangling of Fortran subroutines. This was achieved with the following code:

```
FortranCInterface_HEADER(
  fc_mangle.h
  MACRO_NAMESPACE "FC_"
  SYMBOLS DSCAL DGESV
  )
```

This command will generate the `fc_mangle.h` header file with name-mangling macros, as inferred from the Fortran compiler, and save it into the current binary directory, `CMAKE_CURRENT_BINARY_DIR`. We were careful to set `CMAKE_CURRENT_BINARY_DIR` as an include path for our `math` target. Consider the following generated `fc_mangle.h`:

```
#ifndef FC_HEADER_INCLUDED
#define FC_HEADER_INCLUDED

/* Mangling for Fortran global symbols without underscores. */
#define FC_GLOBAL(name,NAME) name##_

/* Mangling for Fortran global symbols with underscores. */
#define FC_GLOBAL_(name,NAME) name##_

/* Mangling for Fortran module symbols without underscores. */
#define FC_MODULE(mod_name,name, mod_NAME,NAME) __##mod_name##_MOD_##name
```

```
/* Mangling for Fortran module symbols with underscores. */
#define FC_MODULE_(mod_name,name, mod_NAME,NAME) __##mod_name##_MOD_##name

/* Mangle some symbols automatically. */
#define DSCAL FC_GLOBAL(dscal, DSCAL)
#define DGESV FC_GLOBAL(dgesv, DGESV)

#endif
```

The compiler in this example uses underscores for mangling. Since Fortran is case-insensitive, the subroutine might appear in either lowercase or uppercase, justifying the need to pass both cases to the macro. Notice that CMake will also generate macros for mangling symbols hidden behind Fortran modules.

> Nowadays, many implementations of BLAS and LAPACK ship with a thin C layer wrapper around the Fortran subroutines. These wrappers have been standardized over the years and are called CBLAS and LAPACKE, respectively.

Since we have carefully organized the sources into a library target and an executable target, we should comment on the use of the PUBLIC, INTERFACE, and PRIVATE visibility attributes for the targets. These are essential for a clean CMake project structure. As with sources, include directories, compile definitions, and options, the meaning of these attributes remains the same when used in conjunction with target_link_libraries:

- With the PRIVATE attribute, libraries will only be linked to the current target, but not to any other targets consuming it.
- With the INTERFACE attribute, libraries will only be linked to targets consuming the current target as a dependency.
- With the PUBLIC attribute, libraries will be linked to the current target and to any other target consuming it as a dependency.

Building C++ and Python projects using Cython

> The code for this recipe is available at https://github.com/dev-cafe/cmake-cookbook/tree/v1.0/chapter-09/recipe-03 and has a C++ example. The recipe is valid with CMake version 3.5 (and higher) and has been tested on GNU/Linux, macOS, and Windows.

Cython is an optimizing static compiler that allows to write C extensions for Python. Cython is a very powerful tool and uses the extended Cython programming language (based on Pyrex). A typical use case for Cython is speeding up Python code, but it can also be used to interface C/C++ with Python *via* a Cython layer. In this recipe, we will focus on the latter use case and demonstrate how to interface C/C++ and Python using Cython with the help of CMake.

Getting ready

As an example, we will use the following C++ code (`account.cpp`):

```
#include "account.hpp"

Account::Account() : balance(0.0) {}

Account::~Account() {}

void Account::deposit(const double amount) { balance += amount; }

void Account::withdraw(const double amount) { balance -= amount; }

double Account::get_balance() const { return balance; }
```

This code provides the following interface (`account.hpp`):

```
#pragma once

class Account {
public:
  Account();
  ~Account();

  void deposit(const double amount);
  void withdraw(const double amount);
  double get_balance() const;

private:
  double balance;
};
```

Using this example code, we can create bank accounts that start with a balance of zero. We can deposit to and withdraw from an account and also query the account balance using `get_balance()`. The balance itself is a private member of the `Account` class.

Our goal is to be able to interact with this C++ class directly from Python – in other words, on the Python side, we wish to be able to do this:

```
account = Account()

account.deposit(100.0)
account.withdraw(50.0)

balance = account.get_balance()
```

To achieve this, we will need a Cython interface file (we will call this file `account.pyx`):

```
# describe the c++ interface
cdef extern from "account.hpp":
    cdef cppclass Account:
        Account() except +
        void deposit(double)
        void withdraw(double)
        double get_balance()

# describe the python interface
cdef class pyAccount:
    cdef Account *thisptr
    def __cinit__(self):
        self.thisptr = new Account()
    def __dealloc__(self):
        del self.thisptr
    def deposit(self, amount):
        self.thisptr.deposit(amount)
    def withdraw(self, amount):
        self.thisptr.withdraw(amount)
    def get_balance(self):
        return self.thisptr.get_balance()
```

How to do it

Let us look at how to generate the Python interface:

1. Our `CMakeLists.txt` starts out defining the CMake dependency, project name, and language:

```
# define minimum cmake version
cmake_minimum_required(VERSION 3.5 FATAL_ERROR)

# project name and supported language
project(recipe-03 LANGUAGES CXX)
```

```
# require C++11
set(CMAKE_CXX_STANDARD 11)
set(CMAKE_CXX_EXTENSIONS OFF)
set(CMAKE_CXX_STANDARD_REQUIRED ON)
```

2. On Windows, it is best not to keep the build type undefined, so that we can match the build type of this project with the build type of the Python environment. Here we default to the `Release` build type:

```
if(NOT CMAKE_BUILD_TYPE)
  set(CMAKE_BUILD_TYPE Release CACHE STRING "Build type" FORCE)
endif()
```

3. In this recipe, we will also require the Python interpreter:

```
find_package(PythonInterp REQUIRED)
```

4. The following CMake code will allow us to build the Python module:

```
# directory cointaining UseCython.cmake and FindCython.cmake
list(APPEND CMAKE_MODULE_PATH ${CMAKE_CURRENT_SOURCE_DIR}/cmake-cython)

# this defines cython_add_module
include(UseCython)

# tells UseCython to compile this file as a c++ file
set_source_files_properties(account.pyx PROPERTIES CYTHON_IS_CXX TRUE)

# create python module
cython_add_module(account account.pyx account.cpp)

# location of account.hpp
target_include_directories(account
  PRIVATE
    ${CMAKE_CURRENT_SOURCE_DIR}
  )
```

5. Now we define a test:

```
# turn on testing
enable_testing()

# define test
add_test(
  NAME
    python_test
```

```
        COMMAND
          ${CMAKE_COMMAND} -E env
  ACCOUNT_MODULE_PATH=$<TARGET_FILE_DIR:account>
          ${PYTHON_EXECUTABLE} ${CMAKE_CURRENT_SOURCE_DIR}/test.py
        )
```

6. `python_test` executes `test.py`, where we make a couple of deposits and withdrawals and verify the balances:

```python
import os
import sys
sys.path.append(os.getenv('ACCOUNT_MODULE_PATH'))

from account import pyAccount as Account

account1 = Account()

account1.deposit(100.0)
account1.deposit(100.0)

account2 = Account()

account2.deposit(200.0)
account2.deposit(200.0)

account1.withdraw(50.0)

assert account1.get_balance() == 150.0
assert account2.get_balance() == 400.0
```

7. With this, we are ready to configure, build, and test the code:

```
$ mkdir -p build
$ cd build
$ cmake ..
$ cmake --build .
$ ctest

  Start 1: python_test
1/1 Test #1: python_test ..................... Passed 0.03 sec

100% tests passed, 0 tests failed out of 1

Total Test time (real) = 0.03 sec
```

How it works

In this recipe, we have interfaced Python and C++ using a relatively compact `CMakeLists.txt` file, but we have achieved this by using the `FindCython.cmake` and `UseCython.cmake` modules, which have been placed under `cmake-cython`. These modules are included using the following code:

```
# directory contains UseCython.cmake and FindCython.cmake
list(APPEND CMAKE_MODULE_PATH ${CMAKE_CURRENT_SOURCE_DIR}/cmake-cython)
# this defines cython_add_module
include(UseCython)
```

`FindCython.cmake` is included in `UseCython.cmake` and locates and defines `${CYTHON_EXECUTABLE}`. The latter module defines the `cython_add_module` and `cython_add_standalone_executable` functions, which can be used to create Python modules and standalone executables, respectively. Both modules have been downloaded from `https://github.com/thewtex/cython-cmake-example/tree/master/cmake`.

In this recipe, we use `cython_add_module` to create a Python module library. Note how we set the non-standard `CYTHON_IS_CXX` source file property to `TRUE`, so that the `cython_add_module` function will know to compile `pyx` as a C++ file:

```
# tells UseCython to compile this file as a c++ file
set_source_files_properties(account.pyx PROPERTIES CYTHON_IS_CXX TRUE)

# create python module
cython_add_module(account account.pyx account.cpp)
```

The Python module is created inside `${CMAKE_CURRENT_BINARY_DIR}`, and in order for the Python `test.py` script to locate it, we pass the relevant path with a custom environment variable, which is used inside `test.py` to set the `PATH` variable. Note how the `COMMAND` is set to call the CMake executable itself to set the local environment right before executing the Python script. This affords us platform-independence and avoids polluting the environment with spurious variables:

```
add_test(
  NAME
    python_test
  COMMAND
    ${CMAKE_COMMAND} -E env ACCOUNT_MODULE_PATH=$<TARGET_FILE_DIR:account>
    ${PYTHON_EXECUTABLE} ${CMAKE_CURRENT_SOURCE_DIR}/test.py
  )
```

We should also take a look at the `account.pyx` file, which is the interface file between Python and C++ and describes the C++ interface:

```
# describe the c++ interface
cdef extern from "account.hpp":
    cdef cppclass Account:
        Account() except +
        void deposit(double)
        void withdraw(double)
        double get_balance()
```

You can see `except +` in the `Account` class constructor. This directive allows Cython to handle exceptions raised by the C++ code.

The `account.pyx` interface file also describes the Python interface:

```
# describe the python interface
cdef class pyAccount:
    cdef Account *thisptr
    def __cinit__(self):
        self.thisptr = new Account()
    def __dealloc__(self):
        del self.thisptr
    def deposit(self, amount):
        self.thisptr.deposit(amount)
    def withdraw(self, amount):
        self.thisptr.withdraw(amount)
    def get_balance(self):
        return self.thisptr.get_balance()
```

We can see how the `cinit` constructor, the `__dealloc__` destructor, and the `deposit` and `withdraw` methods, are matched with the corresponding C++ implementation counterparts.

To summarize, we have found a mechanism to couple Python and C++ by introducing a dependency on the Cython module. This module can preferably be installed by `pip` into a virtual environment or Pipenv, or by using Anaconda.

There is more

C could be coupled analogously. If we wish to take advantage of constructors and destructors, we could write a thin C++ layer around the C interface.

Typed Memoryviews offer the interesting functionality to map and access memory buffers allocated by C/C++ directly in Python, without creating any overhead: `http://cython.readthedocs.io/en/latest/src/userguide/memoryviews.html`. They make it possible to map NumPy arrays directly to C++ arrays.

Building C++ and Python projects using Boost.Python

The code for this recipe is available at `https://github.com/dev-cafe/cmake-cookbook/tree/v1.0/chapter-09/recipe-04` and has a C++ example. The recipe is valid with CMake version 3.5 (and higher) and has been tested on GNU/Linux, macOS, and Windows.

The Boost libraries offer another popular alternative to interface C++ code with Python. This recipe will show how to use CMake for C++ projects that rely on Boost.Python to expose their functionality as a Python module. We will reuse the example from the previous recipe and attempt to interact with the same C++ implementation (`account.cpp`) as in the Cython example.

Getting ready

While we keep `account.cpp` unchanged, we modify the interface file from the previous recipe (`account.hpp`):

```
#pragma once
#define BOOST_PYTHON_STATIC_LIB
#include <boost/python.hpp>

class Account {
public:
  Account();
  ~Account();

  void deposit(const double amount);
  void withdraw(const double amount);
  double get_balance() const;

private:
  double balance;
};
```

```
namespace py = boost::python;

BOOST_PYTHON_MODULE(account) {
  py::class_<Account>("Account")
      .def("deposit", &Account::deposit)
      .def("withdraw", &Account::withdraw)
      .def("get_balance", &Account::get_balance);
}
```

How to do it

These are the required steps to use Boost.Python with your C++ project:

1. As in the previous recipe, we start by defining the minimum version, the project name, supported language, and the default build type:

```
# define minimum cmake version
cmake_minimum_required(VERSION 3.5 FATAL_ERROR)

# project name and supported language
project(recipe-04 LANGUAGES CXX)

# require C++11
set(CMAKE_CXX_STANDARD 11)
set(CMAKE_CXX_EXTENSIONS OFF)
set(CMAKE_CXX_STANDARD_REQUIRED ON)

# we default to Release build type
if(NOT CMAKE_BUILD_TYPE)
  set(CMAKE_BUILD_TYPE Release CACHE STRING "Build type" FORCE)
endif()
```

2. In this recipe, we depend on the Python and Boost libraries as well as the Python interpreter for testing. The name of the Boost.Python component depends on the Boost version and the Python version, so we probe a couple of possible component names:

```
# for testing we will need the python interpreter
find_package(PythonInterp REQUIRED)

# we require python development headers
find_package(PythonLibs
${PYTHON_VERSION_MAJOR}.${PYTHON_VERSION_MINOR} EXACT REQUIRED)
```

```
# now search for the boost component
# depending on the boost version it is called either python,
# python2, python27, python3, python36, python37, ...

list(
  APPEND _components
    python${PYTHON_VERSION_MAJOR}${PYTHON_VERSION_MINOR}
    python${PYTHON_VERSION_MAJOR}
    python
  )

set(_boost_component_found "")

foreach(_component IN ITEMS ${_components})
  find_package(Boost COMPONENTS ${_component})
  if(Boost_FOUND)
    set(_boost_component_found ${_component})
    break()
  endif()
endforeach()

if(_boost_component_found STREQUAL "")
  message(FATAL_ERROR "No matching Boost.Python component found")
endif()
```

3. With the following commands, we define the Python module and its
   dependencies:

```
# create python module
add_library(account
  MODULE
    account.cpp
  )

target_link_libraries(account
  PUBLIC
    Boost::${_boost_component_found}
    ${PYTHON_LIBRARIES}
  )

target_include_directories(account
  PRIVATE
    ${PYTHON_INCLUDE_DIRS}
  )
```

```
# prevent cmake from creating a "lib" prefix
set_target_properties(account
  PROPERTIES
    PREFIX ""
  )

if(WIN32)
  # python will not import dll but expects pyd
  set_target_properties(account
    PROPERTIES
      SUFFIX ".pyd"
    )
endif()
```

4. Finally, we define a test for this implementation:

```
# turn on testing
enable_testing()

# define test
add_test(
  NAME
    python_test
  COMMAND
    ${CMAKE_COMMAND} -E env
ACCOUNT_MODULE_PATH=$<TARGET_FILE_DIR:account>
    ${PYTHON_EXECUTABLE} ${CMAKE_CURRENT_SOURCE_DIR}/test.py
  )
```

5. The code can now be configured, compiled, and tested:

```
$ mkdir -p build
$ cd build
$ cmake ..
$ cmake --build .
$ ctest

    Start 1: python_test
1/1 Test #1: python_test ...................... Passed    0.10
sec

100% tests passed, 0 tests failed out of 1

Total Test time (real) =   0.11 sec
```

How it works

Instead of depending on the Cython module, this recipe now depends on locating the Boost libraries on the system, in combination with the Python development headers and library.

The Python development headers and library are searched for with the following:

```
find_package(PythonInterp REQUIRED)

find_package(PythonLibs ${PYTHON_VERSION_MAJOR}.${PYTHON_VERSION_MINOR}
EXACT REQUIRED)
```

Note how we first searched for the interpreter and then for the development headers and libraries. Moreover, the search for `PythonLibs` asks for the exact same major and minor versions for the development headers and libraries as were found for the interpreter. This is necessary for ensuring that consistent versions of interpreter and libraries are used throughout the project. However, this command combination will not guarantee that an exactly matching version of the two will be found.

When locating the Boost.Python component, we have met the difficulty that the name of the component that we try to locate depends both on the Boost version and our Python environment. Depending on the Boost version, the component can be called `python`, `python2`, `python3`, `python27`, `python36`, `python37`, and so on. We have solved this problem by searching from specific to more generic names and only failing if no match can be located:

```
list(
  APPEND _components
    python${PYTHON_VERSION_MAJOR}${PYTHON_VERSION_MINOR}
    python${PYTHON_VERSION_MAJOR}
    python
  )

set(_boost_component_found "")

foreach(_component IN ITEMS ${_components})
  find_package(Boost COMPONENTS ${_component})
  if(Boost_FOUND)
    set(_boost_component_found ${_component})
    break()
  endif()
endforeach()
```

```
if(_boost_component_found STREQUAL "")
  message(FATAL_ERROR "No matching Boost.Python component found")
endif()
```

Discovery and usage of the Boost libraries can be tweaked by setting additional CMake variables. For example, CMake offers the following options:

- `Boost_USE_STATIC_LIBS` can be set to `ON` to force the use of the static version of the Boost libraries.
- `Boost_USE_MULTITHREADED` can be set to `ON` to ensure that the multithreaded version is picked up and used.
- `Boost_USE_STATIC_RUNTIME` can be set to `ON` such that our targets will use the variant of Boost that links the C++ runtime statically.

Another new aspect introduced by this recipe is the use of the `MODULE` option to the `add_library` command. We already know from *Recipe 3, Building and linking shared and static libraries*, in *Chapter 1, From a Simple Executable to Libraries*, that CMake accepts the following options as valid second argument to `add_library`:

- `STATIC`, to create static libraries; that is, archives of object files for use when linking other targets, such as executables
- `SHARED`, to create shared libraries; that is, libraries that can be linked dynamically and loaded at runtime
- `OBJECT`, to create object libraries; that is, object files without archiving them into a static library, nor linking them into a shared object

The `MODULE` option introduced here will generate a *plugin library*; that is, a Dynamic Shared Object (DSO) that is not linked dynamically into any executable, but can still be loaded at runtime. Since we are extending Python with our own functionality written in C++, the Python interpreter will need to be able to load our library at runtime. This can be achieved by using the `MODULE` option to `add_library` and by preventing the addition of any prefix (for example, `lib` on Unix systems) to the name of our library target. The latter operation is carried out by setting the appropriate target property, like so:

```
set_target_properties(account
  PROPERTIES
    PREFIX ""
  )
```

One aspect of all recipes that demonstrate the interfacing of Python and C++ is that we need to describe to the Python code how to hook up to the C++ layer and to list the symbols which should be visible to Python. We also have the possibility to (re)name these symbols. In the previous recipe, we did this in a separate `account.pyx` file. When using `Boost.Python`, we describe the interface directly in the C++ code, ideally close to the definition of the class or function we wish to interface:

```
BOOST_PYTHON_MODULE(account) {
  py::class_<Account>("Account")
      .def("deposit", &Account::deposit)
      .def("withdraw", &Account::withdraw)
      .def("get_balance", &Account::get_balance);
}
```

The `BOOST_PYTHON_MODULE` template is included from `<boost/python.hpp>` and is responsible for creating the Python interface. The module will expose an `Account` Python class that maps to the C++ class. In this case, we do not have to explicitly declare a constructor and destructor – these are created for us and called automatically when the Python object is created:

```
myaccount = Account()
```

The destructor is called when the object goes out of scope and is collected by the Python garbage collection. Also, observe how `BOOST_PYTHON_MODULE` exposes the `deposit`, `withdraw`, and `get_balance` functions, and maps them to the corresponding C++ class methods.

This way, the compiled module can be found by Python when placed in `PYTHONPATH`. In this recipe, we have achieved a relatively clean separation between the Python and C++ layers. The Python code is not restricted in functionality, does not require type annotation or rewriting of names, and remains *pythonic*:

```
from account import Account

account1 = Account()

account1.deposit(100.0)
account1.deposit(100.0)

account2 = Account()

account2.deposit(200.0)
account2.deposit(200.0)
```

```
account1.withdraw(50.0)

assert account1.get_balance() == 150.0
assert account2.get_balance() == 400.0
```

There is more

In this recipe, we rely on Boost being installed on the system and so the CMake code tries to detect the corresponding library. Alternatively, we could have shipped the Boost sources together with our project and build this dependency as part of the project. Boost is a portable way to interface Python with C(++). The portability with respect to compiler support and C++ standard however comes at a price: Boost.Python is not a lightweight dependency. In the following recipe, we will discuss a lightweight alternative to Boost.Python.

Building C++ and Python projects using pybind11

The code for this recipe is available at `https://github.com/dev-cafe/cmake-cookbook/tree/v1.0/chapter-09/recipe-05` and has a C++ example. The recipe is valid with CMake version 3.11 (and higher) and has been tested on GNU/Linux, macOS, and Windows.

In the previous recipe, we have used Boost.Python to interface Python with C(++). In this recipe, we will try to interface Python with C++ using pybind11 as a lightweight alternative that makes use of C++11 features and therefore requires a compiler with C++11 support. As an additional variation to the previous recipe we will demonstrate how to fetch the pybind11 dependency at configure time and build our project including a Python interface using the FetchContent approach, which we met in *Chapter 4, Creating and Running Tests, Recipe 3, Define a unit test and linking against Google Test,* and discussed in *Chapter 8, The Superbuild Pattern, Recipe 4, Managing dependencies with a superbuild: III. The Google Test framework.* In *Chapter 11, Packaging Projects, Recipe 2, Distributing a C++/Python project built with CMake/pybind11 via PyPI,* we will revisit this example and show how to package it and make it installable with pip.

Getting ready

We will keep `account.cpp` unchanged with respect to the previous two recipes and only modify `account.hpp`:

```
#pragma once

#include <pybind11/pybind11.h>

class Account {
public:
  Account();
  ~Account();

  void deposit(const double amount);
  void withdraw(const double amount);
  double get_balance() const;

private:
  double balance;
};

namespace py = pybind11;

PYBIND11_MODULE(account, m) {
  py::class_<Account>(m, "Account")
      .def(py::init())
      .def("deposit", &Account::deposit)
      .def("withdraw", &Account::withdraw)
      .def("get_balance", &Account::get_balance);
}
```

We will follow the pybind11 documentation "Building with CMake" (`https://pybind11.readthedocs.io/en/stable/compiling.html#building-with-cmake`) and introduce the pybind11 CMake code using `add_subdirectory`. However, we will not place the pybind11 source code explicitly into our project directory, but rather demonstrate how to fetch pybind11 sources at configure time using `FetchContent` (`https://cmake.org/cmake/help/v3.11/module/FetchContent.html`).

For better code reuse in the next recipe, we will also place all sources into a subdirectory and use the following project layout:

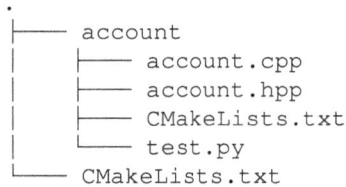

```
.
├── account
│   ├── account.cpp
│   ├── account.hpp
│   ├── CMakeLists.txt
│   └── test.py
└── CMakeLists.txt
```

How to do it

Let us analyze in detail the contents of the various CMakeLists.txt files in this project:

1. The root CMakeLists.txt file contains the familiar header:

```
# define minimum cmake version
cmake_minimum_required(VERSION 3.11 FATAL_ERROR)

# project name and supported language
project(recipe-05 LANGUAGES CXX)

# require C++11
set(CMAKE_CXX_STANDARD 11)
set(CMAKE_CXX_EXTENSIONS OFF)
set(CMAKE_CXX_STANDARD_REQUIRED ON)
```

2. In this file, we also query the Python interpreter that will be used for testing:

```
find_package(PythonInterp REQUIRED)
```

3. We then include the account subdirectory:

```
add_subdirectory(account)
```

4. After that, we define the unit test:

```
# turn on testing
enable_testing()

# define test
add_test(
  NAME
    python_test
  COMMAND
```

```
    ${CMAKE_COMMAND} -E env
ACCOUNT_MODULE_PATH=$<TARGET_FILE_DIR:account>
    ${PYTHON_EXECUTABLE}
${CMAKE_CURRENT_SOURCE_DIR}/account/test.py
  )
```

5. Inside `account/CMakeLists.txt`, we fetch pybind11 sources at configure time:

```
include(FetchContent)
FetchContent_Declare(
  pybind11_sources
  GIT_REPOSITORY https://github.com/pybind/pybind11.git
  GIT_TAG v2.2
)

FetchContent_GetProperties(pybind11_sources)

if(NOT pybind11_sources_POPULATED)
  FetchContent_Populate(pybind11_sources)

  add_subdirectory(
    ${pybind11_sources_SOURCE_DIR}
    ${pybind11_sources_BINARY_DIR}
    )
endif()
```

6. Finally, we define the Python module. Once again we use the MODULE option to add_library. We also set the prefix and suffix properties for our library target to the values PYTHON_MODULE_PREFIX and PYTHON_MODULE_EXTENSION, which are appropriately inferred by pybind11:

```
add_library(account
  MODULE
    account.cpp
  )

target_link_libraries(account
  PUBLIC
    pybind11::module
  )

set_target_properties(account
  PROPERTIES
    PREFIX "${PYTHON_MODULE_PREFIX}"
    SUFFIX "${PYTHON_MODULE_EXTENSION}"
  )
```

7. Let us test it out:

```
$ mkdir -p build
$ cd build
$ cmake ..
$ cmake --build .
$ ctest

  Start 1: python_test
1/1 Test #1: python_test ..................... Passed 0.04 sec

100% tests passed, 0 tests failed out of 1

Total Test time (real) = 0.04 sec
```

How it works

The functionality and use of pybind11 is very similar to Boost.Python, the bonus being that pybind11 is a more lightweight dependency – although we will require C++11 support from the compiler. The interface definition in `account.hpp` is rather similar to that in the previous recipe:

```cpp
#include <pybind11/pybind11.h>

// ...

namespace py = pybind11;

PYBIND11_MODULE(account, m) {
  py::class_<Account>(m, "Account")
      .def(py::init())
      .def("deposit", &Account::deposit)
      .def("withdraw", &Account::withdraw)
      .def("get_balance", &Account::get_balance);
}
```

Again, we can clearly recognize how Python methods are mapped to C++ functions. The library that interprets `PYBIND11_MODULE` is defined in the imported target `pybind11::module`, which we have included using the following:

```cmake
add_subdirectory(
  ${pybind11_sources_SOURCE_DIR}
  ${pybind11_sources_BINARY_DIR}
  )
```

There are two differences with respect to the previous recipe:

- We do not require pybind11 to be installed on the system and therefore do not try to locate it.
- The `${pybind11_sources_SOURCE_DIR}` subdirectory, which contains pybind11 `CMakeLists.txt`, does not exist when we start building our project.

One solution for this challenge is to use the `FetchContent` module, which fetches the pybind11 sources and CMake infrastructure at configure time so that we can reference it using `add_subdirectory`. Using the `FetchContent` pattern, we can now assume that pybind11 is available within the build tree, which allows us to build and link the Python module:

```
add_library(account
  MODULE
    account.cpp
  )

target_link_libraries(account
  PUBLIC
    pybind11::module
  )
```

We use the following command to make sure that the Python module library gets a well-defined prefix and suffix, compatible with the Python environment:

```
set_target_properties(account
  PROPERTIES
    PREFIX ${PYTHON_MODULE_PREFIX}
    SUFFIX ${PYTHON_MODULE_EXTENSION}
  )
```

The rest of the top-level `CMakeLists.txt` file is testing (we use the same `test.py` as in the previous recipe).

There is more

We could have included the pybind11 sources as part of our project source code repository, which would simplify the CMake structure and remove the requirement to have network access to the pybind11 sources at compile time. Alternatively, we could have defined the pybind11 source path as a Git submodule (`https://git-scm.com/book/en/v2/Git-Tools-Submodules`) to simplify the updating of the pybind11 source dependency.

In our example, we have solved this using `FetchContent`, which provides a very compact approach to referencing a CMake subproject without explicitly tracking its sources. Also, we could have solved this recipe using the so-called superbuild approach (see *Chapter 8, The Superbuild Pattern*).

See also

To see how you can expose simple functions, define docstrings, map memory buffers, and find further reading, we refer to the pybind11 documentation: `https://pybind11.readthedocs.io`.

Mixing C, C++, Fortran, and Python using Python CFFI

The code for this recipe is available at `https://github.com/dev-cafe/cmake-cookbook/tree/v1.0/chapter-09/recipe-06` and has C++ and Fortran examples. The recipes are valid with CMake version 3.5 (and higher). Both versions of the recipe have been tested on GNU/Linux, macOS, and Windows.

In the previous three recipes, we have discussed Cython, Boost.Python, and pybind11 as tools to interface Python and C++ providing a modern and clean approach. The main interface in the previous recipes was a C++ interface. However, we may be in a situation where we do not have a C++ interface to hook on to and where we would like to interface Python with Fortran or other languages.

In this recipe, we will demonstrate an alternative approach for interfacing Python using the Python C Foreign Function Interface (CFFI; see also `https://cffi.readthedocs.io`). Since C is the *lingua franca* of programming languages and most programming languages (including Fortran) are able to talk to a C interface, Python CFFI is a tool to couple Python with a large number of languages. A very nice feature of Python CFFI is that the resulting interface is thin and non-intrusive, meaning that it neither restricts the Python layer in language features, nor does it impose any restrictions on the code below the C layer, apart from requiring a C interface.

In this recipe, we will apply Python CFFI to couple Python and C++ *via* a C interface using the bank account example introduced in preceding recipe. Our goal is to arrive at a context-aware interface where we can instantiate several bank accounts, each carrying its internal state. We will conclude this recipe by commenting on how to couple Python and Fortran using Python CFFI. In *Chapter 11, Packaging Projects, Recipe 3, Distributing a C/Fortran/Python project built with CMake/CFFI via PyPI*, we will revisit this example and show how to package it and make it installable with pip.

Getting ready

We will require a couple of files for this recipe. Let us start with the C++ implementation and interface. We will place these in a subdirectory called `account/implementation`. The implementation file (`cpp_implementation.cpp`) is similar to that in previous recipes but contains additional `assert` statements, since we will keep the state of the object in an opaque handle and we will have to make sure that the object is created before we try to access it:

```
#include "cpp_implementation.hpp"

#include <cassert>

Account::Account() {
  balance = 0.0;
  is_initialized = true;
}

Account::~Account() {
  assert(is_initialized);
  is_initialized = false;
}

void Account::deposit(const double amount) {
  assert(is_initialized);
  balance += amount;
}

void Account::withdraw(const double amount) {
  assert(is_initialized);
  balance -= amount;
}
```

```
double Account::get_balance() const {
  assert(is_initialized);
  return balance;
}
```

The interface file (cpp_implementation.hpp) contains the following:

```
#pragma once

class Account {
public:
  Account();
  ~Account();

  void deposit(const double amount);
  void withdraw(const double amount);
  double get_balance() const;

private:
  double balance;
  bool is_initialized;
};
```

In addition, we isolate a C—C++ interface (c_cpp_interface.cpp). This will be the interface we will try to hook into with Python CFFI:

```
#include "account.h"
#include "cpp_implementation.hpp"

#define AS_TYPE(Type, Obj) reinterpret_cast<Type *>(Obj)
#define AS_CTYPE(Type, Obj) reinterpret_cast<const Type *>(Obj)

account_context_t *account_new() {
  return AS_TYPE(account_context_t, new Account());
}

void account_free(account_context_t *context) { delete AS_TYPE(Account,
context); }

void account_deposit(account_context_t *context, const double amount) {
  return AS_TYPE(Account, context)->deposit(amount);
}

void account_withdraw(account_context_t *context, const double amount) {
  return AS_TYPE(Account, context)->withdraw(amount);
}

double account_get_balance(const account_context_t *context) {
```

```
        return AS_CTYPE(Account, context)->get_balance();
}
```

One directory up, under `account`, we describe the C interface (`account.h`):

```
/* CFFI would issue warning with pragma once */
#ifndef ACCOUNT_H_INCLUDED
#define ACCOUNT_H_INCLUDED

#ifndef ACCOUNT_API
#include "account_export.h"
#define ACCOUNT_API ACCOUNT_EXPORT
#endif

#ifdef __cplusplus
extern "C" {
#endif

struct account_context;
typedef struct account_context account_context_t;

ACCOUNT_API
account_context_t *account_new();

ACCOUNT_API
void account_free(account_context_t *context);

ACCOUNT_API
void account_deposit(account_context_t *context, const double amount);

ACCOUNT_API
void account_withdraw(account_context_t *context, const double amount);

ACCOUNT_API
double account_get_balance(const account_context_t *context);

#ifdef __cplusplus
}
#endif

#endif /* ACCOUNT_H_INCLUDED */
```

We also describe the Python interface, which we will comment on below (`__init__.py`):

```
from subprocess import check_output
from cffi import FFI
import os
import sys
```

```
from configparser import ConfigParser
from pathlib import Path


def get_lib_handle(definitions, header_file, library_file):
    ffi = FFI()
    command = ['cc', '-E'] + definitions + [header_file]
    interface = check_output(command).decode('utf-8')

    # remove possible \r characters on windows which
    # would confuse cdef
    _interface = [l.strip('\r') for l in interface.split('\n')]

    ffi.cdef('\n'.join(_interface))
    lib = ffi.dlopen(library_file)
    return lib


# this interface requires the header file and library file
# and these can be either provided by interface_file_names.cfg
# in the same path as this file
# or if this is not found then using environment variables
_this_path = Path(os.path.dirname(os.path.realpath(__file__)))
_cfg_file = _this_path / 'interface_file_names.cfg'
if _cfg_file.exists():
    config = ConfigParser()
    config.read(_cfg_file)
    header_file_name = config.get('configuration', 'header_file_name')
    _header_file = _this_path / 'include' / header_file_name
    _header_file = str(_header_file)
    library_file_name = config.get('configuration', 'library_file_name')
    _library_file = _this_path / 'lib' / library_file_name
    _library_file = str(_library_file)
else:
    _header_file = os.getenv('ACCOUNT_HEADER_FILE')
    assert _header_file is not None
    _library_file = os.getenv('ACCOUNT_LIBRARY_FILE')
    assert _library_file is not None

_lib = get_lib_handle(definitions=['-DACCOUNT_API=', '-DACCOUNT_NOINCLUDE'],
                      header_file=_header_file,
                      library_file=_library_file)


# we change names to obtain a more pythonic API
new = _lib.account_new
free = _lib.account_free
```

```
deposit = _lib.account_deposit
withdraw = _lib.account_withdraw
get_balance = _lib.account_get_balance

__all__ = [
    '__version__',
    'new',
    'free',
    'deposit',
    'withdraw',
    'get_balance',
]
```

This is a handful of files, but, as we will see, most of this interface work is generic and reusable and the actual interface is rather thin. To summarize, this is the layout of our project:

```
.
├── account
│   ├── account.h
│   ├── CMakeLists.txt
│   ├── implementation
│   │   ├── c_cpp_interface.cpp
│   │   ├── cpp_implementation.cpp
│   │   └── cpp_implementation.hpp
│   ├── __init__.py
│   └── test.py
└── CMakeLists.txt
```

How to do it

Let us now use CMake to combine these files to form a Python module:

1. The top-level CMakeLists.txt file contains a familiar header. In addition, we also set the location of our compiled library according to GNU standards:

```
# define minimum cmake version
cmake_minimum_required(VERSION 3.5 FATAL_ERROR)

# project name and supported language
project(recipe-06 LANGUAGES CXX)

# require C++11
set(CMAKE_CXX_STANDARD 11)
set(CMAKE_CXX_EXTENSIONS OFF)
set(CMAKE_CXX_STANDARD_REQUIRED ON)
```

```
# specify where to place libraries
include(GNUInstallDirs)
set(CMAKE_LIBRARY_OUTPUT_DIRECTORY
  ${CMAKE_BINARY_DIR}/${CMAKE_INSTALL_LIBDIR})
```

2. The second step is to include definitions for interfaces and implementation sources under the `account` subdirectory, which we will detail further down:

```
# interface and sources
add_subdirectory(account)
```

3. The top-level `CMakeLists.txt` file concludes with the definition of a test (which requires the Python interpreter):

```
# turn on testing
enable_testing()

# require python
find_package(PythonInterp REQUIRED)

# define test
add_test(
  NAME
    python_test
  COMMAND
    ${CMAKE_COMMAND} -E env
ACCOUNT_MODULE_PATH=${CMAKE_CURRENT_SOURCE_DIR}
ACCOUNT_HEADER_FILE=${CMAKE_CURRENT_SOURCE_DIR}/account/account.h
ACCOUNT_LIBRARY_FILE=$<TARGET_FILE:account>
    ${PYTHON_EXECUTABLE}
${CMAKE_CURRENT_SOURCE_DIR}/account/test.py
  )
```

4. The included `account/CMakeLists.txt` defines the shared library:

```
add_library(account
  SHARED
    implementation/c_cpp_interface.cpp
    implementation/cpp_implementation.cpp
  )

target_include_directories(account
  PRIVATE
    ${CMAKE_CURRENT_SOURCE_DIR}
    ${CMAKE_CURRENT_BINARY_DIR}
  )
```

5. Then we generate a portable export header:

```
include(GenerateExportHeader)
generate_export_header(account
  BASE_NAME account
  )
```

6. Now we are ready to take the Python—C interface for a spin:

```
$ mkdir -p build
$ cd build
$ cmake ..
$ cmake --build .
$ ctest

    Start 1: python_test
1/1 Test #1: python_test ..................... Passed 0.14 sec

100% tests passed, 0 tests failed out of 1
```

How it works

While the previous recipes required us to explicitly declare the Python—C interface and to map Python names to C(++) symbols, Python CFFI infers this mapping on its own from the C header file (in our case, account.h). The only thing we need to provide to our Python CFFI layer is the header file describing the C interface and a shared library containing the symbols. We have done this using environment variable set in the main CMakeLists.txt file, and these environment variables are queried in __init__.py:

```
# ...

def get_lib_handle(definitions, header_file, library_file):
    ffi = FFI()
    command = ['cc', '-E'] + definitions + [header_file]
    interface = check_output(command).decode('utf-8')

    # remove possible \r characters on windows which
    # would confuse cdef
    _interface = [l.strip('\r') for l in interface.split('\n')]

    ffi.cdef('\n'.join(_interface))
    lib = ffi.dlopen(library_file)
    return lib

# ...
```

```
_this_path = Path(os.path.dirname(os.path.realpath(__file__)))
_cfg_file = _this_path / 'interface_file_names.cfg'
if _cfg_file.exists():
    # we will discuss this section in chapter 11, recipe 3
else:
    _header_file = os.getenv('ACCOUNT_HEADER_FILE')
    assert _header_file is not None
    _library_file = os.getenv('ACCOUNT_LIBRARY_FILE')
    assert _library_file is not None

_lib = get_lib_handle(definitions=['-DACCOUNT_API=', '-
DACCOUNT_NOINCLUDE'],
                      header_file=_header_file,
                      library_file=_library_file)

# ...
```

The `get_lib_handle` function opens and parses the header file (using `ffi.cdef`), loads the library (using `ffi.dlopen`), and returns the library object. The preceding file is in principle generic, and can be reused without modification for other projects interfacing Python and C or other languages using Python CFFI.

The `_lib` library object could be exported directly, but we do one additional step so that the Python interface feels more *pythonic* when used Python-side:

```
# we change names to obtain a more pythonic API
new = _lib.account_new
free = _lib.account_free
deposit = _lib.account_deposit
withdraw = _lib.account_withdraw
get_balance = _lib.account_get_balance

__all__ = [
    '__version__',
    'new',
    'free',
    'deposit',
    'withdraw',
    'get_balance',
]
```

With this change, we can write the following:

```
import account
account1 = account.new()

account.deposit(account1, 100.0)
```

The alternative would be less intuitive:

```
from account import lib
account1 = lib.account_new()

lib.account_deposit(account1, 100.0)
```

Note how we are able to instantiate and track isolated contexts with our context-aware API:

```
account1 = account.new()
account.deposit(account1, 10.0)

account2 = account.new()
account.withdraw(account1, 5.0)
account.deposit(account2, 5.0)
```

In order to import the `account` Python module, we need to provide the `ACCOUNT_HEADER_FILE` and `ACCOUNT_LIBRARY_FILE` environment variables, as we do for the test:

```
add_test(
  NAME
    python_test
  COMMAND
    ${CMAKE_COMMAND} -E env ACCOUNT_MODULE_PATH=${CMAKE_CURRENT_SOURCE_DIR}
ACCOUNT_HEADER_FILE=${CMAKE_CURRENT_SOURCE_DIR}/account/account.h
                        ACCOUNT_LIBRARY_FILE=$<TARGET_FILE:account>
    ${PYTHON_EXECUTABLE} ${CMAKE_CURRENT_SOURCE_DIR}/account/test.py
  )
```

In *Chapter 11, Packaging Projects*, we will discuss how to create a Python package that can be installed with pip where the header and library files will be installed in well-defined locations so that we do not have to define any environment variables to use the Python module.

Having discussed the Python aspect of the interface, let us now consider the C-side of the interface. The essence of `account.h` is this section:

```
struct account_context;
typedef struct account_context account_context_t;

ACCOUNT_API
account_context_t *account_new();

ACCOUNT_API
void account_free(account_context_t *context);
```

```
ACCOUNT_API
void account_deposit(account_context_t *context, const double amount);

ACCOUNT_API
void account_withdraw(account_context_t *context, const double amount);

ACCOUNT_API
double account_get_balance(const account_context_t *context);
```

The opaque handle, `account_context`, holds the state of the object. `ACCOUNT_API` is defined in `account_export.h`, which is generated by CMake in `account/interface/CMakeLists.txt`:

```
include(GenerateExportHeader)
generate_export_header(account
  BASE_NAME account
  )
```

The `account_export.h` export header defines the visibility of the interface functions and makes sure this is done in a portable way. We will discuss this point in further detail in *Chapter 10, Writing an Installer*. The actual implementation can be found in `cpp_implementation.cpp`. It contains the `is_initialized` boolean, which we can check to make sure that API functions are called in the expected order: the context should not be accessed before it is created or after it is freed.

There is more

When designing a Python—C interface, it is important to carefully consider on which side to allocate arrays: arrays can be allocated either on the Python side and passed to the C(++) implementation, or they can be allocated on the C(++) implementation that returns a pointer. The latter approach is convenient for situations where the buffer sizes are *a priori* not known. However, returning pointers to arrays allocated C(++)-side can be problematic since it can lead to memory leaks due to Python garbage collection, which does not "see" the allocated arrays. We recommend to design the C API such that arrays can be allocated outside and passed to the C implementation. These arrays can then be allocated within __init__.py, as in this example:

```
from cffi import FFI
import numpy as np


_ffi = FFI()
```

```
def return_array(context, array_len):

    # create numpy array
    array_np = np.zeros(array_len, dtype=np.float64)

    # cast a pointer to its data
    array_p = _ffi.cast("double *", array_np.ctypes.data)

    # pass the pointer
    _lib.mylib_myfunction(context, array_len, array_p)

    # return the array as a list
    return array_np.tolist()
```

The `return_array` function returns a Python list. Since we have done all the allocation work on the Python side, we do not have to worry about memory leaks and can leave the cleanup to the garbage collection.

For a Fortran example, we refer the reader to the following recipe repository: `https://github.com/dev-cafe/cmake-cookbook/tree/v1.0/chapter-09/recipe-06/fortran-example`. The main difference compared to the C++ implementation is that the account library is compiled from a Fortran 90 source file that we account for in `account/CMakeLists.txt`:

```
add_library(account
  SHARED
    implementation/fortran_implementation.f90
  )
```

The context is kept in a user-defined type:

```
type :: account
  private
  real(c_double) :: balance
  logical :: is_initialized = .false.
end type
```

The Fortran implementation is able to resolve symbols and methods defined in the unchanged `account.h` by using the `iso_c_binding` module:

```
module account_implementation

  use, intrinsic :: iso_c_binding, only: c_double, c_ptr

  implicit none

  private
```

```
      public account_new
      public account_free
      public account_deposit
      public account_withdraw
      public account_get_balance

      type :: account
        private
        real(c_double) :: balance
        logical :: is_initialized = .false.
      end type

   contains

      type(c_ptr) function account_new() bind (c)
        use, intrinsic :: iso_c_binding, only: c_loc
        type(account), pointer :: f_context
        type(c_ptr) :: context

        allocate(f_context)
        context = c_loc(f_context)
        account_new = context
        f_context%balance = 0.0d0
        f_context%is_initialized = .true.
      end function

      subroutine account_free(context) bind (c)
        use, intrinsic :: iso_c_binding, only: c_f_pointer
        type(c_ptr), value :: context
        type(account), pointer :: f_context

        call c_f_pointer(context, f_context)
        call check_valid_context(f_context)
        f_context%balance = 0.0d0
        f_context%is_initialized = .false.
        deallocate(f_context)
      end subroutine

      subroutine check_valid_context(f_context)
        type(account), pointer, intent(in) :: f_context
        if (.not. associated(f_context)) then
           print *, 'ERROR: context is not associated'
           stop 1
        end if
        if (.not. f_context%is_initialized) then
           print *, 'ERROR: context is not initialized'
           stop 1
        end if
```

```
  end subroutine

  subroutine account_withdraw(context, amount) bind (c)
    use, intrinsic :: iso_c_binding, only: c_f_pointer
    type(c_ptr), value :: context
    real(c_double), value :: amount
    type(account), pointer :: f_context

    call c_f_pointer(context, f_context)
    call check_valid_context(f_context)
    f_context%balance = f_context%balance - amount
  end subroutine

  subroutine account_deposit(context, amount) bind (c)
    use, intrinsic :: iso_c_binding, only: c_f_pointer
    type(c_ptr), value :: context
    real(c_double), value :: amount
    type(account), pointer :: f_context

    call c_f_pointer(context, f_context)
    call check_valid_context(f_context)
    f_context%balance = f_context%balance + amount
  end subroutine

  real(c_double) function account_get_balance(context) bind (c)
    use, intrinsic :: iso_c_binding, only: c_f_pointer
    type(c_ptr), value, intent(in) :: context
    type(account), pointer :: f_context

    call c_f_pointer(context, f_context)
    call check_valid_context(f_context)
    account_get_balance = f_context%balance
  end function

end module
```

See also

This recipe and solution has been inspired by Armin Ronacher's post, "Beautiful Native Libraries", `http://lucumr.pocoo.org/2013/8/18/beautiful-native-libraries/`.

10
Writing an Installer

In this chapter, we will cover the following recipes:

- Installing your project
- Generating export headers
- Exporting your targets
- Installing a superbuild

Introduction

In previous chapters, we have shown how to configure, build, and test our projects using CMake. Installing projects is an equally important part of the developer's toolbox, and this chapter will demonstrate how to achieve that. The recipes in this chapter cover the install-time operations outlined in the following diagram:

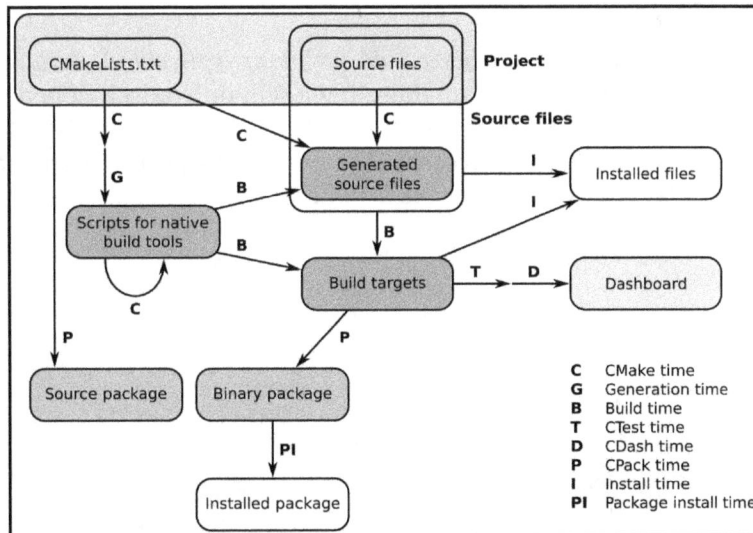

We will walk you through the various steps to be taken in refining the installation of a simple C++ project: from making sure that important files built in your project are copied over to the right directories, to ensuring that other projects depending on your work can detect it using CMake. The four recipes in this chapter will build upon the simple example given in *Chapter 1, From a Simple Executable to Libraries, Recipe 3, Building and linking shared and static libraries*. There we tried to build a very simple library and link it into an executable. We also showed how to build both a static and a shared library out of the same source files. In this chapter, we will go a bit deeper and discuss and formalize what happens at install time.

Installing your project

> The code for this recipe is available at `https://github.com/dev-cafe/cmake-cookbook/tree/v1.0/chapter-10/recipe-01` and has a C++ example. The recipe is valid with CMake version 3.6 (and higher) and has been tested on GNU/Linux, macOS, and Windows.

In this very first recipe, we will introduce our small project and some of the basic concepts that will be used also in the subsequent recipes. Installing files, libraries, and executables is a very basic task, but it can present some pitfalls. We will walk you through these and show you how to effectively avoid many of them with CMake.

Getting ready

The code from *Chapter 1, From a Simple Executable to Libraries, Recipe 3, Building and linking shared and static libraries*, is used almost unaltered: we will only add a dependency on the UUID library. This dependency is conditional, and if the UUID library is not found, we will exclude the code using it *via* the preprocessor. The code is properly organized into its own `src` subdirectory. The layout of the project is as follows:

```
.
├── CMakeLists.txt
├── src
│   ├── CMakeLists.txt
│   ├── hello-world.cpp
│   ├── Message.cpp
│   └── Message.hpp
└── tests
    └── CMakeLists.txt
```

We can already see that we have a root `CMakeLists.txt` with one leaf under the `src` subdirectory and another under the `tests` subdirectory.

The `Message.hpp` header file contains the following:

```
#pragma once

#include <iosfwd>
#include <string>

class Message {
public:
  Message(const std::string &m) : message_(m) {}

  friend std::ostream &operator<<(std::ostream &os, Message &obj) {
    return obj.printObject(os);
  }

private:
  std::string message_;
  std::ostream &printObject(std::ostream &os);
};

std::string getUUID();
```

This is the corresponding implementation in `Message.cpp`:

```
#include "Message.hpp"

#include <iostream>
#include <string>

#ifdef HAVE_UUID
#include <uuid/uuid.h>
#endif

std::ostream &Message::printObject(std::ostream &os) {
  os << "This is my very nice message: " << std::endl;
  os << message_ << std::endl;
  os << "...and here is its UUID: " << getUUID();

  return os;
}

#ifdef HAVE_UUID
std::string getUUID() {
  uuid_t uuid;
```

```
    uuid_generate(uuid);
    char uuid_str[37];
    uuid_unparse_lower(uuid, uuid_str);
    uuid_clear(uuid);
    std::string uuid_cxx(uuid_str);
    return uuid_cxx;
}
#else
std::string getUUID() { return "Ooooops, no UUID for you!"; }
#endif
```

Finally, the sample `hello-world.cpp` executable is as follows:

```cpp
#include <cstdlib>
#include <iostream>

#include "Message.hpp"

int main() {
  Message say_hello("Hello, CMake World!");

  std::cout << say_hello << std::endl;

  Message say_goodbye("Goodbye, CMake World");

  std::cout << say_goodbye << std::endl;

  return EXIT_SUCCESS;
}
```

How to do it

Let us first go through the root `CMakeLists.txt` file:

1. We start, as usual, by requiring a minimum CMake version and defining a C++11 project. Note that we have set a version for our project with the `VERSION` keyword to the `project` command:

```cmake
# CMake 3.6 needed for IMPORTED_TARGET option
# to pkg_search_module
cmake_minimum_required(VERSION 3.6 FATAL_ERROR)
```

```
project (recipe-01
  LANGUAGES CXX
  VERSION 1.0.0
  )

# <<< General set up >>>

set (CMAKE_CXX_STANDARD 11)
set (CMAKE_CXX_EXTENSIONS OFF)
set (CMAKE_CXX_STANDARD_REQUIRED ON)
```

2. The user can define the installation prefix by means of the CMAKE_INSTALL_PREFIX variable. CMake will set a sensible default for this variable: /usr/local on Unix and C:\Program Files on Windows, respectively. We print a status message reporting its value:

```
message (STATUS "Project will be installed to
${CMAKE_INSTALL_PREFIX}")
```

3. By default, we prefer Release configuration for our project. The user will be able to set this with the CMAKE_BUILD_TYPE variable and we check whether that is the case. If not, we set it ourselves to the default, sensible value:

```
if (NOT CMAKE_BUILD_TYPE)
  set (CMAKE_BUILD_TYPE Release CACHE STRING "Build type" FORCE)
endif ()

message (STATUS "Build type set to ${CMAKE_BUILD_TYPE}")
```

4. Next we tell CMake where to build the executable, static, and shared library targets. This facilitates access to these build targets in case the user does not intend to actually install the project. We use the standard CMake GNUInstallDirs.cmake module. This will guarantee a sensible and portable project layout:

```
include (GNUInstallDirs)

set (CMAKE_ARCHIVE_OUTPUT_DIRECTORY
  ${PROJECT_BINARY_DIR}/${CMAKE_INSTALL_LIBDIR})
set (CMAKE_LIBRARY_OUTPUT_DIRECTORY
  ${PROJECT_BINARY_DIR}/${CMAKE_INSTALL_LIBDIR})
set (CMAKE_RUNTIME_OUTPUT_DIRECTORY
  ${PROJECT_BINARY_DIR}/${CMAKE_INSTALL_BINDIR})
```

5. Whereas the previous commands fixed the location of build output *within* the build directory, the following are needed to fix the location of executables, libraries, and include files within the install prefix. These will broadly follow the same layout, but we define the new INSTALL_LIBDIR, INSTALL_BINDIR, INSTALL_INCLUDEDIR, and INSTALL_CMAKEDIR variables, which the users can override, if they are so inclined:

```
# Offer the user the choice of overriding the installation
directories
set(INSTALL_LIBDIR ${CMAKE_INSTALL_LIBDIR} CACHE PATH "Installation
directory for libraries")
set(INSTALL_BINDIR ${CMAKE_INSTALL_BINDIR} CACHE PATH "Installation
directory for executables")
set(INSTALL_INCLUDEDIR ${CMAKE_INSTALL_INCLUDEDIR} CACHE PATH
"Installation directory for header files")
if(WIN32 AND NOT CYGWIN)
  set(DEF_INSTALL_CMAKEDIR CMake)
else()
  set(DEF_INSTALL_CMAKEDIR share/cmake/${PROJECT_NAME})
endif()
set(INSTALL_CMAKEDIR ${DEF_INSTALL_CMAKEDIR} CACHE PATH
"Installation directory for CMake files")
```

6. We report the paths where components will be installed to the user:

```
# Report to user
foreach(p LIB BIN INCLUDE CMAKE)
  file(TO_NATIVE_PATH ${CMAKE_INSTALL_PREFIX}/${INSTALL_${p}DIR}
_path )
  message(STATUS "Installing ${p} components to ${_path}")
  unset(_path)
endforeach()
```

7. The last directives in the root CMakeLists.txt file add the src subdirectory, enable testing, and add the tests subdirectory:

```
add_subdirectory(src)

enable_testing()

add_subdirectory(tests)
```

We now move on to analyze the `src/CMakeLists.txt` leaf. This file defines the actual targets to build:

1. Our project depends on the UUID library. As shown in *Chapter 5, Configure-time and Build-time Operations, Recipe 8, Probing execution,* we can find it with the following snippet:

```
# Search for pkg-config and UUID
find_package(PkgConfig QUIET)
if(PKG_CONFIG_FOUND)
  pkg_search_module(UUID uuid IMPORTED_TARGET)
  if(TARGET PkgConfig::UUID)
    message(STATUS "Found libuuid")
    set(UUID_FOUND TRUE)
  endif()
endif()
```

2. We wish to build a shared library out of our sources and we declare a target called `message-shared`:

```
add_library(message-shared SHARED "")
```

3. The sources for this target are specified with the `target_sources` command:

```
target_sources(message-shared
  PRIVATE
    ${CMAKE_CURRENT_LIST_DIR}/Message.cpp
  )
```

4. We declare compile definitions and link libraries for our target. Note that all are PUBLIC, to ensure that all dependent targets will inherit them properly:

```
target_compile_definitions(message-shared
  PUBLIC
    $<$<BOOL:${UUID_FOUND}>:HAVE_UUID>
  )

target_link_libraries(message-shared
  PUBLIC
    $<$<BOOL:${UUID_FOUND}>:PkgConfig::UUID>
  )
```

5. Then we set additional properties of our target. We will comment upon these shortly.

```
set_target_properties(message-shared
  PROPERTIES
    POSITION_INDEPENDENT_CODE 1
    SOVERSION ${PROJECT_VERSION_MAJOR}
    OUTPUT_NAME "message"
    DEBUG_POSTFIX "_d"
    PUBLIC_HEADER "Message.hpp"
    MACOSX_RPATH ON
    WINDOWS_EXPORT_ALL_SYMBOLS ON
  )
```

6. Finally, we add an executable target for our "Hello, world" program:

```
add_executable(hello-world_wDSO hello-world.cpp)
```

7. The `hello-world_wDSO` executable target is linked against the shared library:

```
target_link_libraries(hello-world_wDSO
  PUBLIC
    message-shared
  )
```

The `src/CMakeLists.txt` file contains also the installation directives. Before considering these, we need to fix the `RPATH` for our executable:

1. With CMake path manipulations, we set the `message_RPATH` variable. This will set `RPATH` appropriately for GNU/Linux and macOS:

```
# Prepare RPATH
file(RELATIVE_PATH _rel ${CMAKE_INSTALL_PREFIX}/${INSTALL_BINDIR}
${CMAKE_INSTALL_PREFIX})
if(APPLE)
  set(_rpath "@loader_path/${_rel}")
else()
  set(_rpath "\$ORIGIN/${_rel}")
endif()
file(TO_NATIVE_PATH "${_rpath}/${INSTALL_LIBDIR}" message_RPATH)
```

2. We can now use this variable to fix the `RPATH` for our executable target, `hello-world_wDSO`. This is achieved by means of a target property. We are also setting additional properties, and we will comment more on these in a moment:

```
set_target_properties(hello-world_wDSO
  PROPERTIES
```

```
MACOSX_RPATH ON
SKIP_BUILD_RPATH OFF
BUILD_WITH_INSTALL_RPATH OFF
INSTALL_RPATH "${message_RPATH}"
INSTALL_RPATH_USE_LINK_PATH ON
)
```

3. We are finally ready to install our library, header, and executable! We use the install command offered by CMake to specify where these should go. Note that the paths are relative; we will elaborate more on this point further below:

```
install(
  TARGETS
    message-shared
    hello-world_wDSO
  ARCHIVE
    DESTINATION ${INSTALL_LIBDIR}
    COMPONENT lib
  RUNTIME
    DESTINATION ${INSTALL_BINDIR}
    COMPONENT bin
  LIBRARY
    DESTINATION ${INSTALL_LIBDIR}
    COMPONENT lib
  PUBLIC_HEADER
    DESTINATION ${INSTALL_INCLUDEDIR}/message
    COMPONENT dev
  )
```

The CMakeLists.txt file in the tests directory contains simple directives to ensure that the "Hello, World" executable runs correctly:

```
add_test(
  NAME test_shared
  COMMAND $<TARGET_FILE:hello-world_wDSO>
  )
```

Let us now configure, build, and install the project and look at the result. As soon as any installation directives are added, CMake generates a new target called install that will run the installation rules:

```
$ mkdir -p build
$ cd build
$ cmake -G"Unix Makefiles" -DCMAKE_INSTALL_PREFIX=$HOME/Software/recipe-01
$ cmake --build . --target install
```

The contents of the build directory on GNU/Linux will be the following:

```
build
├──── bin
│     └──── hello-world_wDSO
├──── CMakeCache.txt
├──── CMakeFiles
├──── cmake_install.cmake
├──── CTestTestfile.cmake
├──── install_manifest.txt
├──── lib64
│     ├──── libmessage.so -> libmessage.so.1
│     └──── libmessage.so.1
├──── Makefile
├──── src
├──── Testing
└──── tests
```

One the other hand, at the install prefix, you can find the following structure:

```
$HOME/Software/recipe-01/
├──── bin
│     └──── hello-world_wDSO
├──── include
│     └──── message
│            └──── Message.hpp
└──── lib64
      ├──── libmessage.so -> libmessage.so.1
      └──── libmessage.so.1
```

This means that the locations given in the installation directives are relative to the `CMAKE_INSTALL_PREFIX` instance given by the user.

How it works

There are three salient points to this recipe that we need to discuss in more detail:

- The use of `GNUInstallDirs.cmake` to define standard locations for the installation of our targets
- The properties set on the shared library and executable targets, in particular the handling of the `RPATH`
- The installation directives

Installing to standard locations

What is a good layout for the installation of your project? As long as you are the only consumer of your project, this question only has limited relevance. However, as soon as you start shipping to the outside world, it will be expected that you provide a sensible layout when installing your project. Fortunately, there are standards that we can adhere to and CMake can help us with that. Effectively, what the `GNUInstallDirs.cmake` module does is to define a set of variables. These variables are the names of the subdirectories where different types of files should be installed. In our example we used the following:

- `CMAKE_INSTALL_BINDIR`: This will give the subdirectory where *user executables* should be located, which is the `bin` directory under the chosen install prefix.
- `CMAKE_INSTALL_LIBDIR`: This expands to the subdirectory where *object code libraries* – that is, the static and shared libraries – should be located. On a 64-bit system, this is `lib64`, whereas on a 32-bit system, it is just `lib`.
- `CMAKE_INSTALL_INCLUDEDIR`: Finally, we used this variable to obtain the correct subdirectory for our C header files. This variable expands to `include`.

The user might, however, want to override these choices. We allowed for that with the following stanza in the root `CMakeLists.txt` file:

```
# Offer the user the choice of overriding the installation directories
set(INSTALL_LIBDIR ${CMAKE_INSTALL_LIBDIR} CACHE PATH "Installation
directory for libraries")
set(INSTALL_BINDIR ${CMAKE_INSTALL_BINDIR} CACHE PATH "Installation
directory for executables")
set(INSTALL_INCLUDEDIR ${CMAKE_INSTALL_INCLUDEDIR} CACHE PATH "Installation
directory for header files")
```

This effectively redefines the `INSTALL_BINDIR`, `INSTALL_LIBDIR`, and `INSTALL_INCLUDEDIR` convenience variables to be used within our project. We also define the additional `INSTALL_CMAKEDIR` variable, but its role will be discussed in detail in the next few recipes.

> The `GNUInstallDirs.cmake` module defines additional variables that will help to place installed files in the expected subdirectories of the chosen install prefix. Please consult the CMake online documentation: `https://cmake.org/cmake/help/v3.6/module/GNUInstallDirs.html`

Target properties and RPATH handling

Let us have a closer look at the properties set on the shared library target. We had to set the following:

- `POSITION_INDEPENDENT_CODE 1`: This sets the compiler flags needed for generating position-independent code. For more details, please consult https://en.wikipedia.org/wiki/Position-independent_code.

- `SOVERSION ${PROJECT_VERSION_MAJOR}`: This is the version of the application programming interface (API) offered by our shared library. Following semantic version, we have decided to set it to be the same as the major version of the project. CMake targets also have a `VERSION` property. This can be used to specify the build version of the target. Note that `SOVERSION` and `VERSION` might differ: we might want to offer multiple builds of the same API over time. We are not concerned with such granular control in this example: setting just the API version with the `SOVERSION` property is enough, CMake will set `VERSION` to the same value for us. For more details on please refer to the official documentation: https://cmake.org/cmake/help/latest/prop_tgt/SOVERSION.html

- `OUTPUT_NAME "message"`: This tells CMake that the base name for the library is just `message` and not the name of the target `message-shared`: `libmessage.so.1` will be generated when building. Proper symbolic links to `libmessage.so` will also be generated, as can be seen from the contents of the build directory and install prefix given previously.

- `DEBUG_POSTFIX "_d"`: This tells CMake to add the `_d` postfix to the generated shared library if we are building the project in a `Debug` configuration.

- `PUBLIC_HEADER "Message.hpp"`: We use this property to set a list of header files, in this case only one, defining the API functions offered by our library. This is primarily intended for Framework shared library targets on macOS but it can also be used on other operating systems and targets, as we have presently done. For more details, please see the official documentation: https://cmake.org/cmake/help/v3.6/prop_tgt/PUBLIC_HEADER.html.

- `MACOSX_RPATH ON`: This sets the directory portion of the "install_name" field of shared libraries to `@rpath` on macOS.

- `WINDOWS_EXPORT_ALL_SYMBOLS ON`: This will force compilation on Windows to export all symbols. Note that this is usually not a good practice and we will show in *Recipe 2, Generating export headers*, how to take care of symbol visibility on different platforms.

Let us now discuss `RPATH`. We are linking our `hello-world_wDSO` executable to `libmessage.so.1`. This means that when the executable is called, the shared library will be loaded. Thus the information on the location of the library needs to be encoded somewhere in order for the loader to do its job successfully. There are two approaches regarding the location of the library:

- It could be made known to the linker by setting environment variables:
    - On GNU/Linux, this would require appending the path to the `LD_LIBRARY_PATH` environment variable. Note that this will most likely pollute the linker path for all applications on your system and might cause symbol clashes (`https://gms.tf/ld_library_path-considered-harmful.html`).
    - On macOS, you can similarly set the `DYLD_LIBRARY_PATH` variable. This suffers from the same pitfalls as `LD_LIBRARY_PATH` on GNU/Linux and the situation can be ameliorated, albeit only partially, by using the `DYLD_FALLBACK_LIBRARY_PATH` variable instead. See the following link for an example of this: `https://stackoverflow.com/a/3172515/2528668`.
- It could be encoded into the executable, using the `RPATH` to set the run-time search path for the executable.

The latter approach is preferable and more robust. However, which path should be chosen when setting the `RPATH` of the dynamic shared object? We need to make sure that running the executable *always* finds the correct shared library, regardless of whether it is run in the build tree or in the install tree. This is achieved by setting the `RPATH` related properties for the `hello-world_wDSO` target to look for a path *relative* to the location of the executable itself, either *via* the `$ORIGIN` (on GNU/Linux) or `@loader_path` (on macOS) variables:

```
# Prepare RPATH
file(RELATIVE_PATH _rel ${CMAKE_INSTALL_PREFIX}/${INSTALL_BINDIR}
${CMAKE_INSTALL_PREFIX})
if(APPLE)
  set(_rpath "@loader_path/${_rel}")
else()
  set(_rpath "\$ORIGIN/${_rel}")
endif()
file(TO_NATIVE_PATH "${_rpath}/${INSTALL_LIBDIR}" message_RPATH)
```

Once the `message_RPATH` variable is set, the target properties will do the rest of the job:

```
set_target_properties(hello-world_wDSO
  PROPERTIES
    MACOSX_RPATH ON
```

```
    SKIP_BUILD_RPATH OFF
    BUILD_WITH_INSTALL_RPATH OFF
    INSTALL_RPATH "${message_RPATH}"
    INSTALL_RPATH_USE_LINK_PATH ON
  )
```

Let us examine this command in detail:

- `SKIP_BUILD_RPATH OFF`: Tells CMake to generate an appropriate `RPATH` so as to be able to run the executable from *within* the build tree.
- `BUILD_WITH_INSTALL_RPATH OFF`: Turns off generating executable targets with their `RPATH` geared to be the same as the one for the install tree. This would prevent us from running the executable from within the build tree.
- `INSTALL_RPATH "${message_RPATH}"`: Sets the `RPATH` for the installed executable target to a path previously computed.
- `INSTALL_RPATH_USE_LINK_PATH ON`: Tells CMake to append linker search paths to the `RPATH` executable.

> More information on how the loader works on Unix systems may be found in this blog post: `http://longwei.github.io/rpath_origin/`.

Installation directives

Finally, let us consider the installation directives. We need to install an executable, one library, and one header file. Executables and libraries are build targets, so we use the `TARGETS` option to the `install` command. Install rules for multiple targets can be set at once: CMake is aware of what kind of targets they are; that is, whether they are executables, shared libraries, or static libraries:

```
install(
  TARGETS
    message-shared
    hello-world_wDSO
```

Executables will be installed in `RUNTIME DESTINATION`, which we set to `${INSTALL_BINDIR}`. Shared libraries are installed to `LIBRARY DESTINATION`, which we set to `${INSTALL_LIBDIR}`. Static libraries would be installed to `ARCHIVE DESTINATION`, which we also set to `${INSTALL_LIBDIR}`:

```
  ARCHIVE
    DESTINATION ${INSTALL_LIBDIR}
```

```
    COMPONENT lib
  RUNTIME
    DESTINATION ${INSTALL_BINDIR}
    COMPONENT bin
  LIBRARY
    DESTINATION ${INSTALL_LIBDIR}
    COMPONENT lib
```

Note that we not only specified DESTINATION, but also COMPONENT. When installing the project with the cmake --build . --target install command, all components were installed, as expected. However, it might be sometimes desirable to only install some of them. This is what the COMPONENT keyword can help us with. For example, to only install libraries, we can run the following:

$ cmake -D COMPONENT=lib -P cmake_install.cmake

Since the Message.hpp header file was set as a public header of the project, we can use the PUBLIC_HEADER keyword to install it along the other targets to the chosen destination: ${INSTALL_INCLUDEDIR}/message. Users of the library can now include the header with: #include <message/Message.hpp>, provided the proper location is passed to the compiler with the -I option.

The various destinations in the installation directives are interpreted as relative paths, unless an absolute path is used. But relative to what? There are different ways in which CMake can compute the absolute path, depending on what tool is triggering the installation. When using cmake --build . --target install, as we have done, paths will be computed relative to CMAKE_INSTALL_PREFIX. However, when using CPack, absolute paths will be computed relative to CPACK_PACKAGING_INSTALL_PREFIX. Usage of CPack will be shown in *Chapter 11, Packaging Projects, Recipe 1, Generating source and binary packages.*

Yet another mechanism is available with Unix Makefiles and Ninja generators: DESTDIR. It is possible to relocate the whole installation tree under the directory specified by DESTDIR. That is, env DESTDIR=/tmp/stage cmake --build . --target install will install the project relative to CMAKE_INSTALL_PREFIX and under the /tmp/stage directory. You can read more here: https://www.gnu.org/prep/standards/html_node/DESTDIR.html.

There is more

Setting the RPATH correctly can be rather tricky, but it is essential for third-party users. By default, CMake sets the RPATH of executables assuming they will be run from the build tree. However, upon installation, the RPATH is cleared, leading to trouble when a user would like to run hello-world_wDSO. Using the ldd tool on Linux, we can inspect the hello-world_wDSO executable in the build tree to see where the loader will look for libmessage.so:

```
libmessage.so.1 => /home/user/cmake-cookbook/chapter-10/recipe-01/cxx-
example/build/lib64/libmessage.so.1 (0x00007f7a92e44000)
```

Running ldd hello-world_wDSO in the installation prefix would result instead in the following:

```
libmessage.so.1 => Not found
```

This is clearly wrong. However, it would be equally wrong to always hardcode the RPATH to point to the build tree or to the installation prefix: any of the two locations could be erased resulting in corrupted executables. The solution presented here sets the RPATH differently for the executable in the build tree and in the installation prefix, so that it will always point to where "it makes sense"; that is, as close to the executable as possible. Running ldd in the build tree shows the same output:

```
libmessage.so.1 => /home/roberto/Workspace/robertodr/cmake-
cookbook/chapter-10/recipe-01/cxx-example/build/lib64/libmessage.so.1
(0x00007f7a92e44000)
```

On the other hand, in the installation prefix, we now get the following:

```
libmessage.so.1 =>
/home/roberto/Software/ch10r01/bin/../lib64/libmessage.so.1
(0x00007fbd2a725000)
```

We have used the CMake install command with the TARGETS signature, since we needed to install build targets. The command has, however, four additional signatures:

- The FILES and PROGRAMS signatures. These are used to install files or programs, respectively. Upon installation, files will be copied and permissions for them set appropriately. That is, for files, read and write permissions to the owner, read permissions to the group and other users and groups. For programs, execution permissions will be additionally granted. Note that the PROGRAMS signature is meant for use with executables that are not build targets. See also: https://cmake.org/cmake/help/v3.6/command/install.html#installing-files.

- The `DIRECTORY` signature. As the name suggests, this is used to install directories. When only a directory name is given, it is, as usual, understood to be relative to the current source directory. Granular control over installation of directories is possible. Please consult the online documentation: `https://cmake.org/cmake/help/v3.6/command/install.html#installing-directories`.

- The `SCRIPT` signature. You can use this one to define custom installation rules within a CMake script. See `https://cmake.org/cmake/help/v3.6/command/install.html#custom-installation-logic`.

- The `EXPORT` signature. We defer discussion of this signature to *Recipe 3, Exporting your targets*.

Generating export headers

The code for this recipe is available at `https://github.com/dev-cafe/cmake-cookbook/tree/v1.0/chapter-10/recipe-02` and has a C++ example. The recipe is valid with CMake version 3.6 (and higher) and has been tested on GNU/Linux, macOS, and Windows.

Let us imagine that the small library that we have introduced has become hugely popular, with many people using it. However, some clients would also like a static library to be available with the installation. Other clients have noticed that all symbols are visible in the shared library. Best practices dictate that shared libraries only expose the minimal amount of symbols, thus limiting the visibility to the outside world of objects and functions defined in the code. We want to make sure that by default all symbols defined in our shared library are hidden from the outside world. This will force contributors to the project to clearly delimit the interface between the library and external codes, since they will have to explicit mark all symbols that also meant to be used outside of the project. As such, we wish to do the following:

- Build both a shared and static library from the same set of source files.
- Ensure that only the visibility of symbols in the shared library is properly delimited.

Recipe 3, Building and linking static and shared libraries, in *Chapter 1, From a Simple Executable to Libraries,* already showed that CMake offers functionality to achieve the first point in a platform-independent way. We did not, however, address the issue of symbol visibility. We will revisit both points with the present recipe.

Getting ready

We will still use mostly the same code as in the previous recipe, but we will need to modify src/CMakeLists.txt and the Message.hpp header file. The latter will include the new, autogenerated header file, messageExport.h:

```
#pragma once

#include <iosfwd>
#include <string>

#include "messageExport.h"

class message_EXPORT Message {
public:
  Message(const std::string &m) : message_(m) {}

  friend std::ostream &operator<<(std::ostream &os, Message &obj) {
    return obj.printObject(os);
  }

private:
  std::string message_;
  std::ostream &printObject(std::ostream &os);
};

std::string getUUID();
```

The message_EXPORT preprocessor directive was introduced in the declaration of the Message class. This directive will let the compiler generate symbols that are visible to the users of the library.

How to do it

Apart from the name of the project, the root CMakeLists.txt file is unchanged. Let us first look at the CMakeLists.txt file in the src subdirectory, where all the additional work actually happens. We will highlight the changes with respect to the file in the previous recipe:

1. We declare our SHARED library target and its sources for the messaging library. Note that compile definitions and link libraries are unchanged:

    ```
    add_library(message-shared SHARED "")
    ```

```
target_sources(message-shared
  PRIVATE
    ${CMAKE_CURRENT_LIST_DIR}/Message.cpp
  )

target_compile_definitions(message-shared
  PUBLIC
    $<$<BOOL:${UUID_FOUND}>:HAVE_UUID>
  )

target_link_libraries(message-shared
  PUBLIC
    $<$<BOOL:${UUID_FOUND}>:PkgConfig::UUID>
  )
```

2. We also set target properties. We have added the
   `${CMAKE_BINARY_DIR}/${INSTALL_INCLUDEDIR}/messageExport.h` header
   file in the list of public headers given as argument to the `PUBLIC_HEADER` target
   property. The `CXX_VISIBILITY_PRESET` and `VISIBILITY_INLINES_HIDDEN`
   properties will be discussed in the next section:

```
set_target_properties(message-shared
  PROPERTIES
    POSITION_INDEPENDENT_CODE 1
    CXX_VISIBILITY_PRESET hidden
    VISIBILITY_INLINES_HIDDEN 1
    SOVERSION ${PROJECT_VERSION_MAJOR}
    OUTPUT_NAME "message"
    DEBUG_POSTFIX "_d"
    PUBLIC_HEADER
"Message.hpp;${CMAKE_BINARY_DIR}/${INSTALL_INCLUDEDIR}/messageExpor
t.h"
    MACOSX_RPATH ON
  )
```

3. We include the standard CMake module `GenerateExportHeader.cmake`
   module and invoke the `generate_export_header` function. This will generate
   the `messageExport.h` header file in a subdirectory of the build directory. We
   will discuss this function and the generated header in more detail very soon:

```
include(GenerateExportHeader)
generate_export_header(message-shared
  BASE_NAME "message"
  EXPORT_MACRO_NAME "message_EXPORT"
  EXPORT_FILE_NAME
"${CMAKE_BINARY_DIR}/${INSTALL_INCLUDEDIR}/messageExport.h"
  DEPRECATED_MACRO_NAME "message_DEPRECATED"
```

```
NO_EXPORT_MACRO_NAME "message_NO_EXPORT"
STATIC_DEFINE "message_STATIC_DEFINE"
NO_DEPRECATED_MACRO_NAME "message_NO_DEPRECATED"
DEFINE_NO_DEPRECATED
)
```

4. The export header should be included whenever the visibility of symbols is to be changed from its default – hidden – value. We have done that in the Message.hpp header file, since we want to expose some symbols in our library. Now we list the ${CMAKE_BINARY_DIR}/${INSTALL_INCLUDEDIR} directory as a PUBLIC include directory of the message-shared target:

```
target_include_directories(message-shared
  PUBLIC
    ${CMAKE_BINARY_DIR}/${INSTALL_INCLUDEDIR}
  )
```

Now we can turn our attention to the generation of the static library:

1. We add a library target to generate the static library. The same sources as for the shared library will be compiled to get this target:

```
add_library(message-static STATIC "")

target_sources(message-static
  PRIVATE
    ${CMAKE_CURRENT_LIST_DIR}/Message.cpp
  )
```

2. We set compiler definitions, include directories, and link libraries, exactly as we did for the shared library target. Note, however, that we added the message_STATIC_DEFINE compile definition. This is to make sure that our symbols are properly exposed:

```
target_compile_definitions(message-static
  PUBLIC
    message_STATIC_DEFINE
    $<$<BOOL:${UUID_FOUND}>:HAVE_UUID>
  )

target_include_directories(message-static
  PUBLIC
    ${CMAKE_BINARY_DIR}/${INSTALL_INCLUDEDIR}
  )

target_link_libraries(message-static
  PUBLIC
```

```
$<$<BOOL:${UUID_FOUND}>:PkgConfig::UUID>
  )
```

3. We also set properties on the `message-static` target. These will be discussed in the next section:

```
set_target_properties(message-static
  PROPERTIES
    POSITION_INDEPENDENT_CODE 1
    ARCHIVE_OUTPUT_NAME "message"
    DEBUG_POSTFIX "_sd"
    RELEASE_POSTFIX "_s"
    PUBLIC_HEADER
"Message.hpp;${CMAKE_BINARY_DIR}/${INSTALL_INCLUDEDIR}/messageExpor
t.h"
  )
```

4. In addition to the `hello-world_wDSO` executable target, which links against the `message-shared` library target, we define another executable target, `hello-world_wAR`. This links against the static library:

```
add_executable(hello-world_wAR hello-world.cpp)

target_link_libraries(hello-world_wAR
  PUBLIC
    message-static
  )
```

5. The installation directives now list the additional `message-static` and `hello-world_wAR` targets, but are otherwise unchanged:

```
install(
  TARGETS
    message-shared
    message-static
    hello-world_wDSO
    hello-world_wAR
  ARCHIVE
    DESTINATION ${INSTALL_LIBDIR}
    COMPONENT lib
  RUNTIME
    DESTINATION ${INSTALL_BINDIR}
    COMPONENT bin
  LIBRARY
    DESTINATION ${INSTALL_LIBDIR}
    COMPONENT lib
  PUBLIC_HEADER
```

```
        DESTINATION ${INSTALL_INCLUDEDIR}/message
        COMPONENT dev
    )
```

How it works

This recipe demonstrates how to set the visibility of symbols for a shared library. The best practice is to keep all symbols hidden by default, explicitly exposing only those symbols that we want to be used by dependents on our library. This is achieved in two steps. First of all, we need to instruct the compiler to hide symbols. Of course, different compilers will have different options available, and directly setting these by hand in our CMakeLists.txt would not be cross-platform. CMake offers a robust and cross-platform way of setting symbol visibility by setting two properties on the shared library target:

- CXX_VISIBILITY_PRESET hidden: This will hide all symbols, unless explicitly marked otherwise. When using the GNU compiler, this adds the flag -fvisibility=hidden for the target.
- VISIBILITY_INLINES_HIDDEN 1: This will hide symbols for inline functions. If using the GNU compiler, this corresponds to -fvisibility-inlines-hidden.

On Windows, this is the default behavior. Recall, in fact, that we needed to override it in the previous recipe by setting the WINDOWS_EXPORT_ALL_SYMBOLS property to ON.

How do we mark the symbols we want to be visible? This is determined by the preprocessor, and we thus need to provide preprocessor macros that expand to visibility attributes that the given compiler on the chosen platform will understand. Once again, CMake comes to the rescue with the GenerateExportHeader.cmake module file. This module defines the generate_export_header function, which we invoked as follows:

```
include(GenerateExportHeader)
generate_export_header(message-shared
  BASE_NAME "message"
  EXPORT_MACRO_NAME "message_EXPORT"
  EXPORT_FILE_NAME
"${CMAKE_BINARY_DIR}/${INSTALL_INCLUDEDIR}/messageExport.h"
  DEPRECATED_MACRO_NAME "message_DEPRECATED"
  NO_EXPORT_MACRO_NAME "message_NO_EXPORT"
  STATIC_DEFINE "message_STATIC_DEFINE"
  NO_DEPRECATED_MACRO_NAME "message_NO_DEPRECATED"
  DEFINE_NO_DEPRECATED
  )
```

The function generates the `messageExport.h` header file, which will contain the preprocessor macros needed. The file is generated in the directory `${CMAKE_BINARY_DIR}/${INSTALL_INCLUDEDIR}`, as requested *via* the `EXPORT_FILE_NAME` option. If this option is left empty, the header file would be generated in the current binary directory. The first argument to this function is an existing target, `message-shared` in our case. Basic invocation of the function only requires passing the name of an existing target. Optional arguments, for fine-grained control of all of the generated macros, can also be passed:

- `BASE_NAME`: This sets the base name of the generated header and macros to the passed value.
- `EXPORT_MACRO_NAME`: This sets the name of the export macro.
- `EXPORT_FILE_NAME`: This sets the name for the export header file generated.
- `DEPRECATED_MACRO_NAME`: This sets the name for the deprecation macro. This is used to mark deprecated code, the compiler will emit a deprecation warning if clients use it.
- `NO_EXPORT_MACRO_NAME`: This sets the name of the no-export macro.
- `STATIC_DEFINE`: This is for the name of the macro to use when also compiling a static library out of the same sources.
- `NO_DEPRECATED_MACRO_NAME`: This sets the name of the macro to be used to exclude deprecated code from being compiled.
- `DEFINE_NO_DEPRECATED`: This instructs CMake to generate preprocessor code to exclude deprecated code from compilation.

On GNU/Linux and using the GNU compiler, CMake will generate the following `messageExport.h` export header:

```
#ifndef message_EXPORT_H
#define message_EXPORT_H

#ifdef message_STATIC_DEFINE
#  define message_EXPORT
#  define message_NO_EXPORT
#else
#  ifndef message_EXPORT
#    ifdef message_shared_EXPORTS
        /* We are building this library */
#      define message_EXPORT __attribute__((visibility("default")))
#    else
        /* We are using this library */
#      define message_EXPORT __attribute__((visibility("default")))
#    endif
```

```
#   endif

#   ifndef message_NO_EXPORT
#     define message_NO_EXPORT __attribute__((visibility("hidden")))
#   endif
#endif

#ifndef message_DEPRECATED
#   define message_DEPRECATED __attribute__ ((__deprecated__))
#endif

#ifndef message_DEPRECATED_EXPORT
#   define message_DEPRECATED_EXPORT message_EXPORT message_DEPRECATED
#endif

#ifndef message_DEPRECATED_NO_EXPORT
#   define message_DEPRECATED_NO_EXPORT message_NO_EXPORT message_DEPRECATED
#endif

#if 1 /* DEFINE_NO_DEPRECATED */
#   ifndef message_NO_DEPRECATED
#     define message_NO_DEPRECATED
#   endif
#endif

#endif
```

We can prepend the classes and functions to be exposed to users with the `message_EXPORT` macro. Deprecation can be achieved by prepending with the `message_DEPRECATED` macro.

The static library is built out of the same sources. However, all symbols are supposed to be visible in the static archive, and as can be seen from the contents of the `messageExport.h` header file, the `message_STATIC_DEFINE` macro comes to the rescue. Once the target has been declared, we set it as a compile definition. The additional target properties on the static library are as follows:

- `ARCHIVE_OUTPUT_NAME` `"message"`: This will ensure that the name of the library file is just message, rather than message-static.
- `DEBUG_POSTFIX` `"_sd"`: This will append the given postfix to the library. This uniquely identifies the library as *static* in a `Debug` configuration.
- `RELEASE_POSTFIX` `"_s"`: This is similar to the previous property, but just appends the postfix for a static library in case the target was built in `Release` configuration.

There is more

It is good practice to hide internal symbols when building a shared library. This means that the library shrinks in size, because what you expose to the user is less than what you have in the library. This defines the Application Binary Interface (ABI), which most of the time should coincide with the Application Programming Interface (API). This is done in two stages:

1. We use the appropriate compiler flags.
2. We mark symbols to be exported with a preprocessor variable (`message_EXPORT`, in our example). When compiling, the hiding will be lifted for these symbols (such as classes and functions).

Static libraries are just archives of object files. Thus one compiles sources into object files and then the archiver bundles them into an archive. There is no notion of ABI: all symbols are visible by default and the visibility flags for the compiler do not affect static archiving. However, if you are going to build a shared and static library from the same source files, you need a way to give meaning to the `message_EXPORT` preprocessor variable that now appears in the code *in both cases*. This is where the `GenerateExportHeader.cmake` module comes in. It will define a header with all the logic for giving the proper definition of this preprocessor variable. For shared libraries, it will be what is needed by the given combination of platform and compiler. Note that the meaning will also change based on whether we are *building* or *using* the shared library. Fortunately, CMake takes care of this for us without further intervention. For static libraries, it will expand to an empty string doing what we expect: nothing.

The attentive reader will have noticed that building the static and shared libraries as shown here will actually require to *compile the sources twice*. This was not an expensive operation for our simple example, but it can clearly become quite onerous, even for projects that are only slightly bigger than our example. Why did we choose this approach over the one using `OBJECT` libraries shown in *Recipe 3, Building and linking static and shared libraries*, in *Chapter 1, From a Simple Executable to Libraries*? `OBJECT` libraries take care of the first step in compiling the library: from sources to object files. In that step, the preprocessor intervenes and will evaluate `message_EXPORT`. Since the compilation of `OBJECT` libraries happens once, `message_EXPORT` is either evaluated to a value compatible with building the shared or the static library. Thus to avoid ambiguities, we chose the more robust approach of compiling twice, letting the preprocessor evaluate the visibility variable correctly.

> For more details on the topic of dynamic shared objects, static archives, and symbol visibility, we suggest reading this article: `http://people.redhat.com/drepper/dsohowto.pdf`.

Exporting your targets

The code for this recipe is available at `https://github.com/dev-cafe/cmake-cookbook/tree/v1.0/chapter-10/recipe-03` and has a C++ example. The recipe is valid with CMake version 3.6 (and higher) and has been tested on GNU/Linux, macOS, and Windows.

We can imagine that our message library has been a huge success in the open source community. People like it a lot and use it in their own projects to print their messages to screen. Users particularly like the fact that each printed message gets a unique identifier. But users would also like the library to be more easily discoverable, once they compile and install it on their systems. This recipe will show how CMake can let us export our targets so that other projects using CMake can pick them up easily.

Getting ready

The source code is unchanged with respect to the previous recipe and the structure of the project is as follows:

```
.
├── cmake
│   └── messageConfig.cmake.in
├── CMakeLists.txt
├── src
│   ├── CMakeLists.txt
│   ├── hello-world.cpp
│   ├── Message.cpp
│   └── Message.hpp
└── tests
    ├── CMakeLists.txt
    └── use_target
        ├── CMakeLists.txt
        └── use_message.cpp
```

Notice that we have added a `cmake` subdirectory containing a `messageConfig.cmake.in` file. This file will contain our exported targets. We have also added a test to check whether the installation and export of the project work as intended.

How to do it

Once again, the root `CMakeLists.txt` file is unchanged with respect to the previous recipe. Moving onto the leaf directory `src` containing our sources:

1. We need to find the UUID library and we can re-use the code used in previous recipes:

```
# Search for pkg-config and UUID
find_package(PkgConfig QUIET)
if(PKG_CONFIG_FOUND)
  pkg_search_module(UUID uuid IMPORTED_TARGET)
  if(TARGET PkgConfig::UUID)
    message(STATUS "Found libuuid")
    set(UUID_FOUND TRUE)
  endif()
endif()
```

2. Next, we set up our shared library target and generate the export header, as shown in the previous recipe:

```
add_library(message-shared SHARED "")

include(GenerateExportHeader)
generate_export_header(message-shared
  BASE_NAME "message"
  EXPORT_MACRO_NAME "message_EXPORT"
  EXPORT_FILE_NAME
"${CMAKE_BINARY_DIR}/${INSTALL_INCLUDEDIR}/messageExport.h"
  DEPRECATED_MACRO_NAME "message_DEPRECATED"
  NO_EXPORT_MACRO_NAME "message_NO_EXPORT"
  STATIC_DEFINE "message_STATIC_DEFINE"
  NO_DEPRECATED_MACRO_NAME "message_NO_DEPRECATED"
  DEFINE_NO_DEPRECATED
  )

target_sources(message-shared
  PRIVATE
    ${CMAKE_CURRENT_LIST_DIR}/Message.cpp
  )
```

3. We set PUBLIC and INTERFACE compile definitions for the target. Note the use of the $<INSTALL_INTERFACE:...> generator expression for the latter:

```
target_compile_definitions(message-shared
  PUBLIC
    $<$<BOOL:${UUID_FOUND}>:HAVE_UUID>
  INTERFACE
    $<INSTALL_INTERFACE:USING_message>
  )
```

4. Next, the include directories are set. Once again note the use of $<BUILD_INTERFACE:...> and $<INSTALL_INTERFACE:...> generator expressions. We will comment on these later on:

```
target_include_directories(message-shared
  PUBLIC
    $<BUILD_INTERFACE:${CMAKE_BINARY_DIR}/${INSTALL_INCLUDEDIR}>
    $<INSTALL_INTERFACE:${INSTALL_INCLUDEDIR}>
  )
```

5. We finish off the shared library target by listing link libraries and target properties. These are unchanged from the previous recipe:

```
target_link_libraries(message-shared
  PUBLIC
    $<$<BOOL:${UUID_FOUND}>:PkgConfig::UUID>
  )

set_target_properties(message-shared
  PROPERTIES
    POSITION_INDEPENDENT_CODE 1
    CXX_VISIBILITY_PRESET hidden
    VISIBILITY_INLINES_HIDDEN 1
    SOVERSION ${PROJECT_VERSION_MAJOR}
    OUTPUT_NAME "message"
    DEBUG_POSTFIX "_d"
    PUBLIC_HEADER
"Message.hpp;${CMAKE_BINARY_DIR}/${INSTALL_INCLUDEDIR}/messageExport.h"
    MACOSX_RPATH ON
  )
```

The same is done for the message-static library target:

1. We first declare it and list its sources:

```
add_library(message-static STATIC "")

target_sources(message-static
  PRIVATE
    ${CMAKE_CURRENT_LIST_DIR}/Message.cpp
  )
```

2. We give PUBLIC and INTERFACE compile definitions, as in the previous recipe, but now using the $<INSTALL_INTERFACE:...> generator expression:

```
target_compile_definitions(message-static
  PUBLIC
    message_STATIC_DEFINE
    $<$<BOOL:${UUID_FOUND}>:HAVE_UUID>
  INTERFACE
    $<INSTALL_INTERFACE:USING_message>
  )
```

3. We list include directories with the same command used for the shared target:

```
target_include_directories(message-static
  PUBLIC
    $<BUILD_INTERFACE:${CMAKE_BINARY_DIR}/${INSTALL_INCLUDEDIR}>
    $<INSTALL_INTERFACE:${INSTALL_INCLUDEDIR}>
  )
```

4. Link libraries and target properties are unchanged with respect to the previous recipe:

```
target_link_libraries(message-static
  PUBLIC
    $<$<BOOL:${UUID_FOUND}>:PkgConfig::UUID>
  )

set_target_properties(message-static
  PROPERTIES
    POSITION_INDEPENDENT_CODE 1
    ARCHIVE_OUTPUT_NAME "message"
    DEBUG_POSTFIX "_sd"
    RELEASE_POSTFIX "_s"
    PUBLIC_HEADER
"Message.hpp;${CMAKE_BINARY_DIR}/${INSTALL_INCLUDEDIR}/messageExpor
t.h"
  )
```

5. Executables are generated with the exact same commands used in the previous recipe:

```
add_executable(hello-world_wDSO hello-world.cpp)

target_link_libraries(hello-world_wDSO
  PUBLIC
    message-shared
  )

# Prepare RPATH

file(RELATIVE_PATH _rel ${CMAKE_INSTALL_PREFIX}/${INSTALL_BINDIR}
${CMAKE_INSTALL_PREFIX})
if(APPLE)
  set(_rpath "@loader_path/${_rel}")
else()
  set(_rpath "\$ORIGIN/${_rel}")
endif()
file(TO_NATIVE_PATH "${_rpath}/${INSTALL_LIBDIR}" message_RPATH)

set_target_properties(hello-world_wDSO
  PROPERTIES
    MACOSX_RPATH ON
    SKIP_BUILD_RPATH OFF
    BUILD_WITH_INSTALL_RPATH OFF
    INSTALL_RPATH "${message_RPATH}"
    INSTALL_RPATH_USE_LINK_PATH ON
  )

add_executable(hello-world_wAR hello-world.cpp)

target_link_libraries(hello-world_wAR
  PUBLIC
    message-static
  )
```

We are now ready to look at the installation rules:

1. We list the installation rules for our targets all together, since CMake can correctly place each of the target in the proper destination. This time, we add the EXPORT keyword so that CMake will generate an exported target file for our targets:

```
install(
  TARGETS
    message-shared
```

```
      message-static
      hello-world_wDSO
      hello-world_wAR
    EXPORT
      messageTargets
    ARCHIVE
      DESTINATION ${INSTALL_LIBDIR}
      COMPONENT lib
    RUNTIME
      DESTINATION ${INSTALL_BINDIR}
      COMPONENT bin
    LIBRARY
      DESTINATION ${INSTALL_LIBDIR}
      COMPONENT lib
    PUBLIC_HEADER
      DESTINATION ${INSTALL_INCLUDEDIR}/message
      COMPONENT dev
    )
```

2. The auto-generated export target file is called `messageTargets.cmake`, and we need to explicitly specify install rules for it. The destination of this file is `INSTALL_CMAKEDIR` defined in the root `CMakeLists.txt` file:

```
install(
  EXPORT
    messageTargets
  NAMESPACE
    "message::"
  DESTINATION
    ${INSTALL_CMAKEDIR}
  COMPONENT
    dev
  )
```

3. Finally, we need to generate the proper CMake configuration files. These will guarantee that a downstream project will be able to find the targets exported by the message library. To do so, we first include the `CMakePackageConfigHelpers.cmake` standard module:

```
include(CMakePackageConfigHelpers)
```

4. We let CMake generate a file containing version information for our library:

```
write_basic_package_version_file(
  ${CMAKE_CURRENT_BINARY_DIR}/messageConfigVersion.cmake
```

```
VERSION ${PROJECT_VERSION}
COMPATIBILITY SameMajorVersion
)
```

5. Using the `configure_package_config_file` function, we generate the actual CMake configuration file. This is based on the template `cmake/messageConfig.cmake.in` file:

```
configure_package_config_file(
    ${PROJECT_SOURCE_DIR}/cmake/messageConfig.cmake.in
    ${CMAKE_CURRENT_BINARY_DIR}/messageConfig.cmake
    INSTALL_DESTINATION ${INSTALL_CMAKEDIR}
    )
```

6. As a last step, we set the install rules for these two auto-generated configuration files:

```
install(
  FILES
    ${CMAKE_CURRENT_BINARY_DIR}/messageConfig.cmake
    ${CMAKE_CURRENT_BINARY_DIR}/messageConfigVersion.cmake
  DESTINATION
    ${INSTALL_CMAKEDIR}
  )
```

What are the contents of the `cmake/messageConfig.cmake.in` template file? The header of this file serves as documentation for its users. Let us look at the actual CMake commands:

1. We start with a placeholder that will be replaced by the `configure_package_config_file` command:

```
@PACKAGE_INIT@
```

2. We include the auto-generated export files for the targets :

```
include("${CMAKE_CURRENT_LIST_DIR}/messageTargets.cmake")
```

3. Then we check whether the static and shared libraries and the two "Hello, World" executables are present with the `check_required_components` function provided by CMake:

```
check_required_components(
  "message-shared"
  "message-static"
```

```
"message-hello-world_wDSO"
"message-hello-world_wAR"
)
```

4. We check whether the target `PkgConfig::UUID` exists. If not, we search again for the UUID library, but only if we are not on Windows:

```
if(NOT WIN32)
  if(NOT TARGET PkgConfig::UUID)
    find_package(PkgConfig REQUIRED QUIET)
    pkg_search_module(UUID REQUIRED uuid IMPORTED_TARGET)
  endif()
endif()
```

Let us try this out:

```
$ mkdir -p build
$ cd build
$ cmake -DCMAKE_INSTALL_PREFIX=$HOME/Software/recipe-03 ..
$ cmake --build . --target install
```

The install tree has the following structure:

```
$HOME/Software/recipe-03/
├── bin
│   ├── hello-world_wAR
│   └── hello-world_wDSO
├── include
│   └── message
│       ├── messageExport.h
│       └── Message.hpp
├── lib64
│   ├── libmessage_s.a
│   ├── libmessage.so -> libmessage.so.1
│   └── libmessage.so.1
└── share
    └── cmake
        └── recipe-03
            ├── messageConfig.cmake
            ├── messageConfigVersion.cmake
            ├── messageTargets.cmake
            └── messageTargets-release.cmake
```

You will notice that a `share` subdirectory has appeared and it contains all the files that we have asked CMake to autogenerate. From now on, the users of our `message` library will be able to locate the `message` library by doing this in their own `CMakeLists.txt` file, provided that they set the `message_DIR` CMake variable to point to the `share/cmake/message` directory in the install tree:

```
find_package(message 1 CONFIG REQUIRED)
```

How it works

This recipe has covered a lot of ground; let us make sense of it. CMake targets are a very useful abstraction for the operations that the build system will perform. Using the `PRIVATE`, `PUBLIC`, and `INTERFACE` keywords, we can set how targets within the same project will interact with each other. In practice, this lets us define how dependencies of target A will affect target B, which depends on A. The full power of this mechanism can be appreciated when other projects want to use a library as a dependency. If the proper CMake configuration files are made available by the library maintainers, then all dependencies can be easily resolved with very few CMake commands.

This problem can be solved by following the pattern outlined in the recipe for the `message-static`, `message-shared`, `hello-world_wDSO`, and `hello-world_wAR` targets. We will analyze the CMake commands for the `message-shared` target alone, but the discussion here is general:

1. Generate your target and lay out its dependencies within the project build. The need to link against the UUID library is a `PUBLIC` requirement for `message-shared`, since it will be used both to build targets within the project and targets in downstream projects. Compile definitions and include directories need to be set both at the `PUBLIC` *or* at the `INTERFACE` level. Some of them will, in fact be needed to build targets within the project, others are only relevant for downstream projects. Moreover, some of these will only be relevant after the project has been installed. This is where the `$<BUILD_INTERFACE:...>` and `$<INSTALL_INTERFACE:....>` generator expressions come in. Only downstream targets *external* to the `message` library will need these, that is they will only be made visible once the target is installed. In our example, the following applies:
   * `$<BUILD_INTERFACE:${CMAKE_BINARY_DIR}/${INSTALL_INCLUDE DIR}>` will expand to `${CMAKE_BINARY_DIR}/${INSTALL_INCLUDEDIR}` only when the `message-shared` library target is used within our project.

- $<INSTALL_INTERFACE:${INSTALL_INCLUDEDIR}> will expand to ${INSTALL_INCLUDEDIR} only when the message-shared library target is used as an exported target within another build tree.

2. Describe the install rules for the target, including the name of the EXPORT file CMake will have to generate.

3. Describe the install rules for the export file CMake has generated. The messageTargets.cmake file will be installed to INSTALL_CMAKEDIR. The NAMESPACE option to the install rule for the target export files will prepend the given string to the name of the targets. This is helpful to avoid potential name clashes between targets from different projects. The INSTALL_CMAKEDIR variable was set in the root CMakeLists.txt file:

```
if(WIN32 AND NOT CYGWIN)
  set(DEF_INSTALL_CMAKEDIR CMake)
else()
  set(DEF_INSTALL_CMAKEDIR share/cmake/${PROJECT_NAME})
endif()
set(INSTALL_CMAKEDIR ${DEF_INSTALL_CMAKEDIR} CACHE PATH
"Installation directory for CMake files")
```

The final part of our CMakeLists.txt generates the configuration files. After including the CMakePackageConfigHelpers.cmake module, this is done in three steps:

1. We call the write_basic_package_version_file CMake function to generate a package version file. The first argument to the macro is the path to the versioning file: messageConfigVersion.cmake. We then specify the version in the Major.Minor.Patch format, using the PROJECT_VERSION CMake variable. Compatibility with newer versions of the library can also be specified. In our case, we guarantee compatibility when the library has the same major version, hence the SameMajorVersion argument.

2. Next, we configure our template file, messageConfig.cmake.in; this file is located in the cmake subdirectory of the project.

3. Finally, we set the install rules for the newly generated files. Both will be installed under INSTALL_CMAKEDIR.

There is more

Clients of the message library are now very happy since they can finally install the library on their system and have CMake discover it for them with minimal modifications to their own CMakeLists.txt:

```
find_package(message VERSION 1 REQUIRED)
```

Clients can now configure their project with the following:

$ cmake -Dmessage_DIR=/path/to/message/share/cmake/message ..

The tests included with our example show how to check that the installation of the targets went according to plan. Looking at the structure of the tests folder we notice the use_target subdirectory:

```
tests/
├──── CMakeLists.txt
└──── use_target
      ├──── CMakeLists.txt
      └──── use_message.cpp
```

This directory contains a small project that uses the exported targets. The interesting part is in the CMakeLists.txt file specifying the tests:

1. We test that the small project can be configured to use the installed library. This is the set up step of the use-target test fixture, as shown in *Chapter 4, Creating and Running Tests, Recipe 10, Using test fixtures*:

```
add_test(
  NAME use-target_configure
  COMMAND
    ${CMAKE_COMMAND} -H${CMAKE_CURRENT_LIST_DIR}/use_target
                     -B${CMAKE_CURRENT_BINARY_DIR}/build_use-target
                     -G${CMAKE_GENERATOR}
                     -Dmessage_DIR=${CMAKE_INSTALL_PREFIX}/${
                     INSTALL_CMAKEDIR}
                     -DCMAKE_BUILD_TYPE=$<CONFIGURATION>
  )
set_tests_properties(use-target_configure
  PROPERTIES
    FIXTURES_SETUP use-target
  )
```

2. We test that the small project can be built:

```
add_test(
  NAME use-target_build
  COMMAND
    ${CMAKE_COMMAND} --build ${CMAKE_CURRENT_BINARY_DIR}/build_use-
target
                      --config $<CONFIGURATION>
  )
set_tests_properties(use-target_build
  PROPERTIES
    FIXTURES_REQUIRED use-target
  )
```

3. The tests of the small projects are also run:

```
set(_test_target)
if(MSVC)
  set(_test_target "RUN_TESTS")
else()
  set(_test_target "test")
endif()
add_test(
  NAME use-target_test
  COMMAND
    ${CMAKE_COMMAND} --build ${CMAKE_CURRENT_BINARY_DIR}/build_use-
target
                      --target ${_test_target}
                      --config $<CONFIGURATION>
  )
set_tests_properties(use-target_test
  PROPERTIES
    FIXTURES_REQUIRED use-target
  )
unset(_test_target)
```

4. Finally, we tear down the fixture:

```
add_test(
  NAME use-target_cleanup
  COMMAND
    ${CMAKE_COMMAND} -E remove_directory
${CMAKE_CURRENT_BINARY_DIR}/build_use-target
  )
set_tests_properties(use-target_cleanup
  PROPERTIES
    FIXTURES_CLEANUP use-target
  )
```

Note that these tests can only be run *after* the project has been installed.

Installing a superbuild

The code for this recipe is available at `https://github.com/dev-cafe/cmake-cookbook/tree/v1.0/chapter-10/recipe-04` and has a C++ example. The recipe is valid with CMake version 3.6 (and higher) and has been tested on GNU/Linux, macOS, and Windows.

Our example `message` library has become a huge success, and many other programmers use it and are very happy with it. You want to use it in your own project too, but are unsure how to manage the dependency properly. You could ship the source code for the message library with your own code, but what if the library is already installed on the system? *Chapter 8*, *The Superbuild Pattern*, showed that this is a typical scenario for a superbuild, but you are unsure on how to install such a project. This recipe will walk you through the details of installing a superbuild.

Getting ready

This recipe will build a simple executable linking against the `message` library. The layout of the project is as follows:

```
├── cmake
│   ├── install_hook.cmake.in
│   └── print_rpath.py
├── CMakeLists.txt
├── external
│   └── upstream
│       ├── CMakeLists.txt
│       └── message
│           └── CMakeLists.txt
└── src
    ├── CMakeLists.txt
    └── use_message.cpp
```

The main `CMakeLists.txt` file coordinates the superbuild. The `external` subdirectory contains CMake instructions to handle the dependencies. The `cmake` subdirectory contains a Python script and a template CMake script. These will be used to fine-tune the installation, the CMake script being first configured and then executed to call the Python script to print the RPATH for the installed `use_message` executable:

```
import shlex
import subprocess
import sys


def main():
    patcher = sys.argv[1]
    elfobj = sys.argv[2]

    tools = {'patchelf': '--print-rpath', 'chrpath': '--list', 'otool': '-
L'}
    if patcher not in tools.keys():
        raise RuntimeError('Unknown tool {}'.format(patcher))
    cmd = shlex.split('{:s} {:s} {:s}'.format(patcher, tools[patcher],
elfobj))
    rpath = subprocess.run(
        cmd,
        bufsize=1,
        stdout=subprocess.PIPE,
        stderr=subprocess.PIPE,
        universal_newlines=True)
    print(rpath.stdout)


if __name__ == "__main__":
    main()
```

Printing the RPATH can easily be done with platform-native tools that we will discuss later on in this recipe.

Finally, the src subdirectory contains the CMakeLists.txt and source file for the actual project we want to compile. The use_message.cpp source file contains the following:

```
#include <cstdlib>
#include <iostream>

#ifdef USING_message
#include <message/Message.hpp>
void messaging() {
  Message say_hello("Hello, World! From a client of yours!");
  std::cout << say_hello << std::endl;

  Message say_goodbye("Goodbye, World! From a client of yours!");
  std::cout << say_goodbye << std::endl;
}
#else
void messaging() {
  std::cout << "Hello, World! From a client of yours!" << std::endl;
```

```
    std::cout << "Goodbye, World! From a client of yours!" << std::endl;
}
#endif

int main() {
  messaging();
  return EXIT_SUCCESS;
}
```

How to do it

We will start by looking at the root `CMakeLists.txt` file, which is coordinating the superbuild:

1. Its preamble is unchanged with respect to the previous recipes. We start by declaring a C++11 project, we set a sensible default install prefix, build type, output directories for our targets, and layout of components in the install tree:

```
cmake_minimum_required(VERSION 3.6 FATAL_ERROR)

project(recipe-04
  LANGUAGES CXX
  VERSION 1.0.0
  )

# <<< General set up >>>

set(CMAKE_CXX_STANDARD 11)
set(CMAKE_CXX_EXTENSIONS OFF)
set(CMAKE_CXX_STANDARD_REQUIRED ON)

if(NOT CMAKE_BUILD_TYPE)
  set(CMAKE_BUILD_TYPE Release CACHE STRING "Build type" FORCE)
endif()

message(STATUS "Build type set to ${CMAKE_BUILD_TYPE}")

message(STATUS "Project will be installed to
${CMAKE_INSTALL_PREFIX}")

include(GNUInstallDirs)

set(CMAKE_ARCHIVE_OUTPUT_DIRECTORY
  ${PROJECT_BINARY_DIR}/${CMAKE_INSTALL_LIBDIR})
set(CMAKE_LIBRARY_OUTPUT_DIRECTORY
  ${PROJECT_BINARY_DIR}/${CMAKE_INSTALL_LIBDIR})
```

```
set(CMAKE_RUNTIME_OUTPUT_DIRECTORY
  ${PROJECT_BINARY_DIR}/${CMAKE_INSTALL_BINDIR})

# Offer the user the choice of overriding the installation
directories
set(INSTALL_LIBDIR ${CMAKE_INSTALL_LIBDIR} CACHE PATH "Installation
directory for libraries")
set(INSTALL_BINDIR ${CMAKE_INSTALL_BINDIR} CACHE PATH "Installation
directory for executables")
set(INSTALL_INCLUDEDIR ${CMAKE_INSTALL_INCLUDEDIR} CACHE PATH
"Installation directory for header files")
if(WIN32 AND NOT CYGWIN)
  set(DEF_INSTALL_CMAKEDIR CMake)
else()
  set(DEF_INSTALL_CMAKEDIR share/cmake/${PROJECT_NAME})
endif()
set(INSTALL_CMAKEDIR ${DEF_INSTALL_CMAKEDIR} CACHE PATH
"Installation directory for CMake files")

# Report to user
foreach(p LIB BIN INCLUDE CMAKE)
  file(TO_NATIVE_PATH ${CMAKE_INSTALL_PREFIX}/${INSTALL_${p}DIR}
_path )
  message(STATUS "Installing ${p} components to ${_path}")
  unset(_path)
endforeach()
```

2. We set the EP_BASE directory property. This will set the layout for the subprojects in the superbuild. All subprojects will be checked out and built under the subprojects folder of CMAKE_BINARY_DIR:

```
set_property(DIRECTORY PROPERTY EP_BASE
${CMAKE_BINARY_DIR}/subprojects)
```

3. We then declare the STAGED_INSTALL_PREFIX variable. This variable points to the stage subdirectory under the build directory. The project will be installed here during the build. This is a way of sandboxing the installation process and gives us a chance to check that the whole superbuild will install with a correct layout:

```
set(STAGED_INSTALL_PREFIX ${CMAKE_BINARY_DIR}/stage)
message(STATUS "${PROJECT_NAME} staged install:
${STAGED_INSTALL_PREFIX}")
```

4. We add the `external/upstream` subdirectory. This contains CMake instructions to manage our upstream dependencies, in our case, the `message` library:

```
add_subdirectory(external/upstream)
```

5. We then include the `ExternalProject.cmake` standard module:

```
include(ExternalProject)
```

6. We add our own project as an external project, invoking the `ExternalProject_Add` command. The `SOURCE_DIR` option specifies that the sources are in the `src` subdirectory. We also pass all appropriate CMake arguments to configure our project. Note the use of `STAGED_INSTALL_PREFIX` as the installation prefix for the subproject:

```
ExternalProject_Add(${PROJECT_NAME}_core
  DEPENDS
    message_external
  SOURCE_DIR
    ${CMAKE_CURRENT_SOURCE_DIR}/src
  CMAKE_ARGS
    -DCMAKE_INSTALL_PREFIX=${STAGED_INSTALL_PREFIX}
    -DCMAKE_BUILD_TYPE=${CMAKE_BUILD_TYPE}
    -DCMAKE_CXX_COMPILER=${CMAKE_CXX_COMPILER}
    -DCMAKE_CXX_FLAGS=${CMAKE_CXX_FLAGS}
    -DCMAKE_CXX_STANDARD=${CMAKE_CXX_STANDARD}
    -DCMAKE_CXX_EXTENSIONS=${CMAKE_CXX_EXTENSIONS}
    -DCMAKE_CXX_STANDARD_REQUIRED=${CMAKE_CXX_STANDARD_REQUIRED}
    -Dmessage_DIR=${message_DIR}
  CMAKE_CACHE_ARGS
    -DCMAKE_PREFIX_PATH:PATH=${CMAKE_PREFIX_PATH}
  BUILD_ALWAYS
    1
  )
```

7. We now add a test for the `use_message` executable, built by the `recipe-04_core` target. This will run the staged installation of the `use_message` executable, that is the one located within the build tree:

```
enable_testing()

add_test(
  NAME
    check_use_message
  COMMAND
```

```
    ${STAGED_INSTALL_PREFIX}/${INSTALL_BINDIR}/use_message
  )
```

8. Finally, we can declare install rules. This time they are rather simple. Since everything needed has already been installed with the correct layout in the staging area, we only need to copy the whole contents of the staging area to the install prefix:

```
install(
  DIRECTORY
    ${STAGED_INSTALL_PREFIX}/
  DESTINATION
    .
  USE_SOURCE_PERMISSIONS
  )
```

9. We declare an additional installation rule with the `SCRIPT` argument. The CMake script `install_hook.cmake` will be executed, but only on GNU/Linux and macOS. This script will print the `RPATH` of the installed executable and run it. We will discuss this in more detail in the next section:

```
if(UNIX)
  set(PRINT_SCRIPT
"${CMAKE_CURRENT_LIST_DIR}/cmake/print_rpath.py")
  configure_file(cmake/install_hook.cmake.in install_hook.cmake
@ONLY)
  install(
    SCRIPT
      ${CMAKE_CURRENT_BINARY_DIR}/install_hook.cmake
    )
endif()
```

You will have noticed that `-Dmessage_DIR=${message_DIR}` has been passed as a CMake argument to our own project. This will correctly set the location of the message library dependency. The value of `message_DIR` is defined in the `CMakeLists.txt` file under the `external/upstream/message` directory. This file handles the dependency on the `message` library – let us see how:

1. We first attempt to find the package. Possibly, the user will have already installed it somewhere on the system and may have passed the `message_DIR` option when configuring:

```
find_package(message 1 CONFIG QUIET)
```

2. If that was indeed the case and `message` was found, we report the location and the version of the target to the user and add a dummy `message_external` target. The dummy target is needed to handle superbuild dependencies correctly:

```
if(message_FOUND)
  get_property(_loc TARGET message::message-shared PROPERTY
LOCATION)
  message(STATUS "Found message: ${_loc} (found version
${message_VERSION})")
  add_library(message_external INTERFACE)  # dummy
```

3. If the library was not found, we will add it as an external project, download it from its online Git repository, and compile it. The install prefix, build type, and installation directories layout are all set from the root `CMakeLists.txt` file, as are the C++ compiler and flags. The project will be installed to `STAGED_INSTALL_PREFIX` and then tested:

```
else()
  include(ExternalProject)
  message(STATUS "Suitable message could not be located, Building
message instead.")
  ExternalProject_Add(message_external
    GIT_REPOSITORY
      https://github.com/dev-cafe/message.git
    GIT_TAG
      master
    UPDATE_COMMAND
      ""
    CMAKE_ARGS
      -DCMAKE_INSTALL_PREFIX=${STAGED_INSTALL_PREFIX}
      -DCMAKE_BUILD_TYPE=${CMAKE_BUILD_TYPE}
      -DCMAKE_CXX_COMPILER=${CMAKE_CXX_COMPILER}
    CMAKE_CACHE_ARGS
      -DCMAKE_CXX_FLAGS:STRING=${CMAKE_CXX_FLAGS}
    TEST_AFTER_INSTALL
      1
    DOWNLOAD_NO_PROGRESS
      1
    LOG_CONFIGURE
      1
    LOG_BUILD
      1
    LOG_INSTALL
      1
    )
```

4. Finally, we set the `message_DIR` directory to point to the location of the freshly built `messageConfig.cmake` file. Note that the path is saved to the CMake cache:

```
if(WIN32 AND NOT CYGWIN)
  set(DEF_message_DIR ${STAGED_INSTALL_PREFIX}/CMake)
else()
  set(DEF_message_DIR
${STAGED_INSTALL_PREFIX}/share/cmake/message)
endif()
file(TO_NATIVE_PATH "${DEF_message_DIR}" DEF_message_DIR)
set(message_DIR ${DEF_message_DIR}
    CACHE PATH "Path to internally built messageConfig.cmake"
FORCE)
endif()
```

We are finally ready to compile our own project and successfully link it against the `message` library, be it already available on the system or freshly built for the purpose. Since this is a superbuild, the code under the `src` subdirectory is a fully standalone CMake project:

1. We declare a C++11 project, as usual:

```
cmake_minimum_required(VERSION 3.6 FATAL_ERROR)

project(recipe-04_core
  LANGUAGES CXX
  )

set(CMAKE_CXX_STANDARD 11)
set(CMAKE_CXX_EXTENSIONS OFF)
set(CMAKE_CXX_STANDARD_REQUIRED ON)

include(GNUInstallDirs)

set(CMAKE_ARCHIVE_OUTPUT_DIRECTORY
  ${CMAKE_BINARY_DIR}/${CMAKE_INSTALL_LIBDIR})
set(CMAKE_LIBRARY_OUTPUT_DIRECTORY
  ${CMAKE_BINARY_DIR}/${CMAKE_INSTALL_LIBDIR})
set(CMAKE_RUNTIME_OUTPUT_DIRECTORY
  ${CMAKE_BINARY_DIR}/${CMAKE_INSTALL_BINDIR})
```

2. We attempt finding the `message` library. Within our superbuild, the configuration will have `message_DIR` correctly set:

```
find_package(message 1 CONFIG REQUIRED)
get_property(_loc TARGET message::message-shared PROPERTY LOCATION)
```

```
message(STATUS "Found message: ${_loc} (found version
${message_VERSION})")
```

3. We are ready to add our executable target, `use_message`. This is built from the `use_message.cpp` source file and links in the `message::message-shared` target:

```
add_executable(use_message use_message.cpp)

target_link_libraries(use_message
  PUBLIC
    message::message-shared
  )
```

4. Target properties are set for `use_message`. Note once again the RPATH fixing:

```
# Prepare RPATH
file(RELATIVE_PATH _rel
${CMAKE_INSTALL_PREFIX}/${CMAKE_INSTALL_BINDIR}
${CMAKE_INSTALL_PREFIX})
if(APPLE)
  set(_rpath "@loader_path/${_rel}")
else()
  set(_rpath "\$ORIGIN/${_rel}")
endif()
file(TO_NATIVE_PATH "${_rpath}/${CMAKE_INSTALL_LIBDIR}"
use_message_RPATH)

set_target_properties(use_message
  PROPERTIES
    MACOSX_RPATH ON
    SKIP_BUILD_RPATH OFF
    BUILD_WITH_INSTALL_RPATH OFF
    INSTALL_RPATH "${use_message_RPATH}"
    INSTALL_RPATH_USE_LINK_PATH ON
  )
```

5. Finally, we set install rules for the `use_message` target:

```
install(
  TARGETS
    use_message
  RUNTIME
    DESTINATION ${CMAKE_INSTALL_BINDIR}
    COMPONENT bin
  )
```

Let us now look at the contents of the `install_hook.cmake.in` template CMake script:

1. The CMake script is executed outside the scope of our main project and hence has no notion of variables or targets defined there. We thus set a variable holding the full path to the installed `use_message` executable. Note the use of `@INSTALL_BINDIR@`, which will be resolved by `configure_file`:

```
set(_executable
${CMAKE_INSTALL_PREFIX}/@INSTALL_BINDIR@/use_message)
```

2. We need to find the executable for the platform-native tool we will use to print the RPATH of the installed executable. We will search for `chrpath`, `patchelf`, and `otool`. The search exits as soon one is found to be installed with an helpful status message to the user:

```
set(_patcher)
list(APPEND _patchers chrpath patchelf otool)
foreach(p IN LISTS _patchers)
  find_program(${p}_FOUND
    NAMES
      ${p}
    )
  if(${p}_FOUND)
    set(_patcher ${p})
    message(STATUS "ELF patching tool ${_patcher} FOUND")
    break()
  endif()
endforeach()
```

3. We check whether the `_patcher` variable is not empty. It would mean no ELF patching tool is available and the operation we want to carry out will fail. We emit a fatal error and alert the user that one of the ELF patching tools needs to be installed:

```
if(NOT _patcher)
  message(FATAL_ERROR "ELF patching tool NOT FOUND!\nPlease install
one of chrpath, patchelf or otool")
```

4. In case one the ELF patching tools was found, we proceed. We invoke the `print_rpath.py` Python script, passing the `_executable` variable as argument. We use `execute_process` for this purpose:

```
find_package(PythonInterp REQUIRED QUIET)
execute_process(
  COMMAND
    ${PYTHON_EXECUTABLE} @PRINT_SCRIPT@ "${_patcher}"
```

```
 "${_executable}"
 RESULT_VARIABLE _res
 OUTPUT_VARIABLE _out
 ERROR_VARIABLE _err
 OUTPUT_STRIP_TRAILING_WHITESPACE
 )
```

5. We check the _res variable for return code. If execution was successful, we print the standard output stream captured in the _out variable. Otherwise, we print the captured standard output and error streams before exiting with a fatal error:

```
if(_res EQUAL 0)
  message(STATUS "RPATH for ${_executable} is ${_out}")
else()
  message(STATUS "Something went wrong!")
  message(STATUS "Standard output from print_rpath.py: ${_out}")
  message(STATUS "Standard error from print_rpath.py: ${_err}")
  message(FATAL_ERROR "${_patcher} could NOT obtain RPATH for
${_executable}")
  endif()
endif()
```

6. We invoke once again execute_process to run the installed use_message executable:

```
execute_process(
  COMMAND ${_executable}
  RESULT_VARIABLE _res
  OUTPUT_VARIABLE _out
  ERROR_VARIABLE _err
  OUTPUT_STRIP_TRAILING_WHITESPACE
  )
```

7. Finally, we report to the user on the result of execute_process:

```
if(_res EQUAL 0)
  message(STATUS "Running ${_executable}:\n ${_out}")
else()
  message(STATUS "Something went wrong!")
  message(STATUS "Standard output from running ${_executable}:\n
${_out}")
  message(STATUS "Standard error from running ${_executable}:\n
${_err}")
  message(FATAL_ERROR "Something went wrong with ${_executable}")
endif()
```

How it works

The superbuild is a very useful pattern in our CMake toolbox. It lets us manage complex projects by separating them into smaller, more manageable subprojects. In addition, we can use CMake as a package manager for the project we are building. CMake can search for our dependencies and, in case they are not found on the system, freshly build them for us. The basic pattern requires three CMakeLists.txt files:

- The root CMakeLists.txt file contains settings shared by the project and the dependencies. It also includes our own project as an external project. In our case, we chose the name ${PROJECT_NAME}_core; that is, recipe-04_core, since the project name recipe-04 is used for the superbuild.
- The external CMakeLists.txt file will attempt to find our upstream dependencies and contains the logic to switch between importing targets or building them, depending on whether the dependencies were found or not. It is good practice to have separate subdirectories for each dependency, containing a similarly structured CMakeLists.txt file.
- Finally, the CMakeLists.txt file for our own project is a standalone CMake project file, since, in principle, we can configure and build it on its own without the additional facilities for dependency management offered by the superbuild.

We will first consider the configuration of the superbuild when the dependency on the message library is not already satisfied:

```
$ mkdir -p build
$ cd build
$ cmake -DCMAKE_INSTALL_PREFIX=$HOME/Software/recipe-04 ..
```

We will let CMake find the library for us, and this is the output we obtain:

```
-- The CXX compiler identification is GNU 7.3.0
-- Check for working CXX compiler:
/nix/store/gqg2vrcq7krqi9rrl6pphvsg81sb8pjw-gcc-wrapper-7.3.0/bin/g++
-- Check for working CXX compiler:
/nix/store/gqg2vrcq7krqi9rrl6pphvsg81sb8pjw-gcc-wrapper-7.3.0/bin/g++ --
works
-- Detecting CXX compiler ABI info
-- Detecting CXX compiler ABI info - done
-- Detecting CXX compile features
-- Detecting CXX compile features - done
-- Project will be installed to /home/roberto/Software/recipe-04
-- Build type set to Release
-- Installing LIB components to /home/roberto/Software/recipe-04/lib64
-- Installing BIN components to /home/roberto/Software/recipe-04/bin
```

```
-- Installing INCLUDE components to
/home/roberto/Software/recipe-04/include
-- Installing CMAKE components to
/home/roberto/Software/recipe-04/share/cmake/recipe-04
-- recipe-04 staged install: /home/roberto/Workspace/robertodr/cmake-
cookbook/chapter-10/recipe-04/cxx-example/build/stage
-- Suitable message could not be located, Building message instead.
-- Configuring done
-- Generating done
-- Build files have been written to:
/home/roberto/Workspace/robertodr/cmake-cookbook/chapter-10/recipe-04/cxx-
example/build
```

As instructed, CMake reports the following:

- The installation will be staged into the build tree. The staged installation is a way of sandboxing the actual installation process. As developers, this is useful for checking that all libraries, executables, and files are installed in the proper location before running the installation commands. For users, it gives the same final structure, but within the build directory. In this way, our project is immediately usable, even without running a proper installation.
- A suitable message library was not found on the system. CMake will then run the commands provided for building the library prior to building our project, in order to satisfy this dependency.

If the library is already at a known location on the system, we can pass the -Dmessage_DIR option to CMake:

```
$ cmake -DCMAKE_INSTALL_PREFIX=$HOME/Software/use_message -
Dmessage_DIR=$HOME/Software/message/share/cmake/message ..
```

And, in fact, the library was found and imported. Only build operations for our own project will be performed:

```
-- The CXX compiler identification is GNU 7.3.0
-- Check for working CXX compiler:
/nix/store/gqg2vrcq7krqi9rrl6pphvsg81sb8pjw-gcc-wrapper-7.3.0/bin/g++
-- Check for working CXX compiler:
/nix/store/gqg2vrcq7krqi9rrl6pphvsg81sb8pjw-gcc-wrapper-7.3.0/bin/g++ --
works
-- Detecting CXX compiler ABI info
-- Detecting CXX compiler ABI info - done
-- Detecting CXX compile features
-- Detecting CXX compile features - done
-- Project will be installed to /home/roberto/Software/recipe-04
-- Build type set to Release
```

```
-- Installing LIB components to /home/roberto/Software/recipe-04/lib64
-- Installing BIN components to /home/roberto/Software/recipe-04/bin
-- Installing INCLUDE components to
/home/roberto/Software/recipe-04/include
-- Installing CMAKE components to
/home/roberto/Software/recipe-04/share/cmake/recipe-04
-- recipe-04 staged install: /home/roberto/Workspace/robertodr/cmake-
cookbook/chapter-10/recipe-04/cxx-example/build/stage
-- Checking for one of the modules 'uuid'
-- Found message: /home/roberto/Software/message/lib64/libmessage.so.1
(found version 1.0.0)
-- Configuring done
-- Generating done
-- Build files have been written to:
/home/roberto/Workspace/robertodr/cmake-cookbook/chapter-10/recipe-04/cxx-
example/build
```

The final installation rule for the project will copy the contents of the staged installation prefix to CMAKE_INSTALL_PREFIX:

```
install(
  DIRECTORY
    ${STAGED_INSTALL_PREFIX}/
  DESTINATION
    .
  USE_SOURCE_PERMISSIONS
  )
```

Note the use of . rather than the ${CMAKE_INSTALL_PREFIX} absolute path, such that this rule can be understood properly also by the CPack tool. Usage of CPack will be shown in *Chapter 11, Packaging Projects, Recipe 1, Generating source and binary packages*.

The recipe-04_core project builds a simple executable target that links against the message shared library. As discussed earlier in this chapter, the RPATH needs to be set properly in order for the executable to run correctly. *Recipe 1* in this chapter showed how to achieve just that with the help of CMake and the same pattern was reused here in the CMakeLists.txt handling the creation of the use_message executable:

```
file(RELATIVE_PATH _rel ${CMAKE_INSTALL_PREFIX}/${CMAKE_INSTALL_BINDIR}
${CMAKE_INSTALL_PREFIX})
if(APPLE)
  set(_rpath "@loader_path/${_rel}")
else()
  set(_rpath "\$ORIGIN/${_rel}")
endif()
file(TO_NATIVE_PATH "${_rpath}/${CMAKE_INSTALL_LIBDIR}" use_message_RPATH)
```

```
set_target_properties(use_message
  PROPERTIES
    MACOSX_RPATH ON
    SKIP_BUILD_RPATH OFF
    BUILD_WITH_INSTALL_RPATH OFF
    INSTALL_RPATH "${use_message_RPATH}"
    INSTALL_RPATH_USE_LINK_PATH ON
  )
```

To check that this is indeed enough, we can use a platform-native tool to print the RPATH of the installed executable. We wrap the call to the tool into a Python script, with is further wrapped into a CMake script. Eventually, the CMake script is invoked as an installation rule with the SCRIPT keyword:

```
if(UNIX)
  set(PRINT_SCRIPT "${CMAKE_CURRENT_LIST_DIR}/cmake/print_rpath.py")
  configure_file(cmake/install_hook.cmake.in install_hook.cmake @ONLY)
  install(
    SCRIPT
      ${CMAKE_CURRENT_BINARY_DIR}/install_hook.cmake
    )
endif()
```

This additional script is executed at the very end of the installation process:

```
$ cmake --build build --target install
```

and on a GNU/Linux system we would see the following output:

```
Install the project...
-- Install configuration: "Release"
-- Installing: /home/roberto/Software/recipe-04/.
-- Installing: /home/roberto/Software/recipe-04/./lib64
-- Installing: /home/roberto/Software/recipe-04/./lib64/libmessage.so
-- Installing: /home/roberto/Software/recipe-04/./lib64/libmessage_s.a
-- Installing: /home/roberto/Software/recipe-04/./lib64/libmessage.so.1
-- Installing: /home/roberto/Software/recipe-04/./include
-- Installing: /home/roberto/Software/recipe-04/./include/message
-- Installing:
/home/roberto/Software/recipe-04/./include/message/Message.hpp
-- Installing:
/home/roberto/Software/recipe-04/./include/message/messageExport.h
-- Installing: /home/roberto/Software/recipe-04/./share
-- Installing: /home/roberto/Software/recipe-04/./share/cmake
-- Installing: /home/roberto/Software/recipe-04/./share/cmake/message
-- Installing:
/home/roberto/Software/recipe-04/./share/cmake/message/messageTargets-
release.cmake
```

```
-- Installing:
/home/roberto/Software/recipe-04/./share/cmake/message/messageConfigVersion
.cmake
-- Installing:
/home/roberto/Software/recipe-04/./share/cmake/message/messageConfig.cmake
-- Installing:
/home/roberto/Software/recipe-04/./share/cmake/message/messageTargets.cmake
-- Installing: /home/roberto/Software/recipe-04/./bin
-- Installing: /home/roberto/Software/recipe-04/./bin/hello-world_wAR
-- Installing: /home/roberto/Software/recipe-04/./bin/use_message
-- Installing: /home/roberto/Software/recipe-04/./bin/hello-world_wDSO
-- ELF patching tool chrpath FOUND
-- RPATH for /home/roberto/Software/recipe-04/bin/use_message is
/home/roberto/Software/recipe-04/bin/use_message:
RUNPATH=$ORIGIN/../lib64:/home/roberto/Workspace/robertodr/cmake-
cookbook/chapter-10/recipe-04/cxx-
example/build/stage/lib64:/nix/store/di389pfcw2krnmh8nmkn55d1rnzmba37-
CMake-Cookbook/lib64:/nix/store/di389pfcw2krnmh8nmkn55d1rnzmba37-CMake-
Cookbook/lib:/nix/store/mjs2b8mmid86lvbzibzdlz8w5yrjgcnf-util-
linux-2.31.1/lib:/nix/store/2kcrj1ksd2a14bm5sky182fv2xwfhfap-
glibc-2.26-131/lib:/nix/store/4zd34747fz0ggzzasy4icgn3lmy89pra-gcc-7.3.0-
lib/lib
-- Running /home/roberto/Software/recipe-04/bin/use_message:
 This is my very nice message:
Hello, World! From a client of yours!
...and here is its UUID: a8014bf7-5dfa-45e2-8408-12e9a5941825
This is my very nice message:
Goodbye, World! From a client of yours!
...and here is its UUID: ac971ef4-7606-460f-9144-1ad96f713647
```

The utilities we suggest to use to work with Executable and Linkable Format (ELF) objects are PatchELF (https://nixos.org/patchelf.html), chrpath (https://linux.die.net/man/1/chrpath), and otool (http://www.manpagez.com/man/1/otool/). The first one works on GNU/Linux and macOS, whereas chrpath and otool are GNU/Linux and macOS specific, respectively.

11
Packaging Projects

In this chapter, we will cover the following recipes:

- Generating source and binary packages
- Distributing a C++/Python project built with CMake/pybind11 *via* PyPI
- Distributing a C/Fortran/Python project build with CMake/CFFI *via* PyPI
- Distributing a simple project as Conda package
- Distributing a project with dependencies as Conda package

Introduction

Up to this point, we have compiled and installed (example) software packages "from sources" – this meant fetching the project *via* Git, and executing the configure, build, test, and install steps manually. However, in practice, software packages are often rather installed using package managers, such as Apt, DNF, Pacman, pip, and Conda. We need to be able to distribute our code projects in various formats: as source archives or as binary installer.

This is what we refer to as packaging time in the now familiar scheme showing the various phases of a project using CMake:

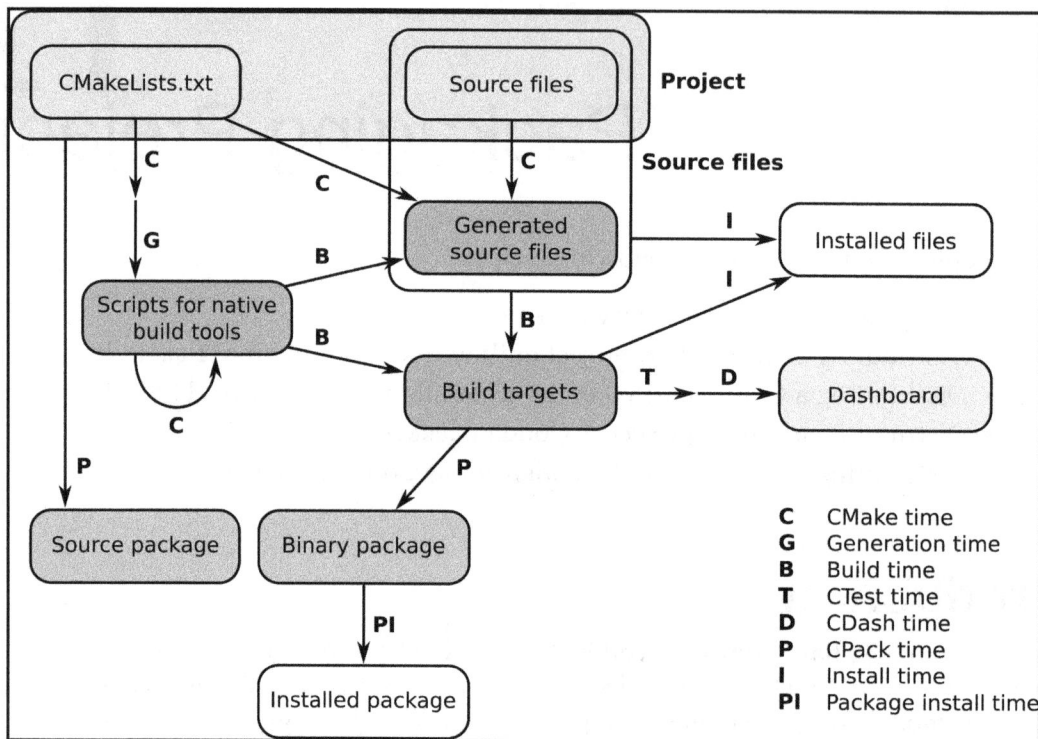

In this chapter, we will explore different packaging strategies. We will first discuss packaging using the tool CPack in the CMake family. We will also provide recipes for packaging and uploading CMake projects to the Python Package Index (PyPI, https://pypi.org) and the Anaconda Cloud (https://anaconda.org) – these are standard and popular platforms for distributing packages *via* the package managers pip and Conda (https://conda.io/docs/), respectively. For PyPI, we will demonstrate how to package and distribute mixed C++/Python or C/Fortran/Python projects. For Conda, we will show how to package C++ projects with dependencies on other libraries.

Generating source and binary packages

The code for this recipe is available at `https://github.com/dev-cafe/cmake-cookbook/tree/v1.0/chapter-11/recipe-01`. The recipe is valid with CMake version 3.6 (and higher) and has been tested on GNU/Linux, macOS, and Windows.

If your code is open source, users will expect to be able to download the sources for your project and build by themselves using your perfectly tailored CMake scripts. Of course, the packaging operation could be done with a script, but CPack offers a more compact and portable alternative. This recipe will guide you through the creation of a number of packaging alternatives:

- **Source code archives:** You can use these formats to ship the source code directly as a compressed archive in your favorite format. Your users will not have to worry about your specific version control system.
- **Binary archives:** Use these to package the freshly built targets into compressed archives in your favorite format. These can be extremely useful, but might not be robust enough to distribute libraries and executables.
- **Platform-native binary installers:** CPack is able to generate binary installers in many different formats, so you can target the distribution of your software to many different platforms. In particular, we will show how to generate installers:
  - In `.deb` format for Debian-based GNU/Linux distributions: `https://manpages.debian.org/unstable/dpkg-dev/deb.5.en.html`
  - In `.rpm` format for Red Hat-based GNU/Linux distributions: `http://rpm.org/`
  - In `.dmg` format for macOS Bundles: `https://developer.apple.com/library/archive/documentation/CoreFoundation/Conceptual/CFBundles/BundleTypes/BundleTypes.html`
  - In NSIS format for Windows: `http://nsis.sourceforge.net/Main_Page`

Getting ready

We will use the source code for the message library presented in *Chapter 10, Writing an Installer, Recipe 3, Exporting your targets*. The project tree consists of the following directories and files:

```
.
├── cmake
│   ├── coffee.icns
│   ├── Info.plist.in
│   └── messageConfig.cmake.in
├── CMakeCPack.cmake
├── CMakeLists.txt
├── INSTALL.md
├── LICENSE
├── src
│   ├── CMakeLists.txt
│   ├── hello-world.cpp
│   ├── Message.cpp
│   └── Message.hpp
└── tests
    ├── CMakeLists.txt
    └── use_target
        ├── CMakeLists.txt
        └── use_message.cpp
```

Since the emphasis in this recipe will be on effective usage of CPack, we will not comment on the source code itself. We will only add packaging directives in CMakeCPack.cmake, which we will discuss in a moment. In addition, we have added INSTALL.md and a LICENSE file: they contain installation instructions and the license for the project and are required by the packaging directives.

How to do it

Let us look at the packaging directives that need to be added to this project. We will collect them in CMakeCPack.cmake, which is included at the end of CMakeLists.txt using include(CMakeCPack.cmake):

1. We declare the name of the package. This is the same as the name of the project and hence we use the PROJECT_NAME CMake variable:

```
set(CPACK_PACKAGE_NAME "${PROJECT_NAME}")
```

2. We declare the package vendor:

```
set(CPACK_PACKAGE_VENDOR "CMake Cookbook")
```

3. The packaged sources will include a description file. This is the plain-text file with the installation instructions:

```
set(CPACK_PACKAGE_DESCRIPTION_FILE
"${PROJECT_SOURCE_DIR}/INSTALL.md")
```

4. We also add a brief summary of the package:

```
set(CPACK_PACKAGE_DESCRIPTION_SUMMARY "message: a small messaging
library")
```

5. The license file will also be included in the package:

```
set(CPACK_RESOURCE_FILE_LICENSE "${PROJECT_SOURCE_DIR}/LICENSE")
```

6. When installing from the distributed package, the files will be placed in the /opt/recipe-01 directory:

```
set(CPACK_PACKAGING_INSTALL_PREFIX "/opt/${PROJECT_NAME}")
```

7. The major, minor, and patch versions of the packages are set as variables for CPack:

```
set(CPACK_PACKAGE_VERSION_MAJOR "${PROJECT_VERSION_MAJOR}")
set(CPACK_PACKAGE_VERSION_MINOR "${PROJECT_VERSION_MINOR}")
set(CPACK_PACKAGE_VERSION_PATCH "${PROJECT_VERSION_PATCH}")
```

8. We set a list of files and directories to be ignored during the packaging operations:

```
set(CPACK_SOURCE_IGNORE_FILES
"${PROJECT_BINARY_DIR};/.git/;.gitignore")
```

9. We list the packaging generators for source code archives – in our case ZIP, to generate a .zip archive, and TGZ, for a .tar.gz archive.

```
set(CPACK_SOURCE_GENERATOR "ZIP;TGZ")
```

10. We also list the binary archive generators:

```
set(CPACK_GENERATOR "ZIP;TGZ")
```

11. We now declare also the platform-native binary installers, starting with the DEB and RPM package generators, only available for GNU/Linux:

```
if(UNIX)
  if(CMAKE_SYSTEM_NAME MATCHES Linux)
    list(APPEND CPACK_GENERATOR "DEB")
    set(CPACK_DEBIAN_PACKAGE_MAINTAINER "robertodr")
    set(CPACK_DEBIAN_PACKAGE_SECTION "devel")
    set(CPACK_DEBIAN_PACKAGE_DEPENDS "uuid-dev")

    list(APPEND CPACK_GENERATOR "RPM")
    set(CPACK_RPM_PACKAGE_RELEASE "1")
    set(CPACK_RPM_PACKAGE_LICENSE "MIT")
    set(CPACK_RPM_PACKAGE_REQUIRES "uuid-devel")
  endif()
endif()
```

12. If we are on Windows, we will want to generate an NSIS installer:

```
if(WIN32 OR MINGW)
  list(APPEND CPACK_GENERATOR "NSIS")
  set(CPACK_NSIS_PACKAGE_NAME "message")
  set(CPACK_NSIS_CONTACT "robertdr")
  set(CPACK_NSIS_ENABLE_UNINSTALL_BEFORE_INSTALL ON)
endif()
```

13. On the other hand, on macOS, a bundle is our installer of choice:

```
if(APPLE)
  list(APPEND CPACK_GENERATOR "Bundle")
  set(CPACK_BUNDLE_NAME "message")
  configure_file(${PROJECT_SOURCE_DIR}/cmake/Info.plist.in
Info.plist @ONLY)
  set(CPACK_BUNDLE_PLIST ${CMAKE_CURRENT_BINARY_DIR}/Info.plist)
  set(CPACK_BUNDLE_ICON ${PROJECT_SOURCE_DIR}/cmake/coffee.icns)
endif()
```

14. We print an informative message to the user on the packaging generators available on the current system:

```
message(STATUS "CPack generators: ${CPACK_GENERATOR}")
```

15. Finally, we include the `CPack.cmake` standard module. This will add a `package` and a `package_source` target to the build system:

```
include(CPack)
```

We can now configure the project as usual:

```
$ mkdir -p build
$ cd build
$ cmake ..
```

With the following command, we can list the available targets (the example output is obtained on a GNU/Linux system with Unix Makefiles as generator):

```
$ cmake --build . --target help
```

```
The following are some of the valid targets for this Makefile:
... all (the default if no target is provided)
... clean
... depend
... install/strip
... install
... package_source
... package
... install/local
... test
... list_install_components
... edit_cache
... rebuild_cache
... hello-world
... message
```

We can see that the `package` and `package_source` targets are available. The source packages can be generated with the following command:

```
$ cmake --build . --target package_source
```

```
Run CPack packaging tool for source...
CPack: Create package using ZIP
CPack: Install projects
CPack: - Install directory: /home/user/cmake-
cookbook/chapter-11/recipe-01/cxx-example
CPack: Create package
CPack: - package: /home/user/cmake-cookbook/chapter-11/recipe-01/cxx-
example/build/recipe-01-1.0.0-Source.zip generated.
CPack: Create package using TGZ
CPack: Install projects
CPack: - Install directory: /home/user/cmake-
```

```
cookbook/chapter-11/recipe-01/cxx-example
CPack: Create package
CPack: - package: /home/user/cmake-cookbook/chapter-11/recipe-01/cxx-
example/build/recipe-01-1.0.0-Source.tar.gz generated.
```

Similarly, we can build the binary packages:

$ cmake --build . --target package

And, in our case, we obtained the following list of binary packages:

```
message-1.0.0-Linux.deb
message-1.0.0-Linux.rpm
message-1.0.0-Linux.tar.gz
message-1.0.0-Linux.zip
```

How it works

CPack can be used to generate many different types of packages for distribution. When generating the build system, the CPack instructions we listed in CMakeCPack.cmake are used to generate a CPackConfig.cmake file in the build directory. When running the CMake command for the package or package_source targets, CPack is automatically invoked with the autogenerated configuration file as argument. Indeed, these two new targets are simple rules that wrap calls to CPack. Much as CMake, CPack also has a concept of generators. Whereas generators in the context of CMake are the tools that will be used to generate the native build scripts, for example, Unix Makefiles or Visual Studio project files, in the context of CPack these are the tools to be used for packaging. We listed these, exercising particular care for the different platforms, using the CPACK_SOURCE_GENERATOR and the CPACK_GENERATOR variables for the source and binary packages, respectively. Thus the Debian packaging utilities will be invoked for the DEB package generator, whereas the appropriate archiving tool on the given platform will be invoked for the TGZ generator. We can invoke CPack directly from the build directory and select which generator to use with the -G command-line option. The RPM package can be generated with the following:

```
$ cd build
$ cpack -G RPM

CPack: Create package using RPM
CPack: Install projects
CPack: - Run preinstall target for: recipe-01
CPack: - Install project: recipe-01
CPack: Create package
CPackRPM: Will use GENERATED spec file: /home/user/cmake-
cookbook/chapter-11/recipe-01/cxx-
```

```
example/build/_CPack_Packages/Linux/RPM/SPECS/recipe-01.spec
CPack: - package: /home/user/cmake-cookbook/chapter-11/recipe-01/cxx-
example/build/recipe-01-1.0.0-Linux.rpm generated.
```

For any distribution, be it source or binary, we need to package only those contents that will be strictly necessary for the end user, hence the entire build directory and any other file related to version control will have to be excluded from the list of files to be packaged. In our example, the exclusion list was declared with the following command:

```
set(CPACK_SOURCE_IGNORE_FILES "${PROJECT_BINARY_DIR};/.git/;.gitignore")
```

We also need to specify basic information about our package, such as the name, a short description, and the version. This information is set by means of CMake variables, which are then passed on to CPack when including the corresponding module.

> Since CMake 3.9 the `project()` command accepts a `DESCRIPTION` field, with a short string describing the project. CMake will set a `PROJECT_DESCRIPTION` which can be reused to set the `CPACK_PACKAGE_DESCRIPTION_SUMMARY`.

Let us look in detail at the instructions for the different kinds of packages we can generate for our example project.

Source archives

In our example, we decided to use the TGZ and ZIP generators for the source archive. These will result in `.tar.gz` and `.zip` archives, respectively. We can inspect the contents of the generated `.tar.gz` file:

```
$ tar tzf recipe-01-1.0.0-Source.tar.gz
```

```
recipe-01-1.0.0-Source/opt/
recipe-01-1.0.0-Source/opt/recipe-01/
recipe-01-1.0.0-Source/opt/recipe-01/cmake/
recipe-01-1.0.0-Source/opt/recipe-01/cmake/coffee.icns
recipe-01-1.0.0-Source/opt/recipe-01/cmake/Info.plist.in
recipe-01-1.0.0-Source/opt/recipe-01/cmake/messageConfig.cmake.in
recipe-01-1.0.0-Source/opt/recipe-01/CMakeLists.txt
recipe-01-1.0.0-Source/opt/recipe-01/src/
recipe-01-1.0.0-Source/opt/recipe-01/src/Message.hpp
recipe-01-1.0.0-Source/opt/recipe-01/src/CMakeLists.txt
recipe-01-1.0.0-Source/opt/recipe-01/src/Message.cpp
recipe-01-1.0.0-Source/opt/recipe-01/src/hello-world.cpp
recipe-01-1.0.0-Source/opt/recipe-01/LICENSE
recipe-01-1.0.0-Source/opt/recipe-01/tests/
```

```
recipe-01-1.0.0-Source/opt/recipe-01/tests/CMakeLists.txt
recipe-01-1.0.0-Source/opt/recipe-01/tests/use_target/
recipe-01-1.0.0-Source/opt/recipe-01/tests/use_target/CMakeLists.txt
recipe-01-1.0.0-Source/opt/recipe-01/tests/use_target/use_message.cpp
recipe-01-1.0.0-Source/opt/recipe-01/INSTALL.md
```

As expected, only the contents of the source tree are included. Notice that the `INSTALL.md` and `LICENSE` files are also included, as specified by means of the `CPACK_PACKAGE_DESCRIPTION_FILE` and `CPACK_RESOURCE_FILE_LICENSE` variables.

> The `package_source` target is not understood by the Visual Studio family of generators: `https://gitlab.kitware.com/cmake/cmake/issues/13058`.

Binary archives

When creating binary archives, CPack will package the contents of the targets described in our `CMakeCPack.cmake` file as described by the installation instructions. Thus in our example the hello-world executable, the message shared library, and the corresponding header files will all be packaged in the `.tar.gz` and `.zip` formats. In addition, also the CMake configuration files will be packaged. This is very useful for other projects that will need to link against our library. The installation prefix used in the package may differ from the one used when installing the project from the build tree. The `CPACK_PACKAGING_INSTALL_PREFIX` variable may be used to achieve this. In our example, we set it to a specific location on the system: `/opt/recipe-01`.

We can analyze the contents of the generated `.tar.gz` archive:

```
$ tar tzf recipe-01-1.0.0-Linux.tar.gz

recipe-01-1.0.0-Linux/opt/
recipe-01-1.0.0-Linux/opt/recipe-01/
recipe-01-1.0.0-Linux/opt/recipe-01/bin/
recipe-01-1.0.0-Linux/opt/recipe-01/bin/hello-world
recipe-01-1.0.0-Linux/opt/recipe-01/share/
recipe-01-1.0.0-Linux/opt/recipe-01/share/cmake/
recipe-01-1.0.0-Linux/opt/recipe-01/share/cmake/recipe-01/
recipe-01-1.0.0-Linux/opt/recipe-01/share/cmake/recipe-01/messageConfig.cmake
recipe-01-1.0.0-Linux/opt/recipe-01/share/cmake/recipe-01/messageTargets-hello-world.cmake
recipe-01-1.0.0-Linux/opt/recipe-01/share/cmake/recipe-01/messageConfigVersion.cmake
```

```
recipe-01-1.0.0-Linux/opt/recipe-01/share/cmake/recipe-01/messageTargets-
hello-world-release.cmake
recipe-01-1.0.0-Linux/opt/recipe-01/share/cmake/recipe-01/messageTargets-
release.cmake
recipe-01-1.0.0-
Linux/opt/recipe-01/share/cmake/recipe-01/messageTargets.cmake
recipe-01-1.0.0-Linux/opt/recipe-01/include/
recipe-01-1.0.0-Linux/opt/recipe-01/include/message/
recipe-01-1.0.0-Linux/opt/recipe-01/include/message/Message.hpp
recipe-01-1.0.0-Linux/opt/recipe-01/include/message/messageExport.h
recipe-01-1.0.0-Linux/opt/recipe-01/lib64/
recipe-01-1.0.0-Linux/opt/recipe-01/lib64/libmessage.so
recipe-01-1.0.0-Linux/opt/recipe-01/lib64/libmessage.so.1
```

Platform-native binary installers

We expect the configuration for each platform-native binary installer to be slightly different. These differences can be managed with CPack within a single CMakeCPack.cmake, as we have done in our example.

For GNU/Linux, the stanza configures both the DEB and RPM generators:

```
if(UNIX)
  if(CMAKE_SYSTEM_NAME MATCHES Linux)
    list(APPEND CPACK_GENERATOR "DEB")
    set(CPACK_DEBIAN_PACKAGE_MAINTAINER "robertodr")
    set(CPACK_DEBIAN_PACKAGE_SECTION "devel")
    set(CPACK_DEBIAN_PACKAGE_DEPENDS "uuid-dev")

    list(APPEND CPACK_GENERATOR "RPM")
    set(CPACK_RPM_PACKAGE_RELEASE "1")
    set(CPACK_RPM_PACKAGE_LICENSE "MIT")
    set(CPACK_RPM_PACKAGE_REQUIRES "uuid-devel")
  endif()
endif()
```

Our example depends on the UUID library, and the CPACK_DEBIAN_PACKAGE_DEPENDS and CPACK_RPM_PACKAGE_REQUIRES options let us specify dependencies between our package and others in the database. We can use the dpkg and rpm programs to analyze the contents of the generated .deb and .rpm packages, respectively.

Note that CPACK_PACKAGING_INSTALL_PREFIX also affects these package generators: our package will be installed to /opt/recipe-01.

CMake truly provides support for cross-platform and portable build systems. The following stanza will create an installer using the Nullsoft Scriptable Install System (NSIS):

```
if(WIN32 OR MINGW)
  list(APPEND CPACK_GENERATOR "NSIS")
  set(CPACK_NSIS_PACKAGE_NAME "message")
  set(CPACK_NSIS_CONTACT "robertdr")
  set(CPACK_NSIS_ENABLE_UNINSTALL_BEFORE_INSTALL ON)
endif()
```

Finally, the following stanza will enable the Bundle packager if we are building the project on macOS:

```
if(APPLE)
  list(APPEND CPACK_GENERATOR "Bundle")
  set(CPACK_BUNDLE_NAME "message")
  configure_file(${PROJECT_SOURCE_DIR}/cmake/Info.plist.in Info.plist
@ONLY)
  set(CPACK_BUNDLE_PLIST ${CMAKE_CURRENT_BINARY_DIR}/Info.plist)
  set(CPACK_BUNDLE_ICON ${PROJECT_SOURCE_DIR}/cmake/coffee.icns)
endif()
```

In the macOS example, we first need to configure a property list file for the package, something achieved by the `configure_file` command. The location of `Info.plist` and the icon for the package are then set as variables for CPack.

> You can read more about the property list format here: `https://en.wikipedia.org/wiki/Property_list`.

There is more

Instead of listing the CPack configuration settings in `CMakeCPack.cmake` as we have done for simplicity, we could have placed the per-generator settings of `CPACK_*` variables in a separate file, such as `CMakeCPackOptions.cmake`, and included these settings into `CMakeCPack.cmake` using `set(CPACK_PROJECT_CONFIG_FILE "${PROJECT_SOURCE_DIR}/CMakeCPackOptions.cmake")`. This file can also be configured at CMake time and then included at CPack time, providing a clean way to configure multi-format package generators (see also: `https://cmake.org/cmake/help/v3.6/module/CPack.html`).

As with all tools in the CMake family, CPack is powerful and versatile and offers much more flexibility and options than what we have shown in this recipe. The interested reader should read the official documentation for the command-line interface to CPack (https:// cmake.org/cmake/help/v3.6/manual/cpack.1.html) and the manual pages, which detail the additional generators that CPack knows how to use to package projects (https:// cmake.org/cmake/help/v3.6/module/CPack.html).

Distributing a C++/Python project built with CMake/pybind11 via PyPI

The code for this recipe is available at https://github.com/dev-cafe/ cmake-cookbook/tree/v1.0/chapter-11/recipe-02. The recipe is valid with CMake version 3.11 (and higher) and has been tested on GNU/Linux, macOS, and Windows.

In this recipe, we will take the pybind11 example from *Chapter 9, Mixed-language Projects, Recipe 5, Building C++ and Python projects using pybind11*, as a starting point, add relevant install targets and pip packaging information and upload the project to PyPI. Our goal will be to arrive at a project that can be installed using pip and runs CMake and fetches the pybind11 dependency under the hood.

Getting ready

To distribute a package *via* PyPI, you will need a user account at https://pypi.org, but it is possible to first exercise with installations from a local path.

We also generally recommend to install this and other Python packages with pip using either Pipenv (https://docs.pipenv.org) or Virtual Environments (https://virtualenv.pypa.io/en/stable/) instead of installing them into the system environment.

Our starting point is the pybind11 example from *Chapter 9, Mixed-language Projects, Recipe 5, Building C++ and Python projects using pybind11*, which contains a top-level CMakeLists.txt file and an account/CMakeLists.txt file that configures the account example targets and uses the following project tree:

```
.
├── account
│   ├── account.cpp
```

```
|    ├── account.hpp
|    ├── CMakeLists.txt
|    └── test.py
└── CMakeLists.txt
```

In this recipe, we will keep `account.cpp`, `account.hpp`, and the `test.py` script unchanged. We will modify `account/CMakeLists.txt` and add a couple of files for pip to be able to build and install the package. For this, we will require three additional files in the root directory: `README.rst`, `MANIFEST.in`, and `setup.py`.

`README.rst` contains documentation about the project:

```
Example project
===============

Project description in here ...
```

`MANIFEST.in` lists files that should be installed along the Python modules and packages:

```
include README.rst CMakeLists.txt
recursive-include account *.cpp *.hpp CMakeLists.txt
```

And, finally, `setup.py` contains instructions for building and installing the project:

```python
import distutils.command.build as _build
import os
import sys
from distutils import spawn
from distutils.sysconfig import get_python_lib

from setuptools import setup


def extend_build():
    class build(_build.build):
        def run(self):
            cwd = os.getcwd()
            if spawn.find_executable('cmake') is None:
                sys.stderr.write("CMake is required to build this
package.\n")
                sys.exit(-1)
            _source_dir = os.path.split(__file__)[0]
            _build_dir = os.path.join(_source_dir, 'build_setup_py')
            _prefix = get_python_lib()
            try:
                cmake_configure_command = [
                    'cmake',
                    '-H{0}'.format(_source_dir),
```

```
                    '-B{0}'.format(_build_dir),
                    '-DCMAKE_INSTALL_PREFIX={0}'.format(_prefix),
                ]
                _generator = os.getenv('CMAKE_GENERATOR')
                if _generator is not None:
                    cmake_configure_command.append('-
G{0}'.format(_generator))
                spawn.spawn(cmake_configure_command)
                spawn.spawn(
                    ['cmake', '--build', _build_dir, '--target',
'install'])
                os.chdir(cwd)
            except spawn.DistutilsExecError:
                sys.stderr.write("Error while building with CMake\n")
                sys.exit(-1)
            _build.build.run(self)

    return build


_here = os.path.abspath(os.path.dirname(__file__))

if sys.version_info[0] < 3:
    with open(os.path.join(_here, 'README.rst')) as f:
        long_description = f.read()
else:
    with open(os.path.join(_here, 'README.rst'), encoding='utf-8') as f:
        long_description = f.read()

_this_package = 'account'

version = {}
with open(os.path.join(_here, _this_package, 'version.py')) as f:
    exec(f.read(), version)

setup(
    name=_this_package,
    version=version['__version__'],
    description='Description in here.',
    long_description=long_description,
    author='Bruce Wayne',
    author_email='bruce.wayne@example.com',
    url='http://example.com',
    license='MIT',
    packages=[_this_package],
    include_package_data=True,
    classifiers=[
        'Development Status :: 3 - Alpha',
```

```
        'Intended Audience :: Science/Research',
        'Programming Language :: Python :: 2.7',
        'Programming Language :: Python :: 3.6'
    ],
    cmdclass={'build': extend_build()})
```

We will place __init__.py into the account subdirectory:

```
from .version import __version__
from .account import Account

__all__ = [
    '__version__',
    'Account',
]
```

We will also place version.py into the account subdirectory:

```
__version__ = '0.0.0'
```

This means that we will arrive at the following file structure for our project:

```
├──── account
│       ├──── account.cpp
│       ├──── account.hpp
│       ├──── CMakeLists.txt
│       ├──── __init__.py
│       ├──── test.py
│       └──── version.py
├──── CMakeLists.txt
├──── MANIFEST.in
├──── README.rst
└──── setup.py
```

How to do it

This recipe builds on top of *Chapter 9, Mixed-language Projects, Recipe 5, Building C++ and Python projects using pybind11.* Let us see how in detail:

First, we extend account/CMakeLists.txt. The only addition is the last directive, which specifies the install target:

```
install(
  TARGETS
    account
```

```
LIBRARY
  DESTINATION account
)
```

And that's it! With the install target and the README.rst, MANIFEST.in, setup.py, __init__.py, and version.py files in place, we are ready to test the installation of our example code which is interfaced using pybind11:

1. For this, create a new directory somewhere on your computer and we will test the installation there.
2. Inside the newly created directory, we run `pipenv install` from a local path. Adjust the local path to point to the directory that holds the setup.py script:

   $ pipenv install /path/to/cxx-example

3. Now we spawn a Python shell inside the Pipenv environment:

   $ pipenv run python

4. Inside the Python shell, we can test our CMake package:

   ```
   >>> from account import Account
   >>> account1 = Account()
   >>> account1.deposit(100.0)
   >>> account1.deposit(100.0)
   >>> account1.withdraw(50.0)
   >>> print(account1.get_balance())
   150.0
   ```

How it works

The ${CMAKE_CURRENT_BINARY_DIR} directory contains the compiled account.cpython-36m-x86_64-linux-gnu.so Python module built using pybind11, but note that its name depends on the operating system (in this case, 64-bit Linux) and the Python environment (in this case, Python 3.6). The setup.py script will run CMake under the hood and install the Python module into the correct path, depending on the selected Python environment (system Python or Pipenv or Virtual Environment). But now we have two challenges when installing the module:

- The naming can change.
- The path is set outside of CMake.

We can solve this by using the following install target, where `setup.py` will define the install target location:

```
install(
  TARGETS
    account
  LIBRARY
    DESTINATION account
  )
```

Here we instruct CMake to install the compiled Python module file into the `account` subdirectory relative to the install target location (*Chapter 10, Writing an Installer,* discusses in detail how the target location can be set). The latter will be set by `setup.py` by defining `CMAKE_INSTALL_PREFIX` to point to the right path depending on the Python environment.

Let us now inspect how we achieve this in `setup.py`; we will start from the bottom of the script:

```
setup(
    name=_this_package,
    version=version['__version__'],
    description='Description in here.',
    long_description=long_description,
    author='Bruce Wayne',
    author_email='bruce.wayne@example.com',
    url='http://example.com',
    license='MIT',
    packages=[_this_package],
    include_package_data=True,
    classifiers=[
        'Development Status :: 3 - Alpha',
        'Intended Audience :: Science/Research',
        'Programming Language :: Python :: 2.7',
        'Programming Language :: Python :: 3.6'
    ],
    cmdclass={'build': extend_build()})
```

The script contains a number of placeholders and hopefully self-explaining directives, but here we will focus on the last directive, `cmdclass`, where we extend the default build step by a custom function, which we call `extend_build`. This function subclasses the default build step:

```python
def extend_build():
    class build(_build.build):
        def run(self):
            cwd = os.getcwd()
            if spawn.find_executable('cmake') is None:
                sys.stderr.write("CMake is required to build this
package.\n")
                sys.exit(-1)
            _source_dir = os.path.split(__file__)[0]
            _build_dir = os.path.join(_source_dir, 'build_setup_py')
            _prefix = get_python_lib()
            try:
                cmake_configure_command = [
                    'cmake',
                    '-H{0}'.format(_source_dir),
                    '-B{0}'.format(_build_dir),
                    '-DCMAKE_INSTALL_PREFIX={0}'.format(_prefix),
                ]
                _generator = os.getenv('CMAKE_GENERATOR')
                if _generator is not None:
                    cmake_configure_command.append('-
G{0}'.format(_generator))
                spawn.spawn(cmake_configure_command)
                spawn.spawn(
                    ['cmake', '--build', _build_dir, '--target',
'install'])
                os.chdir(cwd)
            except spawn.DistutilsExecError:
                sys.stderr.write("Error while building with CMake\n")
                sys.exit(-1)
            _build.build.run(self)

    return build
```

First, the function checks whether CMake is available on the system. The core of the function executes two CMake commands:

```
cmake_configure_command = [
    'cmake',
    '-H{0}'.format(_source_dir),
    '-B{0}'.format(_build_dir),
    '-DCMAKE_INSTALL_PREFIX={0}'.format(_prefix),
]
_generator = os.getenv('CMAKE_GENERATOR')
if _generator is not None:
    cmake_configure_command.append('-G{0}'.format(_generator))
spawn.spawn(cmake_configure_command)
spawn.spawn(
    ['cmake', '--build', _build_dir, '--target', 'install'])
```

Here we have the possibility to change the default generator used by setting the `CMAKE_GENERATOR` environment variable. The install prefix is defined as follows:

```
_prefix = get_python_lib()
```

The `get_python_lib` function imported from `distutils.sysconfig` provides the root directory for the install prefix. The `cmake --build _build_dir --target install` command builds and installs our project in one step in a portable way. The reason why we use the name `_build_dir` instead of simply `build` is that your project might already contain a `build` directory when testing the local install, which would conflict with a fresh installation. For packages already uploaded to PyPI, the name of the build directory does not make a difference.

There is more

Now that we have the local install tested, we are ready to upload the package to PyPI. But, before we do that, make sure that the metadata in `setup.py` (such as the name of the project, and the contact and license information) is reasonable, and that the project name is not already taken on PyPI. It is also good practice to first test upload to and download from the PyPI test instance (`https://test.pypi.org`) before uploading to `https://pypi.org`.

Before the upload, we need to create a file called `.pypirc` in the home directory containing (replace `yourusername` and `yourpassword`):

```
[distutils]account
index-servers=
    pypi
    pypitest
```

```
[pypi]
username = yourusername
password = yourpassword

[pypitest]
repository = https://test.pypi.org/legacy/
username = yourusername
password = yourpassword
```

We will proceed in two steps. First, we create the distribution locally:

```
$ python setup.py sdist
```

In the second step, we upload the generated distribution data using Twine (we install Twine into a local Pipenv):

```
$ pipenv run twine upload dist/* -r pypitest
```

```
Uploading distributions to https://test.pypi.org/legacy/
Uploading yourpackage-0.0.0.tar.gz
```

As a next step, try to install from the test instance into an isolated environment:

```
$ pipenv shell
$ pip install --index-url https://test.pypi.org/simple/ yourpackage
```

Once this is working, we are ready to upload to production PyPI:

```
$ pipenv run twine upload dist/* -r pypi
```

Distributing a C/Fortran/Python project build with CMake/CFFI via PyPI

The code for this recipe is available at https://github.com/dev-cafe/cmake-cookbook/tree/v1.0/chapter-11/recipe-03 and has a C++ and Fortran example. The recipe is valid with CMake version 3.5 (and higher) and has been tested on GNU/Linux, macOS, and Windows.

This recipe is a mashup of the previous recipe and *Chapter 9, Mixed-language Projects, Recipe 6, Mixing C, C++, Fortran, and Python using Python CFFI*. We will reuse many building blocks from the previous recipe, but instead of using pybind11, we will use Python CFFI to provide the Python interface. In this recipe, our goal is to share a Fortran project *via* PyPI, but instead of Fortran, it could equally be a C or C++ project or any language exposing a C interface.

Getting ready

We will start out with the following file tree:

```
.
├── account
│   ├── account.h
│   ├── CMakeLists.txt
│   ├── implementation
│   │   └── fortran_implementation.f90
│   ├── __init__.py
│   ├── interface_file_names.cfg.in
│   ├── test.py
│   └── version.py
├── CMakeLists.txt
├── MANIFEST.in
├── README.rst
└── setup.py
```

The top-level CMakeLists.txt file and all sources below account,
except account/CMakeLists.txt, are unchanged from how they appeared in *Chapter 9, Mixed-language Projects, Recipe 6, Mixing C, C++, Fortran, and Python using Python CFFI*. We will shortly discuss the small changes we need to apply to account/CMakeLists.txt. The README.rst file is identical with the previous recipe. The setup.py script contains one extra line compared to the previous recipe (the line containing install_requires=['cffi']):

```
# ... up to this line the script is unchanged

setup(
    name=_this_package,
    version=version['__version__'],
    description='Description in here.',
    long_description=long_description,
    author='Bruce Wayne',
    author_email='bruce.wayne@example.com',
    url='http://example.com',
```

```
license='MIT',
packages=[_this_package],
install_requires=['cffi'],
include_package_data=True,
classifiers=[
    'Development Status :: 3 - Alpha',
    'Intended Audience :: Science/Research',
    'Programming Language :: Python :: 2.7',
    'Programming Language :: Python :: 3.6'
],
cmdclass={'build': extend_build()})
```

`MANIFEST.in` lists files that should be installed along with the Python modules and packages and contains the following:

```
include README.rst CMakeLists.txt
recursive-include account *.h *.f90 CMakeLists.txt
```

Under the `account` subdirectory, we see two new files. Again, there is a `version.py` file holding the project version for `setup.py`:

```
__version__ = '0.0.0'
```

The subdirectory also holds the `interface_file_names.cfg.in` file, which we will be discussing soon:

```
[configuration]
header_file_name = account.h
library_file_name = $<TARGET_FILE_NAME:account>
```

How to do it

Let usdiscuss the steps necessary to achieve the packaging:

1. We extend `account/CMakeLists.txt` from *Chapter 9, Mixed-language Projects, Recipe 6, Mixing C, C++, Fortran, and Python using Python CFFI*. The only additions are the following directives:

```
file(
  GENERATE OUTPUT
${CMAKE_CURRENT_BINARY_DIR}/interface_file_names.cfg
  INPUT ${CMAKE_CURRENT_SOURCE_DIR}/interface_file_names.cfg.in
  )

set_target_properties(account
  PROPERTIES
```

```
      PUBLIC_HEADER
"account.h;${CMAKE_CURRENT_BINARY_DIR}/account_export.h"
      RESOURCE "${CMAKE_CURRENT_BINARY_DIR}/interface_file_names.cfg"
  )

install(
  TARGETS
    account
  LIBRARY
    DESTINATION account/lib
  RUNTIME
    DESTINATION account/lib
  PUBLIC_HEADER
    DESTINATION account/include
  RESOURCE
    DESTINATION account
  )
```

And that's it! With the install target and the additional files in place, we are ready to test the installation. For this, create a new directory somewhere on your computer and we will test the installation there.

2. Inside the newly created directory, we run `pipenv install` from a local path. Adjust the local path to point to the directory that holds the `setup.py` script:

```
$ pipenv install /path/to/fortran-example
```

3. Now we spawn a Python shell inside the Pipenv environment:

```
$ pipenv run python
```

4. Inside the Python shell, we can test our CMake package:

```
>>> import account
>>> account1 = account.new()
>>> account.deposit(account1, 100.0)
>>> account.deposit(account1, 100.0)
>>> account.withdraw(account1, 50.0)
>>> print(account.get_balance(account1))
150.0
```

How it works

The extension to install mixed-language projects using Python CFFI and CMake compared to *Chapter 9, Mixed-language Projects, Recipe 6, Mixing C, C++, Fortran, and Python using Python CFFI* consists of two additional steps:

1. We require the `setup.py` layer.
2. We install targets such that the header files and the shared library file(s) required by the CFFI layer are installed in the correct paths depending on the selected Python environment.

The structure of `setup.py` is almost identical to the previous recipe, and we refer you to the previous recipe for a discussion of this file. The only addition was a line containing `install_requires=['cffi']` to make sure that installing our example package also fetches and installs the required Python CFFI. The `setup.py` script will automatically install `__init__.py` and `version.py`, since these are referenced from the `setup.py` script. `MANIFEST.in` is slightly changed to package not only `README.rst` and CMake files, but also the header and Fortran source files:

```
include README.rst CMakeLists.txt
recursive-include account *.h *.f90 CMakeLists.txt
```

We have three challenges in this recipe to package a CMake project that uses Python CFFI with `setup.py`:

- We need to copy the `account.h` and `account_export.h` header files as well as the shared library to the Python module location which depends on the Python environment.
- We need to tell `__init__.py` where to locate these header files and the library. In *Chapter 9, Mixed-language Projects, Recipe 6, Mixing C, C++, Fortran, and Python using Python CFFI* we have solved these using environment variables, but it would be unpractical to set these every time we plan to use the Python module.
- On the Python side, we don't know the exact name (suffix) of the shared library file, since it depends on the operating system.

Let us start with the last point: we don't know the exact name, but upon build system generation CMake does and therefore we use the generator expression in `interface_file_names.cfg.in` to expand the placeholder:

```
[configuration]
header_file_name = account.h
library_file_name = $<TARGET_FILE_NAME:account>
```

This input file is used to generate
`${CMAKE_CURRENT_BINARY_DIR}/interface_file_names.cfg`:

```
file(
  GENERATE OUTPUT ${CMAKE_CURRENT_BINARY_DIR}/interface_file_names.cfg
  INPUT ${CMAKE_CURRENT_SOURCE_DIR}/interface_file_names.cfg.in
  )
```

We then define the two header files as `PUBLIC_HEADER` (see also *Chapter 10, Writing an Installer*) and the configuration file as `RESOURCE`:

```
set_target_properties(account
  PROPERTIES
    PUBLIC_HEADER "account.h;${CMAKE_CURRENT_BINARY_DIR}/account_export.h"
    RESOURCE "${CMAKE_CURRENT_BINARY_DIR}/interface_file_names.cfg"
  )
```

Finally, we install the library, header files, and the configuration file to a structure relative to a path defined by `setup.py`:

```
install(
  TARGETS
    account
  LIBRARY
    DESTINATION account/lib
  RUNTIME
    DESTINATION account/lib
  PUBLIC_HEADER
    DESTINATION account/include
  RESOURCE
    DESTINATION account
  )
```

Note that we set `DESTINATION` for both `LIBRARY` and `RUNTIME` to point to `account/lib`. This is important for Windows, where shared libraries have executable entry points and therefore we have to specify both.

The Python package will be able to find these files thanks to this section in `account/__init__.py`:

```
# this interface requires the header file and library file
# and these can be either provided by interface_file_names.cfg
# in the same path as this file
# or if this is not found then using environment variables
_this_path = Path(os.path.dirname(os.path.realpath(__file__)))
_cfg_file = _this_path / 'interface_file_names.cfg'
if _cfg_file.exists():
```

```
        config = ConfigParser()
        config.read(_cfg_file)
        header_file_name = config.get('configuration', 'header_file_name')
        _header_file = _this_path / 'include' / header_file_name
        _header_file = str(_header_file)
        library_file_name = config.get('configuration', 'library_file_name')
        _library_file = _this_path / 'lib' / library_file_name
        _library_file = str(_library_file)
    else:
        _header_file = os.getenv('ACCOUNT_HEADER_FILE')
        assert _header_file is not None
        _library_file = os.getenv('ACCOUNT_LIBRARY_FILE')
        assert _library_file is not None
```

In this case, `_cfg_file` will be found and parsed and `setup.py` will find the header file under `include` and the library under `lib` and pass these on to CFFI to construct the library object. This is also the reason why we have used `lib` as the install target `DESTINATION` and not `CMAKE_INSTALL_LIBDIR`, which otherwise might confuse `account/__init__.py`.

There is more

For follow-up steps for getting the package to the PyPI test and production instances, we refer the reader to the previous recipe since these steps are analogous.

Distributing a simple project as Conda package

The code for this recipe is available at `https://github.com/dev-cafe/cmake-cookbook/tree/v1.0/chapter-11/recipe-04`. The recipe is valid with CMake version 3.5 (and higher) and has been tested on GNU/Linux, macOS, and Windows.

While PyPI is a standard and popular platform to distribute Python packages, Anaconda (`https://anaconda.org`) is more general in the sense that it allows to not only distribute Python or mixed-language projects with a Python interface but also allows packaging and dependency management for non-Python projects. In this recipe, we will prepare a Conda package for a very simple C++ example project configured and built using CMake without dependencies other than C++. In the next recipe, we will prepare and discuss a more complex Conda package.

Getting ready

Our goal will be to package the following simple example code (`example.cpp`):

```cpp
#include <iostream>

int main() {
  std::cout << "hello from your conda package!" << std::endl;

  return 0;
}
```

How to do it

This is how to proceed, step by step:

1. The `CMakeLists.txt` file starts with the minimum version requirement, project name, and supported language:

```cmake
cmake_minimum_required(VERSION 3.5 FATAL_ERROR)

project(recipe-04 LANGUAGES CXX)

set(CMAKE_CXX_STANDARD 11)
set(CMAKE_CXX_EXTENSIONS OFF)
set(CMAKE_CXX_STANDARD_REQUIRED ON)
```

2. We wish to build the `hello-conda` executable, which is built from `example.cpp`:

```cmake
add_executable(hello-conda "")

target_sources(hello-conda
  PRIVATE
    example.cpp
  )
```

3. We conclude `CMakeLists.txt` by defining the install target:

```
install(
  TARGETS
    hello-conda
  DESTINATION
    bin
  )
```

4. We will describe the Conda package in a file called `meta.yaml`, which we will place under `conda-recipe` to arrive at the following file structure:

```
.
├── CMakeLists.txt
├── conda-recipe
│      └── meta.yaml
└── example.cpp
```

5. The `meta.yaml` file consists of the following:

```
package:
  name: conda-example-simple
  version: "0.0.0"

source:
  path: ../ # this can be changed to git-url

build:
  number: 0
  binary_relocation: true
  script:
    - cmake -H. -Bbuild_conda -G "${CMAKE_GENERATOR}" -
DCMAKE_INSTALL_PREFIX=${PREFIX} # [not win]
    - cmake -H. -Bbuild_conda -G "%CMAKE_GENERATOR%" -
DCMAKE_INSTALL_PREFIX="%LIBRARY_PREFIX%" # [win]
    - cmake --build build_conda --target install

requirements:
  build:
    - cmake >=3.5
    - {{ compiler('cxx') }}

about:
  home: http://www.example.com
  license: MIT
  summary: "Summary in here ..."
```

6. Now we can try to build the package:

```
$ conda build conda-recipe
```

7. We will see lots of output on the screen, but once the build is complete, we can install the package. We will do this first locally:

```
$ conda install --use-local conda-example-simple
```

8. Now we are ready to test it – open a new terminal (assuming Anaconda is activated) and type the following:

```
$ hello-conda
```

```
hello from your conda package!
```

9. After the successful test, we can remove the package again:

```
$ conda remove conda-example-simple
```

How it works

The install target in CMakeLists.txt is an essential component to this recipe:

```
install(
  TARGETS
    hello-conda
  DESTINATION
    bin
  )
```

This target makes sure that the binary is installed in ${CMAKE_INSTALL_PREFIX}/bin. The prefix variable is defined by Conda in the build step of meta.yaml:

```
build:
  number: 0
  binary_relocation: true
  script:
    - cmake -H. -Bbuild_conda -G "${CMAKE_GENERATOR}"
-DCMAKE_INSTALL_PREFIX=${PREFIX} # [not win]
    - cmake -H. -Bbuild_conda -G "%CMAKE_GENERATOR%"
-DCMAKE_INSTALL_PREFIX="%LIBRARY_PREFIX%" # [win]
    - cmake --build build_conda --target install
```

The build step configures the project, sets the install prefix to ${PREFIX} (intrinsic variable set by Conda), builds, and installs the project. The motivation to call the build directory build_conda is similar to the previous recipes: a specific build directory name makes it easier to experiment with local installs based on directories that might already contain a directory called build.

By installing the package into the Anaconda environment, we made the executable available to the system.

There is more

The configuration file meta.yaml can be used to specify build, test, and install steps for projects of in principle any complexity. Please refer to the official documentation for an in-depth discussion: https://conda.io/docs/user-guide/tasks/build-packages/define-metadata.html.

For an upload of a Conda package to the Anaconda cloud, please follow the official Anaconda cloud documentation: https://docs.anaconda.com/anaconda-cloud/user-guide/. Also, consider Miniconda as a lightweight alternative to Anaconda: https://conda.io/miniconda.html.

Distributing a project with dependencies as Conda package

The code for this recipe is available at https://github.com/dev-cafe/cmake-cookbook/tree/v1.0/chapter-11/recipe-05. The recipe is valid with CMake version 3.5 (and higher) and has been tested on GNU/Linux, macOS, and Windows.

In this recipe, we will build on the findings of the previous recipe and prepare a more realistic and sophisticated Conda package for an example CMake project that will depend on and utilize the implementation of the DGEMM function, for matrix-matrix multiplication, available in the Intel Math Kernel Library (MKL). Intel MKL is made available as a Conda package. This recipe will provide us with a toolset to prepare and share Conda packages with dependencies.

Getting ready

For this recipe, we will use the same file naming and directory structure as in the previous simple Conda recipe:

```
.
├── CMakeLists.txt
├── conda-recipe
│    └── meta.yaml
└── example.cpp
```

The example source file (`example.cpp`) performs a matrix-matrix multiplication and compares the result returned by the MKL library against a "noddy" implementation:

```cpp
#include "mkl.h"

#include <cassert>
#include <cmath>
#include <iostream>
#include <random>

int main() {
  // generate a uniform distribution of real number between -1.0 and 1.0
  std::random_device rd;
  std::mt19937 mt(rd());
  std::uniform_real_distribution<double> dist(-1.0, 1.0);

  int m = 500;
  int k = 1000;
  int n = 2000;

  double *A = (double *)mkl_malloc(m * k * sizeof(double), 64);
  double *B = (double *)mkl_malloc(k * n * sizeof(double), 64);
  double *C = (double *)mkl_malloc(m * n * sizeof(double), 64);
  double *D = new double[m * n];

  for (int i = 0; i < (m * k); i++) {
    A[i] = dist(mt);
  }

  for (int i = 0; i < (k * n); i++) {
    B[i] = dist(mt);
  }

  for (int i = 0; i < (m * n); i++) {
    C[i] = 0.0;
  }
```

```
double alpha = 1.0;
double beta = 0.0;
cblas_dgemm(CblasRowMajor,
            CblasNoTrans,
            CblasNoTrans,
            m,
            n,
            k,
            alpha,
            A,
            k,
            B,
            n,
            beta,
            C,
            n);

// D_mn = A_mk B_kn
for (int r = 0; r < m; r++) {
  for (int c = 0; c < n; c++) {
    D[r * n + c] = 0.0;
    for (int i = 0; i < k; i++) {
      D[r * n + c] += A[r * k + i] * B[i * n + c];
    }
  }
}

// compare the two matrices
double r = 0.0;
for (int i = 0; i < (m * n); i++) {
  r += std::pow(C[i] - D[i], 2.0);
}
assert(r < 1.0e-12 && "ERROR: matrices C and D do not match");

mkl_free(A);
mkl_free(B);
mkl_free(C);
delete[] D;

std::cout << "MKL DGEMM example worked!" << std::endl;

return 0;
}
```

We also need a modified `meta.yaml`. However, the only change compared to the previous recipe is a line listing the `mkl-devel` dependency under requirements:

```
package:
  name: conda-example-dgemm
  version: "0.0.0"

source:
  path: ../ # this can be changed to git-url

build:
  number: 0
  script:
    - cmake -H. -Bbuild_conda -G "${CMAKE_GENERATOR}"
-DCMAKE_INSTALL_PREFIX=${PREFIX} # [not win]
    - cmake -H. -Bbuild_conda -G "%CMAKE_GENERATOR%"
-DCMAKE_INSTALL_PREFIX="%LIBRARY_PREFIX%" # [win]
    - cmake --build build_conda --target install

requirements:
  build:
    - cmake >=3.5
    - {{ compiler('cxx') }}
  host:
    - mkl-devel 2018

about:
  home: http://www.example.com
  license: MIT
  summary: "Summary in here ..."
```

How to do it

These are the steps to follow to prepare our package:

1. The `CMakeLists.txt` file starts with the minimum version requirement, project name, and supported language:

```
cmake_minimum_required(VERSION 3.5 FATAL_ERROR)

project(recipe-05 LANGUAGES CXX)

set(CMAKE_CXX_STANDARD 11)
set(CMAKE_CXX_EXTENSIONS OFF)
set(CMAKE_CXX_STANDARD_REQUIRED ON)
```

2. We wish to build the `dgemm-example` executable, which is built from `example.cpp`:

```
add_executable(dgemm-example "")

target_sources(dgemm-example
  PRIVATE
    example.cpp
  )
```

3. We then need to locate MKL libraries installed *via* `mkl-devel`. We prepare an `INTERFACE` library called `IntelMKL`. This can be used as any other target and will set include directories, compiler options, and link libraries for any dependent target. The setup is made to mimic what is suggested by the Intel MKL link line advisor (https://software.intel.com/en-us/articles/intel-mkl-link-line-advisor/). First, we set the compiler options:

```
add_library(IntelMKL INTERFACE)

target_compile_options(IntelMKL
  INTERFACE
    $<$<OR:$<CXX_COMPILER_ID:GNU>,$<CXX_COMPILER_ID:AppleClang>>:-m64>
  )
```

4. Next, we search for the `mkl.h` header file and set the `include` directories for the `IntelMKL` target:

```
find_path(_mkl_h
  NAMES
    mkl.h
  HINTS
    ${CMAKE_INSTALL_PREFIX}/include
  )
target_include_directories(IntelMKL
  INTERFACE
    ${_mkl_h}
  )
message(STATUS "MKL header file FOUND: ${_mkl_h}")
```

5. Finally, we locate the libraries and set the link libraries for the `IntelMKL` target:

```
find_library(_mkl_libs
  NAMES
    mkl_rt
  HINTS
    ${CMAKE_INSTALL_PREFIX}/lib
```

```
  )
  message(STATUS "MKL single dynamic library FOUND: ${_mkl_libs}")

  find_package(Threads QUIET)
  target_link_libraries(IntelMKL
    INTERFACE
      ${_mkl_libs}
$<$<OR:$<CXX_COMPILER_ID:GNU>,$<CXX_COMPILER_ID:AppleClang>>:Thread
s::Threads>
      $<$<OR:$<CXX_COMPILER_ID:GNU>,$<CXX_COMPILER_ID:AppleClang>>:m>
  )
```

6. We use the `cmake_print_properties` function to print out useful messages about the `IntelMKL` target:

```
include(CMakePrintHelpers)
cmake_print_properties(
  TARGETS
    IntelMKL
  PROPERTIES
    INTERFACE_COMPILE_OPTIONS
    INTERFACE_INCLUDE_DIRECTORIES
    INTERFACE_LINK_LIBRARIES
  )
```

7. We link the `dgemm-example` target against these libraries:

```
target_link_libraries(dgemm-example
  PRIVATE
    IntelMKL
  )
```

8. We conclude `CMakeLists.txt` by defining the install target:

```
install(
  TARGETS
    dgemm-example
  DESTINATION
    bin
  )
```

9. Now we can try to build the package:

```
$ conda build conda-recipe
```

10. We will see lots of output on the screen, but once the build is complete, we can install the package. We will do this first locally:

```
$ conda install --use-local conda-example-dgemm
```

11. Now we are ready to test it – open a new terminal (assuming Anaconda is activated) and type:

```
$ dgemm-example
```

```
MKL DGEMM example worked!
```

12. After the successful test, we can remove the package again:

```
$ conda remove conda-example-dgemm
```

How it works

The only change in meta.yaml compared to the previous recipe is the mkl-devel dependency. The challenge from the CMake perspective is to locate the MKL libraries that are installed by Anaconda. Fortunately, we know that they are located in ${CMAKE_INSTALL_PREFIX}. The Intel MKL link line advisor available online (https://software.intel.com/en-us/articles/intel-mkl-link-line-advisor/) can be used to look up how to link MKL into our project depending on the platform and compiler chosen. We have decided to wrap this information into an INTERFACE library. This solution is ideal for the case of MKL: the library is not a target created by our project, or any subproject, but it still needs to be dealt with in a possibly very convoluted manner; that is: setting compiler flags, include directories, and link libraries. CMake INTERFACE libraries are targets in the build system, but do not create any build output, at least directly. However, since they are targets, we may set their properties on them. Just as "real" targets, they can also be installed, exported, and imported.

First of all, we declare a new library called IntelMKL with the INTERFACE attribute. We then need to set properties as needed and we follow the pattern of calling the appropriate CMake command on the target with the INTERFACE attribute, using the following:

- target_compile_options, to set INTERFACE_COMPILE_OPTIONS. In our case, -m64 has to be set, but only if using the GNU or AppleClang compilers. Note that we do this with a generator expression.
- target_include_directories, to set the INTERFACE_INCLUDE_DIRECTORIES. These can be set after finding the mkl.h header file on the system. This was done with the find_path CMake command.

- `target_link_libraries`, **to set the** `INTERFACE_LINK_LIBRARIES`. **We** decided to link against the single dynamic library `libmkl_rt.so` and searched for it with the `find_library` CMake command. The GNU or AppleClang compilers will also need to link the executable to the native threading and mathematical libraries. Once again, these cases are elegantly handled with generator expressions.

The properties we have just set on the IntelMKL target can be printed out for the user by means of the `cmake_print_properties` command. Finally, we link against the `IntelMKL` target. As expected, this will set compiler flags, include directories, and link libraries as necessary to compile successfully:

```
target_link_libraries(dgemm-example
  PRIVATE
    IntelMKL
  )
```

There is more

The Anaconda cloud contains a wealth of packages. With the preceding recipes, it is possible and relatively simple to build Conda packages for CMake projects that may depend on other Conda packages. Explore the possibility and share your software packages for others to build on your developments!

12
Building Documentation

In this chapter, we will cover the following recipes:

- Building documentation using Doxygen
- Building documentation using Sphinx
- Combining Doxygen and Sphinx

Introduction

Documentation is essential in all software projects: for users, to explain how to obtain and build the code and to illustrate how to use your code or library effectively, and also for developers, to describe the internal details of your library and to help other programmers get involved with and contribute to your project. This chapter will show how to use CMake to build code documentation, using two popular frameworks: Doxygen and Sphinx.

Building documentation using Doxygen

> The code for this recipe is available at `https://github.com/dev-cafe/cmake-cookbook/tree/v1.0/chapter-12/recipe-01`, and includes a C++ example. The recipe is valid with CMake version 3.5 (and higher) and has been tested on GNU/Linux, macOS, and Windows.

Doxygen (`http://www.doxygen.nl`) is a very popular source code documentation tool. You can add documentation tags as comments in your code. Running Doxygen will extract these comments and create the documentation in a format defined in the Doxyfile configuration file. Doxygen can output HTML, XML, and even LaTeX or PDF. This recipe will show you how to use CMake to build your Doxygen documentation.

Getting ready

We will use a simplified version of the `message` library presented in previous chapters. The source tree is organized as follows:

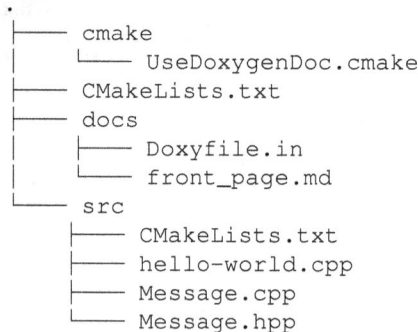

```
.
├── cmake
│   └── UseDoxygenDoc.cmake
├── CMakeLists.txt
├── docs
│   ├── Doxyfile.in
│   └── front_page.md
└── src
    ├── CMakeLists.txt
    ├── hello-world.cpp
    ├── Message.cpp
    └── Message.hpp
```

We still have our sources under the `src` subdirectory, and we have custom CMake modules in the `cmake` subdirectory. Since our emphasis is on the documentation, we have removed the dependency on UUID and simplified the source code. The most significant differences are the numerous code comments in the header file:

```cpp
#pragma once

#include <iosfwd>
#include <string>

/*! \file Message.hpp */

/*! \class Message
 * \brief Forwards string to screen
 * \author Roberto Di Remigio
 * \date 2018
 */
class Message {
public:
  /*! \brief Constructor from a string
   * \param[in] m a message
   */
  Message(const std::string &m) : message_(m) {}
  /*! \brief Constructor from a character array
   * \param[in] m a message
   */
  Message(const char *m) : message_(std::string(m)) {}

  friend std::ostream &operator<<(std::ostream &os, Message &obj) {
```

```
      return obj.printObject(os);
  }

private:
  /*! The message to be forwarded to screen */
  std::string message_;
  /*! \brief Function to forward message to screen
   * \param[in, out] os output stream
   */
  std::ostream &printObject(std::ostream &os);
};
```

These comments are in the format /*! */, and include some special tags, which are understood by Doxygen (see http://www.stack.nl/~dimitri/doxygen/manual/docblocks.html).

How to do it

First, let us discuss the CMakeLists.txt file in the root directory:

1. As should be familiar, we declare a C++11 project, as follows:

```
cmake_minimum_required(VERSION 3.5 FATAL_ERROR)

project(recipe-01 LANGUAGES CXX)

set(CMAKE_CXX_STANDARD 11)
set(CMAKE_CXX_EXTENSIONS OFF)
set(CMAKE_CXX_STANDARD_REQUIRED ON)
```

2. We define the output directories for shared and static libraries and executables, as follows:

```
include(GNUInstallDirs)
set(CMAKE_ARCHIVE_OUTPUT_DIRECTORY
  ${CMAKE_BINARY_DIR}/${CMAKE_INSTALL_LIBDIR})
set(CMAKE_LIBRARY_OUTPUT_DIRECTORY
  ${CMAKE_BINARY_DIR}/${CMAKE_INSTALL_LIBDIR})
set(CMAKE_RUNTIME_OUTPUT_DIRECTORY
  ${CMAKE_BINARY_DIR}/${CMAKE_INSTALL_BINDIR})
```

3. We append the cmake subdirectory to CMAKE_MODULE_PATH. This is required for CMake to find our custom modules:

```
list(APPEND CMAKE_MODULE_PATH "${CMAKE_SOURCE_DIR}/cmake")
```

4. The `UseDoxygenDoc.cmake` custom module is included. We will discuss its content later:

```
include(UseDoxygenDoc)
```

5. We then add the `src` subdirectory:

```
add_subdirectory(src)
```

The `CMakeLists.txt` file in the `src` subdirectory contains the following building blocks:

1. We add a `message` static library, as follows:

```
add_library(message STATIC
  Message.hpp
  Message.cpp
  )
```

2. We then add an executable target, `hello-world`:

```
add_executable(hello-world hello-world.cpp)
```

3. Then, the `hello-world` executable should be linked to the message library:

```
target_link_libraries(hello-world
  PUBLIC
    message
  )
```

In the last stanza in the root `CMakeLists.txt` file, we call the `add_doxygen_doc` function. This adds a new `docs` target that will invoke Doxygen to build our documentation:

```
add_doxygen_doc(
  BUILD_DIR
    ${CMAKE_CURRENT_BINARY_DIR}/_build
  DOXY_FILE
    ${CMAKE_CURRENT_SOURCE_DIR}/docs/Doxyfile.in
  TARGET_NAME
    docs
  COMMENT
    "HTML documentation"
  )
```

Finally, let us look at the `UseDoxygenDoc.cmake` module, where the `add_doxygen_doc` function is defined:

1. We find the `Doxygen` and `Perl` executables, as follows:

```
find_package(Perl REQUIRED)
find_package(Doxygen REQUIRED)
```

2. Then, we declare the `add_doxygen_doc` function. This function understands one-value arguments: `BUILD_DIR`, `DOXY_FILE`, `TARGET_NAME`, and `COMMENT`. We parse these using the `cmake_parse_arguments` standard CMake command:

```
function(add_doxygen_doc)
  set(options)
  set(oneValueArgs BUILD_DIR DOXY_FILE TARGET_NAME COMMENT)
  set(multiValueArgs)

  cmake_parse_arguments(DOXY_DOC
    "${options}"
    "${oneValueArgs}"
    "${multiValueArgs}"
    ${ARGN}
    )

  # ...

endfunction()
```

3. The `Doxyfile` contains all Doxygen settings to build the documentation. A template `Doxyfile.in` is passed as the function argument `DOXY_FILE`, and is parsed into the `DOXY_DOC_DOXY_FILE` variable. We configure the template file, `Doxyfile.in`, as follows:

```
configure_file(
  ${DOXY_DOC_DOXY_FILE}
  ${DOXY_DOC_BUILD_DIR}/Doxyfile
  @ONLY
  )
```

4. We then define a custom target, called `DOXY_DOC_TARGET_NAME`, which will execute Doxygen with the settings in the `Doxyfile` and output the results in `DOXY_DOC_BUILD_DIR`:

```
add_custom_target(${DOXY_DOC_TARGET_NAME}
    COMMAND
      ${DOXYGEN_EXECUTABLE} Doxyfile
    WORKING_DIRECTORY
      ${DOXY_DOC_BUILD_DIR}
    COMMENT
      "Building ${DOXY_DOC_COMMENT} with Doxygen"
    VERBATIM
    )
```

5. Finally, a status message is printed for the user:

```
message(STATUS "Added ${DOXY_DOC_TARGET_NAME} [Doxygen] target to
build documentation")
```

We can configure the project as usual:

```
$ mkdir -p build
$ cd build
$ cmake ..
$ cmake --build .
```

The documentation can be built by invoking our custom `docs` target:

```
$ cmake --build . --target docs
```

You will notice that a `_build` subdirectory will have appeared in the build tree. This contains the HTML documentation that Doxygen has generated from your source files. Opening `index.html` with your favorite browser will show the Doxygen welcome page.

If you navigate to the class list, you can for instance browse the documentation for the `Message` class:

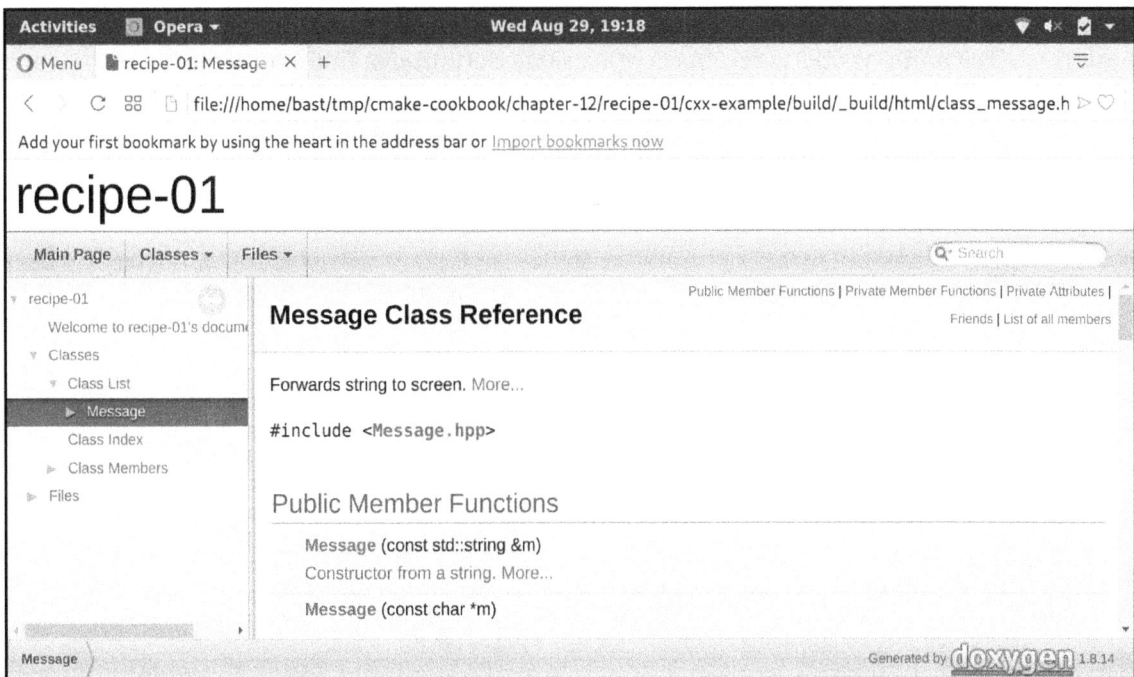

How it works

CMake does not support documentation building by default. However, we can use `add_custom_target` to perform arbitrary operations, and this is the mechanism that we leveraged in the present recipe. The important point to note is that we need to make sure that the tools necessary to build the documentation (Doxygen and Perl in this particular case) are available on the system.

In addition, note that the `UseDoxygenDoc.cmake` custom module only does the following:

* Performs a search for the Doxygen and Perl executables
* Defines a function

The actual creation of the `docs` target is left to a later invocation of the `add_doxygen_doc` function. This is an *explicit is better than implicit* pattern, which we consider a good CMake practice: do not use module inclusion to perform macro-like (or function-like) actions.

We have implemented `add_doxygen_doc` by using a function, and not a macro, in order to limit the scope and possible side-effects of variable definitions. In this particular case, both a function and a macro would work (and would yield the same result), but we recommend preferring functions over macros unless variables in the parent scope need to be modified.

> A new and improved `FindDoxygen.cmake` module was added in CMake 3.9. The convenience function `doxygen_add_docs` was implemented, which will behave as the macro that we have presented in this recipe. For more details, check out the online documentation at `https://cmake.org/cmake/help/v3.9/module/FindDoxygen.html`.

Building documentation using Sphinx

> The code for this recipe is available at `https://github.com/dev-cafe/cmake-cookbook/tree/v1.0/chapter-12/recipe-02`, and includes a C++ example. The recipe is valid with CMake version 3.5 (and higher) and has been tested on GNU/Linux, macOS, and Windows.

Sphinx is a Python program and a very popular documentation system (`http://www.sphinx-doc.org`). When used with Python projects, it can parse the source file for so-called docstrings and automatically produce documentation pages for functions and classes. However, Sphinx is not limited to Python, and can also parse reStructuredText, Markdown plain-text files, and generate HTML, ePUB, or PDF documentation. Coupled with the online Read the Docs service (`https://readthedocs.org`), it offers a great way to quickly get started with writing and deploying documentation. This recipe will show you how to use CMake to build documentation based on Sphinx.

Getting ready

We wish to build a simple website documenting our messaging library. The source tree now looks as follows:

```
.
├── cmake
│   ├── FindSphinx.cmake
│   └── UseSphinxDoc.cmake
├── CMakeLists.txt
├── docs
│   ├── conf.py.in
│   └── index.rst
```

```
└── src
    ├── CMakeLists.txt
    ├── hello-world.cpp
    ├── Message.cpp
    └── Message.hpp
```

We have some custom modules in the `cmake` subdirectory, and the `docs` subdirectory contains the main page for our website in a plain-text reStructuredText format, `index.rst`, and a Python template file, `conf.py.in`, with settings for Sphinx. This file can be autogenerated using the `sphinx-quickstart` utility, which is a part of the Sphinx installation.

How to do it

Compared to the previous recipe, we will modify the root `CMakeLists.txt` file, and will also implement a function (`add_sphinx_doc`):

1. After appending the `cmake` folder to the `CMAKE_MODULE_PATH`, we include the `UseSphinxDoc.cmake` custom module, as follows:

   ```
   list(APPEND CMAKE_MODULE_PATH "${CMAKE_SOURCE_DIR}/cmake")

   include(UseSphinxDoc)
   ```

2. The `UseSphinxDoc.cmake` module defines the `add_sphinx_doc` function. We call this function with keyword arguments, in order to set up our Sphinx documentation build. The custom documentation target will be called `docs`:

   ```
   add_sphinx_doc(
     SOURCE_DIR
       ${CMAKE_CURRENT_SOURCE_DIR}/docs
     BUILD_DIR
       ${CMAKE_CURRENT_BINARY_DIR}/_build
     CACHE_DIR
       ${CMAKE_CURRENT_BINARY_DIR}/_doctrees
     HTML_DIR
       ${CMAKE_CURRENT_BINARY_DIR}/sphinx_html
     CONF_FILE
       ${CMAKE_CURRENT_SOURCE_DIR}/docs/conf.py.in
     TARGET_NAME
       docs
     COMMENT
       "HTML documentation"
     )
   ```

The `UseSphinxDoc.cmake` module follows the same *explicit is better than implicit* pattern that we used in the previous recipe:

1. We need to find the Python interpreter and the `Sphinx` executable, as follows:

```
find_package(PythonInterp REQUIRED)
find_package(Sphinx REQUIRED)
```

2. We then define the `add_sphinx_doc` function with one-value keyword arguments. These are parsed by the `cmake_parse_arguments` command:

```
function(add_sphinx_doc)
  set(options)
  set(oneValueArgs
    SOURCE_DIR
    BUILD_DIR
    CACHE_DIR
    HTML_DIR
    CONF_FILE
    TARGET_NAME
    COMMENT
    )
  set(multiValueArgs)

  cmake_parse_arguments(SPHINX_DOC
    "${options}"
    "${oneValueArgs}"
    "${multiValueArgs}"
    ${ARGN}
    )

  # ...

endfunction()
```

3. The template file, `conf.py.in`, passed as the `CONF_FILE` keyword argument, is configured to `conf.py` in the `SPHINX_DOC_BUILD_DIR`:

```
configure_file(
  ${SPHINX_DOC_CONF_FILE}
  ${SPHINX_DOC_BUILD_DIR}/conf.py
  @ONLY
  )
```

4. We add a custom target, called `SPHINX_DOC_TARGET_NAME`, to orchestrate the documentation building with Sphinx:

```
add_custom_target(${SPHINX_DOC_TARGET_NAME}
  COMMAND
    ${SPHINX_EXECUTABLE}
        -q
        -b html
        -c ${SPHINX_DOC_BUILD_DIR}
        -d ${SPHINX_DOC_CACHE_DIR}
        ${SPHINX_DOC_SOURCE_DIR}
        ${SPHINX_DOC_HTML_DIR}
  COMMENT
    "Building ${SPHINX_DOC_COMMENT} with Sphinx"
  VERBATIM
  )
```

5. Lastly, we print out a status message to the user:

```
message(STATUS "Added ${SPHINX_DOC_TARGET_NAME} [Sphinx] target to
build documentation")
```

6. We configure the project and build the `docs` target:

```
$ mkdir -p build
$ cd build
$ cmake ..
$ cmake --build . --target docs
```

This will produce the HTML documentation in the `SPHINX_DOC_HTML_DIR` subdirectory of the build tree. Once again, you can use your favorite browser to open `index.html` and see the shiny (but still sparse) documentation:

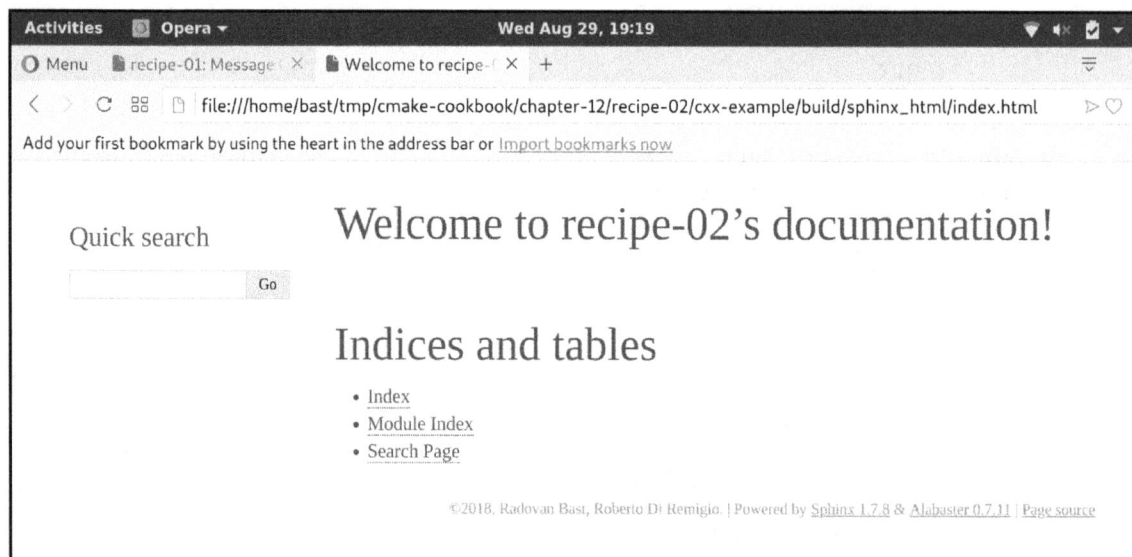

How it works

Once again, we leveraged the power of `add_custom_target` to add an arbitrary build target to our build system. In this case, the documentation will be built using Sphinx. Since Sphinx is a Python program that can be extended with other Python modules, the `docs` target will depend on the Python interpreter. We make sure that dependencies are satisfied by using `find_package`. Note that the `FindSphinx.cmake` module is not yet a standard CMake module; a copy of it is included with the project source, under the `cmake` subdirectory.

Combining Doxygen and Sphinx

The code for this recipe is available at `https://github.com/dev-cafe/cmake-cookbook/tree/v1.0/chapter-12/recipe-03`, and includes a C++ example. The recipe is valid with CMake version 3.5 (and higher) and has been tested on GNU/Linux, macOS, and Windows.

We have a C++ project, and thus, Doxygen is the ideal choice to generate source code documentation. However, we also wish to publish user-facing documentation, explaining, for example, our design choices. We would rather use Sphinx for that, because the generated HTML will also work on mobile devices, and because we can deploy the documentation to Read the Docs (`https://readthedocs.org`). This recipe will illustrate how to use the Breathe plugin (`https://breathe.readthedocs.io`) to bridge Doxygen and Sphinx.

Getting ready

The source tree for this recipe is similar to the two previous recipes:

```
.
├── cmake
│   ├── FindPythonModule.cmake
│   ├── FindSphinx.cmake
│   └── UseBreathe.cmake
├── CMakeLists.txt
├── docs
│   ├── code-reference
│   │   ├── classes-and-functions.rst
│   │   └── message.rst
│   ├── conf.py.in
│   ├── Doxyfile.in
│   └── index.rst
└── src
    ├── CMakeLists.txt
    ├── hello-world.cpp
    ├── Message.cpp
    └── Message.hpp
```

The `docs` subdirectory now contains both a `Doxyfile.in` and a `conf.py.in` template file, with settings for Doxygen and Sphinx, respectively. In addition, we also have a `code-reference` subdirectory.

The files following `code-reference` contain Breathe instructions, to include Doxygen-generated documentation in Sphinx:

```
Messaging classes
=================

Message
-------
.. doxygenclass:: Message
   :project: recipe-03
   :members:
   :protected-members:
   :private-members:
```

This will output the documentation for the `Message` class.

How to do it

The `CMakeLists.txt` file in the `src` directory is unchanged. The only changes in the root `CMakeLists.txt` file are as follows:

1. We include the `UseBreathe.cmake` custom module:

   ```
   list(APPEND CMAKE_MODULE_PATH "${CMAKE_SOURCE_DIR}/cmake")

   include(UseBreathe)
   ```

2. We call the `add_breathe_doc` function. This function is defined in the custom module, and it accepts keyword arguments to set up the combined Doxygen and Sphinx build:

   ```
   add_breathe_doc(
     SOURCE_DIR
       ${CMAKE_CURRENT_SOURCE_DIR}/docs
     BUILD_DIR
       ${CMAKE_CURRENT_BINARY_DIR}/_build
     CACHE_DIR
       ${CMAKE_CURRENT_BINARY_DIR}/_doctrees
     HTML_DIR
       ${CMAKE_CURRENT_BINARY_DIR}/html
     DOXY_FILE
       ${CMAKE_CURRENT_SOURCE_DIR}/docs/Doxyfile.in
     CONF_FILE
       ${CMAKE_CURRENT_SOURCE_DIR}/docs/conf.py.in
     TARGET_NAME
   ```

```
    docs
COMMENT
    "HTML documentation"
    )
```

Let us examine the `UseBreatheDoc.cmake` module. This follows the same explicit is better than implicit pattern that we described in the two previous recipes. The module is described in detail, as follows:

1. The documentation generation depends on Doxygen:

    ```
    find_package(Doxygen REQUIRED)
    find_package(Perl REQUIRED)
    ```

2. We also depend on the Python interpreter and `Sphinx`:

    ```
    find_package(PythonInterp REQUIRED)
    find_package(Sphinx REQUIRED)
    ```

3. In addition, we must also find the `breathe` Python module. We use the `FindPythonModule.cmake` module:

    ```
    include(FindPythonModule)
    find_python_module(breathe REQUIRED)
    ```

4. We define the `add_breathe_doc` function. This function has a one-value keyword argument, which we will parse using the `cmake_parse_arguments` command:

    ```
    function(add_breathe_doc)
      set(options)
      set(oneValueArgs
        SOURCE_DIR
        BUILD_DIR
        CACHE_DIR
        HTML_DIR
        DOXY_FILE
        CONF_FILE
        TARGET_NAME
        COMMENT
        )
      set(multiValueArgs)

      cmake_parse_arguments(BREATHE_DOC
        "${options}"
        "${oneValueArgs}"
        "${multiValueArgs}"
    ```

```
        ${ARGN}
        )

    # ...

endfunction()
```

5. The `BREATHE_DOC_CONF_FILE` template file for Sphinx is configured to `conf.py` in `BREATHE_DOC_BUILD_DIR`:

```
configure_file(
    ${BREATHE_DOC_CONF_FILE}
    ${BREATHE_DOC_BUILD_DIR}/conf.py
    @ONLY
    )
```

6. Correspondingly, the `BREATHE_DOC_DOXY_FILE` template file for Doxygen is configured to `Doxyfile` in `BREATHE_DOC_BUILD_DIR`:

```
configure_file(
    ${BREATHE_DOC_DOXY_FILE}
    ${BREATHE_DOC_BUILD_DIR}/Doxyfile
    @ONLY
    )
```

7. We then add our `BREATHE_DOC_TARGET_NAME` custom target. Note that only Sphinx is run; the necessary calls to Doxygen happen within `BREATHE_DOC_SPHINX_FILE`:

```
add_custom_target(${BREATHE_DOC_TARGET_NAME}
    COMMAND
      ${SPHINX_EXECUTABLE}
          -q
          -b html
          -c ${BREATHE_DOC_BUILD_DIR}
          -d ${BREATHE_DOC_CACHE_DIR}
          ${BREATHE_DOC_SOURCE_DIR}
          ${BREATHE_DOC_HTML_DIR}
    COMMENT
      "Building ${BREATHE_DOC_TARGET_NAME} documentation with
Breathe, Sphinx and Doxygen"
    VERBATIM
    )
```

8. Finally, a status message is printed to the user:

```
message(STATUS "Added ${BREATHE_DOC_TARGET_NAME}
[Breathe+Sphinx+Doxygen] target to build documentation")
```

9. After configuring, we can build the documentation as usual:

```
$ mkdir -p build
$ cd build
$ cmake ..
$ cmake --build . --target docs
```

The documentation will be available in the BREATHE_DOC_HTML_DIR subdirectory of the build tree. After firing up your browser to open the index.html file, you can navigate to the documentation for the Message class:

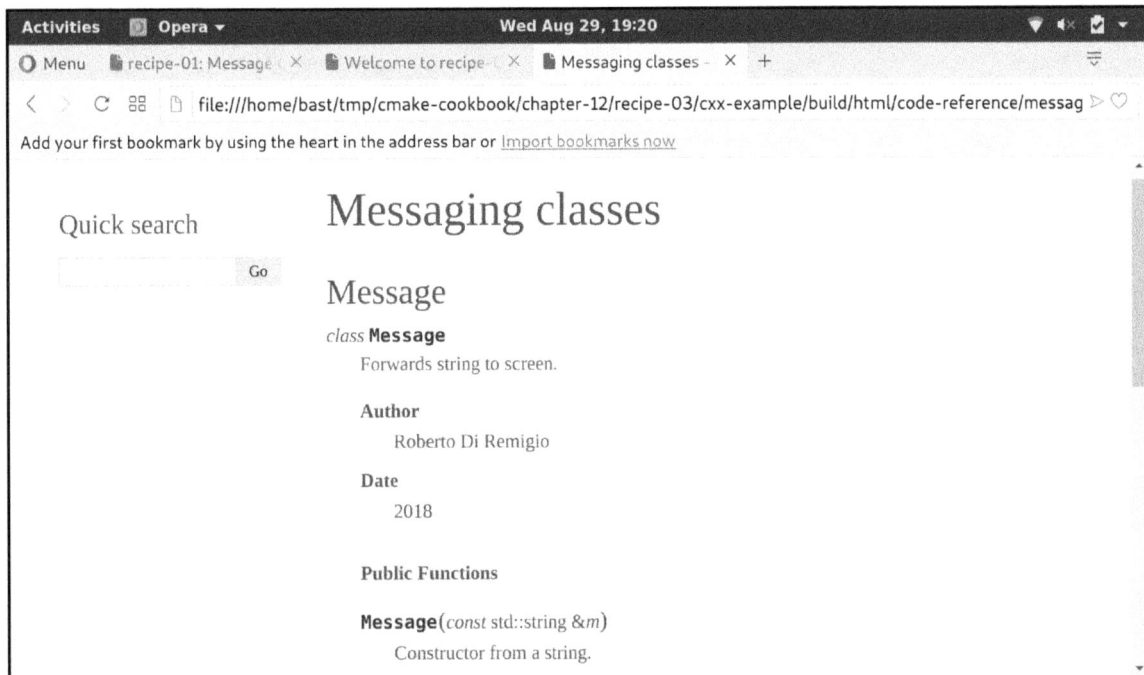

How it works

You will note that both Doxygen and Sphinx are run, despite the fact that only the invocation to Sphinx was given when declaring the custom BREATHE_DOC_TARGET_NAME target. This is thanks to the following settings, defined in the conf.py file for Sphinx:

```python
def run_doxygen(folder):
    """Run the doxygen make command in the designated folder"""

    try:
        retcode = subprocess.call("cd {}; doxygen".format(folder),
shell=True)
        if retcode < 0:
            sys.stderr.write(
                "doxygen terminated by signal {}".format(-retcode))
    except OSError as e:
        sys.stderr.write("doxygen execution failed: {}".format(e))


def setup(app):
    run_doxygen('@BREATHE_DOC_BUILD_DIR@')
```

Doxygen will generate XML output that the Breathe plugin will be able to render in a form consistent with the chosen Sphinx documentation style.

13
Alternative Generators and Cross-compilation

In this chapter, we will cover the following recipes:

- Building a CMake project in Visual Studio
- Cross-compiling a hello world example
- Cross-compiling a Windows binary with OpenMP parallelization

Introduction

CMake does not build executables and libraries on its own. Instead, CMake configures a project and *generates* files used by another build tool or framework to build the project. On GNU/Linux and macOS, CMake typically generates Unix Makefiles, but a number of alternatives exist. On Windows, these are typically Visual Studio project files or MinGW or MSYS Makefiles. CMake includes a wide range of generators for native command-line build tools or integrated development environments (IDEs). You can read more about them at the following link: `https://cmake.org/cmake/help/latest/manual/cmake-generators.7.html`.

These generators can be selected using `cmake -G`, for instance:

```
$ cmake -G "Visual Studio 15 2017"
```

Not all generators are available on every platform and, depending on the platform where CMake runs, typically only a subset is available. To see a list of all available generators on the current platform, type the following:

```
$ cmake -G
```

In this chapter, we will not cycle through all the available generators but we note that most recipes in this book have been tested using the `Unix Makefiles`, `MSYS Makefiles`, `Ninja`, and `Visual Studio 15 2017` generators. In this chapter, we will focus on developing on/for the Windows platform. We will demonstrate how to build a CMake project directly using Visual Studio 15 2017, without using the command line. We will also discuss how to cross-compile a Windows executable on a Linux or macOS system.

Building a CMake project using Visual Studio 2017

The code for this recipe is available at `https://github.com/dev-cafe/cmake-cookbook/tree/v1.0/chapter-13/recipe-01` and has a C++ example. The recipe is valid with CMake version 3.5 (and higher) and has been tested on Windows.

While earlier versions of Visual Studio required developers to edit source code and run CMake commands in different windows, Visual Studio 2017 introduces built-in support for CMake projects (`https://aka.ms/cmake`), which allows for the entire coding, configuring, building, and testing workflow to happen within the same IDE. In this recipe, we will test this and build a simple "hello world" CMake example project directly using Visual Studio 2017, without resorting to the command line.

Getting ready

First, we will use the Windows platform and download and install Visual Studio Community 2017 (`https://www.visualstudio.com/downloads/`). At the time of writing, this version is freely available with a 30-day trial period. The steps which we will follow are also nicely explained in this video: `https://www.youtube.com/watch?v=_lKxJjV8r3Y`.

When running the installer, make sure to select **Desktop development with C++** on the left panel and also verify that **Visual C++ tools for CMake** is checked on the **Summary** panel to the right:

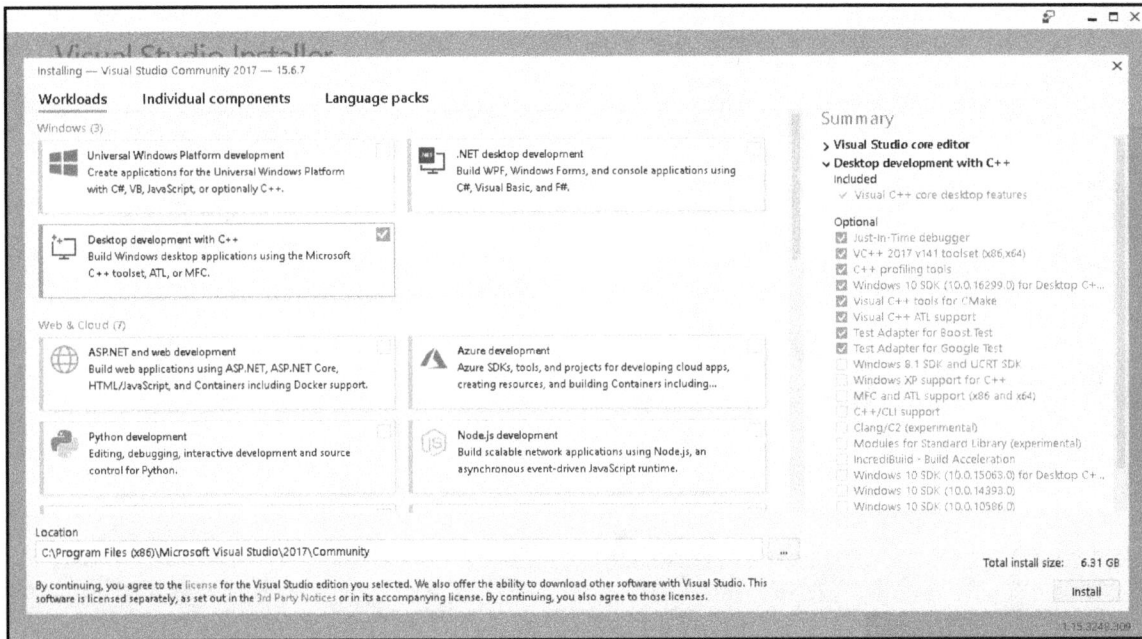

In Visual Studio 2017 15.4, you can also build code for the Linux platform. For this, select **Linux development with C++** under **Other Toolsets**:

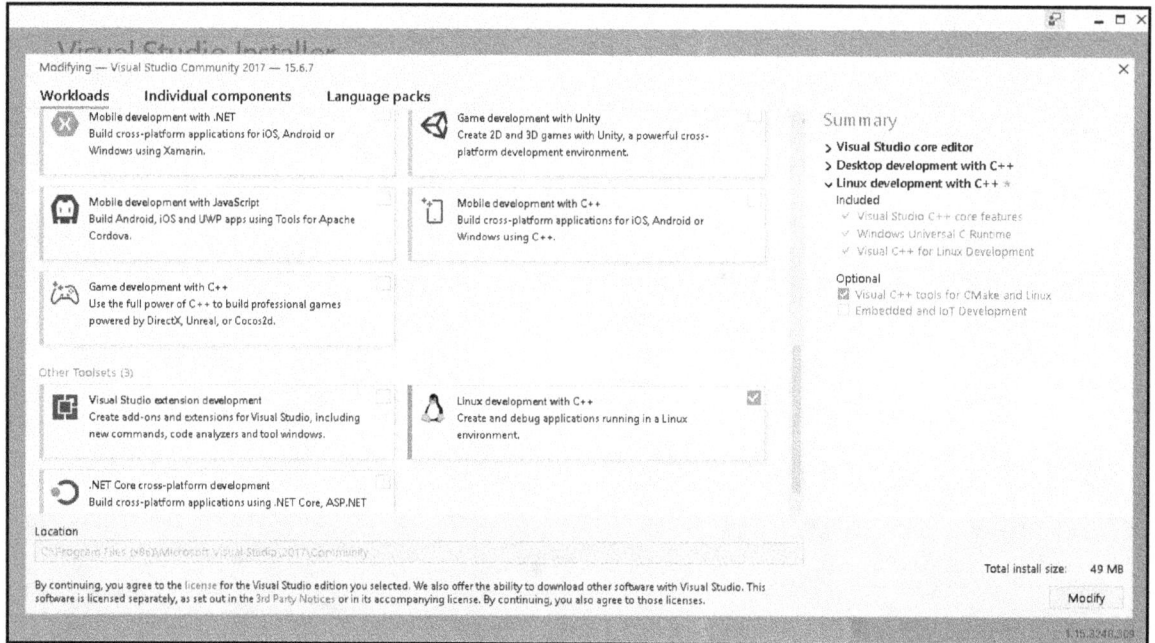

With this option enabled, you can target both Windows and Linux machines from within Visual Studio provided you have configured access to a Linux server. However, we will not demonstrate this approach in this chapter.

In this recipe, we will build a Windows binary on Windows, and our goal will be to configure and build the following example code (`hello-world.cpp`):

```cpp
#include <cstdlib>
#include <iostream>
#include <string>

const std::string cmake_system_name = SYSTEM_NAME;

int main() {
  std::cout << "Hello from " << cmake_system_name << std::endl;

  return EXIT_SUCCESS;
}
```

How to do it

To create the corresponding source code, please follow these steps:

1. Create a directory and place `hello-world.cpp` in the newly created directory.

2. In this directory, create a `CMakeLists.txt` file which contains the following:

```cmake
# set minimum cmake version
cmake_minimum_required(VERSION 3.5 FATAL_ERROR)

# project name and language
project(recipe-01 LANGUAGES CXX)

set(CMAKE_CXX_STANDARD 11)
set(CMAKE_CXX_EXTENSIONS OFF)
set(CMAKE_CXX_STANDARD_REQUIRED ON)

include(GNUInstallDirs)
set(CMAKE_ARCHIVE_OUTPUT_DIRECTORY
  ${CMAKE_BINARY_DIR}/${CMAKE_INSTALL_LIBDIR})
set(CMAKE_LIBRARY_OUTPUT_DIRECTORY
  ${CMAKE_BINARY_DIR}/${CMAKE_INSTALL_LIBDIR})
set(CMAKE_RUNTIME_OUTPUT_DIRECTORY
  ${CMAKE_BINARY_DIR}/${CMAKE_INSTALL_BINDIR})

# define executable and its source file
add_executable(hello-world hello-world.cpp)

# we will print the system name in the code
target_compile_definitions(hello-world
  PUBLIC
    "SYSTEM_NAME=\"${CMAKE_SYSTEM_NAME}\""
  )

install(
  TARGETS
    hello-world
  DESTINATION
    ${CMAKE_INSTALL_BINDIR}
  )
```

3. Open Visual Studio 2017, then navigate to the newly created folder which contains both the source file and `CMakeLists.txt` by the following **File** | **Open** | **Folder**.

4. Once the folder is open, notice how the CMake configure step is run automatically (bottom panel):

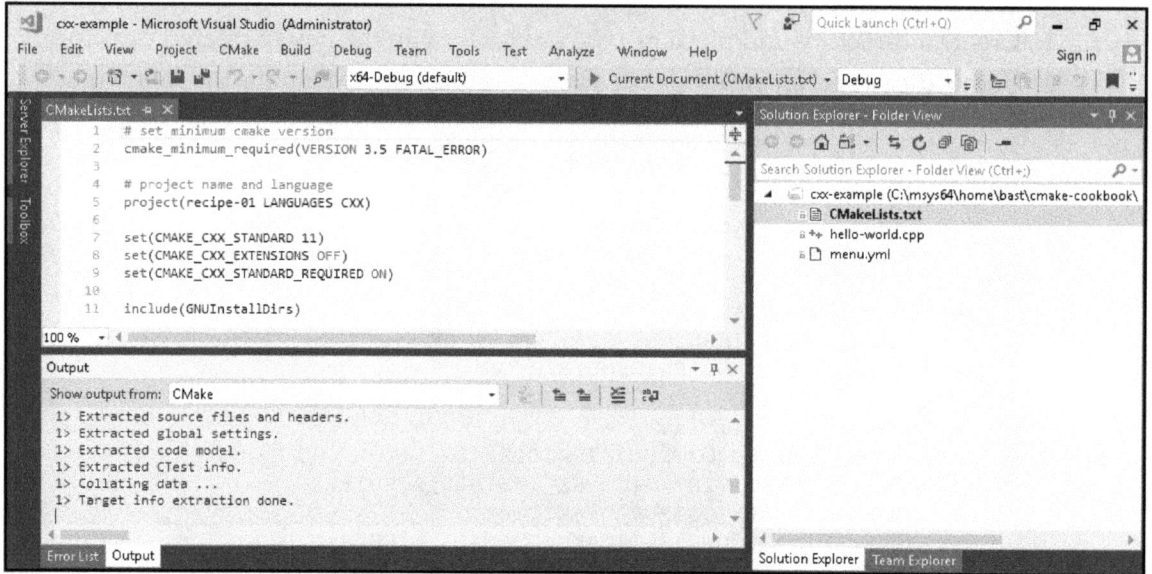

5. Now, we can right-click on CMakeLists.txt (right panel) and select **Build**:

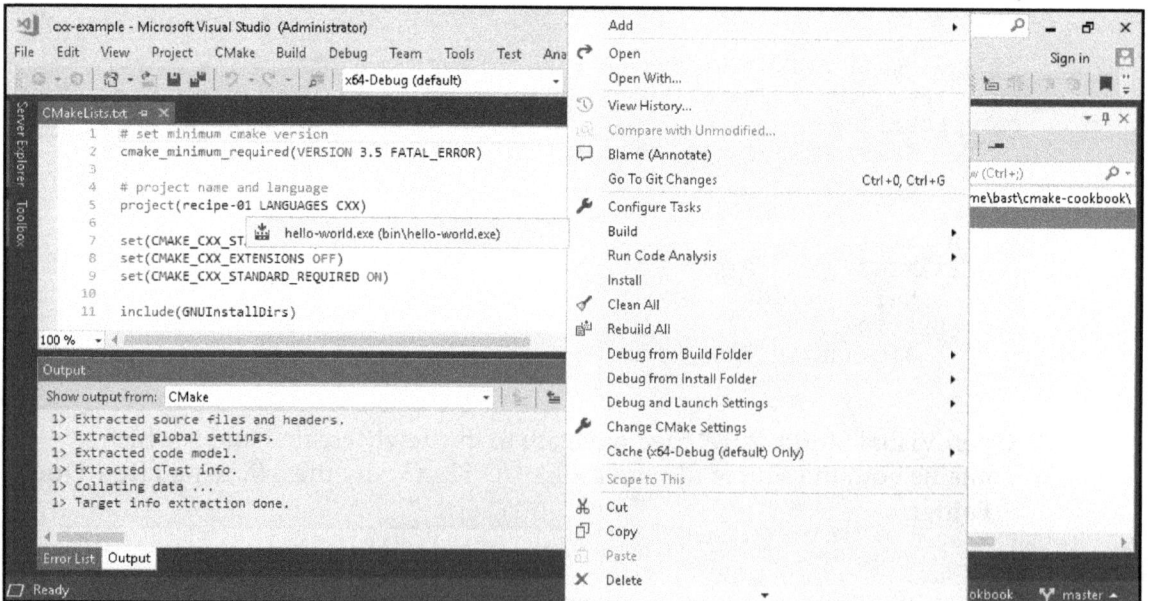

6. This builds the project (see the output on the bottom panel):

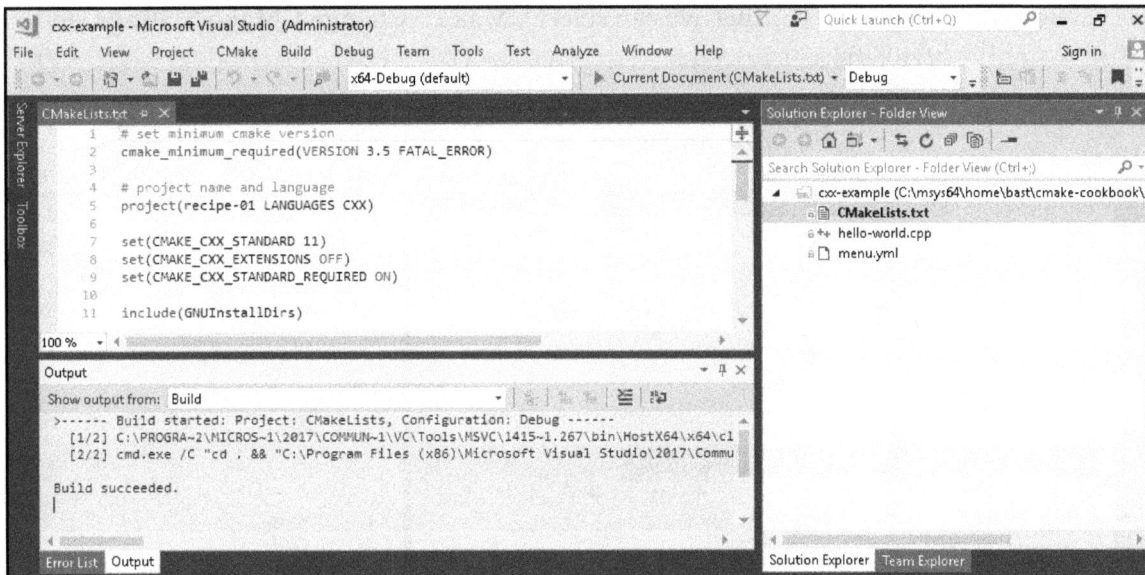

7. This successfully compiled the executable. In the next subsection, we will learn how to locate the executable and possibly change the build and install paths.

How it works

We have seen that Visual Studio 2017 nicely interfaces to CMake, and we have been able to configure and build the code from within the IDE. In addition to the build step, we could have run install or test steps. These are accessible by right-clicking on CMakeLists.txt (right panel).

However, the configuration step was run automatically and we might prefer to modify configuration options. We would also like to know the actual build and install paths so that we can test our executable. For this, we can select **CMake | Change CMake Settings**, and we arrive at the following screen:

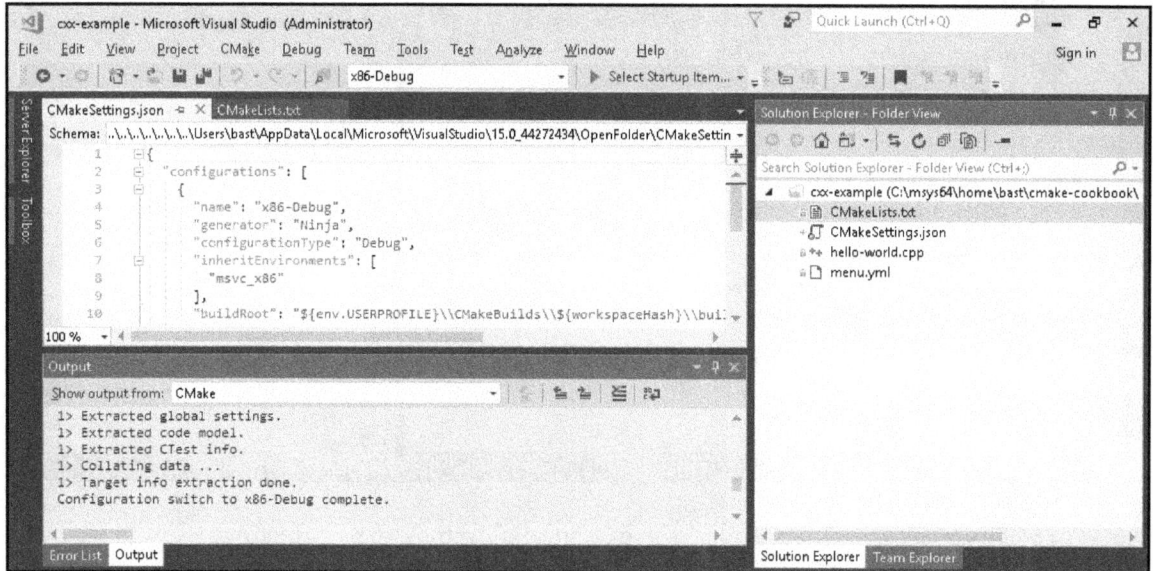

In the top-left panel, we can now inspect and modify the generator (in this case, Ninja), settings, arguments, as well as paths. The build path is highlighted in the preceding screenshot. The settings are grouped into build types (x86-Debug, x86-Release, and so on) and we can toggle between these build types in the middle of the top panel bar.

Now that we know the actual build path, we can test the compiled executable:

```
$ ./hello-world.exe
```

```
Hello from Windows
```

The build and install paths can, of course, be adjusted.

See also

- CMake support in Visual Studio: `https://aka.ms/cmake`
- Visual C++ for Linux Development with CMake: `https://blogs.msdn.microsoft.com/vcblog/2017/08/25/visual-c-for-linux-development-with-cmake/`
- Official documentation for Visual Studio: `https://www.visualstudio.com/vs/features/ide/`

Cross-compiling a hello world example

> The code for this recipe is available at `https://github.com/dev-cafe/cmake-cookbook/tree/v1.0/chapter-13/recipe-01` and has a C++ example. This recipe is valid with CMake version 3.5 (and higher) and has been tested on GNU/Linux and macOS.

In this recipe, we will reuse the "Hello World" example from the previous recipe and cross-compile the code from Linux or macOS to Windows. In other words, we will configure and compile the code on Linux or macOS and obtain an executable for the Windows platform.

Getting ready

We start with a simple hello world example (`hello-world.cpp`):

```cpp
#include <cstdlib>
#include <iostream>
#include <string>

const std::string cmake_system_name = SYSTEM_NAME;

int main() {
  std::cout << "Hello from " << cmake_system_name << std::endl;

  return EXIT_SUCCESS;
}
```

We will also use the unchanged `CMakeLists.txt` from the previous recipe:

```
# set minimum cmake version
cmake_minimum_required(VERSION 3.5 FATAL_ERROR)

# project name and language
project(recipe-01 LANGUAGES CXX)

set(CMAKE_CXX_STANDARD 11)
set(CMAKE_CXX_EXTENSIONS OFF)
set(CMAKE_CXX_STANDARD_REQUIRED ON)

include(GNUInstallDirs)
set(CMAKE_ARCHIVE_OUTPUT_DIRECTORY
  ${CMAKE_BINARY_DIR}/${CMAKE_INSTALL_LIBDIR})
set(CMAKE_LIBRARY_OUTPUT_DIRECTORY
  ${CMAKE_BINARY_DIR}/${CMAKE_INSTALL_LIBDIR})
set(CMAKE_RUNTIME_OUTPUT_DIRECTORY
  ${CMAKE_BINARY_DIR}/${CMAKE_INSTALL_BINDIR})

# define executable and its source file
add_executable(hello-world hello-world.cpp)

# we will print the system name in the code
target_compile_definitions(hello-world
  PUBLIC
    "SYSTEM_NAME=\"${CMAKE_SYSTEM_NAME}\""
  )

install(
  TARGETS
    hello-world
  DESTINATION
    ${CMAKE_INSTALL_BINDIR}
  )
```

To cross-compile the source code, we will need to install a cross-compiler for C++ and optionally for C and Fortran. One option is to use packaged MinGW compilers. As an alternative to packaged cross-compilers, we can also build a suite of cross-compilers from sources using MXE (the M cross environment): `http://mxe.cc`.

How to do it

We will create three files in this cross-compilation "hello world" example following these steps:

1. Create a directory holding `hello-world.cpp` and `CMakeLists.txt`, which we listed previously.

2. Create a `toolchain.cmake` file which contains the following:

```
# the name of the target operating system
set(CMAKE_SYSTEM_NAME Windows)

# which compilers to use
set(CMAKE_CXX_COMPILER i686-w64-mingw32-g++)

# adjust the default behaviour of the find commands:
# search headers and libraries in the target environment
set(CMAKE_FIND_ROOT_PATH_MODE_INCLUDE ONLY)
set(CMAKE_FIND_ROOT_PATH_MODE_LIBRARY ONLY)
# search programs in the host environment
set(CMAKE_FIND_ROOT_PATH_MODE_PROGRAM NEVER)
```

3. Adjust the `CMAKE_CXX_COMPILER` to the corresponding compiler (path).

4. Then, configure the code by pointing `CMAKE_TOOLCHAIN_FILE` to the toolchain file (in this example, the MXE compilers built from sources were used):

```
$ mkdir -p build
$ cd build
$ cmake -D CMAKE_TOOLCHAIN_FILE=toolchain.cmake ..

-- The CXX compiler identification is GNU 5.4.0
-- Check for working CXX compiler: /home/user/mxe/usr/bin/i686-w64-
mingw32.static-g++
-- Check for working CXX compiler: /home/user/mxe/usr/bin/i686-w64-
mingw32.static-g++ -- works
-- Detecting CXX compiler ABI info
-- Detecting CXX compiler ABI info - done
-- Detecting CXX compile features
-- Detecting CXX compile features - done
-- Configuring done
-- Generating done
-- Build files have been written to: /home/user/cmake-
recipes/chapter-13/recipe-01/cxx-example/build
```

5. Now, let us build the executable:

```
$ cmake --build .

Scanning dependencies of target hello-world
[ 50%] Building CXX object CMakeFiles/hello-world.dir/hello-
world.cpp.obj
[100%] Linking CXX executable bin/hello-world.exe
[100%] Built target hello-world
```

6. Note that we have obtained `hello-world.exe` on Linux. Copy the binary to a Windows computer.

7. On a Windows computer, we can observe the following output:

```
Hello from Windows
```

8. As you can see, the binary works on Windows!

How it works

Since we configure and build the code on a host environment (in this case, GNU/Linux or macOS) that is different than the target environment (Windows), we need to provide CMake with information about the target environment which we have encoded in the `toolchain.cmake` file (`https://cmake.org/cmake/help/latest/manual/cmake-toolchains.7.html#cross-compiling`).

First and foremost, we provide the name of the target operating system:

```
set(CMAKE_SYSTEM_NAME Windows)
```

Then, we specify the compiler(s), for instance:

```
set(CMAKE_C_COMPILER i686-w64-mingw32-gcc)
set(CMAKE_CXX_COMPILER i686-w64-mingw32-g++)
set(CMAKE_Fortran_COMPILER i686-w64-mingw32-gfortran)
```

In this simple example, we did not have to detect any libraries or header files but, if we had to, we would specify the root path using the following:

```
set(CMAKE_FIND_ROOT_PATH /path/to/target/environment)
```

The target environment can, for instance, be the one provided by an MXE installation.

Finally, we adjust the default behavior of the find commands. We instruct CMake to search headers and libraries in the target environment:

```
set(CMAKE_FIND_ROOT_PATH_MODE_INCLUDE ONLY)
set(CMAKE_FIND_ROOT_PATH_MODE_LIBRARY ONLY)
```

And to search programs in the host environment:

```
set(CMAKE_FIND_ROOT_PATH_MODE_PROGRAM NEVER)
```

See also

For a more detailed discussion of the various options, see `https://cmake.org/cmake/help/latest/manual/cmake-toolchains.7.html#cross-compiling`.

Cross-compiling a Windows binary with OpenMP parallelization

The code for this recipe is available at `https://github.com/dev-cafe/cmake-cookbook/tree/v1.0/chapter-13/recipe-02` and has a C++ and Fortran example. The recipe is valid with CMake version 3.9 (and higher) and has been tested on GNU/Linux.

In this recipe, we will apply what we have learned in the previous recipe, albeit to a more interesting and realistic example: we will cross-compile a Windows binary which is parallelized using OpenMP.

Getting ready

We will use the unmodified source code from *Chapter 3, Detecting External Libraries and Programs, Recipe 5, Detecting the OpenMP parallel environment*. The example code sums up all natural numbers up to N (`example.cpp`):

```cpp
#include <iostream>
#include <omp.h>
#include <string>

int main(int argc, char *argv[]) {
  std::cout << "number of available processors: " << omp_get_num_procs()
```

```
                    << std::endl;
    std::cout << "number of threads: " << omp_get_max_threads() << std::endl;

    auto n = std::stol(argv[1]);
    std::cout << "we will form sum of numbers from 1 to " << n << std::endl;

    // start timer
    auto t0 = omp_get_wtime();

    auto s = 0LL;
#pragma omp parallel for reduction(+ : s)
    for (auto i = 1; i <= n; i++) {
      s += i;
    }

    // stop timer
    auto t1 = omp_get_wtime();

    std::cout << "sum: " << s << std::endl;
    std::cout << "elapsed wall clock time: " << t1 - t0 << " seconds" <<
std::endl;

    return 0;
}
```

The CMakeLists.txt file is largely unchanged with respect to *Chapter 3, Detecting External Libraries and Programs, Recipe 5, Detecting the OpenMP parallel environment,* except there is an additional install target:

```
# set minimum cmake version
cmake_minimum_required(VERSION 3.9 FATAL_ERROR)

# project name and language
project(recipe-02 LANGUAGES CXX)

set(CMAKE_CXX_STANDARD 11)
set(CMAKE_CXX_EXTENSIONS OFF)
set(CMAKE_CXX_STANDARD_REQUIRED ON)

include(GNUInstallDirs)
set(CMAKE_ARCHIVE_OUTPUT_DIRECTORY
  ${CMAKE_BINARY_DIR}/${CMAKE_INSTALL_LIBDIR})
set(CMAKE_LIBRARY_OUTPUT_DIRECTORY
  ${CMAKE_BINARY_DIR}/${CMAKE_INSTALL_LIBDIR})
set(CMAKE_RUNTIME_OUTPUT_DIRECTORY
  ${CMAKE_BINARY_DIR}/${CMAKE_INSTALL_BINDIR})

find_package(OpenMP REQUIRED)
```

```
add_executable(example example.cpp)

target_link_libraries(example
  PUBLIC
    OpenMP::OpenMP_CXX
  )

install(
  TARGETS
    example
  DESTINATION
    ${CMAKE_INSTALL_BINDIR}
  )
```

How to do it

With the following steps, we will manage to cross-compile an OpenMP-parallelized Windows executable:

1. Create a directory holding `example.cpp` and `CMakeLists.txt`, which we listed previously.
2. We will use the same `toolchain.cmake` as in the previous recipe:

```
# the name of the target operating system
set(CMAKE_SYSTEM_NAME Windows)

# which compilers to use
set(CMAKE_CXX_COMPILER i686-w64-mingw32-g++)

# adjust the default behaviour of the find commands:
# search headers and libraries in the target environment
set(CMAKE_FIND_ROOT_PATH_MODE_INCLUDE ONLY)
set(CMAKE_FIND_ROOT_PATH_MODE_LIBRARY ONLY)
# search programs in the host environment
set(CMAKE_FIND_ROOT_PATH_MODE_PROGRAM NEVER)
```

3. Adjust the `CMAKE_CXX_COMPILER` to the corresponding compiler (path).
4. Then, configure the code by pointing `CMAKE_TOOLCHAIN_FILE` to the toolchain file (in this example, the MXE compilers built from sources were used):

```
$ mkdir -p build
$ cd build
$ cmake -D CMAKE_TOOLCHAIN_FILE=toolchain.cmake ..

-- The CXX compiler identification is GNU 5.4.0
```

```
-- Check for working CXX compiler: /home/user/mxe/usr/bin/i686-w64-
mingw32.static-g++
-- Check for working CXX compiler: /home/user/mxe/usr/bin/i686-w64-
mingw32.static-g++ -- works
-- Detecting CXX compiler ABI info
-- Detecting CXX compiler ABI info - done
-- Detecting CXX compile features
-- Detecting CXX compile features - done
-- Found OpenMP_CXX: -fopenmp (found version "4.0")
-- Found OpenMP: TRUE (found version "4.0")
-- Configuring done
-- Generating done
-- Build files have been written to: /home/user/cmake-
recipes/chapter-13/recipe-02/cxx-example/build
```

5. Now, let us build the executable:

```
$ cmake --build .

Scanning dependencies of target example
[ 50%] Building CXX object CMakeFiles/example.dir/example.cpp.obj
[100%] Linking CXX executable bin/example.exe
[100%] Built target example
```

6. Copy the binary example.exe to a Windows computer.

7. On a Windows computer, we can see the following example output:

```
$ set OMP_NUM_THREADS=1
$ example.exe 1000000000

number of available processors: 2
number of threads: 1
we will form sum of numbers from 1 to 1000000000
sum: 500000000500000000
elapsed wall clock time: 2.641 seconds

$ set OMP_NUM_THREADS=2
$ example.exe 1000000000

number of available processors: 2
number of threads: 2
we will form sum of numbers from 1 to 1000000000
sum: 500000000500000000
elapsed wall clock time: 1.328 seconds
```

8. As we can see, the binary works on Windows and we can observe a speed-up thanks to the OpenMP parallelization!

How it works

We have successfully built an executable for parallel execution on the Windows platform using cross-compilation with a simple toolchain. We were able to specify the number of OpenMP threads by setting OMP_NUM_THREADS. Going from 1 thread to 2 threads, we have observed a reduction of runtime from 2.6 to 1.3 seconds. For a discussion of the toolchain file, please see the previous recipe.

There is more

It is possible to cross-compile for a set of target platforms, for instance, Android. For examples, we refer the reader to https://cmake.org/cmake/help/latest/manual/cmake-toolchains.7.html.

14
Testing Dashboards

In this chapter, we will cover the following recipes:

- Deploying tests to the CDash dashboard
- Reporting test coverage to the CDash dashboard
- Using the AddressSanitizer and reporting memory defects to CDash
- Using the ThreadSanitizer and reporting data races to CDash

Introduction

CDash is a web service used to aggregate the test results reported by CTest during a test run or nightly testing, or in a continuous integration setting. Reporting to the dashboard is what we refer to as **CDash time**, as illustrated by the following diagram:

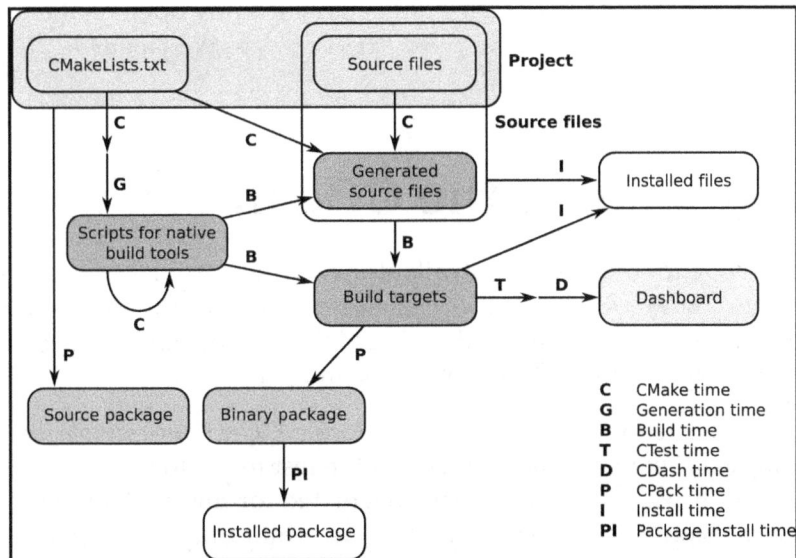

In this chapter, we will demonstrate recipes to report test results to a CDash dashboard. We will discuss strategies for reporting test coverage, as well as memory defects and data races collected with tools such as the AddressSanitizer and the ThreadSanitizer, respectively.

There are two ways to report to CDash: either through the test target of a build or by using a CTest script. We will demonstrate the test target route in the first two recipes and will use the CTest script route in the last two recipes.

Setting up a CDash dashboard

The installation of CDash requires a web server (Apache, NGINX, or IIS) with PHP and SSL enabled, and access to a MySQL or PostgreSQL database server. It is outside of the scope of this book to discuss the setup of a CDash web service in detail; we refer the reader to its official documentation, at `https://public.kitware.com/Wiki/CDash:Installation`.

Installing a CDash instance is not a requirement for producing the recipes in this chapter since Kitware offers two public dashboards (`https://my.cdash.org` and `https://open.cdash.org`). We will reference the former in the recipes.

For readers that decide to install their own CDash instance, we recommend using a MySQL backend, since this seems to be the configuration used by `https://my.cdash.org` and `https://open.cdash.org`, and also seems to be better tested by the community.

> Docker can also be used to provision a CDash instance without too much effort. A request for an official image is currently open on the CDash issue tracker, at `https://github.com/Kitware/CDash/issues/562`.

Deploying tests to the CDash dashboard

> The code for this recipe is available at `https://github.com/dev-cafe/cmake-cookbook/tree/v1.0/chapter-14/recipe-01`, and includes a C++ example. The recipe is valid with CMake version 3.5 (and higher) and has been tested on GNU/Linux, macOS, and Windows.

In this recipe, we will extend the test example of *Recipe 1, Creating a simple unit test*, from *Chapter 4, Creating and Running Tests,* and deploy the test result to `https://my.cdash.org/index.php?project=cmake-cookbook`, which we created for this book on the public dashboard (`https://my.cdash.org`) provided to the community by Kitware.

Getting ready

We will start by reusing the example source code from *Recipe 1, Creating a simple unit test,* in *Chapter 4, Creating and Running Tests,* which sums integers given as command-line arguments. The example consists of three source files: main.cpp, sum_integers.cpp, and sum_integers.hpp. These sources are unchanged. We will also reuse the file test.cpp from *Chapter 4, Creating and Running Tests,* but will rename it to test_short.cpp. We will extend the example with test_long.cpp, containing the following code:

```cpp
#include "sum_integers.hpp"

#include <numeric>
#include <vector>

int main() {
  // creates vector {1, 2, 3, ..., 999, 1000}
  std::vector<int> integers(1000);
  std::iota(integers.begin(), integers.end(), 1);

  if (sum_integers(integers) == 500500) {
    return 0;
  } else {
    return 1;
  }
}
```

We will then organize these files into the following file tree:

```
.
├── CMakeLists.txt
├── CTestConfig.cmake
├── src
│   ├── CMakeLists.txt
│   ├── main.cpp
│   ├── sum_integers.cpp
│   └── sum_integers.hpp
└── tests
    ├── CMakeLists.txt
    ├── test_long.cpp
    └── test_short.cpp
```

How to do it

We will now describe how to configure, build, test, and finally, submit the test results for our example project to the dashboard:

1. The source targets are defined in `src/CMakeLists.txt`, as follows:

```
# example library
add_library(sum_integers "")

target_sources(sum_integers
  PRIVATE
    sum_integers.cpp
  PUBLIC
    ${CMAKE_CURRENT_LIST_DIR}/sum_integers.hpp
  )

target_include_directories(sum_integers
  PUBLIC
    ${CMAKE_CURRENT_LIST_DIR}
  )

# main code
add_executable(sum_up main.cpp)

target_link_libraries(sum_up sum_integers)
```

2. The tests are defined in `tests/CMakeLists.txt`:

```
add_executable(test_short test_short.cpp)
target_link_libraries(test_short sum_integers)

add_executable(test_long test_long.cpp)
target_link_libraries(test_long sum_integers)

add_test(
  NAME
    test_short
  COMMAND
    $<TARGET_FILE:test_short>
  )

add_test(
  NAME
    test_long
  COMMAND
    $<TARGET_FILE:test_long>
  )
```

3. The top-level `CMakeLists.txt` file references the two preceding files, and the new element in this recipe is the line containing `include(CTest)`, which allows us to report to a CDash dashboard:

```
# set minimum cmake version
cmake_minimum_required(VERSION 3.5 FATAL_ERROR)

# project name and language
project(recipe-01 LANGUAGES CXX)

# require C++11
set(CMAKE_CXX_STANDARD 11)
set(CMAKE_CXX_EXTENSIONS OFF)
set(CMAKE_CXX_STANDARD_REQUIRED ON)

# process src/CMakeLists.txt
add_subdirectory(src)

enable_testing()

# allow to report to a cdash dashboard
include(CTest)

# process tests/CMakeLists.txt
add_subdirectory(tests)
```

4. In addition, we create the file `CTestConfig.cmake` in the same directory as the top-level `CMakeLists.txt` file. This new file contains the following lines:

```
set(CTEST_DROP_METHOD "http")
set(CTEST_DROP_SITE "my.cdash.org")
set(CTEST_DROP_LOCATION "/submit.php?project=cmake-cookbook")
set(CTEST_DROP_SITE_CDASH TRUE)
```

5. We are now ready to configure and build the project, as follows:

```
$ mkdir -p build
$ cd build
$ cmake ..
$ cmake --build .
```

6. Having built the code, we can run the test set and report the test results to the dashboard:

```
$ ctest --dashboard Experimental

 Site: larry
```

```
   Build name: Linux-c++
Create new tag: 20180408-1449 - Experimental
Configure project
 Each . represents 1024 bytes of output
 . Size of output: 0K
Build project
 Each symbol represents 1024 bytes of output.
 '!' represents an error and '*' a warning.
 . Size of output: 0K
 0 Compiler errors
 0 Compiler warnings
Test project /home/user/cmake-recipes/chapter-15/recipe-01/cxx-
example/build
 Start 1: test_short
1/2 Test #1: test_short ...................... Passed 0.00 sec
 Start 2: test_long
2/2 Test #2: test_long ...................... Passed 0.00 sec

100% tests passed, 0 tests failed out of 2

Total Test time (real) = 0.01 sec
Performing coverage
 Cannot find any coverage files. Ignoring Coverage request.
Submit files (using http)
 Using HTTP submit method
 Drop site:http://my.cdash.org/submit.php?project=cmake-cookbook
 Uploaded: /home/user/cmake-recipes/chapter-14/recipe-01/cxx-
example/build/Testing/20180408-1449/Build.xml
 Uploaded: /home/user/cmake-recipes/chapter-14/recipe-01/cxx-
example/build/Testing/20180408-1449/Configure.xml
 Uploaded: /home/user/cmake-recipes/chapter-14/recipe-01/cxx-
example/build/Testing/20180408-1449/Test.xml
 Submission successful
```

7. Finally, we can browse the test results in our browser (in this case, the test results are reported to `https://my.cdash.org/index.php?project=cmake-cookbook`):

How it works

A high-level overview of the workflow shows that CTest runs the tests and records results locally in XML files. These XML files are then sent to the CDash server, where they can be browsed and analyzed. We can obtain more details about the passed or failed tests (in this example, there are no failed tests) by clicking on the **2** under **Pass**, as shown in the preceding screenshot. The details, as shown in the following screenshot, record information about the machine that ran the tests, as well as timing information. Again, the test output for individual tests can be browsed online.

Testing started on 2018-04-08 14:49:51

> **Site Name:**larry
> **Build Name:**Linux-c++
> **Total time:**0s
> **OS Name:**Linux
> **OS Platform:**x86_64
> **OS Release:**4.15.13-1-ARCH
> **OS Version:**#1 SMP PREEMPT Sun Mar 25 11:27:57 UTC 2018
> **Compiler Name:**/usr/bin/c++
> **Compiler Version:**7.3.1

2 tests passed.

Name	Status	Time	Summary
test_long	Passed	0s	Stable
test_short	Passed	0s	Stable

Download Table as CSV File

CTest supports three different running submission modes: Experimental, Nightly, and Continuous. We have used `ctest --dashboard Experimental`, and thus, the test results appear under Experimental. The Experimental mode is useful for testing the current state of the code, for debugging a new dashboard script (see Recipes 3 and 4 in this chapter), or for debugging a CDash server or project. The Nightly mode will update (or down-date) the code to the repository snapshot closest to the latest nightly start time, which can be set in `CTestConfig.cmake`; it gives all nightly tests in a project that receives frequent updates a well-defined reference point. For instance, the nightly start time can be set to midnight, Coordinated Universal Time, as follows:

```
set(CTEST_NIGHTLY_START_TIME "00:00:00 UTC")
```

The Continuous mode is useful for a continuous integration workflow and will update the code to the latest version.

> Building, testing, and submitting to the Experimental dashboard can be done with just one command - the `cmake --build . --target Experimental` command.

There is more

In this recipe, we deployed to CDash directly from the test target. It is possible to use a dedicated CTest script instead, and we will demonstrate this approach later in this chapter, in the upcoming Recipes 3 and 4.

CDash allows you to monitor not only whether tests are passing or failing, but also the test timing. You can configure margins for test timing: if a test takes more time than allotted, it will be marked as failing. This is useful for benchmark tests, to automatically detect performance degradation in test timing when refactoring code.

See also

See the official CDash documentation for a detailed discussion of CDash definitions and configuration settings, at `https://public.kitware.com/Wiki/CDash:Documentation`.

Reporting test coverage to the CDash dashboard

> The code for this recipe is available at `https://github.com/dev-cafe/cmake-cookbook/tree/v1.0/chapter-14/recipe-02`, and it includes a C++ example. The recipe is valid with CMake version 3.5 (and higher) and has been tested on GNU/Linux, macOS, and Windows.

In this recipe, we will measure the test coverage and report it to the CDash dashboard, where we will be able to browse the test coverage analysis line-by-line, in order to identify untested or unused code.

Getting ready

We will extend the source code of the previous recipe with a minor change in `src/sum_integers.cpp`, where we will add a function - `sum_integers_unused`:

```cpp
#include "sum_integers.hpp"

#include <vector>

int sum_integers(const std::vector<int> integers) {
  auto sum = 0;
  for (auto i : integers) {
    sum += i;
  }
  return sum;
}

int sum_integers_unused(const std::vector<int> integers) {
  auto sum = 0;
  for (auto i : integers) {
    sum += i;
  }
  return sum;
}
```

Our goal is to detect this unused code with a test coverage analysis, by using gcov (`https:/ /gcc.gnu.org/onlinedocs/gcc/Gcov.html`). Apart from the preceding modification, we will use the unmodified sources of the previous recipe.

How to do it

Through the following steps, we will enable coverage analysis and upload the results to the dashboard:

1. The top-level `CMakeLists.txt` and `tests/CMakeLists.txt` files are unchanged from the previous recipe.
2. We will extend `src/CMakeLists.txt`, with an option to add compile flags for code coverage. This option is enabled by default, as follows:

```cmake
option(ENABLE_COVERAGE "Enable coverage" ON)

if(ENABLE_COVERAGE)
  if(CMAKE_CXX_COMPILER_ID MATCHES GNU)
    message(STATUS "Coverage analysis with gcov enabled")
    target_compile_options(sum_integers
```

```
        PUBLIC
          -fprofile-arcs -ftest-coverage -g
        )
      target_link_libraries(sum_integers
        PUBLIC
          gcov
        )
    else()
      message(WARNING "Coverage not supported for this compiler")
    endif()
  endif()
```

3. We will then configure, build, and deploy to CDash:

```
$ mkdir -p build
$ cd build
$ cmake ..
$ cmake --build . --target Experimental
```

4. This will produce an output similar to the previous recipe, but in addition, the last step will perform a test coverage analysis:

```
Performing coverage
    Processing coverage (each . represents one file):
    ...
    Accumulating results (each . represents one file):
    ...
        Covered LOC: 14
        Not covered LOC: 7
        Total LOC: 21
        Percentage Coverage: 66.67%
Submit files (using http)
    Using HTTP submit method
    Drop site:http://my.cdash.org/submit.php?project=cmake-cookbook
    Uploaded: /home/user/cmake-recipes/chapter-14/recipe-02/cxx-
example/build/Testing/20180408-1530/Build.xml
    Uploaded: /home/user/cmake-recipes/chapter-14/recipe-02/cxx-
example/build/Testing/20180408-1530/Configure.xml
    Uploaded: /home/user/cmake-recipes/chapter-14/recipe-02/cxx-
example/build/Testing/20180408-1530/Coverage.xml
    Uploaded: /home/user/cmake-recipes/chapter-14/recipe-02/cxx-
example/build/Testing/20180408-1530/CoverageLog-0.xml
    Uploaded: /home/user/cmake-recipes/chapter-14/recipe-02/cxx-
example/build/Testing/20180408-1530/Test.xml
    Submission successful
```

5. Finally, we can verify the test results in our browser (in this case, the test results are reported to `https://my.cdash.org/index.php?project=cmake-cookbook`):

How it works

The test coverage analysis is summarized with a percentage of 66.67%. To get further insights, we can click on the percentage and obtain a coverage analysis for the two subdirectories, as follows:

By browsing the subdirectory links, we can inspect the test coverage percentage for individual files, and can even browse a line-by-line summary (for example, `src/sum_integers.cpp`):

```
Coverage File: ./src/sum_integers.cpp

 1        | #include "sum_integers.hpp"
 2        |
 3        | #include <vector>
 4        |
 5      2 | int sum_integers(const std::vector<int> integers) {
 6      2 |   auto sum = 0;
 7   1007 |   for (auto i : integers) {
 8   1005 |     sum += i;
 9        |   }
10      2 |   return sum;
11        | }
12        |
13      0 | int sum_integers_unused(const std::vector<int> integers) {
14      0 |   auto sum = 0;
15      0 |   for (auto i : integers) {
16      0 |     sum += i;
17        |   }
18      0 |   return sum;
19        | }
20        |
```

The green lines have been traversed when running the test suite, whereas the red lines have not. Through this, we can not only identify unused/untested code (with the function `sum_integers_unused`) but can also see how often each line has been traversed. For instance, the code line `sum += i` has been visited 1,005 times (5 times during `test_short`, and 1,000 times during `test_long`). Test coverage analysis is an indispensable companion to automated testing, and CDash provides us with an interface to browse and analyze the results graphically in the browser.

See also

For further reading, we recommend the following blog post, which discusses additional coverage features in CDash: `https://blog.kitware.com/additional-coverage-features-in-cdash/`.

Using the AddressSanitizer and reporting memory defects to CDash

The code for this recipe is available at `https://github.com/dev-cafe/cmake-cookbook/tree/v1.0/chapter-14/recipe-03`, and includes a C++ and a Fortran example. The recipe is valid with CMake version 3.5 (and higher), and has been tested on GNU/Linux and macOS.

AddressSanitizer (ASan) is a memory error detector for C++, C, and Fortran. It can find memory defects, such as use after free, use after return, use after scope, buffer overflows, initialization order bugs, and memory leaks (see `https://github.com/google/sanitizers/wiki/AddressSanitizer`). AddressSanitizer is a part of LLVM, starting with version 3.1, and is a part of GCC, starting with version 4.8. In this recipe, we will fabricate two bugs in our code, which may go undetected in a normal test run. To detect these bugs, we will couple CTest with dynamic analysis by using AddressSanitizer, and will report the defects to CDash.

Getting ready

In this example, we will use two source files and two tests, as follows:

```
.
├── CMakeLists.txt
├── CTestConfig.cmake
├── dashboard.cmake
├── src
│   ├── buggy.cpp
│   ├── buggy.hpp
│   └── CMakeLists.txt
└── tests
    ├── CMakeLists.txt
    ├── leaky.cpp
    └── use_after_free.cpp
```

The file `buggy.cpp` contains two buggy functions, as follows:

```cpp
#include "buggy.hpp"

#include <iostream>

int function_leaky() {
```

```
    double *my_array = new double[1000];

    // do some work ...

    // we forget to deallocate the array
    // delete[] my_array;

    return 0;
}

int function_use_after_free() {

    double *another_array = new double[1000];

    // do some work ...

    // deallocate it, good!
    delete[] another_array;

    // however, we accidentally use the array
    // after it has been deallocated
    std::cout << "not sure what we get: " << another_array[123] << std::endl;

    return 0;
}
```

These functions are exposed in the corresponding header file (buggy.hpp):

```
#pragma once

int function_leaky();
int function_use_after_free();
```

The test source, leaky.cpp, verifies the return code from function_leaky:

```
#include "buggy.hpp"

int main() {
  int return_code = function_leaky();
  return return_code;
}
```

Correspondingly, use_after_free.cpp checks the return value of function_use_after_free, as follows:

```
#include "buggy.hpp"

int main() {
```

```
    int return_code = function_use_after_free();
    return return_code;
}
```

How to do it

We need to compile our code with particular flags to take advantage of ASan. Then, we will run tests and submit them to the dashboard. Let us take a look at how to do this:

1. The buggy library is defined in `src/CMakeLists.txt`:

    ```cmake
    add_library(buggy "")

    target_sources(buggy
      PRIVATE
        buggy.cpp
      PUBLIC
        ${CMAKE_CURRENT_LIST_DIR}/buggy.hpp
      )

    target_include_directories(buggy
      PUBLIC
        ${CMAKE_CURRENT_LIST_DIR}
      )
    ```

2. To the file `src/CMakeLists.txt`, we will add an option and code to sanitize using ASan:

    ```cmake
    option(ENABLE_ASAN "Enable AddressSanitizer" OFF)

    if(ENABLE_ASAN)
      if(CMAKE_CXX_COMPILER_ID MATCHES GNU)
        message(STATUS "AddressSanitizer enabled")
        target_compile_options(buggy
          PUBLIC
            -g -O1 -fsanitize=address -fno-omit-frame-pointer
          )
        target_link_libraries(buggy
          PUBLIC
            asan
          )
      else()
        message(WARNING "AddressSanitizer not supported for this
    compiler")
      endif()
    endif()
    ```

3. The two tests are defined in `tests/CMakeLists.txt` compactly, using a `foreach` loop:

```
foreach(_test IN ITEMS leaky use_after_free)
  add_executable(${_test} ${_test}.cpp)
  target_link_libraries(${_test} buggy)

  add_test(
    NAME
      ${_test}
    COMMAND
      $<TARGET_FILE:${_test}>
    )
endforeach()
```

4. The top-level `CMakeLists.txt` is essentially unchanged with respect to the previous recipes:

```
# set minimum cmake version
cmake_minimum_required(VERSION 3.5 FATAL_ERROR)

# project name and language
project(recipe-03 LANGUAGES CXX)

# require C++11
set(CMAKE_CXX_STANDARD 11)
set(CMAKE_CXX_EXTENSIONS OFF)
set(CMAKE_CXX_STANDARD_REQUIRED ON)

# process src/CMakeLists.txt
add_subdirectory(src)

enable_testing()

# allow to report to a cdash dashboard
include(CTest)

# process tests/CMakeLists.txt
add_subdirectory(tests)
```

5. Also, the `CTestConfig.cmake` file is unchanged:

```
set(CTEST_DROP_METHOD "http")
set(CTEST_DROP_SITE "my.cdash.org")
set(CTEST_DROP_LOCATION "/submit.php?project=cmake-cookbook")
set(CTEST_DROP_SITE_CDASH TRUE)
```

6. In this recipe, we will report to CDash using a CTest script; for this, we will create a file, dashboard.cmake (in the same directory as the main CMakeLists.txt and CTestConfig.cmake), containing the following:

```
set(CTEST_PROJECT_NAME "example")
cmake_host_system_information(RESULT _site QUERY HOSTNAME)
set(CTEST_SITE ${_site})
set(CTEST_BUILD_NAME "${CMAKE_SYSTEM_NAME}-
${CMAKE_HOST_SYSTEM_PROCESSOR}")

set(CTEST_SOURCE_DIRECTORY "${CTEST_SCRIPT_DIRECTORY}")
set(CTEST_BINARY_DIRECTORY "${CTEST_SCRIPT_DIRECTORY}/build")

include(ProcessorCount)
ProcessorCount(N)
if(NOT N EQUAL 0)
  set(CTEST_BUILD_FLAGS -j${N})
  set(ctest_test_args ${ctest_test_args} PARALLEL_LEVEL ${N})
endif()

ctest_start(Experimental)

ctest_configure(
  OPTIONS
    -DENABLE_ASAN:BOOL=ON
  )

ctest_build()
ctest_test()

set(CTEST_MEMORYCHECK_TYPE "AddressSanitizer")
ctest_memcheck()

ctest_submit()
```

7. We will execute the dashboard.cmake script directly. Note how we pass the generator to use with the CTEST_CMAKE_GENERATOR option, as follows:

```
$ ctest -S dashboard.cmake -D CTEST_CMAKE_GENERATOR="Unix
Makefiles"
```

```
Each . represents 1024 bytes of output
  . Size of output: 0K
Each symbol represents 1024 bytes of output.
'!' represents an error and '*' a warning.
  . Size of output: 1K
```

8. The result will appear on the CDash site, as shown in the following screenshot:

How it works

In this recipe, we successfully reported memory bugs to the **Dynamic Analysis** section of the dashboard. We can gain further insights by browsing the defects (under **Defect Count**):

By clicking on the individual links, it is possible to browse the full output.

Note that it is also possible to generate the AddressSanitizer report locally. In this example, we need to set `ENABLE_ASAN`, as follows:

```
$ mkdir -p build
$ cd build
$ cmake -DENABLE_ASAN=ON ..
$ cmake --build .
$ cmake --build . --target test

    Start 1: leaky
1/2 Test #1: leaky ............................***Failed 0.07 sec
    Start 2: use_after_free
2/2 Test #2: use_after_free ...................***Failed 0.04 sec

0% tests passed, 2 tests failed out of 2
```

Running the `leaky` test executable directly produces the following:

```
$ ./build/tests/leaky
```

```
=====================================================================
==18536==ERROR: LeakSanitizer: detected memory leaks

Direct leak of 8000 byte(s) in 1 object(s) allocated from:
    #0 0x7ff984da1669 in operator new[](unsigned long)
/build/gcc/src/gcc/libsanitizer/asan/asan_new_delete.cc:82
    #1 0x564925c93fd2 in function_leaky() /home/user/cmake-
recipes/chapter-14/recipe-03/cxx-example/src/buggy.cpp:7
    #2 0x564925c93fb2 in main /home/user/cmake-
recipes/chapter-14/recipe-03/cxx-example/tests/leaky.cpp:4
    #3 0x7ff98403df49 in __libc_start_main (/usr/lib/libc.so.6+0x20f49)

SUMMARY: AddressSanitizer: 8000 byte(s) leaked in 1 allocation(s).
```

Correspondingly, we can obtain detailed output by running the `use_after_free` executable directly, as follows:

```
$ ./build/tests/use_after_free
```

```
=====================================================================
==18571==ERROR: AddressSanitizer: heap-use-after-free on address
0x6250000004d8 at pc 0x557ffa8b0102 bp 0x7ffe8c560200 sp 0x7ffe8c5601f0
READ of size 8 at 0x6250000004d8 thread T0
  #0 0x557ffa8b0101 in function_use_after_free() /home/user/cmake-
recipes/chapter-14/recipe-03/cxx-example/src/buggy.cpp:28
  #1 0x557ffa8affb2 in main /home/user/cmake-
recipes/chapter-14/recipe-03/cxx-example/tests/use_after_free.cpp:4
  #2 0x7ff1d6088f49 in __libc_start_main (/usr/lib/libc.so.6+0x20f49)
  #3 0x557ffa8afec9 in _start (/home/user/cmake-
recipes/chapter-14/recipe-03/cxx-example/build/tests/use_after_free+0xec9)

0x6250000004d8 is located 984 bytes inside of 8000-byte region
[0x625000000100,0x625000002040)
freed by thread T0 here:
  #0 0x7ff1d6ded5a9 in operator delete[](void*)
/build/gcc/src/gcc/libsanitizer/asan/asan_new_delete.cc:128
  #1 0x557ffa8afffa in function_use_after_free() /home/user/cmake-
recipes/chapter-14/recipe-03/cxx-example/src/buggy.cpp:24
  #2 0x557ffa8affb2 in main /home/user/cmake-
recipes/chapter-14/recipe-03/cxx-example/tests/use_after_free.cpp:4
  #3 0x7ff1d6088f49 in __libc_start_main (/usr/lib/libc.so.6+0x20f49)

previously allocated by thread T0 here:
  #0 0x7ff1d6dec669 in operator new[](unsigned long)
```

```
/build/gcc/src/gcc/libsanitizer/asan/asan_new_delete.cc:82
 #1 0x557ffa8affea in function_use_after_free() /home/user/cmake-
recipes/chapter-14/recipe-03/cxx-example/src/buggy.cpp:19
 #2 0x557ffa8affb2 in main /home/user/cmake-
recipes/chapter-14/recipe-03/cxx-example/tests/use_after_free.cpp:4
 #3 0x7ff1d6088f49 in __libc_start_main (/usr/lib/libc.so.6+0x20f49)

SUMMARY: AddressSanitizer: heap-use-after-free /home/user/cmake-
recipes/chapter-14/recipe-03/cxx-example/src/buggy.cpp:28 in
function_use_after_free()
Shadow bytes around the buggy address:
 0x0c4a7fff8040: fd fd fd fd fd fd fd fd fd fd fd fd fd fd fd fd
 0x0c4a7fff8050: fd fd fd fd fd fd fd fd fd fd fd fd fd fd fd fd
 0x0c4a7fff8060: fd fd fd fd fd fd fd fd fd fd fd fd fd fd fd fd
 0x0c4a7fff8070: fd fd fd fd fd fd fd fd fd fd fd fd fd fd fd fd
 0x0c4a7fff8080: fd fd fd fd fd fd fd fd fd fd fd fd fd fd fd fd
=>0x0c4a7fff8090: fd fd fd fd fd fd fd fd fd fd fd[fd]fd fd fd fd
 0x0c4a7fff80a0: fd fd fd fd fd fd fd fd fd fd fd fd fd fd fd fd
 0x0c4a7fff80b0: fd fd fd fd fd fd fd fd fd fd fd fd fd fd fd fd
 0x0c4a7fff80c0: fd fd fd fd fd fd fd fd fd fd fd fd fd fd fd fd
 0x0c4a7fff80d0: fd fd fd fd fd fd fd fd fd fd fd fd fd fd fd fd
 0x0c4a7fff80e0: fd fd fd fd fd fd fd fd fd fd fd fd fd fd fd fd
Shadow byte legend (one shadow byte represents 8 application bytes):
 Addressable: 00
 Partially addressable: 01 02 03 04 05 06 07
 Heap left redzone: fa
 Freed heap region: fd
 Stack left redzone: f1
 Stack mid redzone: f2
 Stack right redzone: f3
 Stack after return: f5
 Stack use after scope: f8
 Global redzone: f9
 Global init order: f6
 Poisoned by user: f7
 Container overflow: fc
 Array cookie: ac
 Intra object redzone: bb
 ASan internal: fe
 Left alloca redzone: ca
 Right alloca redzone: cb
==18571==ABORTING
```

If we test without the AddressSanitizer (ENABLE_ASAN is OFF by default), no error is reported in the following example:

```
$ mkdir -p build_no_asan
$ cd build_no_asan
```

```
$ cmake ..
$ cmake --build .
$ cmake --build . --target test
```

```
    Start 1: leaky
1/2 Test #1: leaky .......................... Passed 0.00 sec
    Start 2: use_after_free
2/2 Test #2: use_after_free .................. Passed 0.00 sec

100% tests passed, 0 tests failed out of 2
```

Indeed, `leaky` will just waste memory, whereas `use_after_free` may result in non-deterministic failures. One way to debug these failures is to use valgrind (`http://valgrind.org`).

In contrast to the previous two recipes, we have used a CTest script to configure, build, and test the code, and to submit the report to the dashboard. To understand how this recipe works, take a closer look at the `dashboard.cmake` script. First, we define the project name and set the host reporting and the build name, as follows:

```
set(CTEST_PROJECT_NAME "example")
cmake_host_system_information(RESULT _site QUERY HOSTNAME)
set(CTEST_SITE ${_site})
set(CTEST_BUILD_NAME "${CMAKE_SYSTEM_NAME}-${CMAKE_HOST_SYSTEM_PROCESSOR}")
```

In our case, the `CTEST_BUILD_NAME` evaluates to `Linux-x86_64`. In your case, you may observe a different result, depending on your operating system.

Next, we specify paths for the source and build directories:

```
set(CTEST_SOURCE_DIRECTORY "${CTEST_SCRIPT_DIRECTORY}")
set(CTEST_BINARY_DIRECTORY "${CTEST_SCRIPT_DIRECTORY}/build")
```

We could set the generator to `Unix Makefiles`:

```
set(CTEST_CMAKE_GENERATOR "Unix Makefiles")
```

However, for a more portable test script, we prefer to provide the generator *via* the command line, as follows:

```
$ ctest -S dashboard.cmake -D CTEST_CMAKE_GENERATOR="Unix Makefiles"
```

The next code snippet in `dashboard.cmake` figures out the number of available cores on the machine and sets the parallel level of the test step to the number of available cores, in order to minimize the total test time:

```
include(ProcessorCount)
ProcessorCount(N)
if(NOT N EQUAL 0)
  set(CTEST_BUILD_FLAGS -j${N})
  set(ctest_test_args ${ctest_test_args} PARALLEL_LEVEL ${N})
endif()
```

Next, we start the testing step and configure the code, with `ENABLE_ASAN` set to `ON`:

```
ctest_start(Experimental)

ctest_configure(
  OPTIONS
    -DENABLE_ASAN:BOOL=ON
  )
```

The remaining commands in `dashboard.cmake` map to the build, test, memcheck, and submit steps:

```
ctest_build()
ctest_test()

set(CTEST_MEMORYCHECK_TYPE "AddressSanitizer")
ctest_memcheck()

ctest_submit()
```

There is more

The attentive reader will have noticed that we did not search for the AddressSanitizer on our system prior to linking our target against it. A real-world, complete use case would have done that, to avoid unpleasant surprises during the linking stage. We will remind the reader that we showed a method to probe for the availability of sanitizers in *Recipe 7, Probing compiler flags*, in *Chapter 5, Configure-time and Build-time Operations*.

For more AddressSanitizer documentation and examples, see `https://github.com/google/sanitizers/wiki/AddressSanitizer`. AddressSanitizer is not limited to C and C++. For a Fortran example, we refer the reader to the code repository at `https://github.com/dev-cafe/cmake-cookbook/tree/v1.0/chapter-14/recipe-03/fortran-example`.

> CMake utilities to discover sanitizers and adjust compiler flags are available at `https://github.com/arsenm/sanitizers-cmake`.

See also

The following blog post discusses examples of how to add support for dynamic analysis tools, and it inspired the present recipe: `https://blog.kitware.com/ctest-cdash-add-support-for-new-dynamic-analysis-tools/`.

Using the ThreadSanitizer and reporting data races to CDash

> The code for this recipe is available at `https://github.com/dev-cafe/cmake-cookbook/tree/v1.0/chapter-14/recipe-04`, and includes a C++ example. The recipe is valid with CMake version 3.5 (and higher) and has been tested on GNU/Linux and macOS.

In this recipe, we will reuse the approach from the previous example, but use ThreadSanitizer, or TSan, in combination with CTest and CDash, to identify data races and report these to a CDash dashboard. The documentation for ThreadSanitizer can be found online, at `https://github.com/google/sanitizers/wiki/ThreadSanitizerCppManual`.

Getting ready

In this recipe, we will work with the following example code (`example.cpp`):

```cpp
#include <chrono>
#include <iostream>
#include <thread>

static const int num_threads = 16;

void increase(int i, int &s) {
  std::this_thread::sleep_for(std::chrono::seconds(1));
  std::cout << "thread " << i << " increases " << s++ << std::endl;
}
```

```
int main() {
  std::thread t[num_threads];

  int s = 0;

  // start threads
  for (auto i = 0; i < num_threads; i++) {
    t[i] = std::thread(increase, i, std::ref(s));
  }

  // join threads with main thread
  for (auto i = 0; i < num_threads; i++) {
    t[i].join();
  }

  std::cout << "final s: " << s << std::endl;

  return 0;
}
```

In this example code, we start 16 threads, and each of these threads calls the `increase` function. The `increase` function sleeps for one second, then prints and increments an integer, s. We anticipate that this example code will manifest data races, because all threads read and modify the same address, without any explicit synchronization or coordination. In other words, we expect that the final s, which is printed at the end of the code, may differ from run to run. The code is buggy, and we will try to identify the data race with the help of ThreadSanitizer. Without running ThreadSanitizer, we may not see any problems with the code:

```
$ ./example

thread thread 0 increases 01 increases 1
thread 9 increases 2
thread 4 increases 3
thread 10 increases 4
thread 2 increases 5
thread 3 increases 6
thread 13 increases 7
thread thread 7 increases 8
thread 14 increases 9
thread 8 increases 10
thread 12 increases 11
thread 15 increases 12
thread 11 increases 13
```

```
5 increases 14
thread 6 increases 15

final s: 16
```

How to do it

Let us go through the necessary steps in detail, as follows:

1. The file `CMakeLists.txt` starts by defining a minimum supported version, project name, supported languages, and, in this case, a requirement of the C++11 standard:

```
cmake_minimum_required(VERSION 3.5 FATAL_ERROR)

project(recipe-04 LANGUAGES CXX)

set(CMAKE_CXX_STANDARD 11)
set(CMAKE_CXX_EXTENSIONS OFF)
set(CMAKE_CXX_STANDARD_REQUIRED ON)
```

2. Next, we locate the Threads library, define the executable, and link it against the Threads library:

```
find_package(Threads REQUIRED)

add_executable(example example.cpp)

target_link_libraries(example
  PUBLIC
    Threads::Threads
  )
```

3. Then, we offer the option and code to compile and link with support for the ThreadSanitizer:

```
option(ENABLE_TSAN "Enable ThreadSanitizer" OFF)

if(ENABLE_TSAN)
  if(CMAKE_CXX_COMPILER_ID MATCHES GNU)
    message(STATUS "ThreadSanitizer enabled")
    target_compile_options(example
      PUBLIC
        -g -O1 -fsanitize=thread -fno-omit-frame-pointer -fPIC
      )
    target_link_libraries(example
```

```
        PUBLIC
          tsan
        )
  else()
    message(WARNING "ThreadSanitizer not supported for this
compiler")
  endif()
endif()
```

4. Finally, as a test, we execute the compiled example itself:

```
enable_testing()

# allow to report to a cdash dashboard
include(CTest)

add_test(
  NAME
    example
  COMMAND
    $<TARGET_FILE:example>
  )
```

5. The file `CTestConfig.cmake` is unchanged with respect to the previous recipes:

```
set(CTEST_DROP_METHOD "http")
set(CTEST_DROP_SITE "my.cdash.org")
set(CTEST_DROP_LOCATION "/submit.php?project=cmake-cookbook")
set(CTEST_DROP_SITE_CDASH TRUE)
```

6. The corresponding `dashboard.cmake` script is a simple adaptation to TSan from the previous recipe:

```
set(CTEST_PROJECT_NAME "example")
cmake_host_system_information(RESULT _site QUERY HOSTNAME)
set(CTEST_SITE ${_site})
set(CTEST_BUILD_NAME "${CMAKE_SYSTEM_NAME}-
${CMAKE_HOST_SYSTEM_PROCESSOR}")

set(CTEST_SOURCE_DIRECTORY "${CTEST_SCRIPT_DIRECTORY}")
set(CTEST_BINARY_DIRECTORY "${CTEST_SCRIPT_DIRECTORY}/build")

include(ProcessorCount)
ProcessorCount(N)
if(NOT N EQUAL 0)
  set(CTEST_BUILD_FLAGS -j${N})
  set(ctest_test_args ${ctest_test_args} PARALLEL_LEVEL ${N})
endif()
```

```
ctest_start(Experimental)

ctest_configure(
  OPTIONS
    -DENABLE_TSAN:BOOL=ON
  )

ctest_build()
ctest_test()

set(CTEST_MEMORYCHECK_TYPE "ThreadSanitizer")
ctest_memcheck()

ctest_submit()
```

7. Let us take this example for a spin. Once again, we will set the generator passing the CTEST_CMAKE_GENERATOR option:

$ ctest -S dashboard.cmake -D CTEST_CMAKE_GENERATOR="Unix Makefiles"

```
Each . represents 1024 bytes of output
 . Size of output: 0K
Each symbol represents 1024 bytes of output.
'!' represents an error and '*' a warning.
 . Size of output: 0K
```

8. On the dashboard, we will see the following:

9. We can see the dynamic analysis in more detail as follows:

Dynamic analysis started on 2018-04-08 15:44:35

   Site Name: localhost
   Build Name: Linux-x86_64

Name	Status	data race	Labels
example	Failed	2	

How it works

The core ingredients for this recipe are in the following section of CMakeLists.txt:

```
option(ENABLE_TSAN "Enable ThreadSanitizer" OFF)

if(ENABLE_TSAN)
  if(CMAKE_CXX_COMPILER_ID MATCHES GNU)
    message(STATUS "ThreadSanitizer enabled")
    target_compile_options(example
      PUBLIC
        -g -O1 -fsanitize=thread -fno-omit-frame-pointer -fPIC
      )
    target_link_libraries(example
      PUBLIC
        tsan
      )
  else()
    message(WARNING "ThreadSanitizer not supported for this compiler")
  endif()
endif()
```

The ingredients are also in the updated steps in dashboard.cmake:

```
# ...

ctest_start(Experimental)

ctest_configure(
  OPTIONS
    -DENABLE_TSAN:BOOL=ON
  )

ctest_build()
ctest_test()
```

```
set(CTEST_MEMORYCHECK_TYPE "ThreadSanitizer")
ctest_memcheck()

ctest_submit()
```

As in the previous recipe, we can also inspect the output from ThreadSanitizer locally:

```
$ mkdir -p build
$ cd build
$ cmake -DENABLE_TSAN=ON ..
$ cmake --build .
$ cmake --build . --target test

  Start 1: example
1/1 Test #1: example ........................***Failed 1.07 sec

0% tests passed, 1 tests failed out of 1

$ ./build/example

thread 0 increases 0
==================
WARNING: ThreadSanitizer: data race (pid=24563)

... lots of output ...

SUMMARY: ThreadSanitizer: data race /home/user/cmake-
recipes/chapter-14/recipe-04/cxx-example/example.cpp:9 in increase(int,
int&)
```

There is more

It would be a natural step to apply TSan on an OpenMP code, but please note that OpenMP is known to generate false positives under TSan, in some cases. For the Clang compilers, a workaround would be to recompile the compiler itself, and its libomp, with -DLIBOMP_TSAN_SUPPORT=TRUE. In general, using sanitizers in a sensible way may require a recompilation of the entire tool-stack, in order to avoid false positives. This will probably be the case for a C++ project using pybind11; we would need to recompile Python with the sanitizers enabled to get anything meaningful. Alternatively, the Python binding can be left out from the sanitizing by using sanitizer suppression, as explained at https://github.com/google/sanitizers/wiki/ThreadSanitizerSuppressions. This may not be possible if, for example, a shared library is called by both by a sanitized binary and a Python plugin.

See also

The following blog post discusses examples of how to add support for dynamic analysis tools, and it inspired the present recipe: `https://blog.kitware.com/ctest-cdash-add-support-for-new-dynamic-analysis-tools/`.

Porting a Project to CMake

15

In the final chapter of this book, we will combine a number of different building blocks that we have discussed in the previous chapters and apply them to a real-life project. Our goal will be to demonstrate step-by-step how to port a non-trivial project to CMake and discuss the steps involved in such a process. We will provide recommendations for porting your own projects or adding CMake support to legacy code, be it from Autotools, from hand-written configure scripts and Makefiles, or from Visual Studio project files.

To have a tangible and realistic example, we will use the source code behind the popular editor Vim (`https://www.vim.org`) and attempt to port the configuration and compilation from Autotools to CMake.

To keep the discussion and the examples relatively simple, we will not attempt to present a full port to CMake for the entire Vim code with all options. Instead, we will single out and discuss the most important aspects and only build a core version of Vim, without support for a graphical user interface (GUI). Nevertheless, we will arrive at a working version of Vim, configured, built, and tested with CMake and the other tools we have presented in the book.

The following topics will be covered in this chapter:

- Initial steps when porting a project
- Generating files and writing platform checks
- Detecting required dependencies and linking
- Reproducing compiler flags
- Porting tests
- Porting install targets
- Common pitfalls when converting projects to CMake

Where to start

We will first show where to find our example online and then discuss the porting example step by step.

Reproducing the porting example

We will start from the `v8.1.0290` release tag of the Vim source code repository (`https://github.com/vim/vim`) and base our work on the Git commit hash `b476cb7`. The following steps can be reproduced by cloning the source code repository of Vim and checking out that particular version of the code:

```
$ git clone --single-branch -b v8.1.0290 https://github.com/vim/vim.git
```

Alternatively, our solution can be found on the `cmake-support` branch at `https://github.com/dev-cafe/vim` and cloned to your computer using this:

```
$ git clone --single-branch -b cmake-support
https://github.com/dev-cafe/vim
```

In this example, we will emulate a `./configure --enable-gui=no` configuration in CMake, built with the GNU compiler collection.

For comparison with our solution later, and for additional inspiration, we encourage readers to also study the Neovim project (`https://github.com/neovim/neovim`), which is a fork of the traditional Vi editor and provides a CMake build system.

Creating a top-level CMakeLists.txt

As a start, we create a top-level `CMakeLists.txt` in the root directory of the source code repository where we set the minimum CMake version, the project name, and supported languages, in this case C:

```
cmake_minimum_required(VERSION 3.5 FATAL_ERROR)

project(vim LANGUAGES C)
```

Before adding any targets or sources, we can already set the default build type. In this case, we default to the `Release` configuration, which will turn on certain compiler optimizations:

```
if(NOT CMAKE_BUILD_TYPE)
```

```
    set(CMAKE_BUILD_TYPE Release CACHE STRING "Build type" FORCE)
endif()
```

We also use portable install directory variables, as defined for GNU software:

```
include(GNUInstallDirs)
set(CMAKE_ARCHIVE_OUTPUT_DIRECTORY
    ${CMAKE_BINARY_DIR}/${CMAKE_INSTALL_LIBDIR})
set(CMAKE_LIBRARY_OUTPUT_DIRECTORY
    ${CMAKE_BINARY_DIR}/${CMAKE_INSTALL_LIBDIR})
set(CMAKE_RUNTIME_OUTPUT_DIRECTORY
    ${CMAKE_BINARY_DIR}/${CMAKE_INSTALL_BINDIR})
```

As a sanity check, we can already try to configure and build the project, but so far there are no targets so the output from the build step will be empty:

```
$ mkdir -p build
$ cd build
$ cmake ..
$ cmake --build .
```

We will start adding targets in a moment to put more flesh on the bones.

How to allow both conventional configuration and configuration with CMake at the same time

A very nice feature of CMake is that we build *out-of-source*, the build directory can be any directory, and it does not have to be a subdirectory of the project directory. This means that we can port a project to CMake while not intruding into the previous/present configuration and build mechanism. For the migration of a non-trivial project, it is very useful that CMake files can coexist with other build frameworks to allow a gradual migration, both in terms of options, features, and portability, and to allow the developer community to adapt to the new framework. To allow both traditional and CMake configurations to coexist for a while, a typical strategy is to collect all CMake code in CMakeLists.txt files and all auxiliary CMake source files under a cmake subdirectory. In our example, we will not introduce a cmake subdirectory, but rather keep auxiliary files closer to the targets and sources requiring them, but we will take care to keep almost all files used by the traditional Autotools build unmodified, with one exception: we will apply few modifications in order to place autogenerated files under the build directory and not in the source tree.

Capturing a record of what the traditional build does

Before we add any targets to the configuration, it is often useful to first capture a record of what the traditional build does, and save the output of the configuration and the build step into a log file. For our Vim example, this can be done using the following:

```
$ ./configure --enable-gui=no

... lot of output ...

$ make > build.log
```

In our case (the complete content of build.log is not shown here), we are able to verify which sources are compiled and which compile flags are used (-I. -Iproto -DHAVE_CONFIG_H -g -O2 -U_FORTIFY_SOURCE -D_FORTIFY_SOURCE=1). From the log file, we can deduce the following:

- All objects are linked into a single binary
- No libraries are produced
- The executable target is linked against the following libraries: -lSM -lICE -lXpm -lXt -lX11 -lXdmcp -lSM -lICE -lm -ltinfo -lelf -lnsl -lacl -lattr -lgpm -ldl

Debugging the migration

When gradually moving targets and commands to the CMake side, it will be useful to print values of variables using the message command:

```
message(STATUS "for debugging printing the value of ${some_variable}")
```

By adding options, targets, sources, and dependencies while debugging using message, we will inch our way towards a working build.

Implementing options

Find out which options the traditional configuration offers to the users (for example, by running `./configure --help`). The Vim project offers a very long list of options and flags and to keep the discussion in this chapter simple, we will implement only four of the options on the CMake side:

```
--disable-netbeans    Disable NetBeans integration support.
--disable-channel     Disable process communication support.
--enable-terminal     Enable terminal emulation support.
--with-features=TYPE  tiny, small, normal, big or huge (default: huge)
```

We will also ignore any GUI support and emulate `--enable-gui=no`, since it would complicate the example without significantly adding to the learning outcome.

We will place the following options and defaults in `CMakeLists.txt`:

```
option(ENABLE_NETBEANS "Enable netbeans" ON)
option(ENABLE_CHANNEL "Enable channel" ON)
option(ENABLE_TERMINAL "Enable terminal" ON)
```

We will emulate the `--with-features` flag using a variable, `FEATURES`, that can be defined with `cmake -D FEATURES=value`. We make sure that if `FEATURES` is not set, it defaults to "huge":

```
if(NOT FEATURES)
  set(FEATURES "huge" CACHE STRING
    "FEATURES chosen by the user at CMake configure time")
endif()
```

We also make sure that users provide a valid value for `FEATURES`:

```
list(APPEND _available_features "tiny" "small" "normal" "big" "huge")
if(NOT FEATURES IN_LIST _available_features)
  message(FATAL_ERROR "Unknown features: \"${FEATURES}\". Allowed values
are: ${_available_features}.")
endif()
set_property(CACHE FEATURES PROPERTY STRINGS ${_available_features})
```

The last line, containing `set_property(CACHE FEATURES PROPERTY STRINGS ${_available_features})`, has the nice effect that when configuring the project using `cmake-gui`, the user is presented with a selection field for `FEATURES` listing all available features that we have defined already (see also `https://blog.kitware.com/constraining-values-with-comboboxes-in-cmake-cmake-gui/`).

The options can either be placed in the top-level `CMakeLists.txt` (as we have done here) or they can be defined close to the targets that query `ENABLE_NETBEANS`, `ENABLE_CHANNEL`, `ENABLE_TERMINAL`, and `FEATURES`. The former strategy has the advantage that options are listed in one place and one does not need to traverse a tree of `CMakeLists.txt` files to find the definition of an option. Since we have not defined any targets yet, we can start with keeping the options in a central file, but we may later move the option definition closer to the targets to localize scope and arrive at more reusable CMake building blocks.

Start with the executable and very few targets, later localize scope

Let us add some sources. In the Vim example, sources are under `src` and to keep the main `CMakeLists.txt` readable and maintainable, we will create a new file, `src/CMakeLists.txt`, and process this file in its own directory scope by adding this to the main `CMakeLists.txt`:

```
add_subdirectory(src)
```

Inside `src/CMakeLists.txt`, we could start out defining the executable target and listing all sources that we have extracted from `build.log`:

```
add_executable(vim
  arabic.c beval.c buffer.c blowfish.c crypt.c crypt_zip.c dict.c diff.c
digraph.c edit.c eval.c evalfunc.c ex_cmds.c ex_cmds2.c ex_docmd.c
ex_eval.c ex_getln.c farsi.c fileio.c fold.c getchar.c hardcopy.c hashtab.c
if_cscope.c if_xcmdsrv.c list.c mark.c memline.c menu.c misc1.c misc2.c
move.c mbyte.c normal.c ops.c option.c os_unix.c auto/pathdef.c popupmnu.c
pty.c quickfix.c regexp.c screen.c search.c sha256.c spell.c spellfile.c
syntax.c tag.c term.c terminal.c ui.c undo.c userfunc.c window.c
libvterm/src/encoding.c libvterm/src/keyboard.c libvterm/src/mouse.c
libvterm/src/parser.c libvterm/src/pen.c libvterm/src/screen.c
libvterm/src/state.c libvterm/src/unicode.c libvterm/src/vterm.c netbeans.c
channel.c charset.c json.c main.c memfile.c message.c version.c
  )
```

This is a start. In this case, the code will not even configure since the list of sources contains generated files. Before we discuss generated files and link dependencies, we will split this long list up a bit to limit the scope of target dependencies and to make the project more manageable. We will also make it easier for CMake to scan source file dependencies and avoid a very long link line if we group them to targets.

For the Vim example, we can gain further insight into the grouping of sources from `src/Makefile` and `src/configure.ac`. From these files, we can deduce that most sources are basic and required. Some sources are optional (`netbeans.c` should only be built if `ENABLE_NETBEANS` is `ON` and `channel.c` should only be built when `ENABLE_CHANNEL` is `ON`). In addition, we can probably group all sources under `src/libvterm/` and make their compilation optional with `ENABLE_TERMINAL`.

With this, we reorganize the CMake structure to the following tree structure:

```
.
├── CMakeLists.txt
└── src
    ├── CMakeLists.txt
    └── libvterm
        └── CMakeLists.txt
```

The top-level file adds `src/CMakeLists.txt` with `add_subdirectory(src)`. The `src/CMakeLists.txt` file now contains three targets (one executable and two libraries), each carrying compile definitions and include directories. We first define the executable:

```
add_executable(vim
  main.c
  )

target_compile_definitions(vim
  PRIVATE
    "HAVE_CONFIG_H"
  )
```

Then, we define the required sources:

```
add_library(basic_sources "")

target_sources(basic_sources
  PRIVATE
    arabic.c beval.c blowfish.c buffer.c charset.c
    crypt.c crypt_zip.c dict.c diff.c digraph.c
    edit.c eval.c evalfunc.c ex_cmds.c ex_cmds2.c
    ex_docmd.c ex_eval.c ex_getln.c farsi.c fileio.c
    fold.c getchar.c hardcopy.c hashtab.c if_cscope.c
    if_xcmdsrv.c json.c list.c main.c mark.c
    memfile.c memline.c menu.c message.c misc1.c
    misc2.c move.c mbyte.c normal.c ops.c
    option.c os_unix.c auto/pathdef.c popupmnu.c pty.c
    quickfix.c regexp.c screen.c search.c sha256.c
    spell.c spellfile.c syntax.c tag.c term.c
    terminal.c ui.c undo.c userfunc.c version.c
```

```
      window.c
  )

target_include_directories(basic_sources
  PRIVATE
    ${CMAKE_CURRENT_LIST_DIR}/proto
    ${CMAKE_CURRENT_LIST_DIR}
    ${CMAKE_CURRENT_BINARY_DIR}
  )

target_compile_definitions(basic_sources
  PRIVATE
    "HAVE_CONFIG_H"
  )

target_link_libraries(vim
  PUBLIC
    basic_sources
  )
```

Then, we define the optional sources:

```
add_library(extra_sources "")

if(ENABLE_NETBEANS)
  target_sources(extra_sources
    PRIVATE
      netbeans.c
    )
endif()

if(ENABLE_CHANNEL)
  target_sources(extra_sources
    PRIVATE
      channel.c
    )
endif()

target_include_directories(extra_sources
  PUBLIC
    ${CMAKE_CURRENT_LIST_DIR}/proto
    ${CMAKE_CURRENT_BINARY_DIR}
  )

target_compile_definitions(extra_sources
  PRIVATE
    "HAVE_CONFIG_H"
  )
```

```
target_link_libraries(vim
  PUBLIC
    extra_sources
  )
```

The file also optionally processes and links `src/libvterm/` with the following code:

```
if(ENABLE_TERMINAL)
  add_subdirectory(libvterm)

  target_link_libraries(vim
    PUBLIC
      libvterm
    )
endif()
```

The corresponding `src/libvterm/CMakeLists.txt` contains the following:

```
add_library(libvterm "")
target_sources(libvterm
  PRIVATE
    src/encoding.c
    src/keyboard.c
    src/mouse.c
    src/parser.c
    src/pen.c
    src/screen.c
    src/state.c
    src/unicode.c
    src/vterm.c
  )

target_include_directories(libvterm
  PUBLIC
    ${CMAKE_CURRENT_LIST_DIR}/include
  )

target_compile_definitions(libvterm
  PRIVATE
    "HAVE_CONFIG_H"
    "INLINE="
    "VSNPRINTF=vim_vsnprintf"
    "IS_COMBINING_FUNCTION=utf_iscomposing_uint"
    "WCWIDTH_FUNCTION=utf_uint2cells"
  )
```

We have extracted the compile definitions from the recorded `build.log`. The advantage of the tree structure is that targets are defined close to where sources are located. If we decide to refactor the code and rename or move directories, the CMake files describing the targets have the chance to move with the sources.

Our example code still does not even configure (unless this is tried after a successful Autotools build):

```
$ mkdir -p build
$ cd build
$ cmake ..

-- The C compiler identification is GNU 8.2.0
-- Check for working C compiler: /usr/bin/cc
-- Check for working C compiler: /usr/bin/cc -- works
-- Detecting C compiler ABI info
-- Detecting C compiler ABI info - done
-- Detecting C compile features
-- Detecting C compile features - done
-- Configuring done
CMake Error at src/CMakeLists.txt:12 (add_library):
  Cannot find source file:

    auto/pathdef.c

  Tried extensions .c .C .c++ .cc .cpp .cxx .cu .m .M .mm .h .hh .h++ .hm
  .hpp .hxx .in .txx
```

We need to generate `auto/pathdef.c` (and other files), which we will consider in the next section.

Generating files and writing platform checks

It turns out that for the Vim code example, we need to generate three files at configure time, `src/auto/pathdef.c`, `src/auto/config.h`, and `src/auto/osdef.h`:

- `pathdef.c` records the install path, compile and link flags, the user who compiled the code, and the hostname
- `config.h` contains compile definitions that are specific to the system environment
- `osdef.h` is a file containing compile definitions generated by `src/osdef.sh`

This situation is rather common. We will need to configure a file based on CMake variables, perform a number of platform checks to generate config.h, and execute a script at configure time. In particular, the platform checks are very common for projects striving for portability to accommodate the subtle differences between operating systems.

In the original layout, files are generated under the src folder. We do not like this approach and we will do it differently in our example CMake port: these files will be generated in the build directory. The reason for this is that generated files often depend on the chosen options, compiler, or build type and we wish to keep the ability to configure multiple builds with the same source. To enable generation in the build directory, we will have to apply minimal changes to the script which generates one of the files listed before.

How to structure files

We will collect functions that generate these files in src/autogenerate.cmake, include this module, and call these functions in src/CMakeLists.txt before defining the executable target:

```
# generate config.h, pathdef.c, and osdef.h
include(autogenerate.cmake)
generate_config_h()
generate_pathdef_c()
generate_osdef_h()

add_executable(vim
  main.c
  )

# ...
```

The included src/autogenerate.cmake contains other includes for functionality that we will require to probe header files, functions, and libraries, as well as the three functions:

```
include(CheckTypeSize)
include(CheckFunctionExists)
include(CheckIncludeFiles)
include(CheckLibraryExists)
include(CheckCSourceCompiles)

function(generate_config_h)
  # ... to be written
endfunction()

function(generate_pathdef_c)
```

```
   # ... to be written
endfunction()

function(generate_osdef_h)
   # ... to be written
endfunction()
```

We choose to generate files with functions rather than in macros or "naked" CMake code. As we discussed in previous chapters, this sidesteps many pitfalls:

- It lets us avoid files being generated multiple times, in case we accidentally include the module multiple times. As noted in *Recipe 5*, *Redefining functions and macros*, in *Chapter 7*, *Structuring Projects*, we could employ an include guard to protect against accidentally running code multiple times.
- It guarantees full control over the scope of variables defined within the functions. This avoids that these definitions spill out and pollute the main scope.

Configuring preprocessor definitions based on the system environment

The config.h file is generated from src/config.h.in, which contains preprocessor flags that are configured depending on the system capabilities:

```
/* Define if we have EBCDIC code */
#undef EBCDIC

/* Define unless no X support found */
#undef HAVE_X11

/* Define when terminfo support found */
#undef TERMINFO

/* Define when termcap.h contains ospeed */
#undef HAVE_OSPEED

/* ... */
```

An example generated from src/config.h can start like this example (definitions can differ depending on the environment):

```
/* Define if we have EBCDIC code */
/* #undef EBCDIC */

/* Define unless no X support found */
```

```
#define HAVE_X11 1

/* Define when terminfo support found */
#define TERMINFO 1

/* Define when termcap.h contains ospeed */
/* #undef HAVE_OSPEED */

/* ... */
```

A great resource for platform checks is this page: `https://www.vtk.org/Wiki/CMake:How_To_Write_Platform_Checks`.

In `src/configure.ac`, we can examine which platform checks we need to perform to set corresponding preprocessor definitions.

We will make use of `#cmakedefine` (`https://cmake.org/cmake/help/v3.5/command/configure_file.html?highlight=cmakedefine`) and to make sure we do not break the existing Autotools build, we will copy `config.h.in` to `config.h.cmake.in` and change all `#undef SOME_DEFINITION` to `#cmakedefine SOME_DEFINITION @SOME_DEFINITION@`.

In the `generate_config_h` function, we first define a couple of variables:

```
set(TERMINFO 1)
set(UNIX 1)

# this is hardcoded to keep the discussion in the book chapter
# which describes the migration to CMake simpler
set(TIME_WITH_SYS_TIME 1)
set(RETSIGTYPE void)
set(SIGRETURN return)

find_package(X11)
set(HAVE_X11 ${X11_FOUND})
```

Then, we perform a couple of type size checks:

```
check_type_size("int" VIM_SIZEOF_INT)
check_type_size("long" VIM_SIZEOF_LONG)
check_type_size("time_t" SIZEOF_TIME_T)
check_type_size("off_t" SIZEOF_OFF_T)
```

Then, we loop over functions and check whether the system is able to resolve them:

```
foreach(
  _function IN ITEMS
```

```
    fchdir fchown fchmod fsync getcwd getpseudotty
    getpwent getpwnam getpwuid getrlimit gettimeofday getwd lstat
    memset mkdtemp nanosleep opendir putenv qsort readlink select setenv
    getpgid setpgid setsid sigaltstack sigstack sigset sigsetjmp sigaction
    sigprocmask sigvec strcasecmp strerror strftime stricmp strncasecmp
    strnicmp strpbrk strtol towlower towupper iswwupper
    usleep utime utimes mblen ftruncate
    )

    string(TOUPPER "${_function}" _function_uppercase)
    check_function_exists(${_function} HAVE_${_function_uppercase})
endforeach()
```

We verify whether a particular library contains a particular function:

```
check_library_exists(tinfo tgetent "" HAVE_TGETENT)

if(NOT HAVE_TGETENT)
  message(FATAL_ERROR "Could not find the tgetent() function. You need to
install a terminal library; for example ncurses.")
endif()
```

Then, we loop over header files and check whether they are available:

```
foreach(
  _header IN ITEMS
  setjmp.h dirent.h
  stdint.h stdlib.h string.h
  sys/select.h sys/utsname.h termcap.h fcntl.h
  sgtty.h sys/ioctl.h sys/time.h sys/types.h
  termio.h iconv.h inttypes.h langinfo.h math.h
  unistd.h stropts.h errno.h sys/resource.h
  sys/systeminfo.h locale.h sys/stream.h termios.h
  libc.h sys/statfs.h poll.h sys/poll.h pwd.h
  utime.h sys/param.h libintl.h libgen.h
  util/debug.h util/msg18n.h frame.h sys/acl.h
  sys/access.h sys/sysinfo.h wchar.h wctype.h
  )

  string(TOUPPER "${_header}" _header_uppercase)
  string(REPLACE "/" "_" _header_normalized "${_header_uppercase}")
  string(REPLACE "." "_" _header_normalized "${_header_normalized}")
  check_include_files(${_header} HAVE_${_header_normalized})
endforeach()
```

Then, we translate CMake options from the main CMakeLists.txt to preprocessor definitions:

```
string(TOUPPER "${FEATURES}" _features_upper)
set(FEAT_${_features_upper} 1)

set(FEAT_NETBEANS_INTG ${ENABLE_NETBEANS})
set(FEAT_JOB_CHANNEL ${ENABLE_CHANNEL})
set(FEAT_TERMINAL ${ENABLE_TERMINAL})
```

And finally, we check whether we are able to compile a particular code snippet:

```
check_c_source_compiles(
  "
  #include <sys/types.h>
  #include <sys/stat.h>
  int
  main ()
  {
          struct stat st;
          int n;

          stat(\"/\", &st);
          n = (int)st.st_blksize;
    ;
    return 0;
  }
  "
  HAVE_ST_BLKSIZE
  )
```

The defined variables are then used to configure src/config.h.cmake.in to config.h, which concludes the generate_config_h function:

```
configure_file(
  ${CMAKE_CURRENT_LIST_DIR}/config.h.cmake.in
  ${CMAKE_CURRENT_BINARY_DIR}/auto/config.h
  @ONLY
  )
```

Configuring files with paths and compiler flags

We generate `pathdef.c` from `src/pathdef.c.in`:

```
#include "vim.h"
char_u *default_vim_dir = (char_u *)"@_default_vim_dir@";
char_u *default_vimruntime_dir = (char_u *)"@_default_vimruntime_dir@";
char_u *all_cflags = (char_u *)"@_all_cflags@";
char_u *all_lflags = (char_u *)"@_all_lflags@";
char_u *compiled_user = (char_u *)"@_compiled_user@";
char_u *compiled_sys = (char_u *)"@_compiled_sys@";
```

The `generate_pathdef_c` function configures `src/pathdef.c.in`, but we leave out link flags for simplicity:

```
function(generate_pathdef_c)
  set(_default_vim_dir ${CMAKE_INSTALL_PREFIX})
  set(_default_vimruntime_dir ${_default_vim_dir})

  set(_all_cflags "${CMAKE_C_COMPILER} ${CMAKE_C_FLAGS}")
  if(CMAKE_BUILD_TYPE STREQUAL "Release")
    set(_all_cflags "${_all_cflags} ${CMAKE_C_FLAGS_RELEASE}")
  else()
    set(_all_cflags "${_all_cflags} ${CMAKE_C_FLAGS_DEBUG}")
  endif()

  # it would require a bit more work and execute commands at build time
  # to get the link line into the binary
  set(_all_lflags "undefined")

  if(WIN32)
    set(_compiled_user $ENV{USERNAME})
  else()
    set(_compiled_user $ENV{USER})
  endif()

  cmake_host_system_information(RESULT _compiled_sys QUERY HOSTNAME)

  configure_file(
    ${CMAKE_CURRENT_LIST_DIR}/pathdef.c.in
    ${CMAKE_CURRENT_BINARY_DIR}/auto/pathdef.c
    @ONLY
    )
endfunction()
```

Executing shell scripts at configure time

Finally, we generate `osdef.h` using the following function:

```
function(generate_osdef_h)
  find_program(BASH_EXECUTABLE bash)

  execute_process(
    COMMAND
      ${BASH_EXECUTABLE} osdef.sh ${CMAKE_CURRENT_BINARY_DIR}
    WORKING_DIRECTORY
      ${CMAKE_CURRENT_LIST_DIR}
    )
endfunction()
```

In order to generate `osdef.h` in `${CMAKE_CURRENT_BINARY_DIR}/src/auto` instead of `src/auto`, we had to adapt `osdef.sh` to accept `${CMAKE_CURRENT_BINARY_DIR}` as a command line argument.

Inside `osdef.sh`, we check whether this argument is given:

```
if [ $# -eq 0 ]
  then
    # there are no arguments
    # assume the target directory is current directory
    target_directory=$PWD
  else
    # target directory is provided as argument
    target_directory=$1
fi
```

And then, we generate `${target_directory}/auto/osdef.h`. To do so, we also had to adjust the following compilation line inside `osdef.sh`:

```
$CC -I. -I$srcdir -I${target_directory} -E osdef0.c >osdef0.cc
```

Detecting required dependencies and linking

We have now all generated files in place, so let us retry the build. We should be able to configure and compile the sources, but we will not be able to link:

```
$ mkdir -p build
$ cd build
```

```
$ cmake ..
$ cmake --build .

...
Scanning dependencies of target vim
[ 98%] Building C object src/CMakeFiles/vim.dir/main.c.o
[100%] Linking C executable ../bin/vim
../lib64/libbasic_sources.a(term.c.o): In function `set_shellsize.part.12':
term.c:(.text+0x2bd): undefined reference to `tputs'
../lib64/libbasic_sources.a(term.c.o): In function `getlinecol':
term.c:(.text+0x902): undefined reference to `tgetent'
term.c:(.text+0x915): undefined reference to `tgetent'
term.c:(.text+0x935): undefined reference to `tgetnum'
term.c:(.text+0x948): undefined reference to `tgetnum'

... many other undefined references ...
```

Again, we can take the log file from the Autotools compilation and, in particular, the link line as inspiration to resolve the missing dependencies by adding the following code to `src/CMakeLists.txt`:

```
# find X11 and link to it
find_package(X11 REQUIRED)
if(X11_FOUND)
  target_link_libraries(vim
    PUBLIC
      ${X11_LIBRARIES}
    )
endif()

# a couple of more system libraries that the code requires
foreach(_library IN ITEMS Xt SM m tinfo acl gpm dl)
  find_library(_${_library}_found ${_library} REQUIRED)
  if(_${_library}_found)
    target_link_libraries(vim
      PUBLIC
        ${_library}
      )
  endif()
endforeach()
```

Observe how we can add one library dependency to the target at a time and do not have to construct and carry around a list of libraries in a variable, which would produce more brittle CMake code since the variable could get corrupted on the way, in particular for larger projects.

With this change, the code compiles and links:

```
$ cmake --build .

...
Scanning dependencies of target vim
[ 98%] Building C object src/CMakeFiles/vim.dir/main.c.o
[100%] Linking C executable ../bin/vim
[100%] Built target vim
```

We can now try to execute the compiled binary and edit some files with our newly compiled version of Vim!

Reproducing compiler flags

Let us now try to adjust the compiler flags to mirror the reference build.

Defining compiler flags

So far, we have not defined any custom compiler flags, but from the reference Autotools build, we remember that the code was compiled with -g -U_FORTIFY_SOURCE -D_FORTIFY_SOURCE=1 -O2 using the GNU C compiler.

Our first approach could be to define the following:

```
if(CMAKE_C_COMPILER_ID MATCHES GNU)
    set(CMAKE_C_FLAGS "${CMAKE_C_FLAGS} -g -U_FORTIFY_SOURCE -
D_FORTIFY_SOURCE=1 -O2")
endif()
```

And, we would place this code on top of src/CMakeLists.txt, right before generating source files (since pathdef.c uses ${CMAKE_C_FLAGS}):

```
# <- we will define flags right here

include(autogenerate.cmake)
generate_config_h()
generate_pathdef_c()
generate_osdef_h()
```

A slight improvement to the compiler flag definitions would be to define -02 as a `Release` configuration flag and to turn off optimization for a `Debug` configuration:

```
if(CMAKE_C_COMPILER_ID MATCHES GNU)
  set(CMAKE_C_FLAGS "${CMAKE_C_FLAGS} -g -U_FORTIFY_SOURCE
-D_FORTIFY_SOURCE=1")
  set(CMAKE_C_FLAGS_RELEASE "-O2")
  set(CMAKE_C_FLAGS_DEBUG "-O0")
endif()
```

Please verify with `make VERBOSE=1` that the build uses the expected flags.

Scope of compiler flags

In this particular example project, all source files use the same compile flags. For other projects, we may prefer to not define compile flags globally as we have done above, but to define flags individually for each target using `target_compile_options`. The advantage would be more flexibility and more local scope. The price to pay in our example here would probably be unnecessary code duplication.

Porting tests

Let us now discuss how to port tests from the reference build to our CMake build.

Getting started

If the project that is being ported contains a test target or any form of automated testing or test scripts, the first step will again be to run the traditional test step and record the commands used. For the Vim project, the place to start is `src/testdir/Makefile`. It will probably make sense to define tests on the CMake side close to `src/testdir/Makefile` and the test scripts, and we will choose to define tests in `src/testdir/CMakeLists.txt`. To process such a file, we must reference it in `src/CMakeLists.txt`:

```
add_subdirectory(testdir)
```

We should also enable the test target in the top-level `CMakeLists.txt`, right before processing `src/CMakeLists.txt`:

```
# enable the test target
enable_testing()

# process src/CMakeLists.txt in its own scope
add_subdirectory(src)
```

So far, the test target is empty before we populate `src/testdir/CMakeLists.txt` with `add_test` directives. The minimum to specify in `add_test` is a test name and a command to run. The command can be any script written in any language. The essential part for CMake is that the script returns zero if the test is successful and non-zero if the test fails. For more details, we refer the reader to *Chapter 4, Creating and Running Tests*. In the case of Vim, we will need a bit more to accommodate multi-step tests, which we will discuss in the next section.

Implementing a multi-step test

The targets in `src/testdir/Makefile` indicate that the Vim code runs tests as multi-step tests: first the `vim` executable processes a script and produces an output file, then in a second step the output file is compared with a reference file and if these files do not differ, the test is successful. Temporary files are then removed in a third step. This can probably not be fitted into a single `add_test` command in a portable way since `add_test` can only execute one command. One solution would be to define the test steps in a Python script and to execute the Python script with some arguments. The alternative we will present here, which is also cross-platform, is to define the test steps in a separate CMake script and to execute this script from `add_test`. We will define the test steps in `src/testdir/test.cmake`:

```
function(execute_test _vim_executable _working_dir _test_script)
  # generates test.out
  execute_process(
    COMMAND ${_vim_executable} -f -u unix.vim -U NONE --noplugin --not-a-
term -s dotest.in ${_test_script}.in
    WORKING_DIRECTORY ${_working_dir}
    )

  # compares test*.ok and test.out
  execute_process(
    COMMAND ${CMAKE_COMMAND} -E compare_files ${_test_script}.ok test.out
    WORKING_DIRECTORY ${_working_dir}
    RESULT_VARIABLE files_differ
```

```
      OUTPUT_QUIET
      ERROR_QUIET
      )

  # removes leftovers
  file(REMOVE ${_working_dir}/Xdotest)

  # we let the test fail if the files differ
  if(files_differ)
    message(SEND_ERROR "test ${_test_script} failed")
  endif()
endfunction()

execute_test(${VIM_EXECUTABLE} ${WORKING_DIR} ${TEST_SCRIPT})
```

Again, we choose a function over a macro to make sure variables do not escape the function scope. We will process this script, which will call the execute_test function. However, we have to make sure that ${VIM_EXECUTABLE}, ${WORKING_DIR}, and ${TEST_SCRIPT} are defined from outside. These are defined in src/testdir/CMakeLists.txt:

```
add_test(
  NAME
    test1
  COMMAND
    ${CMAKE_COMMAND} -D VIM_EXECUTABLE=$<TARGET_FILE:vim>
                     -D WORKING_DIR=${CMAKE_CURRENT_LIST_DIR}
                     -D TEST_SCRIPT=test1
                     -P ${CMAKE_CURRENT_LIST_DIR}/test.cmake
  WORKING_DIRECTORY
    ${PROJECT_BINARY_DIR}
  )
```

The Vim project has many tests but in this example, we have ported only one (test1) as a proof of concept.

Recommendation for tests

We can give at least two recommendations for porting tests. First, to make sure that the test does not always report success, verify that the test fails if you break the code or change the reference data. Second, add COST estimates to tests so that when run in parallel, longer tests are started first to minimize the total test time (see *Chapter 4, Creating and Running Tests, Recipe 8, Running tests in parallel*).

Porting install targets

We can now configure, compile, link, and test the code, but we are missing the install target, which we will add in this section.

This is the Autotools approach to building and installing code:

```
$ ./configure --prefix=/some/install/path
$ make
$ make install
```

And this is the CMake way:

```
$ mkdir -p build
$ cd build
$ cmake -D CMAKE_INSTALL_PREFIX=/some/install/path ..
$ cmake --build .
$ cmake --build . --target install
```

To add an install target, we add the following snippet in `src/CMakeLists.txt`:

```
install(
  TARGETS
    vim
  RUNTIME DESTINATION
    ${CMAKE_INSTALL_BINDIR}
)
```

In this example, we only install the executable. The Vim project installs a large number of files along with the binary (symbolic links and documentation files). To keep this section digestible, we don't install all other files in this example migration. For your own project, you should verify that the result of the install step matches the install target of the legacy build framework.

Further steps

After a successful port to CMake, the next step should be to localize the scope of targets and variables even further: consider moving options, targets, and variables closer to where they are used and modified. Avoid global variables since they will enforce an order to CMake commands, and this order may not be evident and will lead to a brittle CMake code. One approach to enforcing the separation of variable scopes is to divide larger projects into CMake projects, which are composed using the superbuild pattern (see *Chapter 8, The Superbuild Pattern*). Consider splitting large `CMakeLists.txt` files into smaller modules.

The next steps can be to test the configuration and compilation on other platforms and operating systems in order to generalize and bullet-proof the CMake code and make it more portable.

Finally, when migrating projects to a new build framework, the developer community needs to adapt to it too. Help your colleagues with training, documentation, and code review. The hardest part in porting code to CMake can be to change the habits of humans.

Summary and common pitfalls when converting projects to CMake

Let us summarize what we have achieved in this chapter and what we learned.

Summary of code changes

In this chapter, we have discussed how to port a project to CMake. We have considered the Vim project as an example and added the following files:

```
.
├──── CMakeLists.txt
└──── src
    ├──── autogenerate.cmake
    ├──── CMakeLists.txt
    ├──── config.h.cmake.in
    ├──── libvterm
    │   └──── CMakeLists.txt
    ├──── pathdef.c.in
    └──── testdir
        ├──── CMakeLists.txt
        └──── test.cmake
```

The changes can be browsed online: `https://github.com/dev-cafe/vim/compare/b476cb7...cmake-support`.

This was an incomplete proof of concept port to CMake, where we left out many options and tweaks for simplicity and tried to focus on the most salient features and steps.

Common pitfalls

We would like to conclude this discussion by pointing out some common pitfalls when moving to CMake.

- **Global variables are code smell**: This is true for any programming language, and CMake is no exception. Variables that are carried across CMake files, and in particular "upwards" from leaf to parent `CMakeLists.txt` files, indicate code smell. There is typically a better way to transfer dependencies. Ideally, dependencies should be imported through targets. Instead of assembling a list of libraries into a variable and carrying the variable across files, link to libraries one by one close to where they are defined. Instead of assembling source files into variables, add source files using `target_sources`. When linking to libraries use imported targets when available, instead of variables.

- **Minimize the effect of order**: CMake is not a declarative language, but we should not approach it with an imperative paradigm either. CMake sources that enforce a strict order tend to be brittle. This also connects to the discussion about variables (see previous paragraph). Some order of statements and modules will be necessary, but to arrive at robust CMake frameworks, we should avoid unnecessary enforcement of order.
  Use `target_sources`, `target_compile_definitions`, `target_include_directories`, and `target_link_libraries`. Avoid global scope statements such as `add_definitions`, `include_directories`, and `link_libraries`. Avoid global definitions of compile flags. If possible, define compile flags per target.

- **Do not place generated files outside the build directory**: It is highly recommended to never place generated files outside the build directory. The reason for this is that generated files often depend on the chosen options or compiler or build type, and by writing into the source tree, we give up the possibility to maintain several builds with the same source and we complicate reproducibility of the build steps.

- **Prefer functions over macros**: They have different scopes and the function scope is limited. All variable modifications need to be explicitly marked, which also signals variable redefinitions to the reader. Use a macro when you must but prefer functions if you can.

- **Avoid shell commands**: They may not be portable to other platforms (such as Windows). Prefer using CMake equivalents. If no CMake equivalent is available, consider calling a Python script.

- **In Fortran projects, be careful with the suffix case**: Fortran sources that need to be preprocessed should have an uppercase `.F90` suffix. Sources that are not to be preprocessed should carry the `.f90` suffix.

- **Avoid explicit paths**: This is true both when defining targets and when referencing files. Use `CMAKE_CURRENT_LIST_DIR` when referring to the current path. The advantage of this is that when you move or rename a directory, it will still work.

- **Module includes should not be function calls**: Modularizing the CMake code into modules is a good strategy, but including a module should ideally not execute CMake code. Instead, wrap CMake code into functions and macros and explicitly call these after including the module. This protects against unintended effects when accidentally including a module multiple times and makes the action of executing CMake code modules more explicit to the reader.

Other Books You May Enjoy

If you enjoyed this book, you may be interested in these other books by Packt:

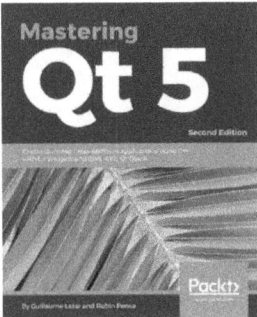

Mastering Qt 5 - Second Edition
Guillaume Lazar, Robin Penea

ISBN: 978-1-78899-539-9

- Create stunning UIs with Qt Widgets and Qt Quick 2
- Develop powerful, cross-platform applications with the Qt framework
- Design GUIs with the Qt Designer and build a library in it for UI previews
- Handle user interaction with the Qt signal or slot mechanism in C++
- Prepare a cross-platform project to host a third-party library
- Use the Qt Animation framework to display stunning effects
- Deploy mobile apps with Qt and embedded platforms
- Interact with a gamepad using Qt Gamepad

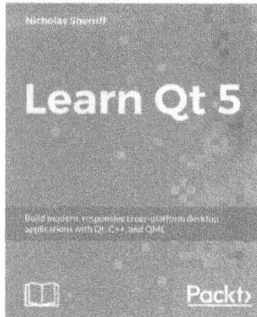

Learn QT 5
Nicholas Sherriff

ISBN: 978-1-78847-885-4

- Install and configure the Qt Framework and Qt Creator IDE
- Create a new multi-project solution from scratch and control every aspect of it with QMake
- Implement a rich user interface with QML
- Learn the fundamentals of QtTest and how to integrate unit testing
- Build self-aware data entities that can serialize themselves to and from JSON
- Manage data persistence with SQLite and CRUD operations
- Reach out to the internet and consume an RSS feed
- Produce application packages for distribution to other users

Leave a review - let other readers know what you think

Please share your thoughts on this book with others by leaving a review on the site that you bought it from. If you purchased the book from Amazon, please leave us an honest review on this book's Amazon page. This is vital so that other potential readers can see and use your unbiased opinion to make purchasing decisions, we can understand what our customers think about our products, and our authors can see your feedback on the title that they have worked with Packt to create. It will only take a few minutes of your time, but is valuable to other potential customers, our authors, and Packt. Thank you!

Index

F

FFTW library 334, 336, 338
files
  configuring, with compiler flags 572
  configuring, with paths 572
  generating 566
  preprocessor, configuring on system
    environment 568
  shell scripts, executing at configure time 573
  structuring 567
FindDoxygen.cmake module
  reference link 498
Fortran libraries
  used, for building C/C++ projects 360, 362, 364
Fortran project build
  distributing, with CMake/CFFI via PyPI 474, 477,
    478
Fortran projects
  building, C/C++ libraries used 354, 355, 357,
    358, 359
  organizing 304, 307, 309, 312, 315
Fortran
  mixing, Python CFFI used 384, 389, 391, 394
functions
  defining 284
  defining, with named arguments 277, 280
  deprecating 286, 288
  redefining 282

G

generator expressions
  used, for compilation 226, 229
  used, for fine-tuning configuration 226, 229
Git hash
  recording, at build time 256, 258
  recording, at configure time 253, 255
global variables
  avoiding, target_sources used 300, 303
Google Test framework 339, 341, 342, 344

H

hello world example
  cross-compiling 517, 519, 521
host processor architecture

discovering 77, 79
host processor instruction set
  discovering 81, 84, 86

I

integrated development environment (IDE) 30
Intel MKL link line advisor
  reference link 487

L

Linear Algebra Pack (LAPACK)
  about 109
  math libraries, detecting 109, 112, 114

M

macros
  defining, with named arguments 277, 280
  deprecating 286, 288
  redefining 282, 284
memory defects
  reporting, to CDash 539, 542, 543, 545, 548
Message Passing Interface (MPI) 120
meta.yaml configuration file
  reference link 483
MPI parallel environment
  detecting 120, 122, 123

O

OpenMP parallel environment
  detecting 115, 117, 119
OpenMP parallelization
  used, for cross-compiling 521, 522, 523, 525
operating system (OS)
  about 68
  discovering 68
options
  presenting, to user 43

P

package_source target
  reference link 462
Pipenv
  reference link 465
platform checks

www.ingramcontent.com/pod-product-compliance
Lightning Source LLC
Chambersburg PA
CBHW081212220326
41598CB00037B/6758